MADONNA'S DROWNED WORLDS

To our families

Madonna's Drowned Worlds

New Approaches to her Cultural Transformations,
1983–2003

Edited by
SANTIAGO FOUZ-HERNÁNDEZ
University of Durham

and

FREYA JARMAN-IVENS
University of Newcastle upon Tyne

ASHGATE

Published by
Ashgate Publishing Limited
Gower House
Croft Road
Aldershot
Hants GU11 3HR
England

Ashgate Publishing Company
Suite 420
101 Cherry Street
Burlington, VT 05401-4405
USA

Ashgate website: http://www.ashgate.com

British Library Cataloguing in Publication Data
Madonna's drowned worlds : new approaches to her cultural
 transformations, 1983–2003. – (Ashgate popular and folk
 music series)
 1. Madonna, 1958– – Criticism and interpretation
 I. Fouz-Hernández, Santiago II. Jarman-Ivens, Freya
 782.4'166'092

Library of Congress Cataloging-in-Publication Data
Madonna's drowned worlds : new approaches to her cultural transformations,
 1983–2003 / edited by Santiago Fouz-Hernández and Freya Jarman-Ivens.
   p. cm. – (Ashgate popular and folk music series)
 Includes bibliographical references and index.
 ISBN 0-7546-3371-3 (alk. paper) – ISBN 0-7546-3372-1 (pbk. : alk. paper)
  1. Madonna, 1958– –Criticism and interpretation. 2. Subculture. I.
Fouz-Hernández, Santiago. II. Jarman-Ivens, Freya. III. Series.

ML420.M1387M28 2004
782.42166'092–dc22

2003062883

ISBN 0 7546 3371 3 (Hbk)
ISBN 0 7546 3372 1 (Pbk)

Typeset in Times by Express Typesetters Ltd, Farnham, Surrey and printed in Great Britain by MPG Books Ltd, Bodmin, Cornwall.

Contents

List of Figures   vii

Notes on Contributors   viii

General Editor's Preface   xi

Acknowledgements   xii

Editors' Notes   xiii

Who's That Girl?

    Introduction: Re-invention? Madonna's drowned worlds
resurface   xv
       Santiago Fouz-Hernández and Freya Jarman-Ivens

Part I: The Girlie Show: Gender Identities

1   Dragging out camp: narrative agendas in Madonna's musical
production   3
    Stan Hawkins

2   Madonna's girls in the mix: performance of femininity beyond
the beautiful   22
    Patricia Pisters

3   Where is the female body? Androgyny and other strategies of
disappearance in Madonna's music videos   36
    Corinna Herr

Part II: Post-Virgin: Sexual Identities

4   Queer hearing and the Madonna queen   55
    Keith E. Clifton

5   What it feels like for two girls: Madonna's play with lesbian
(sub-)cultures   69
    Freya Jarman-Ivens

Part III: Drowned Worlds: Ethnic Identities

6   East is hot! 'Madonna's Indian Summer' and the poetics of
appropriation   91
    Michael Angelo Tata

7   Re-worlding the oriental: critical perspectives on Madonna as
     geisha   104
         Rahul Gairola

8   The day the music died laughing: Madonna and Country   120
         Sean Albiez

9   Crossing the border(line): Madonna's encounter with the Hispanic   138
         Santiago Fouz-Hernández

Part IV: Blond Ambition: Consuming Celebrity

10   Madonna's daughters: girl power and the empowered girl-pop
     breakthrough   161
         David Gauntlett

11   Consuming Madonna then and now: an examination of the
     dynamics and structuring of celebrity consumption   176
         Lisa Peñaloza

Bibliography   193
Index   212

List of Figures

1.1	Organ groove from 'Music'	7
1.2	Dual melodic camp theme from 'Music'	9
3.1	Remedios Varo, *Los Amantes*, 1963	47
11.1	Consuming celebrity	189

Notes on Contributors

Sean Albiez is a senior lecturer in Popular Culture, at the University of Plymouth (UK). His publications include 'Know History! John Lydon, Cultural Capital and the Prog/Punk Dialectic', *Popular Music* (2003), and 'Sounds of Future Past: from Neu! to Numan' in R. Appen and T. Phleps (eds), *Pop Sounds* (Transcript Verlag, 2003). His PhD research examines 'Deutsch-Englisch' connections in 1970s and 1980s electronic music. Broader interests include French electronica, techno and trans-Atlantic flows in electronic music and contemporary Country music.

Keith E. Clifton is Assistant Professor of Musicology at Central Michigan University. He previously held teaching positions at Northwestern University, the University of Northern Iowa and the University of Central Arkansas. A musicologist, lecturer and performer, he has studied at the University of Texas at Austin (BM) and Northwestern University (MM, PhD). A specialist in twentieth-century French music and American music, his work has appeared in *Notes*, *The Opera Journal*, *The Reader's Guide to Music*, *The Journal of Singing* and elsewhere. Forthcoming publications include the book *American Art Song Since 1980: A Guide* for Scarecrow Press and entries in the *Encyclopedia of the Romantic Era* and the *Companion to Modern French Thought*. He has presented lectures and scholarly papers throughout the United States and abroad. Besides Madonna, his research interests in the popular sphere include the musical construction of queer identity, and issues of gender and authorship in the rock group the B52's.

Santiago Fouz-Hernández is a lecturer in Spanish cinema and language at the University of Durham (UK). He has studied at the universities of Santiago de Compostela (Spain) and Newcastle upon Tyne (UK), where he completed an MA and a PhD on issues of masculinity and sexuality in contemporary Spanish and British cinema. He has contributed to various international journals, such as *Leeds Iberian Papers*, *Romance Studies* and *Journal of Iberian and Latin American Studies*, and to books such as *Territories of Desire in Queer Culture* (Manchester University Press, 2000). He is currently planning a book on the male body in contemporary Spanish cinema.

Rahul Gairola is a doctoral student in the Department of English at the University of Washington, Seattle. He received his BA in English, Film and Media Studies from George Mason University and his MA in English from

Rhode Island College. He has also studied at Cornell University, Cambridge University (UK), where he held the 2003–4 Washington Fellowship at Pembroke College, and the Syracuse University London Centre (UK). His work has appeared in the *Journal of Commonwealth and Postcolonial Studies*, *Comparative Literature*, *Popmatters*, *Jouvert*, *South Asian Review* and *Literature & Psychology*. His current interests include ethnic American and world literatures, cultural studies, globalization and postcolonialism. In addition to his work on Madonna, he has written and presented papers on Phish, the Beatles, Cornershop and Duran Duran.

David Gauntlett is Professor of Media and Identities at the Media School, University of Bournemouth. He is the author of the books *Moving Experiences* (John Libbey, 1995), *Video Critical* (John Libbey, 1997) and *TV Living* (with Annette Hill; Routledge, 1999), and editor of *Web.Studies: Rewiring Media Studies in the Digital Age* (Arnold, 2000). His most recent book, *Media, Gender and Identity: An Introduction*, was published by Routledge in 2002. He produces the award-winning website www.theory.org.uk.

Stan Hawkins is Professor of Musicology at the University of Oslo (Norway). Until 1995 he led research and course development in popular music studies at the University of Salford and is noted for his contribution to the field especially in the UK and Scandinavia. He is author of *Settling the Pop Score: Pop Texts and Identity Politics* (Ashgate, 2001). In addition, he is Editor-in-Chief for Popular Musicology Online and the Norwegian chair for the International Association for the Study of Popular Music (IASPM). As a musician, he has been professionally active as a composer and performer in the fields of contemporary music and jazz.

Corinna Herr is a lecturer in Musicology at the Ruhr-Universität Bochum (Germany), teaching music history and popular music with a focus on gender studies. She completed her PhD on *Medeas Zorn: Eine 'starke Frau' in Opern des 17. und 18. Jahrhunderts* [*Medeas Furor, a 'femme forte' in seventeenth- and eighteenth-century opera*], published by Herbolzheim in 2000. She is currently working on a book provisionally entitled *Castratos and Androgynous Popstars in Contexts of Hermeticism and Alchemy*.

Freya Jarman-Ivens is completing a PhD at the University of Newcastle on dissident sexualities and popular music in the late twentieth century, supported by a scholarship from the Arts and Humanities Research Board. She has previously worked on gender issues in fin-de-siècle opera (in which she completed a Masters degree) and Madonna's relationship with her gay audience. Her current research interests and recent papers include the Carpenters and alternative rock music. She is planning a single-authored book on the cultural politics of cover versions.

Lisa Peñaloza is Associate Professor of Marketing at the University of Colorado, Boulder. She completed her doctorate at the University of California, Irvine. Her research views the marketplace as a culture and is concerned with how consumers express culture in their consumer behaviour and, in turn, how marketers negotiate various cultures of consumers. Market subcultures examined in her work relate to ethnicity/race, nationality, gender/sexuality and most recently industry and region in the commodification of Western culture at a Stock Show and Rodeo. Her work has been published in the *Journal of Consumer Research*, *Journal of Marketing*, *Public Policy and Marketing*, *International Journal of Research in Marketing* and *Consumption, Markets and Culture*. Professor Peñaloza is currently working on a project investigating the market beliefs and experiences of Mexican American/Chicano/a consumers in the USA. She is particularly interested in consumption politics and relationships between capitalism and democracy. She teaches in the areas of International Marketing, Marketing Theory and Qualitative Research Methods. Her service activities focus on enhancing the number of under-represented groups among marketing students, practitioners and academics in the USA.

Patricia Pisters is Associate Professor at the Department of Media Studies of the University of Amsterdam (Holland). In 1999 shepublished (with Hannah Bosma) *Madonna: De Vele Gezichten van een Popster*[*Madonna: The Many Faces of a Popstar*]. Her research interests include film theory, popular culture, gender, multi-culturalism, the body and technology. She has recently edited *Micropolitics of Media Culture: Reading the Rhizomes ofDeleuze and Guattari* (Amsterdam University Press, 2001). Other publications include an introduction to media theory, entitled *Lessen van Hitchcock* [*Lessons from Hitchcock*] (2001) and *The Matrix of Visual Culture: Working with Deleuze in Film Theory* (Stanford University Press, 2003).

Michael Angelo Tata received his MA in Creative Writing/Poetry from Temple University, Philadelphia, and his MA in Liberal Studies from the New School for Social Research, New York City, and is in the process of completing his PhD in English Literature through the City University of New York's Graduate Center. He currently teaches courses in American pop culture and aesthetics through the English and Women's Studies Departments at Manhattan's Hunter College. His poetry and criticism have appeared in the journals *Lit*, *Lungfull*, *kenning*, *Bad Subjects*, *Found Object*, *Rhizomes* and *to the quick*, as well as the Critical Studies compilation *From Virgin Land to Disney World: Nature and Its Discontents in the USA of Yesterday and Today* (Editions Rodopi, 2001). His first chapbook of poetry, *The Multiplication of Joy into Integers*, won Iowa's 2002 Blue Light Poetry Prize and appeared in spring 2003.

General Editor's Preface

The upheaval that occurred in musicology during the last two decades of the twentieth century has created a new urgency for the study of popular music alongside the development of new critical and theoretical models. A relativistic outlook has replaced the universal perspective of modernism (the international ambitions of the 12-note style); the grand narrative of the evolution and dissolution of tonality has been challenged; and emphasis has shifted to cultural context, reception and subject position. Together, these have conspired to eat away at the status of canonical composers and categories of high and low in music. A need has arisen, also, to recognize and address the emergence of crossovers, mixed and new genres, to engage in debates concerning the vexed problem of what constitutes authenticity in music and to offer a critique of musical practice as the product of free, individual expression.

Popular musicology is now a vital and exciting area of scholarship, and the Ashgate Popular and Folk Music series aims to present the best research in the field. Authors will be concerned with locating musical practices, values and meanings in cultural context, and may draw upon methodologies and theories developed in cultural studies, semiotics, poststructuralism, psychology and sociology. The series will focus on popular musics of the twentieth and twenty-first centuries. It is designed to embrace the world's popular musics from Acid Jazz to Zydeco, whether high tech or low tech, commercial or non-commercial, contemporary or traditional.

Professor Derek B. Scott
Chair of Music
University of Salford

Acknowledgements

As an edited volume this work would, by definition, have been impossible without all the contributors, and it is to them that our first thanks go, for all their hard work, diligence and co-operation with our schedules. As ever, there are many more people behind the production of this book than those who appear on the contents page, and we would like in particular to thank various people who have been instrumental in this volume's creation. Many thanks go to Ian Biddle of the International Centre for Music Studies at the University of Newcastle upon Tyne. Ian has been of great help from the beginning, and has provided support and advice at every stage, from the proposal to the details of our own chapters, as well as maintaining the project's website. At Ashgate, we would like particularly to thank our editor Heidi May for her assistance with various copyright matters and efficient help throughout the process. Many other people have been of service in our attempts to acquire copyright permission, and whether we were ultimately successful or not our thanks go to those people. Special thanks to Rahul Gairola for securing the copyright permission for the book's cover and to Olivier Tridon for allowing us to reproduce his line drawings of Madonna. On a more personal level, we would like most of all to thank our partners – Christian and Sophie – for their support and patience, especially in the final stages of the preparation of the manuscript.

Editors' Notes

References to films and music videos

Directors of films are referred to in parentheses after the film's title, followed by the year. Music videos are referred to in a similar way, with the director's surname and the year of release in parentheses following the title of a song.

In those chapters where musical material is discussed, namely those by Keith Clifton and Stan Hawkins, the following system is used to describe musical pitch:

A, B, C, D, etc.	Middle C and the octave encompassing it.
A^1, B^1, C^1, D^1, etc.	A, B, C, etc. one octave *above* the middle-C octave.
A^2, B^2, C^2, D^2, etc.	A, B, C, etc. two octaves *above* middle-C.
A_1, B_1, C_1, D_1, etc.	A, B, C, etc. one octave *below* the middle-C octave
(and so on).	

Who's That Girl?

Olivier Tridon

Introduction

Re-invention? Madonna's drowned worlds resurface

Santiago Fouz-Hernández and Freya Jarman-Ivens

In the early 1990s, David Tetzlaff wrote of Madonna: 'never before has a popular performer survived so much hype for so long and continued to attract the fascination of a broad public while staying completely contemporary', adding that reading everything that has been written about Madonna would be like 'mapping the vastness of the cosmos' (1993, p. 239). Over ten years since those remarks, and more than twenty years since her career began, Madonna remains one of the most productive, talked about, loved and hated pop artists in the world. As prolific today as she was then, since 2000 alone Madonna has performed two world tours (the *Drowned World Tour* in 2001, her first tour in eight years; and the *Re-invention Tour* in 2004), released two albums of new material and a second collection of greatest hits, performed in her second play (*Up For Grabs*, Williamson, 2002, in London's West End), released her most extensive photographic portfolio since *Sex* (Klein, 2003),[1] promoted several new fashion trends and continued to appear on countless magazine covers. Tetzlaff's cosmological comparison is surely even more applicable today.

It is widely accepted that the so-called 'Madonna phenomenon' formed a crucial site for the production of a multitude of different modalities of creativity in the 1980s Anglo-American and European pop music scene(s). During that decade Madonna emerged as a role model for women in many different cultures, symbolizing professional and personal independence in a male-dominated society, as well as sexual liberation (see, for example, Lewis, 1990, pp. 123–4; Lugo-Lugo, 2001). Following her playful and (apparently) harmless flirtatiousness in the early stages of her career, the early 1990s saw Madonna focus on more explicit sexual representations, causing controversy first with the 'Justify My Love' video (Mondino, 1990), later with the simultaneous releases of the album *Erotica* and the book *Sex* in 1992, and then with the film *Body of Evidence*, which followed shortly thereafter (Edel, 1993). Thus, Madonna came to be viewed as a somewhat threatening presence, due in no small part to her apparent ability to resist and usurp men's sexual autonomy, an idea highlighted at that time by her playful interaction with lesbianism.[2] This putative danger was reflected in a media backlash, which represented her as a 'tarted-up floozy' and thereby contained the alleged threat in conveniently stereotyped images (see

Schulze, Barton White and Brown, 1993). Around that time, Freddy DeMann (then Madonna's manager) predicted that she would 'throw having children aside – perhaps forever – in the elusive search to be a celebrity' (quoted in Orth, 1992, p. 161). The perceived incompatibility of Madonna's public persona with motherhood seemed to remain in the public consciousness even as she gave birth to her first child in 1996, as suggested by Camille Paglia's views on the supposed 'public concern for the welfare of Madonna's first child' (to which Madonna refers in her *Evita* diaries (1996, 7 May)). However, Madonna's pregnancy and her leading role in *Evita* (Parker, 1996) seemed to facilitate her move away from the controversy of the early 1990s, and this marked the beginning of an unexpected and thorough-going transformation from offensive sex icon and femme fatale into exemplary matriarch and household name.[3] As Savigliano has put it, the acting out of Evita's death was in many ways Madonna's resurrection (1997, p. 159).

Yet those journalists who foresaw that her salvation as an ageing pop artist would come at the cost of leaving behind cutting-edge pop and re-inventing herself as a ballad singer (a prediction that appeared to be confirmed in 1995 by the collection *Something To Remember*, and one substantiated by critics – see Jackson, 1996) seem to have missed the mark somewhat. With the three electronica albums that have followed since then,[4] Madonna has maintained a strong presence in the pop and dance charts in recent years. This exploration of new underground or subcultural music trends (partly motivated by interest in new talents for her own record company, such as Orbit and Mirwais) has characterized most of her work since *Evita*, reflecting a highly tuned sense for the new, the different and the exotic, and for avoiding self-indulgent nostalgia. This was the case with the 2001 *Drowned World Tour*, in which she overlooked most of her old hits and focused instead on more recent material. Yet her past achievements were, in a sense, summarized on that tour in the performance of 'Music'. The original 'Music' video (Åkerlund, 2000) featured a cartoon rendering of Madonna surrounded by buildings named after the titles of her greatest hits, shining in bright neon lights. Although the cartoon character fights and destroys some of the neon signs, as if to insist on her ability to move on, the mere presence of such a long list of hits is a pointed reminder of the longevity of Madonna's success, and her ambivalent relationship with it. Similarly, the live performance of this song encapsulated references to many of her old hits in a remix video (created by Dan-O-Rama), which highlighted various stages of her career:[5] hence, the performances of 'Music' became an appropriate metaphor for Madonna's *own* music. Later, her capacity for transformation and self-reflection was played out in the 2004 *Re-invention Tour*, during which old hits were transformed musically.

Despite the emphasis placed by critics on Madonna's stylistic changes and her exploration of new territories, it is becoming increasingly clear that much of her creative output is also characterized by recurrent themes. Thus, apparently minor details return in a number of ways: bodily gestures reappear in various performances; references are made in songs to earlier hits; musical ideas recur.[6] Extending beyond the regions of Madonna's creative output, certain politics have also persisted throughout her multiplicitous and polyvalent persona(e). One example of this would be her relationship with a kind of (popular) feminism. The unprecedented success that Madonna enjoys as a female recording artist has long invited an understanding of her as a feminist icon, 'something of a role model for girls and young women' (Curry, 1990, p. 16). Indeed, this (pop) feminist posturing seems to have persisted, from early examples such as 'Express Yourself' (1989) to the more recent 'What it Feels Like for a Girl' (from *Music*, 2000). Yet Madonna has also continued to problematize her relationship with feminism (as the videos for those songs would suggest). Distinct feminist approaches would take issue both with the pornographic representations found in her work of the early 1990s, and with her recent celebration of the nuclear family. Madonna has clearly distanced herself from feminism, on one occasion declaring that she is not a feminist, but a 'humanist' ('Madonna on Stage and on the Record', MTV, 2003). Similarly recurring are examples of Madonna's engagement with issues of sexuality or ethnicity. Thus, despite the implicit distance from sexual dissidence marked by her marriage, she has also maintained a subsidiary relationship with queer sexualities in various fictional contexts on the stage (*Up For Grabs*, Williamson, 2002), on film (*Die Another Day*, Tamahori, 2002), and on television (*Will and Grace*, NBC, 2003; MVA, MTV, 2003). Similarly, Madonna continues not only to introduce new ethnicities into her work – recently including images from Japan, the Indian subcontinent and the USA – but also to rework those ethnic representations that were featured in her earlier material. The creative exploration of North American ethnicities, then, newly developed through *Music* (2000) and questioned in *American Life* (2003), forms part of a broader tendency by Madonna to explore Western identities: her appropriation of historical German cinematic figures (Marlene Dietrich, Dita Parlo[7]), references (in interviews) to her own European heritage and engagement with British themes are all evident throughout her career.

Academic responses to these 'subcultural' aspects of Madonna's work have accused her of 'leasing subcultural issues for just as long as the "general public" finds them interesting' and then of dropping them 'as soon as those at the centre have had their fill' (Frank and Smith, 1993b, p. 16); of 'peddling ethnic, feministical and gay ideas to fashion whilst taking none of the risks and absorbing none of the real flak' (O'Hagan, 1993, p. 32); of being a 'colonizer' (hooks, 1992b, p. 159; and 1993, p. 77); of 'subcultural tourism' or even of being a 'Teflon idol' to whom 'nothing sticks' (Tetzlaff, 1993, p. 259). *The Madonna Connection* (Schwichtenberg, 1993a) was arguably a key event in the history of the relationship between the artist and the academy; this was an acceptance, of sorts, of her wider cultural significance and the challenge her personae pose to the field of cultural studies. While Schwichtenberg argued in her introduction that 'academics are typically the last to know about popular phenomena', she was also surely right in adding, 'their reaction to Madonna has proved to be an exception to the rule' (1993b, p. 1). Indeed, this collection was only one of three academic books published that year that focused exclusively on Madonna (see also Frank and Smith, 1993a; Lloyd, 1993), and scholarly interest has since continued unabated (Robertson, 1996; Faith, 1997; Guilbert, 2002). The abundance of critical work on the artist has almost certainly been part of broader developments in methodological trends in academia: the study of popular culture has come a long way since David Riesman described it in 1950 as 'a relatively new field in American social science' (1993, p. 5). This in turn has been part of a shift towards academic interdisciplinarity, and by offering a wide range of texts for analysis – music, video, film, live musical performance, interviews and more – Madonna reveals herself to be an ideal focus for the developing critical resources of popular cultural theory.

Academics working within these fields must face the challenge of precisely how to write about such an intensely pervasive cultural icon as Madonna. This entails primarily the question of how to filter (indeed, *to what extent* to filter) the surplus of popular writing about the subject. Much of this popular writing about Madonna is periodically amalgamated in volumes such as *Desperately Seeking Madonna* (Sexton, 1993); *Madonna: The Rolling Stone Files* (*Rolling Stone*, 1997) or *The Madonna Companion* (Metz and Benson, 1999), but such collections are themselves hampered by the sheer volume of material published, and the intensity with which it is disseminated. The academic might, therefore, choose also to face the popular press head-on, and attempt to stay aware of new developments to whatever extent is possible. Yet there is an inevitable chain of time delays between production by the artist, reception by the media, reception *of* the media (by the academic), the production of analysis and the publication of findings. The novelty of this volume therefore lies not only in its primary focus on newer Madonna material (which has not yet received academic attention), but also in its inflection by the new theoretical approaches adopted by our contributors.

The structural division of this book, with an introduction and four sections named after five of Madonna's concert tours, playfully insists on the theatrical and performative nature of her transformations, and also refers to the length and scope of her career, embodied by those tours. The section entitled 'The Girlie Show' focuses on issues relating to Madonna's exploration of gender identities, an aspect that has dominated previous academic readings of her cultural meaning (see, for example, essays collected in Frank and Smith, 1993a, Schwichtenberg, 1993a or Lloyd, 1993). Whilst earlier interpretations have tended not to focus on musical elements, Stan Hawkins's chapter, which opens this section, considers the roles of music technology and production processes in the continued projection of camp in Madonna's work. Using 'Music' (2000) as his primary object of analysis, Hawkins addresses the interplay of digital editing, musical aesthetics, drag and performance, to argue that Madonna's music is an important part of her deployment of camp. Patricia Pisters concentrates on the persistence of Madonna's relationship with the idea of 'girlhood' and the consistent problematization of feminist themes in her work. Starting with a review of representations of these themes in the early videos and performances, Pisters' chapter culminates in an in-depth analysis of more recent materials that demonstrate some kind of engagement with gender politics and questions of 'the feminine', especially in the song and video 'What it Feels Like for a Girl' (2001) and the *Drowned World Tour*. Corinna Herr considers three video clips ('Open Your Heart' (1986), 'Justify My Love' (1990) and 'Bedtime Story' (1995)) in relation to alchemical and hermeticist traditions, investigating in particular the concepts of androgyny and masquerade, and raising interesting observations about the influence of art deco and surrealism on the videos analysed.

While issues relating to gender and sexuality are strongly linked, we have made a broad division and entitled the second section of this book 'Post-Virgin', as the two chapters in this section deal with matters more strictly related to sexual identities. Whereas much of the previous work on these issues has been influenced by the controversy surrounding *Sex* and *Erotica* in the early 1990s (see Frank and Smith, 1993a), the chapters in this section of our collection analyse subsequent developments. Keith Clifton's chapter is rooted in a ubiquitous focus area of interest in Madonna studies, her relationship with gay men. Starting with a review of Madonna's early connections with disco, he describes *Evita* (1996) as a turning point in her vocal evolution and uses 'Frozen' (1998) as an example of a musical maturity and operatic quality that appeals to a different sector of the gay public. An interesting aspect of Clifton's contribution is his application of classical musicology to the popular text that is Madonna, thus offering a new way of considering her meaning for the gay male community. Freya Jarman-Ivens undertakes an analysis of Madonna's continued and contested deployment of lesbianism, thereby contributing to an area that has attracted considerably less attention within 'queer' approaches to Madonna. In her chapter, Jarman-Ivens looks retrospectively at the artist's more explicit engagement with lesbianism in the early 1990s, and identifies less prominent examples that have emerged since then, ranging from *The Girlie Show* (1993) to *Up For Grabs* (2002), or the lesbo-erotic performance at the 2003 MTV music video awards.[8]

The third section of this book is entitled 'Drowned Worlds', evoking the idea that ethnicity has superseded (although not entirely replaced) sexuality as the focus of Madonna's transformations in recent years, an idea that underscores the emphasis placed on ethnicity by this volume. Although themes of race have been addressed in previous studies on Madonna (for example, Nakayama and Peñaloza, 1993; Scott, 1993), the increasing significance of ethnicities in her work surely invites new analysis, and three of the four essays in this section therefore deal with comparatively recent material. Concentrating specifically on the Hindu iconography that accompanied *Ray of Light* and which characterized much of Madonna's work in 1998, Michael Angelo Tata approaches the range of images contemporary to that album, and explores her apparent eschewal of materialism in favour of Hindu spiritualism and cabbala wisdom. Focusing particularly on a photographic portfolio of Madonna by David LaChapelle published in that year, Tata traces the underlying uniformity of the 'contradictory elements' represented at that time. Rahul Gairola focuses on Madonna's geisha imagery, foregrounded in the *Drowned World Tour* and 'Nothing Really Matters' (Renck, 1999). Reading this alongside other East Asian identities, Gairola's contribution examines the impact of globalization on the commoditization of ethnicity. Whereas Madonna's exploration of intra-Caucasian identities has so far received little academic attention, Sean Albiez addresses these ideas in his study of Madonna's relationship with American identity throughout her career but especially since 'American Pie' (2000), which preceded her move to Britain and her Scottish wedding. Juxtaposing Madonna's *Music* album (musically and visually) with Country music discourse, Albiez explores layers of 'authenticity' and exposes a chain of simulacra in which Madonna's putatively inauthentic appropriation of the cowgirl figure is arguably layered within the questionable authenticity of Country music itself. Noting her apparently inconsistent self-location as a problematically ethnic subject and an exemplary white American, Albiez's conclusion suggests some of the paradoxes of Madonna's version of the 'American dream'. Santiago Fouz-Hernández's chapter explores a racial identity which has recurred perceptibly throughout Madonna's career: he makes use of a wide range of mainly visual material, from 'Borderline' (Lambert, 1984) to *Evita* (Parker, 1996), in his study of Madonna's long-term relationship with Hispanic identities. While critiquing the way in which some of these videos reinforce negative and outmoded stereotypes, he also discusses ways in which they might be understood to subvert Hispanic macho culture. Fouz-Hernández also acknowledges a certain genuineness in Madonna's interest in the Hispanic, which ranges from the Spanish influence on her music to her personal and long-lasting links in real life (most notably her daughter with Carlos León).

As the title 'Blond Ambition' would suggest, the final section of this volume is concerned with aspects of celebrity and consumption. David Gauntlett's primary objective is to identify the role Madonna has played in the reception of female music artists, and her influence on newer pop acts such as Britney Spears and Destiny's Child.[9] Using material from interviews with fans alongside public statements by key female artists, Gauntlett traces the extent to which recent acts have benefited from Madonna's challenges to certain boundaries of acceptability. Employing a similarly sociological approach, Lisa Peñaloza's contribution analyses consumers' attitudes to Madonna as a celebrity. Again, this understanding is updated, and specifically referred back to previous work done in this area, as Peñaloza compares a new survey with an earlier one she had conducted (with Thomas Nakayama, for *The Madonna Connection*). Peñaloza's conclusions in many ways summarize one of the central premises of this volume as a whole when she suggests that Madonna's deployment of subcultural discourses is problematic whether viewed from within the 'mainstream' or from a 'subcultural' location: thus, Madonna and her work emerge as a prism through which audiences are invited to confront ideas of ownership, authenticity, identity and appropriation.

This wide range of readings is undoubtedly appropriate given the extent to which Madonna has become characterized by rapid transformation. The chapters contained in this volume are not only unified by their general subject matter, however: they all represent new ways of thinking about a particularly malleable and reinventable contemporary icon. Although her initial success was in many ways due to her music, and despite her importance as a powerful operator within the music industry, it seems over the years that Madonna has become more famous for simply *being* Madonna than for her cultural products. Our collection seeks to negotiate this interesting and contested position by offering new perspectives on her creative output, as well as concerning itself with her meanings as a celebrity, meanings that will continue to emerge with each new career development and each new 'cultural transformation'. As the subcultural worlds that she has visited – and apparently drowned out with new worlds – resurface here, new complexities in the meanings she generates are constantly emerging. *American Life* suggested a new context against which to explore the apparently contradictory positionings which have characterized her career and works so far. Her own self-questioning lyrics in the single, 'American Life' invited interrogation of her previous objectives. Are the transformations discussed within this book a metaphor for the diversity of America? Does Madonna, through those transformations, live out that diversity? Or is she subsuming difference within an all-inclusive, 'globalizing' label? As the chapters in this collection seem to suggest, any attempt to understand Madonna's meanings must be underscored by a recognition of her complexity, and by an engagement with an overwhelming sense in her oeuvre that, as she would put it, 'nothing is what it seems'.

Notes

1. Also presented as an installation at the Deitch Projects Gallery in Soho, New York, in April and May 2003.
2. For a contemporaneous example of the critical reception of Madonna's interaction with lesbianism, especially as portrayed in *Sex*, see Crimp and Warner, 1993. See also Chapter 5 in this collection for a retrospective analysis by Freya Jarman-Ivens.
3. Whilst the artistic transformation into a more classic-style singer would be only temporary, her ideological transformation would culminate with her focus on spirituality during the late 1990s and a surprising dismissal of her *Sex* book, declaring in 2003 that she was 'just being an ego-driven nutcase!', adding: 'I thought I was

doing a service to mankind, being revolutionary, liberating women, yada yada. I wasn't!' (Ginsberg, 2003, p. 251).

4. *Ray of Light* (1998), *Music* (2000) and *American Life* (2003) were produced by vanguardists William Orbit (1998; 2000) and Mirwais (2000; 2003). Some of the singles from these albums have been remixed by popular DJs such as Above and Beyond, Felix DaHouseCat, Paul Oakenfold and Missy Elliot, also contributing to Madonna's musical currency.

5. This effect was also achieved by the artwork for *GHV2* (2001), which made similar use of a vast range of Madonna images from throughout her career.

6. On bodily poses, compare the cover of the commercially released recording of the *Drowned World Tour* with the *Virgin* tour (see photograph in Metz and Benson, 1999, p. 173) and the *Who's That Girl?* tour (during the performance of 'Who's That Girl?'; available as *Ciao Italia*). On lyrics, see references to 'Vogue' (1990) made in 'Deeper and Deeper' (1992), and to 'Express Yourself' (1989) in 'Human Nature' (1995). On music, as an example, note that direct examples of Spanish musicality are audible as early as 'La Isla Bonita' (1987) and as recently as 'Die Another Day' (2002).

7. German Dita Parlo was a failed Hollywood actress (the irony surely being intentional), who starred in French films of the 1930s, including *L'Atlante* (Vigo, 1934) and *La Grande Illusion* (Renoir, 1937). See Curry, 1990, p. 21, on Madonna's direct references to German cinematic history.

8. Interestingly, Madonna then told David Letterman (CBS, 11 November 2003) that one of the points of the MTV music video award kisses with Britney Spears and Christina Aguilera was to symbolically 'pass on the baton' to the younger artists, a point that intersects with David Gauntlett's contribution to this collection (Chapter 10).

9. Other key evidence of Madonna's influence on new pop acts in the early part of this decade include Kelly Osbourne's cover of 'Papa Don't Preach' (2002); MadHouse's album *Absolutely Mad* (2002), featuring house versions of Madonna hits; and The Androids' humorous homage, '(I'd Rather) Do It With Madonna' (2003), in which they suggest that Madonna is still better and more attractive than any younger female pop act.

PART I

The Girlie Show: Gender Identities

Olivier Tridon

Chapter 1

Dragging out camp
Narrative agendas in Madonna's musical production

Stan Hawkins

Loaded with a wealth of musical surprises, Madonna's tracks transport with them everything we enjoy about pop. Representing an expansive sonic plane, her productions open up an important space for understanding the intricacies of identity at play. The position adopted in this chapter is directed at a search for a theory of constructed performance that concentrates on the issue of style through camp mannerism. In a broad sense, Madonna's musical productions form useful points of departure for working out how identity constructions in pop can entice us into new spaces for social and cultural assimilation. Through all her songs, her musical expression connotes pleasure and enjoyment within a definable socio-historical relationship. It is as if the very effects of production and commercialization – the vital components of pop expression – encapsulate the full trajectories of her personality. To a large extent the link between musical production and pop artists inscribes not just the mechanics of sound reproduction but also the ideas and attitudes that refer to the pop performance as a constructed event. It is on this basis that I want to ground my theoretical discussion of Madonna's performance in a detailed discussion of the relationship between her musical expression and camp.

Musical production is inextricably wrapped up not only in how Madonna chooses to market herself but also in how she wishes to sound. Understood in this way, her recordings shape both her desires and those of the fans who express their feelings through responses to the sound event. Not least, the technologies of studio production construct the personal touches and nuances of whom we hear and how they express themselves. Generally, pop recordings realize the audio dynamics of an ideal performance, where the focus falls on the intensity and presence of musical processes. Because of this, recordings harness stories and in so doing they function as implied narratives that transport the subjectivity of the singer or artist as central character.

What I also want to suggest is that the skill in writing pop songs lies as much in the sound production as in selecting the subject matter of the song. Notably, Madonna's songs are derived from a musical appropriation of production trends emanating from dance culture,[1] which are expressed through her performance. Most crucially, it is her turning to camp that has steadily become a dominant feature of her musical performance. Indeed, her texts are about a narcissistic masquerading which exhibits a sense of self-mockery that is excessive in many ways.[2]

Attached to aesthetic preferences, our enjoyment of music discloses notions of community that have to do with us understanding the functional side of assumptions dealing with taste (see Frith, 1996). Indeed, this also involves the erotic dimension of performance and how it overflows into the spectacular body. Within the confines of this chapter, my employment of the term 'camp pop' is a response to the milieu of popular culture entertainment that symbolizes a celebration of artifice, commerciality and, hence, good and bad taste.[3] At the core of this conception, I would suggest that the aesthetic quality of camp pop designates a move towards a doubleness in which musical expression forms a major part of its construction. In Madonna's case, it is the nature of her brand of pop that explores the potential to which her personality can pertain. Her music relies upon attitude, tone and irony, and is subversive of inflexible social and moral rules. Its positioning therefore suggests a distancing from the constraints of conventional ideas in art and life. For instance, in the visual display of Madonna's role-playing, her videos often imply that sex and gender roles are contrived. In this sense, the theatricalization of Madonna's identity allows for an empathy that is equated with the listener's own sense of submission.

Though her style might mock the seriousness of rock and other musical forms, it still is earnest in its own way. Thus, as much as humour and fun, earnestness forms a crucial ingredient of camp. This is no more evident than in the distortion of prescribed forms of taste and behaviour through the role-playing mechanisms of drag. In Esther Newton's terminology, drag designates role-playing (1999, p. 105) and implies a sex role. In this case, the distancing between the artist and role-playing implicates a degree of superficiality through the switching on and off of these roles at will. Newton states that, in drag, the actor 'should throw himself into it; he should put on a good show; he should view the whole experience as fun, as a camp' (p. 105). Clearly, the doubleness of this strategy is what lies at the heart of drag; it is a system of impersonation through show.

We might pursue the interrelationship of the two terms, camp and pop, which, in their combination, allow for the surplus sensibility of a disposable culture that invokes signifiers of fun and pleasure that are oppositional. On different uses of the terms camp and pop, Andrew Ross (1999) has problematized numerous styles, which include heavy metal, glam rock, punk and rock. His employment of 'pop camp' denotes a cultural and historical periodization of mass culture, with an important focus on the 1960s camp contradictory and layered cultured economy. In debating this concept, Ross emphasizes how camp was 'an antidote to Pop's contagion of obsolescence' (1999, p. 321). There are two matters of interest that build on Ross's critique. The first deals with the idea of stylized performance in pop with all its artificial gesturing. In particular, I am referring to the camp qualities that succeed in winning over the fans by affected performance. For the present argument, I would suggest that it is audiences' specific responses to the performing body that determine the expressive quality of the music. At any rate, when we respond to pop recordings we relate to a repertory of emotional elements that are shaped by moments transported by the logic of musical shape and sound. The second matter concerns the purposefulness of technological seduction in pop through constructs of artificiality and inauthenticity as they are bound up in the recording process itself. Certainly, each time we hear a vocal track within a mix, we react primarily to the technical dialects of audio signal processes and how the voice is recorded. As I have argued in earlier studies, studio production has the most significant effect on the details of sound in a manner that lures us through time into the personal sphere of the performer (see Hawkins, 1997 and 2002). Engineered to ensure that the intended listener achieves a special association with the performer, the recording ultimately concerns the feelings and sentiments of shared communities. What I mean by this is that recordings are about common tastes that help distinguish not only musical styles but also the cultural and social organization of specific musical preferences. From this perspective, then, the power of the recording is manifested in the imaginary process of musical listening.[4] In Madonna's music, the detailed effects of technology are undeniably tied into the full mediation of her star persona, especially as every sound becomes conditional on the fine balance between producer, engineer, artist and, of course, the record company. Since the early 1980s, Madonna's role in the studio has gradually evolved to a point where her input into the final product has become almost total.[5] This is borne out chiefly by the technical processes that reveal not only the artist's collaborative relationship with her team of workers, but also the type of audience for which the music is produced. So, given that it is the audience that permits the communication of musical messages, we might ask to what extent then is camp felt as part of the musical experience. And, if considered as a strategic event that relies on production and reception, how does camp set the limits for what determines a specific response?[6]

As music's rhetoric relies on emotive states and moods, pop artists draw on specific musical traditions to communicate their intentions.[7] While all Madonna's songs share many of the same musical elements,[8] their overall studio conceptions are significantly different. Most of all, the technical editing processes found in her productions disclose important details of compositional processing. There often arises a sense of a new reality through the expressive levels of editing in her music. In most cases, her recordings are collaborative projects in which a range of expert producers becomes part of Madonna's trademark. Indeed, it is the myriad of personal styles and voices that characterize the individuality of each one of her albums, videos and songs.

From one perspective, Madonna's recordings can be read as deconstructions of traditional notions of live performance. Like her image, her musical material is presented in ways that deliberately exceed the bounds of live performance. The studio conditions determining each track are certainly part of the challenge of her 'live' act, as her recordings are realized in ways that make live performances simulated events. This is evident in her concerts, where a high degree of playback creates the illusion of an authenticity that translates into a hyper-artificiality, which is always attached to the recording. In this sense, her style is postmodern in that it becomes a reaction to modernist tendencies and historical periods.[9] Manifested through a strategy of layering sounds and effects, her recordings open up a broad spectrum of possibilities for us to further consider her music as a product of camp pop.

Dragging camp through sound production

If the promo video or live concert focuses our attention on the desired representation of the star, so the sound production always underwrites the pleasures of the text.[10] In Madonna's track 'Music' (2000), the meaning of the song is instantly encoded by one's associations with the artist's voice and image. Posing as a Rhinestone cowgirl on the album sleeve of *Music* (2000), in a construction that can be read as fake, what is presented to us is an outright celebration of camp. From the outset, 'Music'– produced by Madonna and Mirwais Ahmadzï – is charged with dazzling splashes of electronica and top class production tricks.

Quite over the top in its production veneer, the track mediates a camp sensibility through the flashiness of the mix. In particular, the revival of disco style makes this explicit. As each bar builds up into groove patterns that stabilize the feel of the beat, Madonna embraces every rhythmic impulse to play around with titillation. Instead of opening up the song herself, she elects to use an affected, sexy male voice recorded close-up in a sleazy, American drawl: 'Hey Mr DJ, put a record on. I want to dance with my baby.' Phased through heavy reverb, this phrase is tweaked to build up anticipation and tension. Following a reverse cymbal crescendo, the groove revs up with a tightly quantized, funky syncopated figure dominated by a single pitch motif on a low voluptuous Hammond organ tone (Figure 1.1). Sixteen bars of a groove laced with an impressive array of electronic pyrotechnics – high-pitched vocoded flirtatious vocals on the words 'Boogie Woogie. Do you like to?', disco string stabs, dry snares on the second and fourth beats, stereo panning of an intricately spliced-up guitar riff – provide the textural carpet for Madonna's grand entry. Significantly, the regulation of spatial properties in the mix and the textural density of this introduction serve as a warm up for the entire song.[11] From the moment Madonna enters the recording and takes over from the male voice, the processing and

Fig. 1.1   Organ groove from 'Music'

Source: transcribed by the author from *Music* (Warner, 2000)

imaging of her voice in the mix becomes a central feature. Highly quantized, the groove pattern is filled out by a sub-bass accenting the two beats of the funk figure we have already heard (Figure 1.1). On arrival at the first chorus, less than one minute into the song, the word 'music' is cleverly edited through vocoding in a way that contorts Madonna's voice with a joyful earnestness. Instantly, a degree of playfulness emerges from the sonorous elasticity of her vocal phrasing and inflections that discloses the song's camp quality. In fact, 'Music' sets up a horizontal plane of sonic attributes that are related and defined by their imaging in the mix. By this I am suggesting that the imaging of single musical ideas is contingent on the specific physical location of each sound source within the recording itself. In addition, musical imaging concerns the perceived location of these sonic properties from the perspective of the listener.[12] Amongst the many appealing features that stand out in this track's imaging is the variability of sound sources and their means of manipulation within the production, not least through their spatial relationships. As if to make this track an exercise in plotting her control through technical virtuosity and sophisticated engineering, Madonna sets out to show off her production skills unashamedly. Musically, this is instilled as much through a range of technological pyrotechnics as in the features involving pitch, rhythm, timbre and melodic linearity.[13]

As I experience it, the pleasure in 'Music' is based around an erotic sensibility that proposes something quite glamorous and technically ambitious. This occurs within an audio space that is vast, with a myriad of details that challenge our notions of aural reality. In this context, distance relates to where the listener imagines the sound to be and where the front and rear boundaries of the audio image are established by the listener's conception of distance.[14] And it is in this sense that production techniques utilize notions of sonic reality as a form of theatrical distancing and placement. Importantly, sensations of distance in recordings are not just about dynamics, volume or levels of reverberation; they are also about intimacy. In 'Music', the listener is exposed to a composite sound object that is primarily the result of timbral difference and fluctuating levels of reverberation. This is discernible all the way through, as timbres and textures are altered rapidly and in dramatic ways through synthesis and signal processing.[15]

Aesthetically, the effect of this is that certain sounds are located within environments that feel synthetic and mannered and where timbral definition is highly profiled by 'spacey' (as in out of the world) edits and mixes. Indeed, the full galaxy of sounds in 'Music' cntails a compilation of ideas that zigzag in and out of different locations at varying speeds. Constantly mobile, the various sound objects in the mix can be charged with creating the aural fantasy. As repeated hearings of this song soon reveal, musical ideas are pasted and dragged over one another to construct the musical form – a technique controlled by digital editing. Within the many different layers of the mix, the elements of sound (and in this case sound that exists mainly as computer information) are edited in real time, often through meticulous predetermined automation.[16] By this I am referring to digital processes of panning, changes in equalization, alternating fader levels and special effects, all of which form part of the precise edit points that determine the music's fabric and, hence, its feel.[17] In such instances, we are reminded that in pop songs such as 'Music', it is the quest for polished style that is instigated by the intricate mechanics of recording technology in an audio environment that assembles and assumes the artist's authority in any number of guises. Bearing this in mind, I now want to turn to a closer inspection of how the audio image engenders musical relations.

(En)gendering musical relations

Madonna's texts are derived from a unique chemistry that exists between her recorded performance and the spectacle of her construction. Of course, one's own notions of identity are central to any such assumption, and my central argument is that this can be explored further through the flux of structures and gestures. In all the verses of 'Music', Madonna's voice is recorded with relatively little studio treatment: the pitch range is confined to a perfect fifth and her voice is positioned to the front of the mix with few effects. The microphone used, and its close-up effect, produces a special intimacy that sets up a constructed naturalness, which contributes to the erotic sensibility of her voice. In the choruses, there is a significant change to a more synthetic sound (through vocoding) as the pitch range of her melodic phrasing shrinks to a minor third. Contrasting with the verses, the chorus sections are characterized by an unprecedented boost in studio effects. I am referring specifically to the beginning of the first chorus as the vocals are double-tracked and eq'd in a way that dramatizes the effect of sonic contrast.[18]

Teasingly, Madonna distances herself from the intimacy of her verse sections by becoming caught up in a swirl of clever edits. What these digital edits serve as are moments of aural spectacle that bring to the fore an erotic sensuality that is rooted in dance culture. In other words, the subtleties and excesses of musical treatment, especially in terms of skilful editing, endorse the stylistic appropriations and layered rhythmic patterns found in dance music that all have direct associations with the body. In this way, Madonna's musical style guarantees a seductiveness that is about excess through virtuosity – it is this that discloses her camp quality. To expand this point further, I would suggest that musically her camp expression is borne out by countless gestures in the unfolding of the song's compositional form not least through production techniques. One case in point is the thematic material (in its entirety) that culminates in an extended coda-like section which juxtaposes two somewhat disparate melodic riffs, one instrumental, one spoken (Figure 1.2). In the instrumental riff, it is a sense of uncertainty that keeps the momentum of this pattern alive. With a major seventh leap to C♯ via an upper mordent slide (D²), a jarring clash in the tonality of the song occurs, before this discord resolves through B♭¹-C² to A¹. Quite unexpectedly, the dissonance of the C♯ deceives us into a harmonic minor shift, just before the melodic minor descending line is emphasized. The effect of this is to challenge the harmonic stability of the song. That is, the entry of the felicitous pitch C♯², the sharpened seventh degree, is outside the confines of the song's tonality, not least through its late introduction only within the last minute of the song (2:57). Significantly, the occurrence of an altered tone at this point creates something musically different or pseudo-exotic by resting outside the tonal norms of the song.

Mixed to the fore of the track, this instrumental riff is taken up by a crass, analogue-type 1970s moog string synthesizer that boldly pelts out the incessant angular melody to the song's eventual fade-out. Despite excessive reiteration, the interest of this riff is maintained dialogically in the vocoded theme, 'Do you like to?' Instantly, the mismatch of these two lines is sealed through a simultaneous clash of C♯ and C♮. Arguably, while subversive in mannerism, these contrapuntal phrases metamorphose into something alluringly beautiful, quirky and flamboyant, the effect of which is camp. The contrived sensibility of these two phrases results in a pleasure that is caught up in the instrumental timbre, production and memorable tunefulness. Playfully, the exchange between these

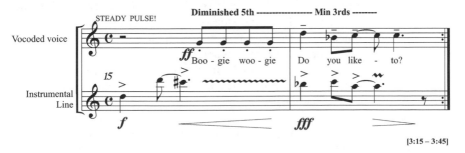

Fig. 1.2 Dual melodic camp theme from 'Music'

Source: transcribed by the author from *Music* (Warner, 2000)

two parts, together with all the other musical events, represents sheer artifice. In a way, it is the pretentiousness of the affected vocal utterance 'Do you like to?' that most enhances the duplicity. In my reading of this, the difference between the two phrases also infers something quite serious, spelling out Madonna's deepest intentions. Through the flashy production of this riff and the meticulous processing, her overall aim is one of extravagance. This is borne out not only in terms of economic investment (as this is a very polished, costly, commercial recording, and one hears this), but also through an attempt to experiment musically. The spirit of disco is expertly captured at this point through stylistic appropriation and innovative technical wizardry. In effect, the blatant reference to disco and funk refutes the traditional domain of rock and other male-based styles. Indeed, the technological expertise found in 'Music' is responsible for contributing to a style that is camp. Elements of digital editing and computer-based approaches to layering one track over the other are constantly daring and yet cheeky. Often to the point of being over-decorative, it is as if the mix liberates artistic expression from taking itself too seriously. This is manifested in the creative implant of non-acoustic instrumental sounds into new contexts, something that emphasizes the constitutive element of postmodern artifice. Indeed, the playfully automated retro-electronic ideas hark back to Kraftwerkian Europop and underlie a sensibility that is more than just ineffable. An almost mocking quality in both melodic gestures (Figure 1.2) belies an attitude that, while disengaged in one respect, is highly reflexive in another.

The coda passage described above is musically flirtatious, not least in terms of the virtuosic quality of its editing. This results in an aesthetic wherein style triumphs over content. Here musical performance is wrapped up in an experience that is exhibitionist in terms of its sponsoring of life as theatre. It is as if the force of all the musical gestures in 'Music' asserts the gregarious and witty nature of hedonism, which nourishes the idea of camp as something intensely pleasurable. At any rate, the compositional processing through digital editing techniques and multi-channel mixing contributes significantly to feeling the music as camp.

Over the past twenty years, Madonna's specific appeal to a gay and bisexual following has been decidedly on the side of pop and dance trends. While the sentimentality found in commercial pop music might determine how well the artist sells, it is also about the complex entanglements of sexual desire, solidarity and pleasure that define taste (see Frank and Smith, 1993b). Paradoxically, camp pop is seldom what it appears to be *musically*. Pop recordings are invariably about painstaking, professional productions that are sophisticated, costly and meticulously calculated before being packaged. Not surprisingly, it is the aesthetics embraced by commercial pop that target specific audience groups. On the social implications of this, Simon Frith (1996) puts forward a particularly persuasive example of the argument that pop can be described as not only collective but also individual in that it functions as a storehouse for reference and quotation. Thus, whether we enter the debate from a sociological or musicological direction, pop songs are attached to sites of consumption that are not only extraordinary but also deeply personal. In fact, what makes artists such as Madonna so compelling to minority audiences can be explained by a gendered reflexivity that overflows into numerous sites from the inner sphere of the subject to the outer parameters of sexual preference.[19]

Several issues arise from these assertions. Within Madonna's performance, I would suggest that aspects of her identity are frequently portrayed as subversive without necessarily destabilizing norms. Entrenched in the spectacle of her videos and colourful live concert performances, her play on gender ambiguity often sets out to deflect non-normative practices while maintaining normative sexuality intact. Yet in the correlations between drag and, say, bi- and homo-inclinations in videos such as 'Vogue' (Fincher, 1990), 'Justify My Love' (Mondino, 1990), 'Erotica' (Baron, 1992), 'Bad Girl' (Fincher, 1993) and 'Human Nature' (Mondino, 1995), her representations constitute a lot more than just futile excursions into gender-bending or trivial displays of subversion.[20] On this basis, we need to ask not only how gendered representation is manifested in pop, but also what happens within dominant heteronormative frames when notions of gender are destabilized.

Within the debates on the socially constructed nature of gender, the problematics of ontology are encountered at the levels of sexuality, gender and language. In short, one of the central issues of queer theory rests on the idea that one is a woman or man only to the extent that one operates within a heteronormative frame (see Butler, 1999, pp. vii–xxvi). But new forms of gendering have gradually arisen in the light of new identities that imply an 'in-between-ness' that has little to do with gender binarisms. These paradoxes have been extensively debated from different standpoints by feminist theorists such as Judith Butler (1993 and 1999), Donna Haraway (1989), Catharine MacKinnon (1987) and bell hooks (1984).

Perhaps the central issue that emerges from many of these debates is the causal link between the distinction of gender and sexuality, and that sexual regulation of gender through heteronormativity cannot be rendered exclusive. Yet, the performance of gender subversion, as Butler argues (1999), indicates little about sexual practice or sexuality. Butler considers performativity as a repetition and a ritual that gains its effect 'through its naturalization in the context of a body', which is part of a larger, culturally sustained temporal entity (p. xv). Although Butler does not decide whether the materiality of the body is constructed or not, she argues for a theory of performativity which underwrites a discourse on gender, and highlights the limitations of gender as a category for analysis. Obviously, one needs to exert caution in any readings of subversive and/or submissive inscriptions of gendered identity in Madonna's texts. For the inquiry into conditions of camp cannot circumvent normative accounts of gender and how these attest to expressions of credibility. From this it would seem that how we proceed to make ethical justifications through the employment of the term 'normative' (without subscribing to a normative gendered world) remains problematic, as the qualification of gender is a fugitive operation when linked to a normative operation of power.

Ultimately, we could say Madonna's musical expression is a confession of calculated constructedness. In various ways, the demonstration of her empowerment in the music industry is a sign that the normative ideals of gender function form uneasy circumscriptions of reality. As I have already suggested, an application of drag to Madonna's performance implies her identity is knowingly unfixed (Tyler, 1991). It is as if in all her texts there is a sense of double inversion as she openly admits her subjectivity is an illusion. This is evident in the structures of impersonation that run through two decades of videos, films and songs that expose the fantasies constituted within the body. In all her texts, a catalogue of imitations symbolize Madonna's drag within the framework of musical performance. Implicit in drag, the act of mimicry accentuates the conflict between the body and its gendered representation. And, in a sense, it is the coupling of aural and visual codes that forms a substantial part of the pleasure derived from the musical sound. I am referring to the pleasure we experience when recognizing the bodily configurations that either conform to or challenge the natural and original. At any rate, it seems that by parodying gender norms, often with blatant sarcasm and caustic wit, drag in Madonna's case exposes the imitative representation of femininity itself. And, through the aid of sound, her expression of femininity results in a degree of normative failure.

Undoubtedly, Madonna's utterance in the chorus of 'Music', when she cries out, 'Music! Makes the people come together! Music! Makes the bourgeoisie and the rebel!' has political implications. In passages such as these Madonna's music, at least on first hearing, conceals nothing and promotes nothing. Could this just be some crass reminder, one might ask, that pop is neither real nor false? Yet, through the very reference to the bourgeoisie there is a suspicion that Madonna seeks to empower herself further through lyrical ingenuity. With such contrived positioning, Madonna's strategy becomes one of distancing, whereby she seeks her inspiration from both contestation and compliance. Clearly, she is part of the anonymity of the bourgeoisie. This becomes even more accented as one moves from 'bourgeois culture proper to its derived, vulgarized and applied forms', which Barthes describes as 'public philosophy' (1973, p. 141). In no uncertain terms, today's bourgeois culture thrives on patterns of consumption linked to the media press, tabloid literature, films and internet chat lines, all of which represent that which the bourgeoisie has made out of their relations with the external world. For Barthes, bourgeois norms are the commercialized and vulgarized truths that have become somewhat archaic. And gradually, through the latter half of the twentieth century, bourgeois culture has narrowed through a type of symbiosis into a common Western ideology. Notably though, Madonna's very flight from the label bourgeois is a process of bourgeois ideology itself, as the bourgeois class seeks to transform the world through technical powers, artistic endeavour and scientific progress.

In her linking of bourgeois culture to camp, Susan Sontag (1999) has considered the issue of social affluence and material gain by questioning the very history of snobbishness. With her put-on arrogance, Madonna often portrays the snob playing out the role of rebel; an act which quickly diffuses any tension by the sheer playfulness of camp. One of the main functions of her performance seems to be to empty reality while still embodying political statements of fact. In other words, in her role as diva she reminds us that contemporary pop culture is about the transition from the real to the artificial where bourgeois ex-nomination can attain full empowerment. This occurs in a context of a perfectible world where, as she tells us, music *makes* the bourgeoisie and the rebel. Certainly, the eloquence of this phrase endorses the buttonholing nature of social politicization through pop. Thus, via memorable melodies, irresistible rhythms and rich mixes, Madonna's texts mobilize and encode qualities that propose ideals, not least in respect to her mainstreaming of difference. By her performing out a multitude of roles she moves effortlessly from one project to the next, capitalizing on the stark differences of gender and spectacularity.

Yet any impressions of gender hardly disclose the constitution of an original blueprint for the camp identity to imitate. Rather, Madonna's identity is about an unfettered access to a construction that is inscribed through fantasy; a fantasy where sex and gender roles are made so superficial that they become, in the end, only a matter of style. No better is this illustrated than when Madonna parodies the cowgirl in her visual promotions of the album *Music* and her *Drowned World Tour* (2001). Through this imagery she fashions herself as an imitation without an original. Here the notion of the loss of the 'normal', which in this case is the quintessential patriarchal construction of the male, parodies its own occasion for empowerment as we realize the fallacy of originality itself. In this sense, Madonna's strategy of drag through the cowboy can be both provocative and troublesome. As her performances over the last twenty years have achieved parodic displacement through disruptive repetitions, they have become re-circulated as powerful voices of a cultural hegemony. In other words, her output proposes a reconsideration of the reception of the feminine and the masculine to the extent that when camp is played out through drag, it symbolizes a radical statement that pertains to survival within rigid social structures and systems. Put differently, she impersonates in ways that poke fun at the restrictive nature of normative identification. Good proof of this can be found in the theatricality of her pop videos where her challenging of the male gaze signifies a queering of femininity on many fronts.[21] Like Bette Davis's films, the stylized mannerisms found in Madonna's videos exude a calculated authority and self-sufficiency that serves as a powerful channel for political commentary.[22]

Vocal authorship and notions of pleasure

When considering the potential of Madonna's gender transformations from one album, film or video to the next, we might say that these different representations are located in stylized repetitions of acting that expose the effect of her identity as a tenuous cultural construction. As her vocal expression forms part of her theatrical enactment, so it contributes to the stacking up of Madonna as coherent subject. Mostly, it is in the exuberance of her voice that her sentiments are realized.

Further, there is always a sense that Madonna's performances are never inconsequential. It is as if they are regulated to tell stories within a mobile frame that seeks to consolidate the subject at the same time as transgressing conventions. Thus, a central element of her aesthetic lies in the manner her narratives are presented to us – an element that exposes the phantasmic effect of a camp identity. Always, her affected mannerisms engage our attention by escorting us through a maze of performative possibilities that proliferate gender configurations within and outside the domain of compulsory categories.

More generally, I would suggest that incorporating identity politics within any consideration of the musical text forms an important part of theorizing the mediation of pleasure through sonic process. To this end, the control of narrative function within musical discourse is important, not least through the symbiosis of music, production and language. Sean Cubitt explores this issue through discussing the conditions of identification in the amplified voice: 'The amplified voice is an ideal form, an image like a mirror image. It is like us yet bigger, more perfect, almost godlike; like Socrates' daemon, it is more coherent and more fully in control of its identity than we often feel ourselves to be' (2000, p. 155). As Cubitt points out, there can be little doubt that the listener's active engagement with the amplified voice grants access to a wealth of emotions. Turning to Lacan's mirror phase metaphor, Cubitt insists that the amplified voice connects us through an idealized image with our inner and exterior worlds. Moreover, he points out how melodies and tunes can be interpreted as processes of signification that produce the subject as an 'effect of language' (p. 156), thus signifying a lack and absence.[23] Cubitt stresses the point that desire is always manifested through language, whose effect is something truly human. In this way, signifying practices in music inhabit that area between our social worlds and desire where '[t]here is a deal of play between the conscious enjoyment of presence and the activity of the unconscious about absence, a play that underlies the pleasure of listening' (p. 157). Underlying the pleasures in listening then, the chasm between language and consciousness or being makes up the discursive field of struggles of exchange. And, while Madonna's identity is constructed for itself, it always underwrites the determination of her purpose.

In the song 'Human Nature', from the *Bedtime Stories* album (1994), Madonna makes explicit a number of strong sentiments that deal with survival, romance, revenge, seduction and manipulation (see Hawkins, 1997, pp. 36–65). In their overdubbing, the music material in this song harnesses a wealth of discrete musical elements shaped by pitch, harmony, rhythm and sonic textures, all of which communicate the subject's desire. As the song develops, Madonna's voice entices us into a soundscape that concentrates on a representation of her femininity and struggle for empowerment. Challenging patriarchal masculinity head on, she delivers the phrase, 'And I'm not sorry / I'm not your bitch, don't hang your shit on me.' Her whispers to an imaginary confidante are heightened by the poignancy of the melodic phrase, 'Express yourself don't repress yourself.'[24] Demanding respect from those who have scorned her in the past, not least the music press, her vocal expression by the mid-1990s, when this song was recorded, is more confident, balancing between insincerity and parody, and between contempt and mirth.

There can be little doubt that her recordings to date have permitted her fans to join her in an experience that pursues pleasure on many different levels. Not unlike the opera heroine, there is always some element of melodrama in Madonna's delivery that helps identify the struggle between the female and her world.[25] In the 'Human Nature' video clip (Mondino, 1995), a personal and historical struggle is inscribed through theatrical representation and the high visibility of drag. Musically, this is borne out by the staticity of harmonic structures, which flirt with unlikely harmonic shifts (D♮s superimposed over B major chord progressions). These are set against rough jungle-bass riffs that weigh down the low register in a menacing manner. Similarly, in the kit tracks, the punches of the kick drum and snares become tantalizing metaphors of the narrative, while the employment of door-slamming samples abruptly blend into the percussion sounds to drive home the aggression of Madonna's delivery. Situated in the foreground of the mix, the vocal close-ups always promise intimacy. Indeed, the vocal amplification is erotic through close-up mic-ing and effects processing, as much as through the style of delivery as studio processing. Moreover, the manner by which she alternates between sung and spoken vocal phrases helps solicit an array of nuances that tantalize us and heighten our enjoyment.

In the video clip of this song, the erotic dimension of the music is evoked through the black latex-clad, androgynous bodies that provide important points for queering identification. A visualization of the layering of rhythmic grooves through lurid choreography captures Madonna and her troupe facing the camera full on, as they flaunt their sexuality with a serious defiance that verges on the pornographic. Structured by the musical form itself, the 'Human Nature' video is generally marked by quick edits that are in sync with the beat. What stands out most here is the highly narcissistic camera shots of the feline choreography, with strong hints at sadomasochistic and dominatrix trickery. Both the strong rhythmic drive and the melodic shapes in the lead vocals empower Madonna, completing her desire for herself by inverting the male gaze. Throughout the video, the focus is on androgyny, which is supported by layered musical ideas consisting of slippery melodic shapes, fragmentary samples and oiled rhythmic gestures. In such moments we are reminded of how the androgyne succumbs to the power of a camp sensibility. Behind the beauty of the androgynous troupe of dancers in 'Human Nature', the height of sexual appeal and desire lies in the idea of going against normative representations, which perhaps represents the most compelling side of Madonna's strategy of queering. Thus, queering in its nature, this video signals one in a line of spectacular constructions that raises a series of questions concerning the political purpose of musical expression and the alliances that exist between sexuality and subjectivity.

Watch me doing this camp, faggy stuff!

Gender categorization has been addressed to varying degrees in all the scholarly studies based around Madonna (see, for example, Frank and Smith, 1993a; Schwichtenberg, 1993a). In being able now to call her own shots, twenty years on in an extraordinary career, Madonna has inscribed her identity by her own take on mainstream pop. Pamela Robertson has argued how Madonna's self-presentation and reception can be traced back to the significant changes in post-1960s camp (1996, p. 136). In particular, her mainstreaming of camp has contributed to the introduction of queer politics into popular culture, not least through appropriation. On the issue of appropriation, Robertson has suggested that this intersects with the problems of mainstreaming, something that lends itself to the currency of difference in identity politics. Robertson offers an argument for evaluating difference within queer self-conceptions: 'If difference has been reified by queer and non-queer culture alike that is because we still cling to some belief that there are real differences and that some of these matter deeply' (pp. 137–8). If we accept Robertson's notion, Madonna's antics of queering are indeed problematic in terms of her reconceptualization of gender and sex identities and, moreover, her relegating of gay politics into a discourse on style. For Robertson, there is a difficulty in deciding who owns camp and whether heterosexual camp is indeed camp at all. At the core of her critique is a cautious approach to the definition of camp and the ongoing struggles that underlie appropriation. Robertson insists that context cannot be removed from any definition of camp. In much pop, camp constitutes the main part of a commercialized directive, and hence stands as a dominant social and historical marker. Certainly, the 'Madonna phenomenon' has offered a window on the political arena of gender parody and drag culture from the mid-1980s onwards. While her texts indeed appropriate film divas such as Dietrich, Davis, West or Garbo, it is the context within which she has revitalized camp that is most relevant. Robertson maintains that Madonna opens up important debates on camp today (1996, p. 119), to the point that she flags up some of the central concerns in the changing roles of women and the rearticulation of feminist orthodoxies through post-feminism (see Whiteley, 2000).

Sontag's position on camp is that its sensibility signifies a triumph of style over content and irony over tragedy through its consistent experience of the world (Sontag, 1999, p. 62). This is evident in the bulk of pop music and pop art, where camp quickly converts the serious into the banal, fusing the gap between low and high cultures. To return to an earlier point, pop texts can be perceived as pleasure-filled forms of entertainment catering for mass audiences, and yet they can also serve as antidotes to the disposability of commercial products. Compared to serious forms of rock (I am referring specifically to cock-rock styles, artists and groups), it is obvious that pop possesses a more flippant, glitzy and excessive quality that is consciously superficial and knowingly limp-wristed.[26]

Ever since the launch of MTV, Madonna's songs have captured an ideology of entertainment that is remarkably stylized and commercially exploitative. Indeed, her brand of pop sets out to conceal the ramifications of its technical and economic production by diverting our focus onto the immediacy of pleasurable experience. Ultimately, Madonna's texts are a platform for advertising. They cannot avoid promoting the pop commodity in the knowledge that it is disposable once consumed. Yet this is only part of the story, as I have argued elsewhere (Hawkins, 2002, pp. 1–35). As Madonna's identification advocates a policy of impersonation and transgressive display, her expression becomes a mechanism for her to address the interrelationships between the music industry, social politics and her own camp sensibility.

Of course, Madonna's political plight might well signify little more than a showcase for accessing more publicity and personal gain, with her narcissistic traits masking, as some critics have argued, an average musical talent (see Frith, 1993, p. 88). By (arguably) not confronting 'real' difference, Madonna's queering translates into a contrived, superficial, yet dangerous appropriation of the Other's more serious political and social mission. Pandering to the male gaze (even if this is an ironic gesture in itself), and getting us to revel in the delights of watching her playing out her 'camp and faggy stuff', she easily becomes just another hag on tour. So, rather than subversive, her politics can be interpreted as cranky appropriations of marginal practices that all too quickly convert into a dubious Bakhtinian carnival of intrigue and spectacle.

The problematics of this point are debated by Butler (1993) as she challenges the meaning behind such intentions. Investigating the subversive quality of drag, especially in heterosexual contexts, Butler sets out to describe how drag functions as high het entertainment. She also directs our attention to drag's control of boundaries against the possible threat of queerness. Heterosexual privilege, she argues, in taking on many different mantles, produces a type of drag that ultimately fortifies heterosexual desire. Significantly, Butler's diagnosis of drag presumes that displacement and gender appropriation are not simply 'reducible to a heterosexual matrix and the logic of repudiation' (1993, p. 127). This is because drag is always about the inclusion of the Other that was originally desired, but is now hated.

In one respect, Butler's premise is similar to Robertson's reading of Madonna as a woman seeking to conceal 'the actual powerlessness of subcultural groups through her performance of agency and power' (Robertson, 1996, p. 134). Nonetheless, Butler and Robertson would surely agree that Madonna also provides valuable recourse to a cultural critique of identity politics, not least in terms of the strategic functioning of camp as both a political and a critical force. Elaborating on this assertion, I would emphasize that reading Madonna as a camp icon needs to accommodate her musical expression as a dominant part of the queering process, whether this be through production techniques or compositional form.

Clearly, the struggle to situate herself in the centre of a male-dominated industry has involved her targeting mainstream as much as subcultural audiences. In this sense, her appropriation of camp through musical style is about (re)defining herself as adversarial. To contextualize this further, post-1970s pop recognized the subcultural part of the market and its keenness to have a share in the mainstream market. This probably stands as the most constituent hallmark of camp pop in the 1980s and 1990s. As Robertson argues, camp signifies that of 'difference and alienation from the dominant' (1996, p. 129), not least through its transience. In the end, the politics of Madonna are also about survival through the constant shifting and crossover forms of spectacle. And, by dragging out different forms of identification, her performances cannot fail to challenge circumscriptions of sexual stereotypes in pop culture.

Finally, in returning to the theoretical starting point of this chapter, Madonna's produced sound is contingent on a specific camp expression. Forever reliant on polished productions that are driven by the compositional layering of catchy grooves, the zeal of her music ultimately lies in the spectacle and theatricality of a survivalist fantasy. Ever since the early 1980s, her songs have been in hot pursuit of the latest developments in the dance scene, with a strong tendency towards flashy musical textures and gestures. Not least, the musical trends she has developed and appropriated have been consonant with an aestheticism that embraces humour, self-mockery and eroticism. As a means of dealing with the music industry's male-driven, hostile environment, her agency has undercut the very conventions that have excluded female artists to a large extent. So, rather than tears, it is more scornful laughter and pursed-lip determination that has characterized her agency. Most of all, her unique blend of camp can be perceived as an attempt to disavow the control mechanisms of a male-driven music industry. Obsessed with surface and style, a sensibility in her musical expression emerges that struggles to distinguish between the ludicrous and the serious, often at its own peril. Further, her identity depends so much on stylistic changes from one album to the next that it reinforces her resistance to the dominant ideologies that have traditionally subverted female composers and performers.[27] As a key element of her expression, her productions abound with a form of performance that is open to ironic and affected imitation.

What seems most remarkable about her career so far is how her play on identification has dragged in so many differences all at once. This alone has had a significant impact on the trends in pop music that have emerged in the past decades. If, in Pamela Robertson's words, 'Madonna's reception, both positive and negative, suggests that camp can still be a political and critical force' (1996, p.138), then there is a definite need to recognize her music's central contribution to this dynamic process. This is surely because the thrill of all her musical productions are complicated circumstances and contradictions that subscribe to identity formation and make musical gestures socially meaningful and, best of all, thoroughly enjoyable.

Notes

1. By 'dance culture' I am referring to the proliferation of styles that have emerged since disco in the 1970s, which have dominated the Club scene and trends in youth culture. Notably, the musical practices emanating from dance culture are linked to mainstream and subcultural formations that are demarcated by the advances in the technological development of musical production.

2. It is different forms of conception that conflate musical evaluations and disclose humour as being present or not. As arguments centred on taste make clear, any form of response to music cannot be made in abstraction (Frith, 1996).

3. For the intellectual, camp pop can be evaluated as good on the basis of bad taste. Sontag's formulations of camp (1999) address the currency of bad taste (in the right circumstances!) with all the egalitarian implications that are associated with democratic mandates. My position on camp is post-Sontagian and informed by the work of scholars such as Andrew Britton, Richard Dyer, Jack Babuscio, Andrew Ross and Pamela Robertson. However, Sontag's work must be acknowledged as groundbreaking in its opening up of camp as a topic, not least amongst heterosexuals.

4. My employment of the term 'the imaginary process' in listening refers to more than just what music might mean, because it makes provision for the fantasy through which musical meaning often occurs. Not only does music summon forth physical responses to sound, but it also embodies an awareness that brings music into its own domain of reality. Put differently, the act of fantasizing or escaping through music can be directly associated with the imaginary process of listening, the auditory effects of which are attributed to a range of sensory modes. For a critique on the idea of imagining music and the processes entailed in this, see Cook, 1990, pp. 71–121.

5. This is evident from the countless interviews with producers and engineers who have worked with Madonna. In two of her CD productions, *Ray of Light* (1998) and *Music* (2000), both William Orbit and Mirwais Ahmadzï emphasize the strong input Madonna makes into the studio production itself. For example, see Mirwais's interview (Rideout, 2001).

6. Note that I prefer the use of the term 'message' in this instance to 'product' as message implies that there are different ways by which to receive the music.

7. For an in-depth discussion of the nature of this process through the discourse of identity politics, see my studies on Madonna, Morrissey, Annie Lennox, Prince and the Pet Shop Boys in Hawkins (2002).
8. Here I am referring to the parameters of binary and ternary form, chord progressions, synth-based instrumentation and melodic structure.
9. In my other studies on Madonna I have taken up the problematic issue of reading her as both a modernist and a postmodernist subject. See Hawkins, 1997 and 2002.
10. In this context I am referring to Barthesian notions of pleasure and *jouissance*. Barthes has raised important questions relating to the expressive levels that produce pleasure both in the text and through performance (1973 and 1975).
11. By spatial properties I am referring to specific qualities of sound that are controlled through the recording process. The spatial control of sound highlights the impact of a small or large musical idea as well as distinguishing one sound from another. Spatial attributes of sound are realized through the interrelationships of location and distance within the mix. The stereo location of sound encompasses the lateral location of musical ideas at any lateral point within a given horizontal plane. The differentiation of one sonic property from the other in the mix of 'Music' is often used for dramatic impact and, moreover, to reinforce notions of reality (as in the sound of Madonna's 'real' voice) and unreality (as in the quality of her 'vocoded' voice). Within the recording process, sounds always exist at various distances, providing a spatial impression of the performance context. The precise control of spatial properties has a significant effect on the music and becomes a source for evaluating artistic expression.
12. By sonic properties I am referring to all the parameters of musical coding, which include melody, rhythm, harmony, instrumentation, pitch, tonal inflection, dynamic usage and phrase schemes, that are profiled through their contrast with one another in the mix.
13. Melodic linearity relates to the patterns and contours of notes that organize melodic events. This term helps explain the succession of pitches and their distribution horizontally.
14. Of course, how we determine distance in a recording will vary considerably from one listener to the next depending on the individual's knowledge of sound sources: to a person who does not know the sound of a shakahuchi this might appear far away when in fact it is placed 'near'.
15. For musical composition purposes, synthesis is the process of producing streams of samples by algorithmic means, while signal processing is about converting and transforming samples. Audio applications of signal processing include manipulating the dynamic range, mixing, filtering and equalizing, time-delay effects (chorus effect, flanging, phasing, echoes), spatial projection, reverberation and noise reduction.
16. Here I am referring to digital recording where specialized computers and software are used for editing the sound signals. The track 'Music' serves as a testament to state-of-the-art digital editing, whereby degrees of creativity can be measured by the sheer magnitude of edit points. In editing, the producers and engineers must be technically proficient in an artistic manner in order for the music to convince.
17. Usually the sound engineer or producer seeks out specific edit points in the first mixes of a performance and tries out and experiments before 'performing' the edit into the final mix. Edit points are where two segments are joined and are calculated by estimating the specific sound that will result from this process. In working out the particular edit the engineer or producer will consider all the musical events carefully to decide where an edit point can be inserted. The major part of the track 'Music' has been rearranged through editing processes.

18. An equalizer is employed to boost certain frequencies or virtually eliminate others. Equalization as a process compensates for the irregularities in certain frequency responses and controls the shape of the response curve. The form of control is flexible in 'Music'.

19. By minority audiences I am referring to audiences that fall outside the mainstream definitions of heteronormativity. However, I am not excluding mainstream audiences from this categorization and I am fully aware of the dangers of essentializing any such definitions. This issue is taken up in considerable detail in my other studies. See Hawkins, 2002.

20. Drag is the parody of an original gender identity and is a double inversion whereby appearance becomes illusory. While the outer appearance might be masculine, for example, the inner quality is feminine. As a parodic identity, drag is a complicated process which can be considered, in certain cases, as an uncritical degradation and appropriation of stereotyping women. The distinction between the anatomical side of the performer and the gender being performed is that which defines drag. By imitating gender, the performer of drag denaturalizes gender and sex. This results in a fluidity of identity which suggests an open-ness to reconstruction. See Butler, 1999, pp. 174–80.

21. I have dealt in some detail with this issue by considering the implications of ironic intent in Madonna's videos. Like Mae West, Madonna constructs her identity around a sensibility that satirizes notions of narcissism. Her videos can be read as statements of resistance and empowerment. See Hawkins, 2002, pp. 48–52.

22. Jack Babuscio (1999) analyses camp theatricality in film stars such as Bette Davis and Judy Garland. He emphasizes the double aspect of performance and how this becomes a key element for attracting a disproportionately large gay following. By virtue of the intense theatricality of their roles in cinema, the hyperbolic personae of these stars project stylized touches that function as ironic social and cultural commentaries.

23. Cubitt argues that the presence of the subject in the song is indeed about an absence. In his reading of the song 'Maybellene' by Chuck Berry, he applies Lacan's category of alienation to the division of the subject's presence to itself and its presence in terms of signification. It is the play between conscious enjoyment of presence and that of the unconsciousness of absence that emphasizes where the pleasure of listening lies (2000, pp. 156–8).

24. Perhaps the most striking reference is to her song 'Express Yourself' (1989), the main phrase of which is repeated in 'Human Nature' (1995).

25. In Chapter 4 of this volume Keith Clifton deals more with the parallels between Madonna and operatic sensibilities.

26. In Sontag's account (1999), camp mocks the critic through its exclusive affiliation to gay subculture. Placed within context, I do not consider Sontag's position in danger of limiting the scope of camp, an accusation of her work waged by others (Robertson, 1996; Newton, 1999; Ross, 1999).

27. Susan McClary (1991) has dealt with this in her groundbreaking feminist critique of musicology, in which she has turned to a personal reading of Madonna's strategies of empowerment.

Chapter 2

Madonna's girls in the mix
Performance of femininity beyond the beautiful

Patricia Pisters

In a comic strip featured in *Desperately Seeking Madonna* (Sexton, 1993) two police investigators visit a girl in hospital, the victim of a crime and the third in a series of similar attacks. One of the investigators remarks that the assailant seems to pick his targets according to their resemblance to Madonna yet none of the victims looks alike since Madonna constantly changes her own image: one of the captions reads: 'one of the key elements of Madonna's success has been her ability to constantly stay fresh and new' (p. 128). The first victim looks like Madonna before her global stardom, the second like the star at the time of her first and second albums, and this, the third victim, is a *True Blue* look-alike; the next one, they surmise, will surely resemble a *Like a Prayer*-Madonna. The comic strip dates from the time of the album *Like a Prayer* (1989), yet the 'joke' underlines the extent to which Madonna's ability to continually transform herself has taken on the status of a trope or cultural pattern, invoked with extraordinary frequency in Madonna journalism and in scholarship interested in figuring her as the postmodern artist *par excellence*. However, apart from her ability to change and renew herself, there are also many recurring themes in her songs and videos which suggest that there is a continuity amongst the many changes: Madonna's oeuvre constantly revisits a number of core thematics that include self-respect, control, love, sexuality, religion and/or spirituality, and plays with these themes in highly accessible – but nevertheless contested – ways. This chapter is an attempt to examine these thematics in terms of the questions they raise about 'authenticity' and 'performativity', drawing in particular on Jean Baudrillard's theorization of the *simulacrum* and recent critical strands in feminist theory.

'What it Feels Like for a Girl', from *Music* (2000), makes reference to a recurring idea in Madonna's work, namely her thoughts about what might be termed 'girlhood' and, more broadly speaking, femininity: the *Who's That Girl?* (1987) and *The Girlie Show* (1993) tours or the songs 'Like a Virgin' (1984), 'Material Girl' (1985), 'Papa Don't Preach' (1986), 'Who's That Girl?' (1987), 'Dear Jessie' (1989), 'Bad Girl' (1993), 'Little Star' (1998) and 'Candy Perfume Girl' (1998) all insist on the idea of 'girlhood' as powerfully productive. Indeed, since the beginning of her career, Madonna has clearly inspired many female pop artists, including the Spice Girls, Britney Spears and Kelly Osbourne.[1] Like all the issues she tackles, it is difficult to categorize these girl-tropes neatly: Madonna's girls do not only have many faces, but also embody very different meanings, very different imaginations of how to do cultural work with femininity. The album version, the video clip and the live performances of 'What it Feels Like for a Girl', for example, together present a very rich embodiment and performance of many different aspects of femininity and the position of women in contemporary media.

This is amply demonstrated in *I Dream of Madonna*, where girls and women talk about their relationship to Madonna. One of the dreams is described as follows:

> I went to the grocery store and while I was in line at the checkout, noticed that Madonna was a few people in front of me. She wasn't adult though; she was about twelve years old and had a girlfriend with her. I enthusiastically said hello to her and told her that she should come to Roller Town sometime with me. She thought that would be cool. While I was talking to her I was thinking, how could this twelve-year-old girl offend anyone? (Turner, 1993, p. 62)

This dream articulates two central aspects of the way Madonna has been understood and appropriated by women: on the one hand, Madonna is perceived mostly as a good girlfriend and, on the other, she is the girl that offends everyone. The first view is a feature of many other dreams in Turner: 'I was in my room when Madonna jumped out of one of my posters and "Into the Groove" was playing. We started dancing and laughing and got to be really good friends' (1993, p. 68). The extent to which her female consumers feel this kind of intimate connection suggests that Madonna has been able to generate in many of her listeners a deep sense of affinity with her, the intensity of which seems relatively unique in contemporary global star practice. I will deal with this issue by looking at different feminist strategies and reactions to Madonna's work in order to comment on some of the ways in which the various conceptions of what girls *can* or *should* be have changed since second-wave feminism in the 1970s. Madonna's contentious status as 'offensive' girl will be explored here by examining several of the debates that have raged around that status. While it has long been clear that her performances may be seen as playful games with the audience, Madonna continues to shock and surprise. Here I will discuss the questions raised by post-modernist debates that have to do with the ways in which Madonna appropriates and transforms conventions, and the way in which she fundamentally questions authenticity in her performances, which can be seen as simulations.

The third section of this chapter looks at the use of multimedia forms that has been central to Madonna's success. The combination of the different layers of a range of media types means her songs and videos are never unambiguous, despite their musical accessibility and the articulacy of their lyrics. I will specifically consider this in the context of female eroticism (a topic that has itself generated much debate in relation to Madonna) to say something about the multi-layered messages Madonna has generated in her work concerning femininity. Finally, focusing on the contrast between the rather mellow album version of 'What it Feels Like for a Girl', the unexpected harshness of the banned video clip and the rich layers of meanings in the stage performance of the song, I will explore how all the above-mentioned aspects of Madonna's work merge here in yet another new way. New light is shed on Madonna's latest questions and statements about 'girlhood' and feminism by the juxtaposition of the apparently passive dissatisfaction expressed in the audio, with the aggressive action of the video and the erotic context of the live performance.

Girlhood and feminism: 'Like a Virgin' and 'Express Yourself'

It is thus clear that, from the beginning of her career, Madonna has been seen to influence women and girls, both professionally and personally. Her sloppy new-wave look from the period around 'Lucky Star' (1983) and 'Like a Virgin' was immediately imitated by thousands of girls: during the *Virgin* tour (1985) the audience seemed to consist mainly of Madonna 'wannabes' and look-alikes. According to Lisa Lewis, in her study on female music artists at the beginning of the MTV period, for many young girls, imitating Madonna meant creating a space and identity of their own (1990, p. 213). Madonna was both what Lewis calls an 'access sign' and a 'discovery sign' (p. 109). As an 'access sign', Madonna demonstrated that girls can have access to areas that are traditionally forbidden or unavailable to them, such as the music industry. She was one of the central female proponents of early MTV, and used the music video to enter and conquer a space for women in the music industry, which has since become more accessible terrain for women. Also, at the narrative level of her videos, Madonna accesses 'boy zones', like the streets ('Borderline' (Lambert, 1984); 'Papa Don't Preach' (Foley, 1986)), thereby representing women outside of the confines of domestic spaces (Lewis, 1990, p. 122). As a 'discovery sign', Madonna offered from the beginning a positive model of female sexuality and bodily pleasure. Her free style of dressing, speaking and behaving encouraged for many female fans a discovery of their identity and body (pp. 122–3).

Yet the emancipatory potential of Madonna has spawned many debates among feminists adopting a range of positions. Buikema and Smelik (1993) note that it is possible to distinguish at least three theoretical currents in feminist debates. A first group of feminists could be called feminists of equality; a second group of feminists foregrounds differences between men and women; a third group consists of feminists who want to deconstruct altogether the distinction we make between male and female.[2] Exemplified by the work of Simone de Beauvoir, amongst others, feminism of equality focuses on the battle for equal rights (in education, jobs, access to media and so on). We have already seen how, in some respects, Madonna endorses this feminist position, because she has gained access to traditionally male-dominated areas and is seen to be in complete control of her career. Another dream described by Turner describes these aspects of equality and control in relation to Madonna: 'I had a dream that Madonna's real name was Boswana. Everyone who knew her called her that. It's because she's the boss' (1993, p. 34). Yet this current of feminism has also violently condemned many mainstream representations of women as passive objects of desire. A prominent example of such a position is perceptible in film theory, in Laura Mulvey's (1975) critique of classical Hollywood cinema as degrading of women, by focusing on their 'to-be-looked-at-ness'. From such a position Madonna has been criticized for her presentation of her female body as an object of desire. Equality feminism seeks avant-garde strategies of resistance, trying to break away from the traditional image of women and sexuality, and while Madonna embodies female success in a male-dominated industry, she also remains in the popular mainstream and often seems to present herself as hyper-feminine and as someone 'to be looked at'.

From the position of those feminists who promote difference, however, it is precisely Madonna's representation of female sexuality that can be praised, in Lewis's terms, as 'discovery signs' (1990). This group of feminists does not struggle for equality but wants to emphasize and value the differences between men and women. However, sexual expression is, of course, only one aspect of female identity. Indeed, the critique of Madonna from this feminist position would be that she may champion some positive aspects of femininity but 'overlooks' others. Her sometimes aggressive image of 'bossiness' and directness, for example, has not always been appreciated and has encouraged the view of many that her work is more about unfettered ego than about productive engagement with gender politics. In addition, until the birth of her daughter in 1996, it was often said that Madonna was not naturally maternal, or that motherhood was a convenient part of a public relations exercise for her (Leonardi and Pope, 1996, p. 221): and yet, for difference feminists, motherhood is another difference to be valued.

Both of the feminist positions noted so far lead ultimately to a critique of the very ground of our conceptions of masculinity and femininity. Thus, a third group of feminists argues that gender is not essential, but a social and cultural construct. Such 'deconstructive feminism', typified by the work of Judith Butler (1990), works with the notion of gender as performance, and it is this type of feminism with which Madonna has most often been associated. The fact that her visual image is in a constant state of modification is a statement about the constructedness of femininity in her work, and very often she has destabilized masculinity and femininity by playing different 'gender-bending' roles, as in 'Express Yourself' (Fincher, 1989). Although she has demonstrated that sexual stereotypes can be challenged, one of the main criticisms of Madonna from this deconstructive angle is that she herself always remains clearly a white, slim and conventionally attractive woman (see hooks, 1992b; Bordo, 1993), undoubtedly playing with femininity, but only within the safe boundaries of conventional (and commercial) attractiveness.

The deconstructive 'gender-bending' approach has been associated with the free play and self-reflexivity of images in postmodernism, which has often been denounced as a superficial, meaningless and apolitical performance, rendering images and representations rather empty, soulless and meaningless. The same has been said about Madonna's 'Express Yourself' (Smelik, 1992). However, upon re-examination it becomes clear that the video accompanying this song might also relate to several core political questions raised by feminism: 'Come on girls!' are the first words in the video clip of 'Express Yourself' and, clearly, Madonna is interpellating girls;[3] but what exactly is this message, and how does she convey it? In her male suit and grabbing her crotch, Madonna invites women to 'express and respect themselves', apparently espousing gender fluidity as a road to gender equality: 'Don't go for second best', she tells women, 'you deserve the best in life'; if not 'you're better off on your own'. Yet Madonna does not just invite women to be independent, but also to look for a 'big strong hand' that can 'lift you to a higher ground'. The video clip for this song also shows Madonna in a highly feminine silk green dress, dancing provocatively, crawling lusciously on her hands and knees and even being tied to a bed: these are not obviously empowering positions, except in the sense that women might be seen as in control because of their seductive powers (although a more negative connotation of this construction of female sexuality is the way in which sexually assertive women might also be perceived as dangerous). To anxieties expressed about her being tied down in the video, Madonna has responded that 'the video ... does not exploit women because she chained *herself* to the bed' (Robertson, 1996, p. 134, her emphasis). The lyrics here make the message even more ambiguous: 'You don't need diamond rings or eighteen carat gold / Fancy cars that go very fast you know they never last, no, no.' Here she seems to be casting doubt on the more overtly performative aspects of the video, making the case also for an 'authentic' connectivity between the genders: 'Make him express himself.' It is clear, then, that Madonna deliberately complicates the possible readings that can be made of her work. She can rarely be consigned to a stable category: when one thinks she is pleading for equality, she foregrounds hyper-femininity and difference; when one thinks she is relying on binaristic or stable representations of sexuality, she simultaneously deconstructs those binarisms. In short, she is semantically slippery.

Postmodern play, simulacra and simulations: *Truth or Dare?*

By eluding stable categorization, Madonna also demonstrates that postmodern play with images is not to be seen simply as a superficial game: her work appropriates images from twentieth-century media and transforms them in such a way as to lend them productive new meanings. Her strategy is not so much to engage in a clear-cut resistance, but to appropriate and transform mainstream culture from within: hers is not a revolutionary feminism. The primary visual references in 'Express Yourself' are to Fritz Lang's film *Metropolis* (1926; Curry, 1990, p. 21). The film is set in a hyper-modern city in which the world is divided between the rich elite who live above the ground and own all the buildings and factories, and the workers who live under the ground and who are mere labour machines. The son of the rich factory owner falls in love with a working-class girl, Maria. Because this relationship is potentially dangerous for the class division, the boy's father commands a scientist to invent a robot who is identical to Maria, but who is evil and creates chaos (in contrast to the real Maria). Finally, the evil Maria is burned like a witch and the good Maria reunites, through her love (heart), the workers (hands) and the capitalist elite (mind). The film ends with the words: 'Without the heart there can be no understanding between the hand and the mind.' With this, the status quo is re-established and a clear distinction between body (workers, hand, labour) and mind (elite, intellect, capital) and between good (Maria, love, order) and evil (Robot Maria, hate, chaos) is maintained (see Morton, 1993). The line that ends *Metropolis* is repeated at the end of 'Express Yourself'. In the video clip, however, Madonna neither repeats the binary oppositions of the film, nor simply reverses the power positions (between workers and owners, or between men and women). Both men and women are looking and being looked at, active and passive; categories are blurred, and the body/hand and the mind/head are not separated forces in society to be regulated by the heart/love of a 'good girl'. Instead, the heart, hand and head are to be in balance in everybody, male or female.

'Express Yourself' is an example of the conflicting ways in which Madonna appropriates and transforms popular images and ideas. Because of her emphasis on performance, play and masquerade, it has often been said that Madonna is merely fake, that nothing about her is sincere (see Lentz, 1993; Schulze et al., 1993). Again, it is interesting to see how Madonna's own work challenges this by questioning the very concepts of performance and authenticity that are crucial to the construction of a star's image and credibility. Questions surrounding Madonna's authenticity were particularly raised with the release of *Truth or Dare* (Keshishian, 1991), the docu-film that followed the artist on her *Blond Ambition* tour (1990). As Pribram (1993) has argued, the film's distinction between the on-stage performances in colour and the backstage images in black and white creates the expectation that what we see in colour is pure performance – Madonna the artist – and the black and white footage is an image of the 'real' and 'true' Madonna. In another sense, however, the backstage images are as constructed as the colour images, an idea that brought into question the extent to which Madonna's 'true self' would ever be revealed.[4]

Arguably, Madonna does not show her real 'self' but toys with the idea of authenticity and our desire to know the true person behind the star. Yet this is not just a meaningless teasing of the audience: apparently knowing that everything is always already mediated, she seems to question the very concept of authenticity. As she has said in interview 'I'm revealing what I wanna reveal ... While you *can* argue that I chose to show what I wanna show, I can also say that *what* I chose to show is very revealing' (quoted in Pribram, 1993, p. 190, her emphasis).

Baudrillard has proposed that postmodern culture is saturated with images that are referring to *each other*, instead of referring to a true and authentic 'reality' that exists underneath the image, and he uses the term 'simulacra', which he takes from Plato, to denote these images, copies of copies with no underlying 'real'. In the process of simulating the 'real', the difference between reality and fiction is elided:

> To simulate is not to feign: Someone who feigns an illness can simply go to bed and pretend he is ill. Someone who simulates an illness produces in himself some of the symptoms. Thus, feigning leaves the reality principle intact: the difference is always clear, it is only masked, whereas simulation threatens the difference between 'true' and 'false', between 'real' and imaginary. (Poster, 1988, pp. 167–8)

In this world of simulacra and simulations the most appropriate strategy is seduction, an eloquent free play with simulacra that generates an extraordinary sense of intense semiosis: in seduction, 'things make events all by themselves, without any mediation, by a sort of instant commutation [or] rather metamorphosis ... Fashion is a splendid form of metamorphosis' (Poster, 1988, p. 102–13). When Madonna's work simulates and seduces (in the form of fashionable metamorphoses and playful references to all kinds of existing images), she renders the question of the 'real' or 'authentic' Madonna void, and articulates instead the textual Madonna. Instead of presenting us with some core 'truth', she demonstrates that all images are constructed but nevertheless have real effects: reality and performance start to blend into each other.

Multimedia strategies in 'Justify My Love'

In the examples I have raised so far, in which Madonna's work affirms, transforms and destabilizes questions of 'girlhood' in and through performance, she uses various layers of contemporary media to convey her always ambiguous (and potentially confusing) messages. The music, the lyrics and the images of her videos are often contrasted, and another example of Madonna's multimedia strategies can be seen in her video 'Justify My Love' (Mondino, 1990), which was banned from MTV but released commercially. This video can be seen as a contested and challenging statement about female sexuality. This is far from an ordinary pop song: although it has a very simple tonal structure and the same bass line and the same chords are repeated over and over, there is little melodic interest, and Madonna speaks more than she sings. What is most striking about the music is the tonal colour of both the instruments and the voices (see Bosma and Pisters, 1999, pp. 32–47). The repetitive, almost hypnotic chords of the synthesizer are pared down, austere: they seem to 'moan' a little, perhaps because they are open fifths (the first and fifth tone together, with no third), played in parallel. Parallel fifths have long been excluded from use in Western art music, and have been associated with improper harmonic texture (see Scholes, 1993, pp. 451–2), a tradition which has been used to suggest improper behaviour.[5] Another characteristic of the production values is the articulation of phonic (and, by implication, physical) space. The drums sound rather squashed and dry, close and confined, filtered using a number of by then commonplace processes. The androgynous voices on the other hand sound distant, remote, 'elsewhere'. The visual images function in combination with the words to suggest a similar spatial ambiguity: the rooms of the Royal Monceau Hotel in Paris (where the video was filmed) are disconnected from each other, small and intimate, while the words evoke motion, distance and travelling. As for vocal aspects of the recording, the very fact that Madonna speaks more than she sings, and is recorded in such a way as to make her voice seem close to us, set against the sparse texture, is far from conventional since in Western music it is often the male voice that speaks and the female voice that sings ecstatically.[6] Opposed to Madonna's speaking voice, which suggests control, there are also a lot of wordless sounds of breathing and soft moaning, which again evoke proximity and intimacy.[7] In the background an androgynous voice (Lenny Kravitz) is singing 'ah, ah'. Here we find a vocal deconstruction of gender, together with a play with spatiality. Seduction, intimacy, control and freedom are in interplay with each other in the different media layers: voice, music and image. In both words and images perhaps the most striking theme is that of sexual ambiguity and the undermining of stereotypical sex roles. Madonna still looks hyper-feminine, but at the same time she is also active and in control, not just a passive object of the gaze: 'Not like this', 'Tell me your dreams', 'That's right'. In contrast to many rock songs, which are often associated with male sexuality (see Frith, 1996, p. 143), there is no sense of musical climax in 'Justify My Love', and the song has therefore been described as a long foreplay (Whiteley, 1997, p. 265). In short, 'Justify My Love' plays with musical conventions, utilizing the latest developments in recording techniques (filtering, compression, etc.) to produce a rich and subtle deconstruction of the 'standard' strophic pop song, undoing thereby the kinds of gender conventions to which less radical songs invariably acquiesce, and yet simultaneously refusing to take up a unified subject position. In this, the track exemplifies some of the ways in which popular culture can engage in strikingly disruptive and radicalizing cultural work.

'What it Feels Like for a Girl': beyond victimization and beyond the beautiful

Many aspects of 'being a girl' are raised in Madonna's work and it is this 'being' that is crucial: Madonna's work is not about simply overturning the status quo, although it undoubtedly has radical implications, but more about the articulation of feminine experience, exemplified, as we shall see, in the track 'What it Feels Like for a Girl'. Various topics such as love, sexuality, materiality, self-respect, independence and dependency, and expressing oneself have been noted here. Even in cases when Madonna's work challenges the stereotypes, for instance by demanding that men express themselves, it never seems to call simply for role reversals: indeed, as we have already seen, role reversal always marks out an ambiguity that was always already there, and a refusal of categorical stability is at the forefront of most of Madonna's work. When *Ray of Light* (1998) was released, the softness and melodic sounds of the music seemed surprising, and even her videos seemed subdued and uncontroversial: it seemed that the 'bad girl' had finally become a wise and peaceful mother. But the controversy started again with the next album, *Music*, when the video of 'What it Feels Like for a Girl' was released (Ritchie, 2001). The album version of the song starts with a sample from the film *The Cement Garden* (Birkin, 1993). The voice of Charlotte Gainsbourg speaks softly:

> Girls can wear jeans, cut their hair short, wear shirts and boots. It's OK to be a boy. But for a boy to look like a girl is degrading because you think that being a girl is degrading. But secretly you'd like to know what it is like, wouldn't you? What it feels like for a girl?

Madonna's singing voice enters, 'Silky smooth, lips as sweet as candy' and 'Hair that twirls on finger tips so gently', with the music suitably soft and mellow, seeming to acquiesce to archetypically 'feminine' vocalities and musical practices. In one sense, the song seems to invite boys to imagine themselves as girls, with all the hyper-feminine elements that are traditionally associated with being a girl: this is 'girlhood' for the boys, it would seem. But she continues: 'Strong inside but you don't know it / Good little girls they never show it / When you open up your mouth to speak / Could you be a little weak?' Here the demand for girls not to show themselves too strong and too independent, because it might frighten the boys too much, would seem to underline the first impression of this track as feminine imagined through the eyes of hegemonic masculinity. On this point, Madonna has declared:

> Our generation [of women] certainly has been encouraged to grab life by the balls, be super-independent, get a great education, follow our dreams, kick ass, all that stuff, and I feel like I woke up one day holding the golden ring and realized that smart, sassy girls who accomplish a lot and have their own cash and are independent are really frightening to men. I felt like, 'Why didn't somebody tell me? Why didn't

somebody warn me?' And that's also what that song is about – swallowing that bitter pill. (Sischy, 2001b)

Thus emerges a new sense to the song's meaning, that of the consequences of emancipation, perhaps a 'post-feminist' position. The album version of 'What it Feels Like for a Girl' suggests 'soft' and perhaps melancholic aspects of femininity, but responses to the song's video clip did not parallel this apparently traditional positioning: after its first airing, the video was banned in the USA. Neither putative blasphemy nor sexuality caused offence with this video (as they had done with 'Like a Prayer' (Lambert, 1989) or 'Justify My Love', for instance); 'What it Feels Like for a Girl' was considered, rather, to be too violent. For the video, the music was re-mixed (by Above and Beyond) so that it is no longer delicate and melodic, but hard and rhythmic. Charlotte Gainsbourg's sample is repeated in the middle of the song, but Madonna's text has disappeared and all that remains is the refrain: 'Do you know what it feels like for a girl in this world?' Madonna's character wears an earring that reads 'lady' and her shoes are high-heeled, but that seems to be the greatest extent to which traditional female roles are played out in the video. Madonna states: 'The video shows my character acting out a fantasy and doing things girls are not allowed to do. This is an angry song and I wanted a matching visual to it and an edgy dance mix' (quoted in Scharff, 2001).

So, a song that invites boys to 'feel like a girl' and exposes regrets about perhaps being too independent is changed by the video images and the re-mixed music into the fantasy of a woman behaving like a 'bad boy'. Of course Madonna's husband, Guy Ritchie, director of testosterone-driven films such as *Lock, Stock and Two Smoking Barrels* (1998) and *Snatch* (2000), was a more than suitable director to help her act out this angry fantasy. However, this anger is not just a jealous response to what 'girls are not allowed to do' (but boys can). The video seems to suggest that the anger is also a reaction to what boys (who are positioned as thinking it is degrading to be female) can do to girls: it is an act of redress that we see here. Madonna's character in the video winks at three lecherous and arrogant young men who stop next to her at a traffic light. She then drives into their car, steals another car, drives aggressively, robs a man at a cash machine, points a (water) gun at police officers and sets fire to a gas station. By appropriating stereotypical 'rebellious' masculine behaviour, she turns the tables of violence back on the men for whom such behaviour is constructed as 'natural'. Here, the men are at the receiving end of the violence, a position that is usually reserved for women, as depicted in the cartoon strip from *Desperately Seeking Madonna* mentioned at the beginning of this chapter.

In the *Drowned World Tour* (2001) Madonna's Spanish performance of the song ('Lo que siente la mujer') also initially emphasized the 'feminine' sensuality of the song found on the album version. Yet, in her traditional 'gender-bending' style, a further sense of ambiguity was introduced in the live performance to disturb gendered norms: the Spanish dress worn by Madonna in the performance incorporates a pair of trousers; the masculine-looking dancers to whom she sings are women; and the male flamenco dancer who appears on stage after this song (during the performance of 'La Isla Bonita') has long hair and wears a corset.[8] Traditional gender categories are thus confused, hyped and distorted in all kinds of ways, although, as anticipated by critics such as hooks (1992b) and Bordo (1993), Madonna once again remains conventionally sexy and attractive, confining her 'rebellion' to that same safe space mentioned above in the analysis of 'Express Yourself'. The presentation of violence as both a fantasy and an act of revenge in 'What it Feels Like for a Girl' was also reproduced in the *Drowned World Tour*, not only in that song but also in 'Mer Girl' (from *Ray of Light*), which precedes the first (fragmentary) hearing of 'What it Feels Like for a Girl'. In both performances there are accompanying visual images that suggest a new position for women in Madonna's work, a position beyond victimization. In 'Mer Girl' Madonna sings about the death of her mother ('I ran from my house ... From my mother who haunts me ... I ran to the cemetery / And held my breath / And thought about your death'), or perhaps her own death ('And the ground gave way beneath my feet / And the earth took me in her arms / Leaves covered my face'). In the live performance, the quiet and subtle performance of 'Mer Girl' is interrupted by a much wilder performance of 'Sky Fits Heaven' (also from *Ray of Light*), in which Madonna swings through the air and uses martial arts to fight against her opponents. When the second part of 'Mer Girl' starts, Madonna's face appears on a large video screen at the back of the stage. In contrast to her clear dominance in the 'Sky Fits Heaven' fight scenes, Madonna's face is battered, her make-up is smeared and her nose is bleeding; here we see Madonna again at the receiving end of violence, cipher of the archetypal feminine victim. It is possible to see this image as a comment on the performance of her *own* aggression in the live performance of 'Sky Fits Heaven' and in the video of 'What it Feels Like for a Girl', perhaps as the reason for her 'revenge'. But when she sings one of the last verses of 'Mer Girl' on stage, 'And I smelt her burning flesh / Her rotting bones / her decay', Madonna on screen wipes the blood off her nose, and then smiles, almost wickedly, returning the audience's gaze with almost brazen confidence. With this smile, she seems to indicate not only that the suffering of pain through violence can be a performance, but also that she is beyond victimization: after everything has happened, she will retain control of her own subjectivities.

At the end of this live performance of 'Mer Girl', Madonna aggressively reclaims the stage: she pulls off her wig, grabs a gun and 'shoots' her dancer before she disappears into the floor, like a Faustian demon. Here, we see Madonna playing out both her 'male' fantasy and her violent revenge fantasy from the 'What it Feels Like' video clip. While she is backstage changing her costume, a semi-instrumental version of that song is played over the images of a manga animation. The narrative of the animation seems to deal once more with male violence against a female victim, representing it this time as sexual, and proposing it as 'monstrous'. At the very end of the animation, however, the preceding scenes are revealed as 'staged'. A director in the animation shouts, 'Everyone, we have to move the camera.' The actor, literally configured as a monster, who has 'raped' a girl apologizes to the actress, and she responds, 'Oh no, it's all right.' Yet the girl's sharp intake of breath during the animated section suggests that perhaps the whole act was *not* a simulation, and that she either lost her virginity or the 'monster' came on her. Yet, as the smile on Madonna's face on the screen during 'Mer Girl' signified, here we have a girl who is beyond victimization. She even seems to fantasize about it: not only is the rape act staged for a film set, but at the very end of the animation the girl is seen to wake up from a dream – the film set was part of her dream.

Baudrillard's ideas about simulacra, simulations and seduction are apposite here and are helpful in understanding how the studied ambiguity of Madonna's oeuvre reveals concerns about the nature of mediated subjectivity. The manga animation in itself is a simulacrum, an 'empty' image that only refers to other images. Within the image there is a simulation within the simulation – the film set – yet even that simulation is further falsified, because it appears to be contained within the girl's dream. Here, we have a succession of simulations that raise questions about gendered behaviour and the possibilities of making statements about this behaviour through playful performance: how are we to make sense of this chain of simulacra? The position 'beyond victimization', suggested by Madonna's live performance of 'Mer Girl' and the manga animation accompanying 'What it Feels Like for a Girl', can also be understood in Baudrillardian terms as refusing any subject position at all, for to do so would be to be 'still', available, open to appropriation. According to Baudrillard, in this world of simulacra and performance we already live after the apocalypse: 'everything has already been liberated, changed, undermined' (1989, p. 34). Yet this is no cause for anxiety: in fact it can be liberating. In a similar way, I would like to propose that Madonna's *Drowned World Tour* expresses something of this post-apocalyptic feeling (after the world has drowned?). It is full of simulacra and seductions and, moreover, with her battered face on screen during the performance of 'Mer Girl', the manga animation and the video of 'What it Feels Like for a Girl', Madonna's work seems to embrace Baudrillardian ethics:

> Seduction, like fashion, is a happy form, beyond the beauty of desire: 'I am not beautiful, I am worse.' Seduction uses signs that are already simulators to make them into falser than false. It displaces them, turns them into traps and produces a splendid effect snatched from the imperative veracity of signs, and even of desire, which is no longer at stake. (Gane, 1993, p. 113)

Thus, Madonna's work is no longer an articulation of her feminine subject as the beautiful centre of her 'gender-bending' performances. She still seduces, but no longer as an object and subject of desire. Her work now ensnares us in the layers of her performances that become 'falser than false'. By doing so, her work makes an extreme statement about the epistemological fluidity of contemporary culture, a fluidity in which debilitating constrictive gender roles and brutalizing violence can only be overcome through hyper-conscious performances.

The banning of the video for 'What it Feels Like for a Girl', however, demonstrates that performances are taken to have real effects and, especially, that there are still many rules governing gendered behaviour. The video is too violent ... for a girl: despite the water guns, the humour and the tongue-in-cheek aspects of the performance, girls don't wink at men, don't drive too fast, don't expose their anger, don't steal. To a certain extent, men are not supposed to do that either, but the average Hollywood movie or hip-hop clip seems to foreground such behaviour in men (Eminem's hyperbolic representations of violence would be a clear example); it is accepted and even glorified, and women are very often at the receiving end of this violence. Refusing a position of victimization by 'taking revenge', Madonna seems once more to advocate a feminism of equality. But, as Sue Scharff (2001) rightly remarks, it is difficult to get your message across when your right to rage, even a fantasy of rage, is censored.

With the album version, the video clip and the staged performances of 'What it Feels Like for a Girl' Madonna has explored a plethora of female identities and subject positions: she deals explicitly and yet ambiguously with feminism (articulated through the three approaches to feminine experience outlined in this chapter: (i) femininity for boys; (ii) post-feminist consequences of emancipation; (iii) revenge fantasies); she plays with cultural tropes in her performances, which as such become simulacra (*The Cement Garden*, gendered behaviour, manga-animated violence); and she uses multi-media layers (lyrics, music, video images, animation and *mise-en-scène* of stage performance) to create a productive ambiguity. As in so much of Madonna's work, 'What it Feels Like for a Girl' refuses categorical stability and demonstrates some of the ways in which popular culture continues to problematize hegemonic subject positions. With this song, video and stage performance, Madonna's work continues to express and remix the textual Madonna and all its 'girlie' aspects and to blur the distinction between star persona and living subject. In so doing, her work continues to force us to think about our experiences of contemporary life, so intensely mediated by audiovisual media and performance strategies. Madonna's work 'seduces', to use Baudrillard's term, by playing out all kinds of gender-ambiguities and actively problematizing the epistemological grounds on which gender is constructed. The video and live performance of 'What it Feels Like for a Girl' seem to have added another layer to her performance: aggression and victimization are highly self-conscious performances that keep on displacing gender divisions and subject positions.

This chapter has shown how Madonna's work explicitly problematizes authenticity and performance and how, to that end, her work draws in particular on tropes of feminine experience to work through some of the complexities of the post-feminist predicament. Madonna's oeuvre is no radically politicalized project working for a clear ideological outcome, but her work does suggest a continuous preoccupation with gender politics and their destabilization. In this sense, her work demonstrates the radicalizing potential of creative strategies that do not sit squarely in the explicitly political or commercial arena: the seduction that her work affords is thus grounded in what might be termed a productive politics of pleasure. She is not simply an object of desire, not simply a figure of fascination, but she is also, in her multitude of textual personae, and in her self-ironizing and knowing self-aggrandizing, a tantalizing puzzle. Taking Baudrillard's hyper-reality to its extreme conclusion, Madonna is not simply 'beautiful' but 'worse'.

Acknowledgements

I would like to thank the editors of this book and Dr Ian Biddle (International Centre for Music Studies, University of Newcastle upon Tyne) for their help and feedback on this chapter.

Notes

1. In Chapter 10 of this volume David Gauntlett deals specifically with this topic.
2. There are many other feminist configurations, including lesbian feminism, radical feminism and ecological feminism, but the three positions mentioned here are particularly relevant for understanding the different critiques waged by feminists against Madonna.
3. As Keith Clifton argues in Chapter 4 of this collection, the opening line could also have meaning for gay men.
4. In the film itself, Warren Beatty asserted that Madonna 'doesn't want to live off camera'.
5. My thanks to Hannah Bosma for this observation in particular relation to the robber's song in *Ronja Räubertochter* (Danielsson, 1984).
6. See, for example, modern R&B music, in which male rapping is often contrasted with female singing.
7. See Chapter 3 in this volume for Corinna Herr's comments on Madonna's use of speech and *sprechgesang*, which is half-spoken, half-sung.
8. See Chapter 9 by Santiago Fouz-Hernández for more on Hispanic elements in Madonna's work.

Chapter 3

Where is the female body?
Androgyny and other strategies of disappearance in Madonna's music videos

Corinna Herr

One of the most noticeable aspects of Madonna's music videos is the (sexual) presentation of her body. This seems to be a general strategy of her work, and some have argued that it is the only one (see Frank and Smith, 1993a). Yet, more detailed analysis reveals that there is clearly more than this lying just beneath the surface. Patton argues that 'music videos provide important raw material for the *bricolage* construction of memory links' (1993, p. 91). This observation is significant, as it emphasizes that there may be more than one message behind music videos, and even small features – which the spectator does not necessarily perceive initially – might later emerge as important.

Discussions of Madonna in gender studies seem broadly divided between those who reclaim her for a feminist analysis, and those who believe that she is only helping to reinforce stereotypes of gender binarisms.[1] In this chapter, I aim to show how these polarizations have arisen, and to determine to what extent Madonna can be seen as the conventional model of 'womanliness'. I also want to show how the concept of masquerade functions meaningfully in her work, and how Madonna's treatment of this idea both espouses and rejects the stereotype of 'womanliness'. My demonstration of this point involves the 'search' for Madonna's body, which always seems to be presented prominently in her music videos but which, on closer examination, 'disappears' more often than we are initially aware of.

I will also argue that there is a connection, hitherto unacknowledged, between queerly sexualized images in Madonna's video clips and certain concepts in the history of ideas. As I will argue, some of these concepts – like hermeticism, androgyny, surrealism and structures of the so-called New Age[2] – may be found by looking more closely at Madonna's images of herself.

The conception of masquerade is, I will argue, one of the most important features in Madonna's work, but what does this exactly mean? In what senses do voice and body function as masks, and what analyses might be extrapolated from this? Joan Riviere was one of the first to propose the idea of 'womanliness as a masquerade' (1929). Riviere describes the case of a female patient who, in public performance, assumes first a role then socially defined as 'masculine' by speaking before the audience (p. 305). In order to achieve the applause and reassurance of the men present in the audience, the patient then assumes a 'feminine' role by 'flirting and coquetting with them in a more or less veiled manner' (p. 305). Riviere sees this last role not so much as a play-act, but as a mask, which she defines as a distinguishing feature of 'womanliness': 'the reader may now ask how I define womanliness or where I draw the line between genuine womanliness and the masquerade. My suggestion is not, however, that there is any such difference; whether radical or superficial, they are the same thing' (p. 306; see also Weissberg, 1994, p. 10).

There are two ways of understanding this in order to comprehend better the concept of 'womanliness as a masquerade'. It is significant that Riviere's interpretation is constructed outside of the notions of 'sex' and 'gender' as biological and socially defined categories respectively, as generally acknowledged today. Riviere's work suggests that a woman's 'female identity' – which, in this case, has to be consistent with her (biological) sex as well as her (social) gender – serves as a mask to enable her survival in a male-dominated world. Riviere infers that 'real womanliness' cannot involve a consistent identity, in contrast to real masculinity – a 'real male identity' – which Riviere apparently does not doubt.[3] Her theory presupposes an essentialist definition of the biological 'sex' and in some cases (the male ones) does not include the category of 'gender'. So the traditionally binaristic construction of gender is very much present in Riviere's argumentation; furthermore, she surpasses it by reclaiming the essentialism, which in turn implies that security and consistency are available exclusively for the male population.[4] The second possibility is that suggested by Judith Butler (1990), who argues that there is no direct correlation between biological sex and gender identity, but that gender identity is always socially defined. Butler thus concludes that the 'gendered subject' is also defining its sexual identity (pp. 9–10). In this model there remains no sense of 'real' female and male identities; only constructed identities.

Both possibilities are inferred by E. Ann Kaplan in her identification of some interpretative possibilities with respect to Madonna's work (1993, pp. 150, 156). Clearly extrapolating from Butler's work, Kaplan describes 'the theory that the Madonna image usefully adopts one mask after another to expose the fact that there is no "essential" self and therefore no essential feminine but only cultural constructions' (1993, p. 160). Kaplan calls this the 'mask as mastery'. She also writes of the 'mask as deception', by which she means Madonna's use of masquerade to reproduce 'patriarchal modes and fantasies' (p. 160), thereby inferring Riviere's construction (but without explicitly mentioning Riviere). Kaplan moves on quickly from both theories, as she focuses on offering 'an analysis of Madonna as commodity, an analysis of how commodity relations interface with an oppositional politics', integrating 'subjectivity and gender issues' (p. 160). In my opinion, however, it has not been sufficiently shown (by

Kaplan or other scholars) how Madonna uses the concept of masquerade alongside other concepts of thought (such as hermeticism and the New Age) or of art (such as surrealism) or media techniques to show how identity might be perceived as a cultural construction. Kaplan aims to demonstrate her theories on Madonna by referring to some of her music videos, but the truly subversive qualities of Madonna's music and images might become clearer through a thorough analysis of some of her clips.

The constructions and applications of 'womanliness as masquerade' help to expose the construction of historically binaristic gender identities. Yet most of the arguments are based almost exclusively on representations of the body, which is surely only one possible way in which gendered representations are constructed. For example, Monika Bloss demonstrates that some voice categories contribute to gendered representations by referring to the high-pitched crying and shouting of Little Richard and the falsetto voices of the Bee Gees, Prince and Michael Jackson as implying the 'other' sex, and as closely connected with female hysteria (2001, p. 200). Bloss criticizes such masquerades as constructing androgyny as primarily 'male' and patriarchal (p. 196). But especially in the realm of late twentieth-century popular music, both female and male performers play with the notion of gender, and especially androgyny. Apart from Madonna and those performers named by Bloss, Marilyn Manson is a notable example of this new playful kind of gender representation. In the case of Manson, however, a self-created artificial and androgynous personality seems sometimes to substitute his 'real' personality completely, as can be seen in his own writings (Manson with Strauss, 1998, pp. 128–9). Wicke argues that 'the most remarkable thing about the [category of the] popular in the 20th century is the medialization of the musical and the turn to the body' (2001, p. 41).[5] The tendency noted by Wicke has become more pertinent with the increasing significance of visual media in popular music, which now relies heavily on the music video. Thus, disguise and masquerade have become ever more important factors to support – or oppose – the (musical) representation of the self. I will now turn to three of Madonna's videos to illustrate some of the points raised so far.[6]

'Open Your Heart': 'womanliness as a masquerade'

As I have noted, Madonna's body often seems to be the focus of her videos. In 'Open Your Heart' (Mondino, 1986) the representation of the body is certainly comparable to that found in, for example, 'Erotica' (Baron, 1992) and 'Express Yourself' (Fincher, 1989).[7] But in 'Open Your Heart' we ultimately witness the disappearance of Madonna's body through a flight into androgyny.

Out of the three levels of the music video – text (lyrics), music and visual image – it is the visual image that we remember mostly, as visual perception makes a more immediate and lasting impression on us than auditory perception. In comparison with this visual emphasis, text and music seem to stay in the background. The music in 'Open Your Heart' is relatively conventional in terms of rhythmic, melodic and harmonic structure. The multifunctional use of the voice is, however, remarkable. We often find in Madonna's songs a tendency to half-speak and half-sing:[8] in this case it is a whisper ('Watch out!') at the beginning of the song. Furthermore, the background vocals are also sung by Madonna, adding another layer to her vocal function.

In the text, the narrator tries to make another person love her (although the female voice suggests a female narrator, we cannot presuppose this as there is no textual indication of gender identities): 'Open your heart to me, darling / I'll give you love if you, you turn the key.' She seems not only demanding but nearly threatening: 'Don't try to run, I can keep up with you'; 'I'll make you love me.'

In terms of visual imagery, the female body is perhaps the most prominent feature: at the beginning of the video we are immediately confronted with the sight of a woman, with markedly sexual attributes, on a cardboard decoration, as the giant picture fills the screen. The picture is a reproduction of Tamara de Lempicka's art deco painting *Andromeda* (1929), in which the disproportionate size of its subject is apparent even in the original; she dominates the frame of the painting.[9] This first hint of excess in terms of female bodily visibility is then confirmed in the peep-show that forms the next image, in which Madonna, as a strip-artist, is central.

Two visual worlds seem to interact in the video for 'Open Your Heart': the sphere of the boy outside the building and the sphere of the stripper inside. Only in the final scene do both realms merge, when woman and child meet and leave together. The little boy in his oversized suit and hat is forced to wait outside the building, as the ticket-collector will not let him in. While waiting, he watches the pin-up girls in the window by closing one eye, then the other, his eyelids imitating the rising and falling of shutters in the 'real' peep-show. Madonna (among others) is seen on a poster on the wall of the building, with short black hair. At the beginning of the show we watch Madonna remove her dark wig and reveal her 'real' (dyed) blonde hair. With this sign, which symbolizes that 'everything is a masquerade', the show begins. In Madonna's show, her gestures, dance, clothes and the presentation of her body show the body clearly as an object of desire. The public is shown in isolated cabins, the audience at the peep-show. We see some men, an androgynous couple and a 'masculine' looking woman. The gestures of the boy in front of the building continue to be reflected in the 'reality' of the adults inside. These people are shown in detail, and we notice their strange faces and gestures. They receive their satisfaction not through action but by watching, as voyeurs.[10] The window shutters of their cabins open and close. A real striptease is only hinted at, by Madonna removing her long gloves at the end of the show. In the last scene of the video we see Madonna in front of the building – still as a blonde, but with a more 'masculine' hairstyle. She wears a suit and hat similar to those of the boy. After she kisses the child on the mouth, they dance together towards the horizon, while the ticket-collector runs behind them and seems to call after them. But his voice must not disturb Madonna's song: what he has to say can be found as a subtitle on the screen: 'Ritorna, ritorna Madonna, abbiamo ancora bisogno di te' ('Come back Madonna, we still need you'). The silhouettes of Madonna and the boy seem to merge while dancing and are eventually indistinguishable from each other.

In this video clip, gender and the female body seem to be little more than playthings. 'Womanliness' here is false and masked (covered), as well as a mask (covering), there is another layer of something – which in turn might be nothing more than another mask. The first sign for this are the cardboard women, who are not shown in a 'realistic' manner, but present female forms in the exaggerated style of art deco. Madonna herself is masked at the beginning by her dark wig. In fact, we find her in three different masks: with the black wig at the beginning of the show; as a blonde at the show; and in the man's suit and hat after the show. We cannot say which one of these Madonnas is the 'real one', but I would like to suggest that it is none of them. All images of the woman we see are only constructed: womanliness as a masquerade.

Yet, we do not find the masquerade only in the visual image. The sense of self in the song's lyric is unequivocal: there is no change of levels; there is only one 'I'.[11] But Madonna's voice, which articulates this 'I', is not only one voice: as I have noted, the voice is present at least three times in different forms (as speech, as lead vocals and as background vocals, in which we of course find further melodic lines and 'voices'). Vocal diversity is also achieved by our not seeing Madonna singing all the time. Her style of singing seems controlled and emotionless, demonstrated by the lack of expression and dynamics in her voice. A contrast thus seems to be built between the music and the visual action. In a texture of different, changing images and visual levels, only the music seems to be a constant element. As Susan McClary observes, 'the music in music videos is largely responsible for the narrative continuity and the affective quality ... even if it is the visual images we remember correctly' (1991, p. 161).

The numerous levels of Madonna's masquerade reveal different levels of the 'feminist' message of this video.[12] At first, as I have shown, the focus lies clearly on the presentation of the body, and Madonna seems a passive object of the active male gaze (see Mulvey, 1975). But this voyeuristic male gaze is itself being exposed to the audience watching the video: we are watching the voyeurs, and are voyeurs in that way. But in the combination of our gaze with that of one of the video voyeurs, the situation is changed again: now we ourselves are the voyeurs, alongside those in the video. Furthermore, not only are we watching Madonna, but Madonna is watching us. At the moment of her singing 'I think that you're afraid to look in my eyes' she is looking not only at the fictional audience, but at us, the 'real' audience:[13] it is we who are gazed at. Already at this moment the female body on the screen seems to vanish as we become objects of the gaze. And at the end of the video, Madonna's body also vanishes physically behind the men's suit and in the darkness. This 'escape to androgyny' (McClary, 1991, p. 162) is the second disappearance of her body.

Madonna's masquerades are mostly based on 'media' construction.[14] The mass media render possible the extremely rapid change of body – and gender – presentation. Wicke states that 'no longer does the musical structure initiate the bodily agency as a moment of music-making, but the self-presentation of the body becomes the starting point of the whole performance' (2001, p. 44).[15] But Wicke also notes the continuing importance of the music, as it provides a physical experience which is impossible without the combination of sound, rhythm and movement (p. 55). The use of the (video or film) camera in representation – the 'medialization' of vocal and bodily performance – reveals the radical aspects of the masquerade. The 'real thing' is not something behind the veil, but masquerade is the 'real thing': womanliness *is* a masquerade. But if this is the case, should we conclude that, in Riviere's theory and Madonna's performance in 'Open Your Heart', the whole construction of gender is now devoid of its (culturally constructed) essentialism? Only the body and the voice of the woman (Madonna) perform the masquerade, and thus seem to disappear: male bodies here are always clearly visible as male. So, even in this apparent androgyny, the binarism of gender persists.

'Justify My Love': masculinity as a masquerade?

It is important to note that apparent androgyny in Madonna's work does not always dissolve into traditional gender binarisms. I will now turn to the 'Justify My Love' and its video (Mondino, 1990) as an example of some other ways in which Madonna has employed the concept of androgyny. While the lyrics of the song seem disjointed and directionless, some phrases clearly function as a signal for action, which is often played out visually. For example, Madonna refuses to be kissed while the lyrics direct – 'not like that'; at 'kiss me, that's right, kiss me', she is seen kissing her sexual partners. The music does not function at a clearly meaningful level either. One perceives no 'catchy tune', or indeed any tune at all at first, as the singing voice enters late. The primary structural motif is rhythmic, overlaid with sustained instrumental chords. This is the case throughout at least the first third of the whole song; there are no sung stanzas. Various types of voice are used by Madonna in this song. The first is her spoken voice, talking in intervals in a dark, hoarse sound (over her second voice, which intermittently moans and sighs), while the music stays a background rhythm. After an entirely spoken first stanza (the first seventeen bars of text), the singing voice finally enters for the refrain, '... for you / To justify my love', but for only six beats. Here, another Madonna sings in a higher voice and, as in (for example) 'Like a Virgin' (1984), her voice at this point seems (technologically) deprived of deeper frequencies. At the key words 'Justify my love' both voices meet and sing/speak together. The refrain is repeated, and the second stanza is as the first, with speech and rhythm emphasized. The song ends with the chorus.

Madonna's style of singing in 'Justify My Love' seems much more controlled and feels more distant than in 'Open Your Heart'. The background groaning, which is intended to remind the listener of copulation, is a key memorable feature. So, in the same way that the spectators were turned into voyeurs in 'Open Your Heart', here the listeners are turned into voyeurs acoustically.[16] This seems important as the image of the voyeur is a recurrent feature in Madonna's work. In 'Open Your Heart', the music video provides us with the vision of ourselves as voyeurs, but we also understand the importance of the acoustics in music videos: sound and music are not merely a background for visual images, but constitute a meaningful level in themselves. As we have seen, this may be achieved through the meaning of the words (as, for example, signals for action) or through the music itself, which in this case includes an important affective quality, not entirely provided by the melody or harmony.

Visually the audience sees many 'strange' images.[17] While Madonna walks down the hotel corridor we see through open doors men and women in sexual positions, sometimes practising bondage. After a stranger has 'rescued' Madonna by kissing her, she is seen with others in one of the hotel rooms. There is no question of 'real' gendered identity – womanliness or masculinity – in this room. Everyone is watching everybody else: masculine looking women and men with make-up watch as Madonna and the stranger have sex.[18] The unfocused images provided by the camera serve to strengthen this manifold masquerade.[19] The peak of the masquerade is an androgynous pair of 'men' painting moustaches on each other to 'recover' their masculinity symbolically, while Madonna laughs at this 'masculinity as a masquerade'.[20] As in 'Express Yourself', the end of the video is marked by a sentence which appears on the screen: 'Poor is the man whose pleasure depends on the permission of another', echoing a line previously spoken by Madonna in the song.[21] This fulfils a similar function to that of a literary epigraph (although in literature it normally appears at the beginning of the text): it expresses the essence of a text, or the meaning behind something else. Moreover, these words in their literal sense ('do what you want') are the axiom of an occult tradition, which in the twentieth century includes also the Satanists and their leader Alistair Crowley, whose influence is also felt in the New Age (Hanegraaff, 1996, pp. 87–8, 90).[22]

The scandal concerning the 'Justify My Love' video, the ban by MTV and the first showing of the clip on *Nightline* is well-documented (Henderson, 1993, pp. 107–10; Schwichtenberg, 1993c, pp. 129–30). But what is really so shocking about the clip? Why did this produce such a scandal in America? First, we must consider the possibility that the scandal was orchestrated by Madonna and her media advisers. In terms of the clip itself, the video is very artfully constructed, and masquerade is put to the extreme, even if Madonna herself is less involved in the action and watches with a perceptible sense of amusement. But her laughter destabilizes the establishment, the patriarchy and the reign of gender binarism, and this is possibly the most scandalizing aspect of this video.[23]

Masquerade and androgyny are themselves structures that endanger the hegemonic binarism of gender. Madonna's presentation of these structures is clearly subversive. Even though, in 'Open Your Heart', we seem to find merely a conventional image of womanliness, the presentation itself is highly subversive and this is reinforced by the flight into androgyny. So here we have the inheritance of a very old and hidden tradition of what has always been a subversive structure. It seems, by the reactions to 'Justify My Love', that it is still just as subversive and revolutionary.

In 'Justify My Love', apart from the masquerade, it is androgyny – the rapprochement of the two sexes towards another – which serves to further the disappearance of the female body. In this clip we find different 'types' of androgyny. First, there is a unique 'third' sex; a sexual form different from the dichotomous male and female, and this is represented through 'feminized' men and 'manly' women.[24] But in 'Justify My Love', as in 'Open Your Heart', we also find androgynous twins, which might represent an older Platonic conception of androgyny. Also one perceives the affinities between androgyny and masquerade. Here, masquerade is the means by which androgyny is symbolized: the men have dressed themselves up to give the impression of 'effeminacy' and the women have painted themselves moustaches to seem 'masculine'.

Both concepts, masquerade and androgyny, are perceptible in ancient Greek tradition. While the idea of masquerade has been maintained since then, in theatre and opera, the idea of androgyny has become more hidden, but its tradition is equally long. In Plato's 'Symposium' the participants of a banquet hold speeches on the subject of 'eros'. Plato invokes the historical figure of Aristophanes, who shows us in his speech the image of three godlike races from mythical times. These descend as 'double creatures', combinations of male-male, female-female and male-female beings from the sun, earth and moon. But the gods were afraid of the competition of these 'perfect creatures' and they decided to cut them apart. Since their separation mankind has yearned for a reunion (Aurnhammer, 1986, pp. 9–15). Already in Ovid the Platonic image is subtly changed: the androgynous ideal is no longer necessarily the combination of two beings, but it can exist in one person by the rapprochement of the two sexes in one being. This kind of androgyny has been present in literature and the arts continuously throughout the centuries and is important for current discussions of the concept in gender studies (see Bock and Alfermann, 1999).

While the epigraph of 'Justify My Love' may point towards the concept of occultism, the structure of androgyny suggests an affinity with the ideas of hermeticism, a concept closely connected with – or even the root of – the occult.[25] The hermetic discourse is historically an agglomeration of ideas that can be traced back to an arcane text, the *Corpus Hermeticum* (1991; see Hanegraaff,

1996). The central figure in the hermetic tradition is Hermes Trismegistus, founder of the arcane arts of magic, alchemy and astrology (Seligmann, 1988, pp. 104–10; Hanegraaff, 1996, pp. 315, 390). Hermetic ideas have been disseminatcd through the history of ideas (although not primarily through representatives), but the tradition has been a mostly hidden and subversive part of our culture. A structurally important feature of this type of thought is the combination of antithetical powers, and a significant example of this is the concept of androgyny. Androgyny has been an important feature for alchemy, as the alchemical process is one of several possibilities of woman and man's reunion into one of Plato's 'double' creatures: 'The so-called chymical marriage, the binding of the two polarities male and female is the term in hermetic-alchemistic symbolism for the chemical or spiritual act of creation, which is necessary for the birth of everything new' (Biedermann, 1991, p. 117).[26] The chymical marriage leads to the birth of the androgyne.[27] The androgynous ideal is a combination of two people from opposite sexes, and the result of the chymical marriage is the hermaphrodite, the perfect human being with all the virtues of man and woman.

Androgyny has been an important part of gender discourses throughout the centuries (Aurnhammer, 1986). More recently, in the New Age movement, both androgyny and hermeticism have been seen to be adapted:

> Although 'polarity-holism' has many dimensions, the association of the two poles with masculine and feminine appears to be particularly strong in the minds of New Age adherents … [This] logically tends towards the androgyne … [and is] most characteristic of what might be called 'mainstream' New Age. (Hanegraaff, 1996, p. 153)[28]

For the New Age, androgyny is a path to the ideal society (Hanegraaff, 1996, pp. 338–9). From the 1980s the New Age movement became an increasingly visible feature of society, with celebrities such as Shirley MacLaine adopting the movement's beliefs (see Hanegraaff, 1996, pp. 109–10). Even though Madonna never explicitly adopted 'New-Age music', her 'esoteric' image seen in the videos for 'Ray of Light' (Åkerlund, 1998) and (especially) 'Frozen' (Cunningham, 1998) provides a subtle link to this movement. More hidden connections to this movement, and also to surrealism, become clearer in the next section.

'Bedtime Story': everything is a masquerade in the surrealistic realm of signs

Visual references to surrealist paintings seem to be a key to Madonna's world of images, featuring in the videos for 'Justify My Love' and 'Open Your Heart', as well as in 'Bedtime Story' (Romanek, 1995). In this video concepts of the New

Age are also adapted (not only) through the recurrence of androgyny. The New Age dreams of a perfect world, and these dreams are being presented by Madonna as a 'bedtime story', as an occasion for dreaming.[29]

While in 'Justify My Love' words still seem to be able to function – as signal, explanation, epigraph – in 'Bedtime Story' 'words are useless'. Only music and image seem to have representative function, with most importance placed on the visual image: this is indicated by the words 'welcome – lucid', which are not sung, but shown on a monitor at the beginning of the clip. Madonna appears lying on a bed, seemingly the subject of an experiment. The intense light shines through Madonna's pale body, which seems to vanish into its surroundings. In this image, there are affinities to the New Age as well as to hermeticism, as the pale body seems almost entirely light and no longer bound to the earth. An analogy to this can be seen in the ideal body of hermeticism, the 'body of light'. Followers of this movement aim to achieve this ideal body while still on earth. New Age adepts have also been identified as 'beings of light', and their new era is called 'The Age of Light' (Hanegraaff, 1996, pp. 341–4). But this era can only be achieved through a 'higher level of consciousness': this 'super-consciousness' that is available in the Age of Light can only be achieved by leaving the consciousness behind (p. 341), which might – in the realm of the New Age – also include the dream.[30] In the video clip, the process of leaving the consciousness behind seems to be achieved by drugs. This is implied by an image in the video of a liquid substance dripping through a funnel and the frequent image of the poppy plant (*papaver somniferum*) in the dream, either as capsules (lying in a vase on a table, while a little girl is reading a book) or as whole plant – we perceive later a young man with a bouquet of poppies (see also Mertin, 1999, pp. 158–9). Drugs, of course, are frequently associated with the New Age movement, and all sorts of herbs – including papaver plants – were crucial ingredients in alchemical experiments.[31] The *papaver somniferum*, an opiate, has been especially important to New Age adepts in the process of enlarging their visions of Christ (see Dohm, 2000, pp. 78–9).

As in 'Justify My Love', the music in 'Bedtime Story' does not function at a meaningful level: the listener is unable to easily perceive a coherent musical structure. The first sound we hear seems to be another of Madonna's whispers ('ah'), but the sound is distanced through technology, so we can no longer tell whether it is really a human sound. From *Erotica* (1992) onwards, Madonna's style of singing has been criticized as singing 'with a sense of caution' (Frith, 1993, p. 89), but in 'Justify My Love' her singing already seems more controlled and more distant from the listener than in 'Open Your Heart'.[32] There might, however, be more to it than just a lack of technique, as Frith claims for Madonna's version of 'Fever' (p. 89). This might instead, especially in *Erotica*, be seen as a desire to advance to another level of singing, to try to say something now more by her style of singing than by using a multitude of (her own) voices, like she did in 'Open Your Heart' (as I have shown). In 'Bedtime Story' especially, we hear a voice thickened through technological manipulation, and music that seems, by its disjointed structure, to imply an ethereal or even cosmological reference. The slow tempo of the music and its decrescendo transform the textual description of 'vanishing into the unconsciousness' into (audible) action.

The treatment of the text too, fits into this pattern. Although the language is semantically and syntactically in order, the words are so disjointed that their meaning is hard to identify for the listener. This is most marked in the passage 'Words are useless, especially sentences', as the words are sung with so many rests in between that it is nearly impossible for the listener to re-adjoin them without the help of the printed lyrics. The first words of the song, 'Let's get unconscious honey', are the signal for the surrealistic images that dominate this music video. Surrealist art was inspired in part by psychoanalytic theories, and here Madonna exposes this connection in her music video. The super-consciousness of the New Age, which is mostly based on concepts of the psychoanalyst Carl Gustav Jung,[33] is here transformed into the unconscious worlds of surrealism, which is itself connected with early Freudian and Jungian concepts (see Janet A. Kaplan, 1983, p. 109).

If we find reminders and even images of Tamara de Lempicka in 'Open Your Heart' and 'Justify My Love', in 'Bedtime Story' there are images that refer equally to surrealist art. For example, the image of the pregnant woman out of whose stomach white doves rise reminds us not only of the Belgian surrealist René Magritte, but also of Frida Kahlo's work, especially *My Birth* (1932).[34] We can identify at least one other image as a citation of a specific surrealistic painting, *Los amantes* (1963), by the Spanish-Mexican artist Remedios Varo. In this painting (Figure 3.1), two people are sitting on a bench and holding hands. The figure on the right is clothed in a man's suit; the figure on the left wears a dress. Each head has been replaced by a mirror and it is only by their bodies and clothes that they can be identified as male and female. Janet A. Kaplan's interpretation is that they see 'not their partner, but a reflection of themselves' (1983, p. 109). This interpretation is based on the fact that, as mirrors, the heads now primarily reflect and are unable to express anything that is not already there. Nevertheless, this interpretation does not explain all levels of the painting. First, the figures are not looking at themselves, but at the viewer. Second, it is not clear from the painting which head is in which mirror – the female head on the female body or vice versa. This is further problematized by the fact that the heads are so similar, or perhaps even identical. Again, the concept of androgyny comes to the fore.

The 'decapitation' of the couple in Varo's painting has a model in the 'chymical marriage', which was described in 1616 by Johann Valentin Andreae (1973). The hero of Andreae's work, Christian Rosencreutz, is bidden to a royal wedding in a castle. The bride and bridegroom willingly allow themselves to be decapitated and are brought into a 'laboratory'. After a complicated procedure the couple are

Fig. 3.1 Remedios Varo, *Los Amantos*, 1963

Source: © VG Bild-Kunst, Bonn 2002

brought back to life (see Cersowsky, 1990, pp. 108–29). The text by Andreae is a key work in seventeenth-century hermetical and alchemical literature. It has been mentioned and adapted, among others, by Jung in his *Mysterium conjunctionis* (1963; see also Cersowsky, 1990, p. 292), and might therefore be known by Varo (though perhaps not by Madonna).[35] The links to alchemy and hermeticism are nevertheless present – even if they are unconsciously presented.

Concerning Varo's picture, Janet A. Kaplan also suggests that 'the narcissist attraction [between the two figures] is so great that it generates steam, which rises, condenses, and falls back down as rain, creating a flood that swirls around their legs' and is likely to drown them (1983, p. 109). In Madonna's video adaptation, these two people, who are sitting in the same position as Varo's with their hands held a little higher, are already sitting *under* water. The possibility of 'expression' instead of mere 'reflection' is made more distinct as the figures sing. The two figures now wear the same clothes – in contrast to Varo's painting – and the heads are not round as Varo's mirrors, but hexagonal. Here, evidently the faces are identical. The heads are now entirely indistinguishable from each other; the change in their expressions when they are singing is not significant. The androgynous twins we found in 'Open Your Heart' and 'Justify My Love' are not only cited, but drawn into the very centre of this video. Thus, in 'Bedtime Story', Madonna is returning to the Platonic concept of androgyny, the combination of two bodies. By contrast, in the other two videos, the twins are only a passing reference and the important concept is that of the unique 'third' androgynous sex. But the Platonic conception of the rapprochement of the two sexes, which we also find in Varo's picture, is radically changed again: in Madonna's version, it is the reflection of only one woman – a duplication of the perfection, one might infer. This couple sits in a 'drowned world' (possibly a precursor to the *Drowned World Tour* in 2001); but this world is not destroyed, another subtle change from Varo's painting. Also, the flood might signify something more: just as the elements of earth and air seemed to govern the first images of Madonna's pale lucid body, and seemed to announce the 'New Age of Light' (see Hanegraaff, 1996, p. 341–4), here the element water might also imply transformation rather than destruction:[36] These people are not drowning (as Varo has shown them) but sitting quietly in their world, which is a new world for new bodies. When the New Age speaks of 'The Age of Aquarius', it indicates the arrival of a new era.[37] The video takes this concept in its literal sense and to its logical conclusion: Aquarius is represented by the water carrier and these people are sitting in a 'drowned world'. In the next image the androgynous couple is drawn out to a multitude of bodies: around these images we see a cube with monitors on its six sides, each of which shows a face again – but this time it is Madonna's face, not as a blonde as in the beginning, but with dark, short hair. Now the reproduction multiplies again: this is embodied by an oriental-looking man with a high Turkish hat, who at first divides in two, but in the end we see at least eight of him, dancing. While 'womanliness' might here be indicated by his wide robe, which whirls around him as he dances, we must also remember that in the history of gendered identities, the feminization of the oriental 'other' is a recurrent issue (see Bowers, 2002; Solie, 2001).

The citation of Varo's painting seems carefully chosen by Madonna. Varo is one of the few female surrealistic painters, and her work is 'virtually unknown in the United States and Europe' (Janet A. Kaplan, 1983, p. 7). Hence, the choice seems not to have been made by chance. Varo's is a 'secret world … a reality apart' (p. 1), where there is an overlapping of the natural and the technological, and especially in this painting the connections towards the occult and hermeticism are strong, as we have already seen. In 'Bedtime Story', we find hints of the creation of a 'new world', filled with magic and symbols, which signify nothing but themselves, rendered possible only by technology. Varo believed in magic, 'held a mystical belief in forces beyond the self' (Janet A. Kaplan, 1983, p. 2), and in other works looked also to alchemy, astrology and the occult (p. 5; see also pp. 104–5). All this is linked to the beliefs of the New Age, which itself refers structurally to the arcane world of hermeticism (see Hanegraaff, 1996), of which magic, mysticism and alchemy are important parts. Real masks with Madonna's face on them, swimming on the sea, are further references to the masquerade. This also implies a link back to the psychoanalytical roots of 'womanliness as a masquerade'. But in this case not only womanliness or masculinity is masquerade. In this surrealist realm of signs *everything* is a masquerade: logic and identities are questionable, and while the whole world seems to consist of signs, gender identity is particularly brought into question. Although this world consists of auto-referential signs, it is not the hostile world of simulacra described by Baudrillard (1988).[38] This new world, symbolized by the 'new bodies under water' in 'Bedtime Story', is the hopeful world of the hermetic adepts, the surrealists and the New Age: a world beyond in a new era.

Madonna's transformations and cultural thought

Madonna's music videos always contain different layers of ideas and structures and various discourses. The hermetical and alchemical connections have not previously been noted, but this reading shows another fascinating aspect of Madonna's work. There are surely even more hermetical ideas, besides androgyny, behind some of Madonna's images, which will demand future investigation. For example, in her music videos 'Fever' (Sednaoui, 1993) and 'Rain' (Romanek, 1993) some of the four elements (in these videos, fire and water) are again of paramount importance. Alongside other implications contained within these songs and their respective videos (such as the Japanese visual references in 'Rain' or the fact that 'Fever' is a cover version), these points remain significant in the context established by this chapter: fire and water are important ingredients of the alchemical process, and gold (shown in 'Fever' as part of Madonna's body) is, of course, its final aim. In Madonna's golden body we also find analogies to Gustav Klimt's 'golden women':[39] the body may be seen as armour, but it also (as in Klimt) fades away into its surroundings. This also happens to Madonna's 'water-body' in 'Rain' and, as I have shown here, to her 'air-body' in 'Bedtime Story'.[40]

The search for the female body in Madonna's music videos has revealed its disappearance (by a flight into androgyny) and, in the end, its loss into a world of signs where nothing seems to be real any longer. This process is rendered possible only through the medium itself, and in the medium we also find further affinities to hermetical structures. An important idea in the *Corpus Hermeticum* is the possible ubiquity of the human spirit: this ubiquity is to a great extent achieved by video-technique and by its dissemination via the Internet, and not only with regard to the spirit but to a (virtual) bodily 'reality'. This also is implied in 'Bedtime Story': Madonna shows us a world of which she is not necessarily a part, but to which she nevertheless seems to be attracted. Perhaps this world, shown by Madonna, is one way to an ideal society. It is rendered possible through the disappearance, and simultaneous multiplication, of the female body through masquerade and androgyny, which are both important features in Madonna's and (post-) modern cultural transformations.

Acknowledgements

A shorter version of this text is published in German as 'Madonnas Maskeraden im Kontext von Gender und Hermetik' in Annette Kreutziger-Herr and Katrin Losleben (eds) (2003), *Frau.Musik.Sprache: Texte aus der Hochschule für Musik und Theater Hannover*, Hanover: Hochschule für Musik und Theater. For help with the English version and style, I would especially like to thank Eva Rieger, Santiago Fouz-Hernández and Freya Jarman-Ivens. Thanks also to Tanja Möller for the preparation of the Varo still.

Notes

1. Although E. Ann Kaplan states that she has 'never been able to locate these negative articles' (1993, p. 155), when reading the essays in Frank and Smith (1993a), a highly critical tendency is easy to perceive. See also Barber-Kersovan, 2000, p. 277–8. In this chapter I will not aim to contradict these views, or to 're-establish' the value of Madonna's work. I aim instead to point out certain important issues in the history of ideas which can also be found in her music videos, and which have thereby become a part of (post)modern culture (and arguably show a certain depth to Madonna's work as well).

2. The New Age movement 'constitutes a major phenomenon in popular religion' (Hanegraaff, 1996, p. 1) and its cultural significance cannot be doubted; nevertheless the term is vague. The movement is rooted in the 'so-called counterculture of the 1960s', but is still relevant in the early 1990s (p. 10), and probably later, as we see in Madonna's reception of it in the 'Bedtime Story' video (Romanek, 1995). See the remainder of this chapter, especially the section on that video.

3. For more on 'stable', 'natural' masculine identities, as opposed to 'constructed/able' feminine identities, see Halberstam, 1998.

4. Riviere does not describe any different degrees of gender identity, although they had previously been analysed by the German Magnus Hirschfeld in 1918 (see Sykora, 1999).

5. 'Das "auffälligste Merkmal des Populären in der Musik des 20. Jahrhunderts" ist die "Medialisierung des Musikalischen" und gleichzeitig eine "Wendung zum Körper".'

6. In the description of the first two videos I will concentrate on details relevant to the concept of masquerade. For more detailed analyses, see Henderson, 1993; E. Ann Kaplan, 1993; Patton, 1993; and Schwichtenberg, 1993c.

7. For more on bodily representation in 'Open Your Heart', see Schulze et al., 1993.

8. The musicological term for this is *sprechgesang*, from the German.

9. Thanks to Santiago Fouz-Hernández and Freya Jarman-Ivens for the identification of the picture.

10. On the voyeuristic male gaze, see McClary, 1991, p. 162, and Mulvey, 1975.

11. The song was co-written by Madonna, Gradner Cole and Peter Rafelson. What I refer to here is not the authorial 'I', but the narrative (vocal) 'I'.

12. On this topic, see Bordo, 1993, pp. 287–9. For a more general analysis of feminism in Madonna's work, see also Chapter 2 by Patricia Pisters in this volume.
13. On this point, see McClary, 1991, p. 162, and Grigat, 1995, pp. 33–4. For more on Madonna's defiance of the male gaze, see Bordo, 1993, p. 283, and Fiske, 1987a, p. 19.
14. Bloss describes a similar process in the work of Annie Lennox (2001, p. 198).
15. 'Nicht mehr der "musikalische Ablauf" setzt den Rahmen für das körperliche Agieren als Moment des Musizierens, sondern die körperliche Selbstinszenierung sowie die kalkulierte Präsentation eines bestimmten Körperbildes werden zum Ausgangspunkt und Träger von Bewegungsabläufen.'
16. Barber-Kersovan describes, in a general way and without reference to any specific video, how listeners to Madonna's music are turned into 'acoustic voyeurs' (2000, p. 269). (Madonna 'drängt mit ihrer bis ins Detail kontrollierten Präsentation den Zuhörer in die Rolle eines akustischen Voyeurs'.)
17. For a comprehensive reading of the images in 'Justify My Love', see Henderson, 1993, pp. 110–13.
18. This image again recalls Tamara de Lempicka's paintings, especially her *Group of Four Nudes* (1932).
19. For a reading of this clip within a film history context, see Schwichtenberg, 1993c, pp. 138–9.
20. See also similarly androgynous images in *Sex* (1992; including one of Madonna painting a man's lips). On masculinity as a masquerade, concerning the video 'Vogue' (Fincher, 1990), see also Patton, 1993, pp. 84–7, although the concept is not explicitly identified.
21. In 'Express Yourself', the epigraph reads 'Without the heart there can be no understanding between the hand and the mind'. See Patricia Pisters in this collection (Chapter 2) for a reading of that video.
22. This reference to a connection with the Satanist movement is not meant as a negative judgement, nor even a judgement at all. Indeed, the positive implications of the axiom ('do what you want') are also felt: they engender a (feminist) liberation in the contexts of the occult that is also present in Madonna's early music videos, especially 'Like a Prayer' (Lambert, 1989). On occultism and its connection to hermeticism, see Hanegraaff, 1996, pp. 421–42.
23. In my view, Madonna's laughter is also a final sign of the subversion presented in this music video. This contrasts with an interpretation by Henderson who, in her analysis, dismisses the importance of the concept of irony, on the grounds of its being 'ambiguous' (1993, pp. 112–13).
24. On the 'third sex', see Sykora, 1999.
25. The term 'occult' emerged only in the nineteenth century and has been used rather unspecifically (see Hanegraaff, 1996, pp. 421–42). For a survey of the concept of hermeticism, see Hanegraaff, 1996, pp. 388–96.
26. 'Chymische Hochzeit, die Vereinigung der polaren Gegensätze ist, in der hermetisch-alchimistischen Symbolik Bezeichnung des chemischen oder geistigen "Schöpfungsaktes", der für die "Geburt" alles Neuen nötig ist.'
27. 'Die sexuelle Symbolik, die in kaum verhüllter Form die Bilderwelt der Alchemie beherrscht, führt in konsequenter Ausprägung, zu der vorstellung des Androgyns, in dem die ursprünglich angelegten Gegensätze harmonisch auf spiritueller Ebene aufgelöst und zu einer höheren Ganzheit geführt worden sind' (Biedermann, 1991, p. 119). On alchemy, see Hanegraaff, 1996, pp. 394–5, 398–9.
28. For a survey of the connection of New Age and hermeticism, see Hanegraaff, 1996.

29. For a comprehensive reading of this video, see Mertin, 1999, pp. 139–48, 157–62. Mertin concentrates on Christian symbolism in the video, but fails to see a link either to surrealism or to the New Age and the concept of androgyny. See also Bullerjahn, 2001, pp. 225–6.
30. On the unconscious and its parallel to dreams in the New Age, see Hanegraaff, 1996, pp. 214–15.
31. See Hanegraaff, 1996, p. 11, on the use of psychedelic drugs.
32. See Chapter 4 by Keith Clifton in this volume for more on Madonna's vocal development.
33. See Brumlik, 1993, p. 7, on Jung and super-consciousness. On the influence of C.G. Jung's theories on the New Age, see Hanegraaff, 1996, pp. 496–513.
34. See Magritte's *The Man with the Bowler* (1964), where we see the white dove in front of – or instead of? – the man's face. It is known that Madonna collects surrealist paintings and is particularly fond of the Mexican painter Frida Kahlo. Kahlo's pictures of birth visions may have been particularly significant for Madonna at the time of the 'Bedtime Story' video, as she was still trying to become pregnant. Madonna actually owns *My Birth* and is particularly fond of it. See Bullerjahn, 2001, p. 226.
35. Although most surrealists were influenced primarily by Freud, it is known that Varo 'could not help but be influenced by the predominating theories of Freud and Jung' (Janet A. Kaplan, 1983, p. 109). Varo also 'studied mystic disciplines and read metaphysical texts' (p. 104), so she may have known Andreae from her own studies.
36. The four elements earth, air, water and fire are acknowledged not only in hermeticism but in most early modern thought, and their significance in the context of the present chapter should therefore be clear.
37. 'New Age believers generally see the coming of the New Age as closely connected to large astronomical cycles, which are interpreted astrologically. Thus, the last ca. 2000 years, dominated by Christianity, are referred to as the Age of Pisces ... The Age of Aquarius, which will follow the Age of Pisces, will also last approximately 2000 years, presumably to be followed by yet another and quite different Age.' These two millennia will be characterized by the position of the earth in the zodiacal system (Hanegraaff, 1996, p. 102). On the New Age as 'Age of Aquarius' and as new era, see pp. 331–56. On the zodiacal system, see Biedermann, 1991, pp. 475–7.
38. Nevertheless, in Schwichtenberg's reading of Baudrillard, his theory can also be seen as a 'challenge to the male/female polarities of sexual difference, which have by now proved to be an impasse for feminist theory' (1993c, p. 133). My reading of 'Bedtime Story' follows this line of argument.
39. See, for example, *Judith I* (1901) or *Wasserschlangen I* (1904/07). See Karentzos, 2002 on Klimt's 'golden women'.
40. Some of these ideas are further developed in my forthcoming book, provisionally entitled *Castratos and Androgynous Popstars in Contexts of Hermeticism and Alchemy.*

PART II

Post-Virgin: Sexual Identities

Olivier Tridon

Chapter 4

Queer hearing and the Madonna queen

Keith E. Clifton

> So much controversy has swirled around my career this past decade that very little attention ever gets paid to my music. The songs are all but forgotten.
> (*Something to Remember* liner notes, 1995)

Given her enviable status as one of the most successful pop stars American culture has ever produced, we might assume that critical acclaim has consistently accompanied Madonna's commercial success, and yet the quotation above illustrates that respect for her artistic work has been fickle. Madonna's transformational imagery, lovers and sexual escapades have provided ample fodder for tabloid-style commentary, with little or no attention paid to her skills as a songwriter and performer. In this essay I intend to move beyond accepted stereotypes into the realm of serious discourse concerning Madonna's artistic merits. With the releases of *Ray of Light* (1998) and *Music* (2000), appearing more than a decade after her eponymous debut album (1983), Madonna's work began to attract serious attention. Prior to these albums, two important collections, *Deconstructing Madonna* (Lloyd, 1993), and *The Madonna Connection* (Schwichtenberg, 1993a), grappled with similar issues, providing a significant foundation for later Madonna studies.[1]

While not gifted with an especially powerful or wide-ranging voice, Madonna has worked to expand her artistic palette to encompass diverse musical, textual and visual styles and various vocal guises, all with the intention of presenting herself as a mature musician. This transformation is arguably as significant to Madonna's artistic development as the more obvious external changes of hairstyle, wardrobe or make-up.

Especially in her usage of the voice, Madonna's self-transformation is paramount and deliberate. We may perceive audible changes from the squealing sex kitten of the early years (in 'Material Girl' (1984) and 'Dress You Up' (1984)), through passionate balladeer in the 1990s ('Take a Bow' (1994)), to energetic disco-style diva ('Music'(2000)), and rapper ('American Life' (2003)). Madonna's vocal metamorphosis has proven to be a central and yet under-theorized aspect of her career, culminating in the long-awaited *Evita* (Parker,

1996), a role for which she endured months of voice lessons with coach Joan Layder in order to transform herself into a 'legitimate' singer.[2]

Equally significant is Madonna's longstanding identification with the gay community and especially gay men, where songs such as 'Express Yourself' (1989) resonate strongly. When Madonna sings 'Come on girls, do you believe in love?', there is a sense that she is singing as much for her gay audience as for heterosexual females.[3] The gay attraction to Madonna includes her ubiquitous transformations of image, liberated sexuality and elaborate and often campy stage antics. But there is another connection that has been overlooked: Madonna's voice itself. Drawing on recent queer theory concerning the phenomenon of the opera queen (Koestenbaum, 1993; Morris, 1993; Robinson, 1994), I will consider the symbiotic relationship between Madonna and what I have termed her 'Madonna Queens' within the gay community.

This chapter examines Madonna's songs and performance style, showing how both have evolved significantly over the years. I have selected for detailed commentary five songs that represent a cross-section of her vocal styles: 'Material Girl' (1984), 'Papa Don't Preach' (1986), 'I'd Be Surprisingly Good for You' (1996), 'Frozen' (1998) and 'Music' (2000). Within these songs, and others mentioned in this chapter, specific trends emerge that may be labelled 'Madonna's vocal tropes'; such categories as 'nostalgic', 'electronic' or 'little-girl voice' would be included. By shifting her vocal timbre and inflection, Madonna consistently redefines the 'Madonna sound' in much the same way as she has redefined the 'Madonna look', making it difficult to establish a single prevailing vocal style. Through an examination of Madonna as composer, arranger and singer, we discover that this artist is anything but one-dimensional.

'Give Me One More Chance': Madonna, the critics and the academy

Madonna's stormy relationship with the critics is a well-established and crucial aspect of her remarkable career. From Susan Baker's dismissal of Madonna as a mere 'porn queen in heat' (cited in McClary, 1991, pp. 148, 204),[4] to Camille Paglia's quasi-canonization of the artist as the future of feminism (1992), critics have been bitterly divided on her artistic merits.[5] Her apparent desire to push the boundaries of America's puritanical sexual codes has required that the music sometimes takes second place to social and political agendas.

In the field of musicology, serious discussion of Madonna has been even rarer than in the popular press. Musicologists seem to have been reluctant to address popular culture, and especially music of the 1980s and 1990s, an era frequently viewed as musically insignificant. An important step was made with the publication of Susan McClary's groundbreaking collection of essays *Feminine Endings* (1991), which included the first musicological article to discuss Madonna as a serious artist. In her analysis of several key songs – including 'Live to Tell' (1986) and 'Like a Prayer'(1989) – McClary notes the lack of critical consensus where Madonna is concerned, as well as the 'automatic dismissal of her music as irrelevant' (p. 148).

McClary assaults the stereotype of dance-inspired music as feminine and weak, versus stronger, masculine rock styles. She writes:

> It is for this reason that dance music in general usually is dismissed by music critics, even 'serious' rock critics. Recall the hysterical scorn heaped upon disco when it emerged, and recall also that disco was the music that underwrote the gay movement, black urban clubs, *Saturday Night Fever*'s images of working-class leisure, and other contexts that did not conform to the cherished ideal of (white, male, heterosexual, middle-class) rebel rock. (1991, p. 153)[6]

The subtext of McClary's argument is unambiguous: music by artists such as Madonna or Prince, with their frequent use of dance idioms and subsequent association with gay or sexually liberated audiences, is seen as somehow inferior to 'real' rock and roll. But Madonna's music refuses to be defined by narrow boundaries of gender, sexuality or anything else. Fluidity is paramount; or, as McClary states, Madonna the artist 'refuses to be framed by a structure that will push her back into submission or annihilation' (1991, p. 152).

Madonna and her queer audience

In the same way that musicologists have reluctantly embraced new modes of thinking about popular music, these same scholars have been equally hesitant, until relatively recently, in grappling with similar issues in classical music. Again, McClary has challenged this conservatism through her reinterpretation of works such as Bizet's *Carmen* and Tchaikovsky's *Symphony No. 4 in F Minor* (1991, pp. 69–79). One example of musicologists adopting these new methodologies, however, is in the study of opera, where the phenomenon of the 'opera queen' has attracted attention. Forming a significant financial and audience base for modern opera houses, gay men maintain a visible presence at opera performances. The opera house has become a highbrow substitute for the gay bar scene, especially for men who do not fit the 'stud' stereotype of perfectly chiselled bodies and (real or manufactured) youth. As one who has spent years at the opera as audience member and observer, I can state without hesitation that the typical gay opera patron is less concerned with fulfilling these stereotypes. The opera house, at times a highly cruisy environment, becomes a 'safe space' for all types of gay men. Mitchell Morris confirms the concept of the opera house as protective space when he states that 'as long as the opera house provides a space – a closet, we might say – in which the spirit may soar free, everyday injustices seem to matter much less' (1993, p. 186).

The fetishistic connection between gays and opera singers has been the subject of important work, especially from Wayne Koestenbaum (1993), Morris (1993) and Paul Robinson (1994). Single-minded devotion to one diva is a central tenet of the opera queen, and as Koestenbaum has written in his campy diatribe on opera and gay men, 'The opera queen must choose one diva. The other divas may be admired, enjoyed, even loved. But only the diva can reign in the opera queen's heart; only one diva can have the power to describe a listener's life' (1993, p. 19). Morris amplifies the same sentiment when he states that 'central to a true opera queen's aesthetic is the cult of the singer' as favoured singers form 'a homosocial bond between gay men, just as women typically serve to establish such a bond between straight men' (1993, pp. 187–8).[7]

The definition of a 'queen' may also be applied (with care) to popular music. Many gay men profess a strong, almost obsessive devotion to a particular artist, while others are attracted to a wider spectrum of artists and styles. The archetypal gay man, craving variety in his fashion, music and romantic lives, is well provided for by Madonna. Across her career, and even within a single album, there is a tremendous range of styles and lyrical content: Madonna has consistently refused to be placed into a single, stable category. This creates a complex paradox, for just as an opera queen will admire Maria Callas or Joan Sutherland, that same queer listener may profess a similar devotion to Tina Turner, Cher or k. d. lang. It is precisely her fluidity and flexibility that allows the 'Madonna Queen' to reserve a special place for her in their imagination. In the album *Music* (2000), for example, Madonna runs the gamut from techno-inspired dance music, to serious ballads, to quasi-Western anthems. Koestenbaum's contention that opera singers often touch listeners on a deep personal level is crucial here.[8] Throughout her career, Madonna has written from personal experience, covering everything from the strained relationship with her father ('Oh Father' (1989)) to the birth of daughter Lourdes ('Little Star' (2000)), and we see an emotional exchange similar to that identified by Koestenbaum thereby occurring between a pop singer and her audience.

Madonna's association with the gay community is also well documented in the popular and academic press. Writing about Madonna's association with the camp aesthetic, Pamela Robertson discusses the ways she 'foregrounds her identification with both African American and gay male culture' (1999, p. 270) and how 'in numerous interviews, she states her identification with gay men, self-identifying as a fag-hag' (p. 281).[9] Madonna consistently brings aspects of marginalized cultures – black, gay, lesbian, Hispanic – to the core of her work. The emphasis on Madonna as an icon for gay men should not detract from her substantial lesbian following. As Michael Musto puts it, Madonna is 'the great leveller ... the first superstar to appeal equally to both camps' (quoted in Henderson, 1993, p. 121). Her ability to appropriate various cultures has been criticized in some quarters, with Madonna accused of 'subcultural tourism' (Tetzlaff, 1993, p. 259): one who visits but never intends to stay (Faith, 1997, pp. 88–9). And yet it is her resistance to such narrow constraints that makes her appealing to a gay audience: Madonna is an artist who 'shimmies into our fag imagination' (Musto quoted in Henderson, 1993, p. 112).

For many gay men, Madonna has become an icon with a conscience. Her richer vocal sound and complex lyrics, evident post-*Evita* on *Ray of Light* (1998), *Music* (2000) and some of the tracks on *American Life* (2003), mirrors the socio-cultural shift in her gay listeners, as many gay men have rejected the excesses of the 1980s – such as drug use and casual sex – in favour of more mature life choices. Her evolving artistry parallels the evolution of gay culture from the 1980s to the present. Madonna has presented herself – in public, at least – in the same way, as she has abandoned her previous hedonism in favour of a new role as doting wife and mother. And yet the boundaries between the old and new Madonna remain fluid, as they do for gay men in general. The serious spirituality of *Ray of Light* has given way in *Music* to a rebirth of the dance-style *jouissance* of her early years. Madonna foregrounds topics that gay men can relate to, and she does so without prejudice, covering everything from drag and vogueing, to Western rodeo culture.[10]

The Madonna sound: the early years

The circumstances surrounding Madonna's early years in the music business are well known to her fans: the departure from Michigan for New York City, the gigs as a drummer and singer, the big break on the dance hit 'Everybody' (1983). Madonna has always been self-conscious about her voice, especially when compared to her vocal idols, a group that includes Ella Fitzgerald, Prince and Chaka Khan. In various interviews, Madonna has discussed the singers and styles that most influenced her, with a frequent emphasis on classic soul. She states that 'Ella Fitzgerald has an incredible voice. She's the greatest. Joni Mitchell ... Patsy Cline ... Chaka Khan – I love her voice. I love all the old soul singers – Marvin Gaye, Frankie Lymon, Sam Cooke' (St. Michael, 1990, p. 39).[11]

The release of her first album, *Madonna* (1983), announced that a major pop star had arrived, but one not yet fully formed artistically. Her vocal style and lyrics appear similar to those of other pop stars of the period (such as Paula Abdul, Debbie Gibson and Taylor Dayne), most of whom have not gone on to enjoy the same success as Madonna, perhaps suggesting that Madonna's later artistic developments exceed those of her early contemporaries and have played a part in her success. The songs on *Madonna* reveal several key trends that have continued to define her success, including a strong dance-based idiom, catchy hooks, highly polished arrangements and Madonna's own vocal style. In songs such as 'Lucky Star' (1983) and 'Burning Up' (1983, her first video for MTV), Madonna introduced a style of upbeat dance music that would prove particularly appealing to future gay audiences. The bright, girlish vocal timbre of these early years became somewhat passé in Madonna's later work, which, as I shall argue below, was a deliberate choice.

The release of *Like a Virgin* (1984) was the defining moment of her early career. Not only had Madonna the musical artist arrived, but Madonna the sexual one as well, especially after her appearance on the 1984 MTV music awards, where she sang the album's title song while rolling around the stage suggestively clad in a white wedding dress. The album itself foreshadows several trends in Madonna's later work, including references to classical styles (the pizzicato synthesizer line that opens 'Angel'); potential controversy ('Dress You Up' as lightning rod for the Parent's Music Resource Center); and retro styles ('Shoo-Bee-Doo', Madonna's homage to Motown).

The song from the *Like a Virgin* album that best exemplifies Madonna's early style is 'Material Girl'. Here, Madonna is in complete control of all aspects of her art, including the appropriation of Marilyn Monroe imagery in the video.[12] The song opens with Madonna using a 'little-girl' voice, a timbre employed to great effect on the first album.[13] But following the first verse, Madonna abruptly switches to a richer, more mature sound for the chorus ('We are living in a material world'). The new vocal style, along with a denser instrumental texture, give extra weight to the meaning of the song, namely, that she is in charge of the discourse. The robotic male back-up chorus solidifies her status as the focal point of the song. The coda to 'Material Girl', again featuring the male chorus chanting in unison, further highlights her control. While the men repeat the line 'Living in a material world' in a low monotone, Madonna adds commentary of her own: clearly, *she* is in charge and the men must bow to *her* wishes. In many ways, 'Material Girl' represents the antithesis of the misogynistic imagery evident in numerous songs of the period. We are reminded, for example, of the (in)famous video for Robert Palmer's 'Addicted to Love' (1986), where the female 'band' is depicted as a group of nameless automatons who merely support the sexualized image Palmer depicts: Madonna turns the table on this stereotype.[14]

Madonna grows up

Madonna's complex relationship with her father was a focal point of the controversial (and perhaps exaggerated) documentary film *Truth or Dare* (Keshishian, 1991). Losing her mother at such a young age may have caused Madonna to view men with scepticism, perhaps accounting in part for her dysfunctional romantic relationships prior to meeting Guy Ritchie. The trope of fatherhood is frequently evoked in Madonna's work, as evidenced by songs such as 'Oh Father', 'Papa Don't Preach', or 'Mother and Father' (2003). In Madonna's artistic career, 'Papa Don't Preach' is a significant milestone, appearing on *True Blue* (1986), an album frequently referred to as her first mature artistic statement.[15] The song introduced a new seriousness to Madonna's music.

The opening synthesizer riff, programmed to imitate the sound of classical strings, lends an air of gravity unprecedented in Madonna's oeuvre at the time. Madonna has acknowledged the influence of classical music, and has spoken in particular about her love for Chopin and Mozart (St. Michael, 1990, p. 36).[16] Prior to the present study, Madonna's employment of classical styles has been largely ignored. 'Papa Don't Preach' begins with music of a distinctly Vivaldian flair, as the fast tempo and classical-style chord progression prepares the listener for the substantive lyrics to follow. The opening chords, presented twice in antecedent/consequent phrases, could easily appear in a Baroque work, as both chords and melody emphasize tonic, submediant and flattened leading-tones: Fm---|E♭---|D♭---|Cm---|D♭-E♭-|Fm---|D♭-E♭-|Fm---. The flourishes in the right hand of the synth line further reinforce the sense of urgency. An unusual choice for a pop song, the tonic key of F minor has a history in classical music of expressing extreme pathos, as in Beethoven's *Appassionata* sonata, and the key therefore constructs a disjuncture between 'pop' and 'classical' realms, underlined in 'Papa Don't Preach' by the instrumentation in the introduction. This introduction sounds anxious and unstable, perhaps representative of the adult realm occupied by the father. For the next section, the sound of dance music is evoked as a powerful beat is hammered out by the instruments. Thus, in a few short bars two very different worlds collide, emphasizing the central conflict of the lyrics.

With Madonna's vocal entrance, we immediately perceive a sound different from that found in her previous work: mature, centred and in a lower range than 'Material Girl'. This 'anti-little-girl voice' establishes the central tension of the lyrics – between a woman in trouble who wants to be taken seriously and the father who still views her as a child.[17] She addresses her father directly, asking him to talk to her as an adult, not the 'little girl' he still perceives her to be ('You should know by now that I'm not a baby'; 'I may be young at heart, but I know what I'm saying'). The transition to the chorus ('The one you warned me all about') employs a more dramatic, almost pained vocal style and a higher range, leading inexorably to cries of 'Please' followed by the powerful chorus ('Papa, don't preach'), where Madonna switches to a 'pleading voice'. Here, she cries out the song's main hook in a high voice.

Madonna's employment of a variety of musical styles is evident throughout the song, including the Spanish-inspired bridge section, one of the earliest recorded examples of Madonna's penchant for Hispanic music.[18] While the narrative of 'Papa Don't Preach' concerns a young woman and the decision to abort or keep her new baby, clearly framed within a heterosexual context, the song may contain a queer subtext as well. How many gay men and lesbians can relate to a moment when they have decided to come out to a conservative, homophobic parent, only wishing that their father (or mother) would accept them unconditionally? In her unique way, Madonna is speaking to and for a larger audience than even she may have intended. Her new voice reinforces these diverse meanings, giving voice to realistic and painful emotions previously untapped in her recordings.

'You Must Love Me': Madonna's greatest challenge

Even before undertaking serious voice study in preparation for the *Evita* project (1996), Madonna's music of the late 1980s and early 1990s reveals the growing depth of her artistry. In songs such as 'Express Yourself' (1989) and 'Till Death Do Us Part'(1989), Madonna explored subject matter with a mature musical and vocal style far removed from her earliest efforts.

But not all critics welcomed her new artistic path. In his critique of the *Erotica* album (1992) – Madonna's most maligned project, especially due to its association with the *Sex* book – Simon Frith describes Madonna's early 1990s voice in no uncertain terms:

> By disco standards, Madonna's voice is a thin instrument. There's not much body in it; her vocal chords don't, in themselves, make enough noise to defy a rhythm track. She gets her effects not by switching gear but by switching register, and, whether she's singing from mouth or throat or chest, when she pushes her voice it becomes shrill and petulant. (1993, p. 88)

While few, including the singer herself, would proclaim that Madonna's voice is an exceptionally powerful instrument, his characterization of her voice as 'thin' applies only to certain situations and fails to account for the major strides Madonna made over the course of her early albums. Such criticism may well have fuelled Madonna's enthusiasm for improving the quality and sound of her voice, at any price. Receiving the role of Eva Perón in the film adaptation of *Evita* proved to be the motivation she needed to do just that. Madonna campaigned relentlessly for the part, realizing that she had stiff competition from more established actresses such as Michelle Pfeiffer and Glenn Close (Taraborrelli, 2001, p. 244). Madonna envisioned that *Evita* would fulfil two significant functions in her career: to establish her as a serious actress and as a serious singer.[19]

In order to transform herself into a singer able to cope with the tremendous demands of the show, Madonna began voice lessons in 1996 with New York voice teacher Joan Layder, who had previously coached Patti LuPone – one of the most celebrated exponents of the role. In their private sessions, Layder focused on strengthening Madonna's upper range in anticipation of the demands of *Evita*: 'She had to use her voice in a way she'd never used it before ... *Evita* is real musical theatre – it's operatic, in a sense. Madonna developed an upper range that she didn't know she had' (Taraborrelli, 2001, p. 249). Madonna approached this latest challenge with great enthusiasm, later remarking that 'I suddenly discovered that I had been using only half my voice' (p. 250).[20] The hard work soon paid off in a more mature and balanced vocal sound. Writing for *USA Today*, Edna Gundersen noted that *Evita* represented Madonna's 'finest singing to date' (1999, p. 75).

Evita represents the culmination of Madonna's obsession with Hispanic culture.[21] Responses to the final results were mixed, although there can be no doubt that she had come a long way vocally and dramatically. While Madonna won the 1996 Golden Globe award for best actress, the reviews of Madonna's musical performance varied widely. Writing for *Rolling Stone*, Elysa Gardner stated that Madonna was 'hindered by the thin tone and limited range of her voice' and that her version of 'Don't Cry for Me Argentina' was 'curiously tentative' (1997, p. 253). Certainly Madonna does not possess the vocal strength that artists such as LuPone have brought to the role, but then this was one of the few times that Madonna had appeared with full orchestra rather than a pop/rock band.

Arguably, Madonna's strongest musical moments in *Evita* are the intimate ones, especially the death scene and its accompanying song 'You Must Love Me', which exposes her newly strengthened high register. The highlight of the soundtrack, however, is the duet 'I'd Be Surprisingly Good For You' with stage veteran Jonathan Pryce as Juan Perón. Here, Eva tries to convince Juan that a relationship between them would benefit his cause. Sometimes accused of manipulating the people in her life to advance her career, Madonna is playing a woman accused of the same thing.[22] Her vocal quality in this song may be labelled 'seductive', a quiet, somewhat breathy style already evident in songs such as 'Justify My Love'. Here the sound is more mature, as she effectively controls the extremities of range required in the duet (from $F\sharp_1$ to C^1). The higher tessitura is especially well-manipulated, as she trims the voice to a near-whisper for the seminal line 'I'm not talking of a hurried night, a frantic tumble and a shy goodbye.'

'Veronica Electronica' faces her critics

Madonna's efforts to transform the quality of her voice for *Evita* provide a career milestone that continues to resonate in her recent work. After *Evita*, Madonna was ready to put her new voice and mature artistry to work on a full-length album of original songs. *Ray of Light*, the first collection of new material since *Bedtime Stories* in 1994, provided such a challenge. While the album has experienced its share of criticism – for example from Tamara Ikenberg of the *Los Angeles Times*, who refers to Madonna's new sound as 'Veronica Electronica' (1999, p. 167) – *Ray of Light* may be the most acclaimed album of her career.[23] With its complex tapestry of styles, moods and sounds, *Ray of Light* is a major artistic statement, its seriousness of purpose comparable to the earlier *Like a Prayer* (1989). Produced with the assistance of techno-guru William Orbit, *Ray of Light* reveals several different sides of Madonna's musical personality, from Byrds-like folk in 'Swim' to the techno dance beats of 'Nothing Really Matters' and the spiritual undertones of 'Shanti/Ashtangi'. In describing the project as a whole, Orbit has said that Madonna 'didn't want to lose her identity. She just wanted to expand her sound' (quoted in Taraborrelli, 2001, p. 302). And Madonna herself has commented that 'I just feel like I'm shedding layers. I'm slowly revealing who I am' (quoted in Powers, 1999, p. 81).

'Frozen' clearly displays Madonna's musical evolution. Written in F minor, the same key as the earlier 'Papa Don't Preach' (1986), 'Frozen' is rife with allusions to classical music. These include sweeping string riffs, restrained vocals sung largely without vibrato, perhaps recalling medieval sacred chant, and classical chordal progressions. The lyrics reflect Madonna's fascination with those who refuse to communicate their true feelings, a topic already familiar in songs ranging from 'Express Yourself' (1989) to 'Take a Bow' (1994). The song reveals Madonna's artistic depth, refusing to be defined by one prevailing vocal mould. A closer examination reveals its complexity in more detail:

Introduction: Opens with austere, classical style string riff at a low dynamic level. The chord progression emphasizes tonic, subdominant, submediant and flattened leading-tone chords. Note that the stable dominant chord (C Major) is conspicuously absent: F minor–E♭–D♭maj⁷–E♭–F minor (with 4–3 suspension). For the second phrase, which includes a dramatic crescendo, rhythm and ambient electronic effects are added gradually to enhance the mysterious mood.

Verse One: Madonna enters tentatively in medium range ('You only see what your eyes want to see'), then descends to F_1 to highlight the refrain ('You're frozen, when your heart's not open'). The sudden shift to a lower register serves to amplify the alienation and sorrow implicit in the refrain.

Chorus: Light dance rhythm and ambient sounds are added as Madonna shifts to a medium range and a more controlled vocal style – while retaining a certain passion – for the repeated musical hook, 'If I could melt your heart.'

Verse Two: Similar musical style to verse one, but with more visceral textual imagery ('Love is a bird, she needs to fly').

Bridge: Broad, quasi-operatic string lines provide instrumental commentary on the lyrics. Although abbreviated in the radio version, the album presents this bridge twice for dramatic effect. Each phrase concludes with an incomplete dominant (C Major chord without E♮), maintaining the tension of the song.

Coda: Combination of passionate vocals, techno beat, and string riff to create a powerful *mélange* of styles. The song ends with a string ostinato that simply fades away, without fully resolving to the tonic chord.

By employing a lower vocal range, lush harmonies and instrumentation, and expressive lyrics, 'Frozen' emerges as Madonna's most operatic song, an aria in popular form. Although not primarily a dance song, the subtle dance beat and unresolved conclusion produce a visceral effect not unlike Richard Dyer's concept of disco's 'whole body eroticism' (1990, p. 413).

The video of 'Frozen' (Cunningham, 1998) also reflects Madonna's new spiritual and artistic path. Filmed in the California desert, Madonna is clad in a stark black dress to become a 'virtual angel of death' (Powers, 1999, p. 82). The imagery is mysterious and haunting. The song was also performed in Part Two of the *Drowned World Tour* (2001). Dressed in a Jean-Paul Gaultier black kimono with enormous sleeves creating a span of about fifty feet, Madonna appeared onstage as a kabuki-like figure.[24] As the song progresses, she gradually breaks loose from the sleeves, perhaps symbolic of an escape from oppression.[25]

Like so much of her work, 'Frozen' may employ a gay subtext. The lyrics are surely resonant for many gay men and lesbians who have come out to parents or loved ones, only to find rejection or, in many cases, banishment. Madonna could easily be addressing homophobic parents when she states repeatedly that 'You're frozen, when your heart's not open.' The grand sweep of the music recalls works of the Romantic period, or certain Neo-Romantics such as Samuel Barber and his *Adagio for Strings*. A further connection may be Romantic opera, where Madonna's music seems to invoke the lyricism of Verdi and Puccini. Since gay 'opera queens' are likely to favour opera from this period, 'Frozen' may recall works such as *Madama Butterfly* or *Aida* for some of these listeners. Her vocal style invites us to experience the pathos she describes, with the queer listener as a target audience.

'Hey Mr DJ'

The phenomenal success of *Ray of Light* exerted enormous pressure on Madonna to create a suitable follow-up album. The result was *Music*, an album that found her returning to the dance idiom that made her famous, and the gay audience that has always supported her. Although Madonna never completely abandoned writing dance music, the albums from 1989 until 1996 (*Like a Prayer* to *Evita*) show her exploring a more mature sound. *Music* is filled with images and themes familiar to queer listeners, including the retro disco milieu of the title song and 'Paradise (Not for Me)', a sequel to 'Frozen' in its classical sweep and sophisticated electronic effects.

Music opens with the title song, one of the catchiest singles of her career.[26] An androgynous voice asks the DJ to 'put a record on' as the dance beat begins. Above this foundational beat, with its clapped backbeat pattern, Madonna's voice is electronically manipulated as it asks 'Do you like to boogie woogie?' The use of casual, even campy speech ('I wanna dance wis' my baby') may further reinforce a connection with gay listeners. As Leap (1995 and 1996) and Chesebro (1981) have shown, the employment of camp language within gay culture provides a method by which homosexuals may distance themselves from the dominant culture and establish their own identities.

For the verses, Madonna returns to her normal voice in medium range, leading to the chorus with its strong dance groove. For the hook of the song – 'Music makes the people come together' – Madonna employs a higher and more urgent voice as a means to entice her listeners into the dance. As Mary Ann Wright has suggested, the dance club (the milieu Madonna evokes) is a safe space that allows for, and celebrates, all varieties of expression (1998, p. 240). Brian Currid amplifies this sentiment when he writes that 'all the dancers of the club, dancing (coincidentally) to a black musical form, enact their "togetherness", without any consciousness of race, class, or gender difference' (1995, p. 184). Like a great disco anthem, the constant beat commands us to get up and dance, which appears to be Madonna's intention.

The song provides a cross-section of Madonna's artistic range, as she sings in several styles, some natural and some electronically manipulated, that refuse confinement. To my ears, 'Music' is an expression of gratitude to her loyal audience of 'Madonna Queens'. The endless loop form invites repetition as it would in a disco environment, recalling Dyer's concept of the 'endlessly repeated phrase which drives beyond itself' (1990, p. 414). Even the opening phrase of the chorus, here functioning simultaneously as the hook of the song, mirrors one of Madonna's early hits recorded almost two decades before: 'Everybody' (1983). In this song, written in A minor, the melody begins on G, the flattened leading note, and rises to the second scale degree on the syllable 'bo' of 'everybody' to highlight the chorus (G-A-B-A; '*Everybody*, come on dance and sing'). In 'Music', Madonna begins on a higher pitch (scale degree three) and then descends, emphasizing the half step between scale degrees three and two (B♭-A; '*Music* makes the *people* come to*gether*'). In the choruses of both 'Music' and 'Everybody', Madonna is defining her artistic credo, that music has the power to overcome divisions of race, gender and sexuality.

Throughout her career, Madonna's manipulation of her voice shows us that, by refusing to be defined in one way, she has in fact opened up a space for new kinds of musical analysis. Her legacy lies in bringing the marginal, the forgotten and the oppressed to the centre of American popular culture. Her staunch refusal to accept the artistic status quo serves as a model for others in the music business. Morris's summary statement concerning the 'opera queen' could apply with equal potency to Madonna's work. He writes:

> If the members of an oppressed minority find on stage adequate and cathartic representations of an emotional state central to their affective lives as shaped by the repressive social order surrounding them, it is no wonder they invest so heavily in the art form. (Morris, 1993, p. 192)

At the twentieth anniversary of Madonna's first album, fans, audiences and critics were still as keen to analyse her latest moves, coinciding with the release of *American Life*. Whatever new voices she employs in the future, or styles she appropriates, for many of us, a good sense of 'queer hearing' will be required to decipher the messages hidden just beneath the surface.

Notes

1. See also Frank and Smith, 1993a.
2. On Madonna's transformation to a 'legitimate' singer, compare Holden (1999), Milano (1999) and Taraborrelli (2001, p. 249).
3. In this song and others, Madonna's discourse mimics exaggerated gay speech patterns. Gay men, especially in relaxed social occasions, sometimes refer to each other camply as 'honey', 'darling' or 'girl'. See Patricia Pisters in this volume for a feminist reading of this song (Chapter 2).
4. As a member of the Parents' Music Resource Center, Susan Baker led the crusade in the mid-1980s to bring parental warning stickers to rock albums, a practice that continues to the present day.
5. Paglia defends 'Justify My Love' as 'pornographic', 'decadent' and 'fabulous' (1992, p. 3).
6. Dance music, and especially disco, is currently enjoying a Renaissance of sorts among music scholars. See Morris, forthcoming.
7. Morris defines the opera queen as 'any member of that particular segment of the American gay community that defines itself by the extremity and particularity of its obsession with opera' (1993, p. 184). In a related article, Paul Robinson refers succinctly to such men as 'voice fetishists' (1994, p. 285).
8. See in particular Koestenbaum, 1993, p. 10.
9. Mitchell Morris's article, concerning the 1980s duo The Weather Girls and their hit 'It's Raining Men' (1983), addresses issues that relate to Madonna and her gay audience. He writes that 'The Weather Girls helped teach some of us about possible aspects of being gay, and this was true in the image they projected, the lyrics and structure of the song, and its place in the musical texture that defined the culture of disco' (1999, p. 215). The same song has since been covered by ex-Spice Girl Geri Halliwell (2001), another artist with a substantial gay following.
10. Overall, I see much of the *Music* album as distinctly camp. I would also suggest that the cover art itself is camp, notably Madonna's combination of Western clothing with expensive shoes and bright red high heels. In particular, there is a clear evocation of Judy Garland – a major gay icon – in the artwork, by means of a single red (ruby) shoe. For further commentary regarding Madonna and Country music, see Chapter 8 by Sean Albiez in this collection. On Madonna's musical construction of camp, especially in 'Music', see Chapter 1 by Stan Hawkins.
11. The influence of soul on Madonna's music is clearly evident, especially on the album *Bedtime Stories* (1994). A song with a particularly strong soul groove is 'Secret', where Madonna's seductive vocal style recalls such singers as Roberta Flack and Tina Turner. In addition, 'Take a Bow' was co-written by prominent soul artist Kenneth 'Babyface' Edmonds, who also sings back-up on the track.
12. Madonna has acknowledged her fascination with Monroe (Worrell, 1999, pp. 40–41). Like Madonna herself, Monroe was often stereotyped as a 'dumb blonde' unable to produce serious artistic work.
13. The concept of a 'little-girl voice' is also discussed by McClary in regard to the songs 'Like a Virgin' and 'True Blue' as ironic commentaries on a woman who sings one way but actually means something else (1991, p. 155).
14. See also 'Girls On Film' (Godley & Creme, 1981) and 'Hungry Like the Wolf' (Mulcahy, 1982), both by Duran Duran; 'Just a Gigolo' by Dave Lee Roth (Roth, 1985); and 'Girls, Girls, Girls' by Mötley Crüe (dir. unknown, 1987).
15. In reviewing *True Blue* for the *Chicago Tribune*, Greg Kot said that the album 'expanded Madonna's musical horizons' and that the project signalled her 'transition

from pop star to pop artist' (1999). In the *Los Angeles Times*, Robert Hilburn complimented Madonna's improved voice, noting that 'the most obvious growth is in the control and character in Madonna's singing' (1999).

16. On her love for Chopin and Mozart, Madonna has stated that 'they have some real sweet feminine quality about a lot of their music' (St. Michael, 1990, p. 36). Madonna employs a similar riff (and eventual dance groove) to 'Papa Don't Preach' in her title song for the James Bond film *Die Another Day* (Tamahori, 2002).

17. The conflict between father and daughter is made more potent by the video, starring actor Danny Aiello as the father. Madonna has stated that the little girl in the video is a composite of aspects of her relationship with her own father. Another powerful statement concerning the father/daughter bond can be found on the track 'Oh Father' (1989).

18. Another would be 'La Isla Bonita', which also appears on the *True Blue* album (1986). Others songs include 'Who's That Girl?' (1987), 'Spanish Eyes' (1989), 'I'm Going Bananas' (1990), and 'To Have and not to Hold' (1998). For detailed commentary regarding Madonna's treatment of Hispanic cultures, see Chapter 9 by Santiago Fouz-Hernández in this collection.

19. At the time of *Evita*, Madonna stated that 'I really want to be recognized as an actress' (Taraborrelli, 2001, p. 243). She had further problems on the set as many Argentinians viewed the casting of a pop music star as antithetical to the memory of their beloved Eva.

20. The filming schedule for *Evita* was altered somewhat to accommodate Madonna's vocal health. As Taraborrelli writes, Madonna 'would sing only in the afternoon, and every other day. Days off were allocated for her to rest her voice' (2001, p. 251). References to vocal training can be found in Taraborrelli, 2001, pp. 248–50, *passim*.

21. Again, see Fouz-Hernández in this volume (Chapter 9) for more on the role of *Evita* in Madonna's relationship with Hispanic identities.

22. For a comparison between Madonna and Perón, see Taraborrelli, 2001, p. 245.

23. *Ray of Light* has been compared favourably to *Like a Prayer* from almost a decade before. Both albums received largely favourable reviews, and both appeared at the end of their respective decades following a period of backlash.

24. Kabuki refers to one of three styles of traditional Japanese theatre, the others being Noh and Bunraku. With plots concerning love and duty, kabuki shows feature actors dressed in elaborate costumes and make-up, often in vivid colours.

25. For a lively behind-the-scenes examination of this tour, see Gordinier, 2001.

26. For a more extensive discussion of the song, see Chapter 1 by Stan Hawkins in this collection.

Chapter 5

What it feels like for two girls
Madonna's play with lesbian (sub-)cultures

Freya Jarman-Ivens

When considering Madonna from a critical academic perspective, I have found myself consistently ambivalent regarding her interaction with her gay audience, and largely in agreement with critic Michael Musto: 'After an hour's private session with [Madonna], we're ... mad at her for ripping us off, but somehow thanking her for noticing us, legitimizing us' (quoted in Henderson, 1993, p. 122). Throughout her habitual transformations, Madonna's incorporation of gay male iconography into her oeuvre seems little more than the inauthentic usage of a marginalized style that became almost fashionable in its otherness: to suggest cynically that she was capitalizing on 'gay chic' would not seem unreasonable, given her legendary history of repeated subcultural transformations. Academic studies of Madonna's relationship with gay (sub-)cultures have tended either to confine the word 'gay' to meaning 'gay men', as opposed to a definition inclusive of lesbians (Curry, 1990; Henderson, 1993; Robertson, 1996), or to annex lesbian (sub-)cultures to gay male culture (Andermahr, 1994).[1] There is certainly much to discuss on that subject,[2] as her appropriation of gay male iconography functions at every level of her act: song lyrics ('In This Life' (1992)); stage acts (such as parts of *The Girlie Show* tour (1993)); video images (such as 'Vogue' (Fincher, 1990)); public support for AIDS charities; and personal relationships (most notably with openly gay actor Rupert Everett both in fiction (*Next Best Thing* (Schlesinger, 2000)) and real life; and with gay-porn star Tony Ward). Further to these tangible manifestations of gay male imagery in Madonna's work – often received enthusiastically by the gay male community – she arguably functions within a 'camp sensibility', somehow tapping into a particularly gay male modus operandi.[3] It is not my project here to discount such a proposition, nor to undo the work of those who have focused on gay men over lesbians as Madonna's 'chosen ones'. Perhaps, as a lesbian, I am jealous of the greater interest generally afforded to gay men than to lesbians. I am not, however, envious of Madonna's apparent focus on gay men: it is my contention that she engages in equally interesting and complex ways with lesbianism. References to Madonna's interaction with lesbian (sub-)cultures tend merely to acknowledge the 'lesbian chic' which, perhaps, Madonna could not have avoided engaging with, such was its popular cultural appeal in the early 1990s.[4]

A typical observation is that Madonna 'flirted' with lesbianism in her work at that time: an alleged relationship with Sandra Bernhard; lesbian group sex in *Sex* (1992); butch or androgynous women by her side on stage (see the 'boyish girls' who danced in *The Girlie Show*[5]) and video (for example, 'Justify My Love' (Mondino, 1990)).[6] hooks identifies this 'flirting' as a mechanism by which Madonna maintains her (white, Western) power, and therefore accuses Madonna of inauthenticity (1993, p. 72), while Lentz notes Madonna's 'deployment of fantasy as a way of distancing herself from the stigma of the queer sexual practices she depicts' (1993, pp. 156–7). Yet the idea of Madonna's 'flirtation' with lesbianism does not go nearly far enough to explore the complexities of the relationship, especially as lesbianism itself is an intricate network of discourses and sub-discourses. Perhaps I should be less mistrusting of Madonna herself and more specifically critical of the construction (both popular and academic) of Madonna as a gay male icon, to the exclusion of the many sapphic facets of her work. My propositions, then, are these: first, that 'lesbian subculture' is not a coherent (sub-)culture at all – it is far from reducible to a single-levelled concept, consisting instead of a wide range of subcultures and discourses; second, that Madonna has engaged, knowingly and (perhaps) also unknowingly, with many of these (sub-)cultures; and finally that, far from being an extension of her relationship with gay male (sub-)cultures, the relationship Madonna has formulated with lesbian (sub-)cultures is unique and of interest in itself.

Within the group of individuals who constitute so-called 'lesbian (sub-) cultures', there are arguably as many different experiences of 'lesbianism' as there are lesbians.[7] Indeed, the sheer variety of lesbian experience precludes an easy definition. According to Healey, 'The definition of a lesbian as being someone "who did not fuck men" was both negative and hardly a reflection of the diversity of the lesbian world' (1996, p. 82). So lesbian experience may well involve sex with men, or celibacy by choice. Furthermore, the apparently oxymoronic notion of the 'male lesbian' has also emerged in recent years (see Fischer, 2002, p. 12).[8] Beyond such all-inclusive political correctness, however, we must recognize that, in practice, various recurring behavioural themes exist within lesbian (sub-)cultures that characterize those who practise them to a greater or lesser extent. There are recognizable patterns within lesbian (sub-)cultures that may be described as lesbian identities, and key discourses that inform and police those identities. To enable a discussion of Madonna's engagement with such paradigms, it is essential first to identify the paradigms themselves.

As Henderson astutely observes, 'framing' the lesbian reception of Madonna as a cultural icon are those debates commonly referred to as the 'sex wars' (1993, p. 115). These discursive battles have been waged over the political implications of pornography and various sexual practices, especially sadomasochism (S/M). As the title of Healey's (1996) book *Lesbian Sex Wars* implies, these debates have not been restricted to either lesbian or feminist politics. While they have emerged from a broadly feminist political environment, they are also inextricably linked with the lesbian political landscape. These debates, then, are battles of control over the construction of who is (or is not) a lesbian and what is (or is not) lesbian sex. They address issues such as penetration and lesbian sexuality, butch/femme and the construction of lesbian identity, separatism and political lesbianism. The 'lesbian sex wars' provide a clear window into ways in which Madonna engages with lesbian (sub-)cultures, and by addressing these discourses I shall make some initial observations. However, there are other (perhaps less obviously 'lesbian') modes of interaction between Madonna's work and lesbian (sub-)cultures that will also be identified here.

Sapphism and the sisterhood

The well-established link between lesbianism and feminism, through the sex wars, itself forms the first point at which Madonna's career intersects with lesbian discourses. Lesbian and feminist politics have a long history of agreement (and disagreement), especially visible in so-called 'second-wave feminism'.[9] Healey describes how lesbianism and feminism were united at a fundamental level in the 1970s by a common political aim: 'The political theory of lesbian feminism transformed lesbianism from a stigmatized sexual practice into an idea and a political practice that posed a challenge to male supremacy and its basic institution of heterosexuality' (1996, p. 29). Jeffreys sums this up when she writes that, at that time, 'Any woman could be a lesbian' (1994, p. vii). This notion of 'lesbian feminism' as a political affiliation 'which was nothing whatsoever to do with lesbians or lesbian sex' (Healey, 1996, p. 30) potentially masks the truth regarding the number of sexually defined lesbians who were involved with the second-wave feminist movement. Yet a distinct pattern emerges, in which lesbians engage in feminist politics:

> Lesbians were attracted to the feminist movement in the 1970s just as they had been attracted to suffrage campaigning seventy years before. Again for lesbians, equal wages and equal access to education were of particular importance since lesbians could not rely on being supported by a male partner. The feminist attack on conventional notions of femininity also presumably attracted lesbians, who felt constricted by the beautiful, passive, domestic and heterosexual image of women which was still held up as the model of good womanhood. (Hamer, 1996, p. 194)[10]

Beyond the analysis of their political relationship, the two identities have also long been conflated in the popular imagination: as Louise Carolin notes, 'in the mid-1980s it wasn't only your man in the street and my father who thought that "lesbian" and "feminist" were synonymous terms' (1995, p. 36). With these visible links in mind, we must surely reconsider the (much-debated) construction of Madonna as a (pop-)feminist icon.[11] At the beginning of her career, Madonna was repeatedly compared with Cyndi Lauper, whose 'Girls Just Want To Have Fun' (1983) quickly became an early pop-feminist anthem as a 'powerful cry for access to the privileged realm of male adolescent leisure and fun' (Lewis quoted in Stein, 1994, p. 20). The contemporaneous releases of Lauper's hit and Madonna's 'Holiday' (her first international hit, in 1983) symbolized a battle between these two charismatic solo female artists that characterized the pop-music scene through 1984 (see O'Brien, 2002, pp. 228–30). This, combined with the fact that Madonna's style of clothing at this time clearly resembled Lauper's, inevitably intensified comparisons between the two women. Might this have been the embryonic stage of the popular link between Madonna and a type of feminism? Madonna's success quickly overtook Lauper's, and the sheer relentlessness of her success has surely been a major factor in the popular construction of Madonna as a feminist icon, as she enjoys respect and autonomy within the male-dominated music industry. Furthermore, as Curry argues, she represents the highly valued attributes of health, wealth and beauty, and 'on this level alone ... Madonna should have become something of a role model for girls and young women' (1990, p. 16).

More in-depth feminist analysis of her career reveals the ways in which this construction of Madonna has emerged. In particular, within Lewis's model of 'access' and 'discovery' signs, for female fans, Madonna represents access to male privileges. For Lewis, female musicians in female address videos 'symbolically ... execute take-overs of male space, effect the erasure of sex roles, and make demands for parity with male-adolescent privilege. They rework the ideological stance of male privilege into a redress of grievances for girls by appropriating the richness of signification that the image of "the street" holds for boys and men' (1990, p. 109).[12] Considering not only the surface of Madonna's text (individual performances, songs, videos), but also her 'cumulative star image', Curry explains how Madonna might be read as 'a parody of the dominant patriarchal culture which produces her as a commodity' (1990, p. 16). Madonna's image as a whole thus functions on a more complex level than the individual texts. So while specific songs ('Express Yourself' (1989), 'Till Death Do Us Part' (1989)) and videos (such as 'What it Feels Like for a Girl' (Ritchie, 2001)) may well invite feminist readings, it is the extra- and inter-textual interpretative possibilities that endorse a reading of Madonna as a feminist icon, and support 'exceptional interest [in Madonna] as a female cultural icon' (p. 17).[13] On its own, this construction of Madonna as (pop-)feminist icon does not offer an unequivocal connection between the star and lesbianism. However, given the perceptible popular link between lesbianism and feminism, the first points of association are emerging here, and we can start to see how Madonna engages with discourses in lesbian (sub-)cultures.

Waiting for the right man?

I want to move now from this general debate to identifying specific lesbian (sub-)cultural discourses that Madonna has invoked, usually through particular visual styles. Madonna is undoubtedly most notorious for those images that accompanied the simultaneous releases of the album *Erotica* and the book *Sex* in 1992. The pornographic iconography that characterized the two products generated images of Madonna in a (i)conical-breasted basque during the *Blond Ambition* tour (1990), and as Dita Parlo in *Sex* (later replayed in *The Girlie Show* tour). Madonna's dominatrix imagery forces us to confront two particularly hard-fought sex wars – those surrounding pornography and sadomasochism – which relate interestingly with lesbian (sub-)cultures, as I discuss below in relation to the 'Human Nature' video (Mondino, 1995). While pornography dominated American feminist debate in the early 1980s, the politics of lesbian sadomasochism was a dominant topic for discussion by British feminists (Healey, 1996, pp. 92–3).

The notorious *Blond Ambition* look consisted of a long, blonde, taut ponytail placed high on Madonna's head,[14] fishnet tights and a pink satin basque with constructed conical breasts. The highly hetero-sexualized image called upon many of the codes of straight pornography, codes foregrounded by her wearing them as outer-garments. This intense heterosexuality is not apparently connected with a lesbian context of consumption, but we must remember the contemporaneous representations (1988–91) of Madonna and her relationship with openly bisexual comedienne Sandra Bernhard which, while far from being unequivocally sexual, must surely be one of Madonna's clearest interactions to date with lesbian (sub-)cultures. The question here is, how does her display of such apparently extreme heterosexuality impact upon – or, how is it *impacted upon by* – the climate of debate surrounding Madonna's sexuality generated by her relationship with Bernhard? One potentially productive interpretation can be found in the vestimentary codes accompanying the *Blond Ambition* look, whilst re-locating the imagery alongside that found in *Sex*. A connection thus emerges between Madonna's act at this time and heterosexual pornography, in which a well-established theme is the scene of two women initiating sexual contact between themselves and being brought to climax by an intervening male. Played out in this classic scene are anxieties that 'real' lesbians leave men redundant. Thus we see the effacement of the 'real' lesbian by the traditionally attractive (blonde-haired, large-breasted, perfectly made-up) and available woman, exposing the conditions upon which this scene is predicated: that lesbian sexual activity must only occur between women who are *attractive to* and *conquerable by* men. Madonna played both of these roles within the fusion of hyper-hetero style and (possible) bisexuality: she defined herself as desirable through clearly coded mechanisms of dress and gesture; and she presented herself as available through the photographs in *Sex* and an already long history of high-profile boyfriends (Sean Penn, Warren Beatty and Tony Ward by that time). Thus, the image she presents of supposedly 'real' lesbian behaviour is highly problematized. This challenge did not, however, seem to affect significantly the message taken by gay and lesbian communities from Madonna's relationship with Bernhard. The lack of clarification from either woman certainly did not detract from the rumours surrounding the nature of the relationship. Indeed, they seemed to delight in, encourage and even generate the media's desire for elucidation: in 1988, on *The Late Show with David Letterman*, the pair appeared together, keen to talk about themselves and boasting about visits to lesbian bars (see Taraborrelli, 2001, p. 152); in April 1989, Bernhard dedicated her 'lesbian version' of Billy Paul's 'Me and Mrs. Jones' to Madonna at a charity concert; in May that year, Madonna and Bernhard publicly fondled each other while singing a 'lesbian version' of Sonny and Cher's 'I Got You Babe' at another charity event (see Bego, 1992, p. 229).

Although both women apparently courted the media's interest in their relationship at the time, with Bernhard openly claiming to have slept with both Madonna and Sean Penn (Taraborrelli, 2001, p. 152), they have also both denied since that the relationship was ever sexual. Bernhard declared in 1990, 'We're friends and that's it' (Bego, 1992, p. 230). Madonna's apparently outright denial of the sexual nature of the relationship came in 1991, when she told *Rolling Stone*: 'Let me put it this way: I've certainly had fantasies of fucking women, but I'm not a lesbian' (Fisher, 1997, p. 185). Yet this seemingly unproblematic declaration is still open to being claimed by lesbians, since it came moments after Madonna admitted having done 'the finger-fucking thing' (p. 185), leaving some room for interpretation: 'not being a lesbian' does not preclude 'finger-fucking' and other same-sex activity. Despite the ambiguous nature of her relationship with Bernhard, the overriding message taken by Madonna's gay audiences seems to have been that Madonna directly championed same-sex relationships. Affected consumers of Madonna at this time either understood that she and Bernhard did have a sexual relationship, or that they may as well have had – since Madonna's response seemed to be that of someone who could or would have such an affair. For many gays and lesbians, the high-profile nature of the relationship and rumours made 'lesbianism just a little less invisible' (Pokorny, 1989, p. 10), perhaps regardless of what 'really' happened. One young gay man, clearly assuming the relationship to have been sexual, believed it to have affected the way in which his own sexuality was perceived: 'Once Madonna had had sex with a woman, [homosexuality] was, like, legal' (quoted in Teeman, 2000, p. 63). Taraborrelli's cynical analysis of this is that the relationship was a convenient 'promotional hook' for Madonna. He writes, 'Madonna was well aware that many of her staunchest supporters were homosexual men, and that even a hint that she herself was gay would only strengthen their loyalty and devotion' (2001, p. 153). This adds an interesting dimension because it suggests that, although Madonna was engaging with lesbian (sub-)cultures by means of her relationship with

Bernhard, her concern was more for the support of gay men than for any implications for a lesbian audience. Madonna was also alleged to have been in a sexual relationship with Jennifer Grey (star of *Dirty Dancing* (Ardolino, 1987)), thus intensifying rumours of Madonna as possibly bisexual (Bego, 1992, p. 211).

While Madonna's allegedly lesbian relationships seem to engage directly and positively with lesbianism, there are also more negative implications contained within this image. The early to mid-1990s saw much experimentation with homosexuality and the widespread public emergence of bisexuality and the fashionable 'lipstick lesbian' (neo-femme?).[15] Through her enigmatic lack of confirmation regarding her relationships with Bernhard and Grey, Madonna clearly benefited from the newly increased public acceptance of female bisexuality, and one might view this cynically as commercial exploitation. Furthermore, bisexuality is still a problematic concept in the gay community, and in this way Madonna plays to a straight audience titillated by sexual otherness, rather than (or, at best, alongside) a lesbian audience looking for a positive role model. Bisexuality is seen by many either as a refusal to come out as completely gay or as appropriation of a passing fashion (see McAuley, 1995, p. 30). In addition, 'lipstick lesbians' are not always felt to be 'real' lesbians (Ainley, 1995, pp. 151, 154), being particularly subject to the image of lesbians as 'needing the right man',[16] and there is the apparently increasing phenomenon of the 'hasbian', a woman 'who tried the same sex when it was cool but now prefer[s] men' (*Cosmopolitan*, 2003, p. 119). Perhaps in the case of Madonna these stereotypes are indeed borne out; her previous turbulent relationship with Sean Penn recalls the idea that lesbians have had a 'bad experience' with men, and she returned fairly quickly to the heterosexuality from whence she came (with Warren Beatty), apparently underlining her status by means of motherhood (with Carlos Léon) and marriage (to Guy Ritchie), traditionally heterosexual institutions. Thus, following an initially positive reaction to the Bernhard rumours from some political gays and lesbians, Madonna's longer-term return to heterosexuality arguably represented a public undermining of her relationship with lesbianism, or at least the playing out of some more negative stereotypes of lesbian behaviour.[17]

'Nothing like a good spanky'

The second infamous sex war that particularly interacts with lesbian (sub-)cultures, and which Madonna has repeatedly visited, is that regarding sadomasochism. This, of course, is far from an exclusively lesbian practice, but as Hart and Dale argue: 'While heterosexual S/M sexuality has thrived rather quietly and uneventfully throughout the centuries, gay, and particularly lesbian, S/M has generated heated debates both between the dominant culture and gay and lesbian subcultures, as well as within gay and lesbian subcultures' (1997, p. 341). The apparently greater visibility of gay and lesbian sadomasochistic practices makes them particularly significant within broader debates surrounding S/M, and within the present context. In addition, it is precisely the non-exclusivity of sadomasochism that informs most interestingly the lesbian political responses to this expression of sexuality. Debate surrounding lesbian sadomasochism has been largely informed by feminist discussions within a heterosexual context. Heterosexual sadomasochism is figured as a way in which men exercise sexual power over women, and anti-S/M lesbian feminists have thus concluded that 'S/M is a powerful base of male domination', violently misogynistic, and therefore inappropriate in a lesbian context (Healey, 1996, p. 107).[18]

For Loulan, the rejection of sadomasochism by parts of the lesbian community is related to the historical alliance between lesbianism and feminism:

> We 'keep score' ... making certain that everyone is treated fairly; always ... ensuring that everything equals out in the end. Even as feminists, we still adhere to this role. When it comes to sex, we often continue to apply these rules. If I make love to you, you have to make love back to me. And that's where S/M lesbians differ – they don't apply these rules, at least not in the same way. (1990, p. 145)

Loulan adds that while 'the concept that partners should be equal in sex is important in a world set up to make women inferior', there has been a tendency for this to become a more oppressive policing of lesbian sexual activity: 'there is tremendous pressure for both women in a couple to do and like the same kinds of sex acts. There is pressure for each to initiate the same amount. There is concern that one cannot be more dominant than the other' (p. 75). Madonna has very clearly maintained a position of dominance throughout her career, allowing herself to be viewed as in control of her changing image, her music and her representation in the media. Robertson observes that 'throughout her various incarnations, Madonna asserts her own power and independence, in the economic sphere and in terms of authorship' (1996, pp. 126–7), which, as we have seen, is one factor in the construction of Madonna as (pop-)feminist icon. Furthermore, it is the foundation of Madonna's play with sadomasochistic style: her Dita Parlo persona may be read as a sexualized version of a role Madonna had already been playing, that of a woman 'in complete charge of her life' (Stephen Bray quoted in Allen, 1999, p. 152).

Beyond Madonna's visual interaction with sadomasochistic style, at least one of her songs, 'Hanky Panky' (1990), deals directly with sadomasochistic themes: 'I'll settle for the back of your hand somewhere on my behind / Treat me like I'm a bad girl, even when I'm being good to you / I don't want you to thank me, you can just spank me /... / Tie my hands behind my back and, ooh, I'm in ecstasy.' On *I'm Breathless* (1990), the song is performed in an almost comical style, employing a range of musical and performative devices that feel somewhat parodic, although it is not always clear what exactly is being parodied. The big-band instrumentation and chorus-girl-style backing group reference the era in which *Dick Tracy* is set (Beatty, 1990; the film which inspired the album), and highlight the image of the gangster's moll which Madonna (as Breathless Mahoney) plays in the film. The type of sadomasochistic sexuality played out in 'Hanky Panky' is markedly dissimilar to that suggested by Dita Parlo and the stage antics of the *Blond Ambition* tour (1990). The song is far too upbeat to give any air of seriousness to the subject matter, and the overall sense is of parody and irony. This does not necessarily lessen the importance of the song, as it arguably introduces sadomasochism into the mainstream in a non-threatening manner. Yet, lack of seriousness simultaneously invites a reading of this song as, on some level, mocking or even 'inauthentic'. However, there is a sense in which 'Hanky Panky' reveals 'authentic' sadomasochistic discourse, when Madonna sings 'I just like things a little rough and you'd better not disagree', thereby revealing a level of control over the situation. Consensual S/M relies on the 'top' playing only within the limits agreed to by the 'bottom', who is always able to end the fantasy scene and ultimately has a large part of control in the sadomasochistic interaction. Control, consent and power are not monopolized by one partner in the S/M scenario, and despite the parodic sense of 'Hanky Panky', Madonna thus engages with meaningful sadomasochistic discourse. Such problematizing of power relations may also connect Madonna's stance here more clearly with lesbian (S/M) discourse, in that the lesbian context implies its own challenge to the traditionally perceived S/M power relations (that is, heterosexual and male dominant).

Madonna also juxtaposed sadomasochism and parody in the video for 'Human Nature', and there are parts of this clip that also display specifically lesbian S/M. While sections of the video present themselves as being 'serious', there are key points at which humour and parody are introduced. During the second verse, Madonna is chained to a chair by two masked men, and pulls faces of mock annoyance. Throughout the bridge into the chorus, these images are interspersed with Madonna teasing and taunting a woman tied by her hands to a bar above her head, and at her ankles. Here, Madonna carries a crop-like implement in her hand which she uses variously for whipping and tickling the bound woman. She laughs at the woman, and there are moments when this seems malicious or sadistic but, in the moments when Madonna turns to the camera, the laughter also seems to be gleeful, out of pure amusement with the situation. Madonna's movement across the screen seems disjointed and accelerated, rather resembling a silent film, and this further distances the action from anything 'serious'. The character Madonna adopts in these scenes returns later in the video with a leather-clad Chihuahua, an image bordering on the ridiculous that confirms the presence of a cheeky sense of humour within this video.[19] As in the song 'Hanky Panky', the humour in this video can be perceived as being challenging and liberatory, as well as having a potentially dissociative function for Madonna. Roberts notes that, 'Through [feminist] humor, an audience can be manipulated into seeing or at least laughing at gender stereotypes or patriarchal conventions', and that 'using humor can make a feminist message appealing to a wide audience' (1990, p. 173). Similarly, 'Human Nature' introduces an otherwise controversial subject into a mainstream context, defusing the threat through laughter, although this neutralizing strategy may also be interpreted as effecting Madonna's own distance from the subject.[20]

Performative masculinity

So far, we have seen how Madonna engages with lesbian (sub-)cultures through political discourses, but beyond this there are other, more empirical senses in which her work draws from recurring themes in lesbian (sub-)cultures. One such theme is that of lesbian history,[21] and the way in which Madonna plays with this reveals further themes, one of which is drag king culture. Drag discourses were particularly richly embodied by Madonna in the video for 'Express Yourself' (Fincher, 1989).[22] Wearing a pin-striped men's suit, Madonna initially invites multiple readings of women wearing men's clothing. A conventional view of such practice, based on the male-dominance of Western culture, is that women don male attire for primarily cultural reasons: 'According to most doctors, male transvestites derive sexual excitement – and erections – from wearing women's underclothing, but women are regarded as having not *sexual* but *cultural* desires – desires that the culture and its doctors understand' (Garber, 1993, p. 45, her emphasis). This is paralleled in Halberstam's description of the idea that whereas 'femininity reeks of the artificial' (1998, p. 234), masculinity 'just is' and 'tends to define itself as nonperformative' (p. 236). Thus, it becomes difficult to perform masculinity: 'Women dressing as men is not the *performance* that men dressing as women is' (Silberman, 1997, p. 182, his emphasis). Madonna fundamentally challenges this, since her cross-dressing is *part of a performance* and is therefore at one level necessarily performative.

In terms of lesbian (sub-)cultures and history, the significance of this becomes clear through an analysis of the specific style of clothing that Madonna chooses to wear in her performance. Although there has not developed an extensive drag king culture to parallel that of the drag queens (Halberstam, 1998, p. 234), female-to-male cross-dressing was a popular form of entertainment in early twentieth-century England: 'Drag kings ruled Britain's stages throughout the hey-day of music-hall as mass entertainment. "Male impersonators", as they were billed, became hugely popular acts ... Every hall had at least one such act' (Bingham, 1997, p. 26). The popularity of women wearing men's clothing was also a common element of Hollywood films in the early twentieth century: Josef von Sternberg, for instance, directed seven films starring Marlene Dietrich – several of which featured the star in men's clothing.[23] Sternberg's intention was apparently to give Dietrich appeal to the female audience, and make her more than a sex symbol for consumption by men (Kobal, 1968, p. 49). During the Hollywood Production Code era, which lasted from 1933 to 1962, 'male impersonation died out as a mainstream theatrical practice', despite sustained female-to-male cross-dressing in cinema (Halberstam, 1998, p. 234). Thus, once the Code was lifted, female cross-dressing had lost much of the cultural presence that it had once enjoyed, and it might be argued that Dietrich's cross-dressing thus became an integral part of her style to a point that might not be accepted in today's cinema.[24]

Given the casual prevalence with which women now wear clothing designed for men, or clothing inspired by menswear designs, making a point about gender through clothing has perhaps become more difficult. Furthermore, it is important to note that female-to-male cross-dressing and male impersonation are not necessarily indicative of, or connected with, lesbian sexuality. Bingham records that, with a few notable exceptions, 'it's impossible to establish lesbian sexuality for most [male impersonators]'. She also describes the phenomenon as 'undoubtedly queer, even if not all of its practitioners were known for certain to be lesbian' (1997, p. 26). In this context, then, Madonna's reference to this style of performance may also be read as 'undoubtedly queer', but perhaps distanced from a lesbian context. As a consequence, if Madonna wishes to retrieve the drag king/male impersonator image, her choice of clothing must be defined as obviously and exclusively (or at least primarily) male, and the details of her chosen style therefore become significant. In the 'Express Yourself' video, Madonna's choice of clothing resembles closely that worn by men in the early decades of the twentieth century: indeed, it is particularly evocative of the era in which *Metropolis* was made (Lang, 1926; the film that inspired Madonna's video). Thus, while she foregrounds the gendered-ness of vestimentary codes outside of any historical context, she underlines her point by referencing a period in the history of male impersonation and female-to-male cross-dressing through her choice of a tailored men's suit in a classic pin-stripe. In addition, Madonna ensures the possibility for a clearly lesbian reading of her performance through the monocle that accessorizes the suit. Many interpretations of this feature are surely possible through the application of various theoretical models, but at a pragmatic level we can see a clear link between the monocle and lesbian history.[25] Garber notes that '[t]he tuxedo, the cigarette, the cropped haircut, and the monocle are the most recognisable and readable signs of the lesbian culture of Paris [in the twenties]' (1993, p. 153). Perhaps the monocle especially is reminiscent of this era and culture since tuxedos, cigarettes and cropped haircuts have withstood changes in fashion where the monocle has not, and it has therefore retained a definite historically locating power. Moreover, it is specifically associated with Lady Una Troubridge, the long-time lover of Radclyffe Hall (Doan, 1998, p. 676), thus affording it a distinctly lesbian signification. However, we must remember that we read with hindsight and be cautious in assuming a lesbian interpretation of Madonna's cross-dressing in this style. As Doan observes, 'in England in the 1920s, fashion-conscious women of all sexual persuasions were obliged to "cross-dress" by donning boyish or mannish attire and by cutting their hair short' (1998, p. 667) and 'codes such as smoking, short hair, and hands in pockets denoted a particular fashion rather than a sexual identity' (p. 675). While Garber's (1993) interpretation draws our attention to the monocle as a proto-lesbian signifier, Doan disputes the inevitability of these connotations (1998, p. 679). My analysis of the instability of these signifiers is that, overall, Madonna references a 'golden age' of cross-dressing, 'a time of unprecedented cultural confusion over gender and sexual identity' (p. 665), and that in so doing, she opens up a free space for lesbian interpretation.

In Madonna's cross-dressing, then, we see a coded engagement with lesbian history through drag and fashion. Madonna further played with this connection in *The Girlie Show* tour, when she performed an early hit in a Berlin cabaret style – singing 'Like a (w)irgin' in a heavy German accent. During the performance, she wore top hat and tails, and played (more than) suggestively with a walking cane. The overplayed accent and $\frac{3}{4}$ time signature, underscoring a circus-style orchestration, give the piece a strong sense of parody (and performativity). With respect to the present chapter, what is most interesting is not the parody itself but *what* she is parodying. The image of Madonna at this point in the show is clearly referencing Marlene Dietrich's style, through the accent and tuxedo which, significantly, is worn – as Dietrich did in *Morocco* (von Sternberg, 1930) – with full-length trousers rather than feminizing stockings, in the style of Hollywood chorus girls.[26] The reference to Dietrich is underlined at the end of Madonna's performance of 'Like a Virgin', when the song transitions into the first verse of 'Falling in Love Again', which Dietrich made famous in *Der Blaue Engel* (von Sternberg, 1930). Madonna thereby reinforces the theme, introduced in the 'Express Yourself' video, of female-to-male cross-dressing in a 1930s style. Images of Weimar Berlin have a long-standing history in Madonna's work, from 'Open Your Heart' (see Curry, 1990, p. 19) to more recent work, such as the *Vanity Fair* photo session published in October 2002 (Daly, 2002). The contexts of 1930s Germany and cross-dressing intersect in Madonna's choice of Dietrich as a reference, which is itself significant: specific scenes in Dietrich's films combine with her own tendency towards trousers – off-screen as well as on – to make her a particularly meaningful icon for gay men and lesbians.[27] Thus, another layer is added to Madonna's engagement here with lesbianism.

The significance of lesbian discourse in this section of *The Girlie Show* emerges during the next song, 'Bye Bye Baby'. Madonna is joined by two female dancers, also wearing tuxedos and carrying canes, and the three cross-dressed women are entertained by three other female dancers, dressed in basques and heels. During the song, the 'dancing girls' tease the cross-dressed women, rubbing themselves on their thighs and using the canes as phallic props; they proceed to challenge the 'men's' signifiers of masculinity, throwing the canes to the floor and removing their top hats, and ultimately pushing them to the floor.[28] In response, the 'men' slap the girls and simulate sex with them. After the song, the 'men' swagger about the stage, grabbing their crotches and otherwise adopting exaggerated macho mannerisms. Here, Madonna exhorts her cross-dressed colleagues to 'Fuck those dames', proclaiming 'We ain't gonna cry for no broads' and ultimately asserting, 'We fuck women!'

It is clear that throughout her career Madonna has continually played with issues of sexuality, often generating significant controversy in the process. This was especially the case in the early to mid-1990s, mostly surrounding *Erotica* and *Sex*, but since then analysis of her engagement with lesbian (sub-)cultural discourses has been somewhat reduced to this particular period, and specifically the allegedly sexual relationship with Sandra Bernhard in the late 1980s (and into the early 1990s). What I have explored here are some of the ways in which Madonna has associated more broadly with lesbian discourses through sadomasochism, cross-dressing, feminism and even heterosexual pornographic iconography. Since then, obvious engagement by Madonna with such tropes has been somewhat less documented. As I have noted, Madonna's marriage to film director Guy Ritchie seemingly symbolizes a move away from her 'lesbian flirtations' of the early 1990s, by means of a traditionally important signifier of heterosexuality, a 'tighten[ing] up [of] the nuclear family' (Ratliff, 2003): are we to suppose that Madonna has ended her relationship with lesbian (sub-)cultures?

Yet she continues to associate herself with many of the same lesbian (sub-)cultural themes that she had begun to explore in previous years: her early (putative) feminist politics re-emerge in the song 'What it Feels Like for a Girl', and its accompanying video.[29] It is also worth noting the 'Impressive Instant' section of the *Drowned World Tour* (2001) as a further example of Madonna's playful insistence on masculinity as 'performable': here, the dancers place a spurting hose between Madonna's legs, rendering her phallic and ejaculatory. A similar scene was included at the end of the (withdrawn) 'American Life' video (Åkerlund, 2003), in which Madonna sprays the audience with water from a hose gun. Both scenes are further examples of an image in *Sex*, described by Andrew Ross as evoking 'female ejaculation, the great open secret of lesbian subculture in the early 90s' (1993, p. 58), a description which reminds us that female masculinity and lesbianism are allied, but not necessary mutually implicit. More direct appropriation of lesbian iconography has also resurfaced, but there is a noticeable difference in Madonna's presentation of this theme. In the play *Up For Grabs* (Williamson, 2002), Madonna's character kissed a female dotcom entrepreneur. On the surface, this signalled a return to her sexually fluid stage antics of the previous decade. Yet closer examination reveals a degradation of lesbian sexuality here: Madonna's heterosexual character, Loren, is desperate to sell a painting at any emotional cost to herself, and agrees to have sex with the entrepreneur, a potential buyer, to increase the sale value of the painting. Ultimately, the two women do not consummate this agreement, perhaps suggesting a rather less positive approach to lesbianism.[30] Madonna's other notable lesbian foray in 2002 was in the Bond film *Die Another Day* (Tamahori, 2002), in which Madonna had a cameo role as a lesbian fencing instructor. Apparently, Madonna 'demanded that her character … be a lesbian simply because she does not want to kiss star Pierce Brosnan in the script' (pop-music.com, 2003). Madonna's role presents a challenge to the highly heterosexualized world of the Bond films, and yet the representation of lesbianism here is far from unproblematic (not least because the character's sexuality is more 'understood', than made overt). If the rumour is to be believed concerning how the character came to be defined as a lesbian, then a critical audience must surely wonder to what extent Madonna is playing here on a classic trope: that of a woman being constructed as a lesbian because she fails to fulfil an arrogant male assumption about his own desirability to women.[31] In this formation, Madonna's character in *Die Another Day* 'must' be a lesbian precisely in order to avoid Bond's appeal believably. Thus, while she challenges the heteronormativity of Bond's world, she simultaneously dismisses lesbianism as an autonomous sexual identity, one that may exist without alteritous reference to heterosexuality.

Alongside these open engagements with lesbianism, it might also be argued that Madonna's latest role as wife and mother is perhaps not so far from contemporary lesbian (sub-)cultures, since a kind of 'reclamation' of marriage and motherhood by lesbians has begun in recent years. Although it is important to note the presence of an anti-gay-marriage movement from *within* the community (see Carpenter, 2002; Douglas, 2002), the late 1990s saw what might be termed a 'gayby boom' (see Brill, 2001, p. 1) and gay and lesbian couples fight to have their relationships legally recognized. Beyond the marriage/motherhood question, Madonna's visual style has also remained associable with lesbian (sub-)cultures, again in a historical context. Since her marriage to Ritchie and their purchase of a Wiltshire stately home, she has been seen to adopt codes of Scottish/English aristocracy, completing her 'lady of the manor' image with a Barbour tweed hunting vest, moleskin Burberry trousers, a field coat, knee-length breeches and a shooting cap (see Boshoff, 2003, p. 17). The aristocratic tweed style and quasi-cropped hair, also seen in the *Vanity Fair* photographs (Daly, 2002), bears a not insignificant resemblance to early twentieth-century masculine women. Ethel Mannin's portrayal of Georgian female masculinity demonstrates the particular relevance of tweed: 'Usually when people describe a woman as "masculine" they imply a ... clumsy, thick-ankled, untidily tweed-clothed hoyden' (quoted in Doan, 1998, p. 685). *The Birmingham Post*'s contemporary description of Radclyffe Hall further evokes the *Vanity Fair* images of Madonna: 'Miss Hall affects a mannish mode of dress, and has what many people consider the best shingle in London. Her hair is of gold, and cropped as closely as a man's, a natural ripple in it being the only break in its sleek perfection' (quoted in Doan, 1998, p. 685).

Marriage, motherhood and tweed are, in themselves, hardly prominent and unambiguous signs of a continuing relationship by Madonna with lesbian (sub-)cultures, especially given the significant debates concerning appropriation, assimilation and ownership of the first two of these matters. In the context of this equivocalness, the persistence of Madonna's subtle detachment from queer texts is pertinent. What remains, then, are interacting strands of a relationship with 'queer' in Madonna's work. Initially, we see the apparent recurrence of lesbianism throughout her career, as in *Up For Grabs* or *Die Another Day* in 2002, or the notorious MTV MVA kisses in 2003. On closer examination, however, the simplicity of such imagery is consistently obstructed by her repeated detachment from it, a detachment that is played out in Madonna's personal life, as she staunchly maintains her position as 'Mrs Ritchie'. Yet in the final analysis, as Madonna continues to use an increasing variety of subcultural colours on her palette, her texts are always open to multiple readings by a similar variety of subcultures, however unconvincing some of her appropriations may be. Whichever way we choose to look at it, what is clear from this study is that new readings are always ready to be found, and claimed.

Acknowledgements

I would to thank Santiago Fouz-Hernández for all his valuable comments, but specifically for bringing me up to date with the history of Madonna's career, as I have not been familiar with her work since the late 1980s. Santiago has been instrumental in acquainting me particularly with *Up For Grabs*, *Die Another Day*, *The Girlie Show* and the *Drowned World Tour* (notably the 'Impressive Instant' section), key events in Madonna's sapphic story which I would otherwise have missed. Thanks also go to my supervisor and friend Ian Biddle, for his ever-helpful comments.

Notes

1. See Hamer, 1996, p. 206, on how this problem seems to pervade lesbian and gay studies.
2. This is suggested in other chapters in this collection, particularly in Chapter 4, Keith Clifton's contribution.
3. See Stan Hawkins in this collection (Chapter 1) for more on Madonna and camp. The gay male community's devotion to Madonna has apparently become established enough in the popular imagination to generate some humour: in an episode of the American sitcom *Will and Grace*, in which Madonna made a guest appearance (NBC, 24 April 2003), Jack (a regular gay character on the show) comments to Madonna's character, 'as a gay man, I'm awfully drawn to you', prompting knowing laughter and applause from the studio audience. See also The Androids' video, '(I'd Rather) Do It with Madonna' (2003) or Jonathan Ross's band, Four Poofs and a Piano, on the night of his interview with Madonna (BBC1, 2 May 2003).
4. See, for example, *LA Law*'s (NBC, 1986–94) CJ (Amanda Donohoe), one half of America's first prime-time lesbian kiss in 1991; the UK's counterpart in 1993 on *Brookside* (Channel 4, 1982–2002); the television show *OUT* (later renamed *Out on Tuesday*; Channel 4, 1989–92); k. d. lang's Grammy-winning album *Ingénue* (1992).

5. A scanned copy of the advert for 'Androgynous/boyish girls' as dancers for *The Girlie Show* is archived at <http://www.geocities.com/Hollywood/Heights/8484/girlie.html>, last visited 22 April 2003. Visible on the commercially released filmed performance, many of the female dancers are indeed 'boyish' or 'androgynous'. One dancer has such small breasts that, when she appears topless in the performance of 'Deeper and Deeper', it is only on close examination that her sex is determinable. Also significant in *The Girlie Show* is Madonna's simulated group lesbian sex. Having descended into an uninhibited orgy by the end of 'Deeper and Deeper', the beginning of 'Why's It So Hard?' finds Madonna and two female dancers simulating sex, raised on a podium above other intertwined combinations of men and women, an image that recalls the group lesbian photographs in *Sex*.

6. It is worth noting here some of the more recent developments in this area of Madonna's visual output. Some of the female dancers in the *Drowned World Tour* (2001), for example, were noticeably 'butch'. Also, the (withdrawn) video for 'American Life' (Åkerlund, 2003) invites fruitful lesbian analysis. Most interesting for the present study is a female character dressed in a tight white vest and Y-fronted underpants. This character is last seen doing chin-ups, a classically male work-out exercise.

7. Because of the problematic nature of the word 'subculture', I write of '(sub-)cultures'. For an overview of the politics of 'subcultures', see Gelder and Thornton, 1997.

8. Until further work has been done on the subject of 'male lesbians', I do not include this concept in my own research, as they do not self-identify as women: by their own definition they are 'male'. I understand their identity to be elsewhere on a spectrum of sexuality and accept the traditional view of lesbians as necessarily self-identified women. On a somewhat related topic, see Halberstam on the pattern of female-to-male transsexuals finding temporary refuge in the label 'lesbian' (1998, pp. 150–51).

9. Second-wave feminism 'was foreshadowed by the publication of Betty Friedan's *The Feminine Mystique* in 1963' (Hamer, 1996, p. 193). First-wave feminism is generally taken as those activities pertaining to women's rights taking place at the beginning of the twentieth century, the suffragette movement, for instance. The existence and definition(s) of 'third-wave feminism' are currently undergoing debate: see <http://www.iftr.org.uk/news/2002/twf.html>, last visited 26 January 2003. A combination of factors – including the widespread cultural rejection of lesbianism prior to the Stonewall riots, and the tendency towards 'pomo-sexuality', the deconstruction of sexual categories at the turn of the millennium – mean that second-wave feminism coincided with a moment of particular visibility in lesbian history.

10. See also Ainley, 1995, pp. 45–57, for more on the relationship between lesbianism and feminism.

11. 'Pop-feminism' denotes 'popular feminism' which implies the dilution of feminist theory for a mass-market (see David Gauntlett (Chapter 10) in this volume). See also hooks, 1993; Queen, 1993; Faith, 1997, pp. 50–74.

12. 'Female address video' is Lewis's (1990) term for a music video produced with a female audience in mind.

13. See Patricia Pisters in this volume (Chapter 2) for more on Madonna and feminist discourses, in particular her discussion of Lewis's 'discovery' and 'access' signs. For academic feminist readings of Madonna, see hooks, 1993; Queen, 1993; Faith, 1997, pp. 50–74.

14. Madonna wore the ponytail (a clip-on accessory) during the early part of the *Blond Ambition* tour, mainly on the Japanese leg. In other performances, Madonna wore her hair in a short, permed style. Both hairstyles are visible in *Truth or Dare* (Keshishian,

1991), the docu-film that follows Madonna and her crew for the duration of the tour. The ponytail has become far more symbolic of this period of Madonna's career than the perm: various representations of Madonna since then evidence this, including the humorous spoof of *Truth or Dare* by British comediennes Dawn French and Jennifer Saunders, entitled *In Bed With French and Saunders* (BBC2, 11 March 1993).

15. See O'Sullivan for an attempt 'to fasten down ... the way in which lesbianism has surfaced as a fashion item and as part of what's naughty and trendy in the 1990s' (1994, p. 78).

16. Ainley implies this stereotype by quoting one lesbian who feels she could have been 'saved' from lesbianism (in favour of the 'lesser' fate of bisexuality) by 'some suitable men' (1995, p. 177).

17. It is worth noting that Madonna's friendship with Sandra Bernhard – which had dissolved following Bernhard's accusations that Madonna had 'stolen' her then girlfriend Ingrid Casares (Taraborrelli, 2001, pp. 221–2) – seems to have developed again (as of spring 2003), perhaps partly due to a common interest in the cabbala. Bernhard was noted to have been present in the audience for Madonna's appearance on *Will and Grace* (NBC, 24 April 2003), arguably inviting recollections of their friendship in the early 1990s, and all the speculation that generated.

18. This point has been challenged by the pro-S/M lobby: the argument that lesbian sadomasochism reinforces heterosexual power relations relies on heterosexist modes of analysis and does not consider the potential for specifically lesbian interrelations as opposed to heterosexual interactions. See Healey, 1996, p. 107.

19. Madonna clearly seems to be taking on a 'character' role at this point in 'Human Nature', as her image in these scenes is radically different from that adopted throughout the rest of the video. The 'silent movie'-type motion also separates this 'Madonna' from the other. A similar identity-splitting strategy is used in many of Madonna's videos, a recent and obvious example being 'Die Another Day' (Traktor, 2002), in which two Madonnas fight each other. See also the 'real' versus cartoon Madonnas in 'Music' (Åkerlund, 2000) in terms of questioning 'real' identity. A lack of space precludes further analysis of Madonna's association between sadomasochism and ironic humour, although it would surely be productive.

20. It may be worth noting that Madonna adopts the 'bottom' role in the heterosexual S/M scenes in 'Human Nature', but is instead (able to be) positioned as the 'top' in the lesbian scenes, thus replaying the lesbian anti-S/M argument that sadomasochism reinforces male-dominant power relations. Compare this with her role in *Body of Evidence* (Edel, 1993), as a female S/M 'top'. The ultimate suicide of her character in that film might be read not only as poetic justice for the crime of murder she apparently committed, but as a broader type of 'justice' for her 'deviant' sexual inclinations. Her 'deviance' might include sadomasochism, sexual dominance as a woman and the intersection of these, which is the reversal of male-dominant S/M roles (as perceived by anti-S/M feminists: Breslow (1999) argues that there is no statistical difference between men and women in terms of S/M roles adopted). While Madonna's 'top' role in *Body of Evidence* may also present some challenges to her apparent tendency towards the uncritical playing-out of hetero-centric S/M stereotypes, the effect of these challenges is lessened somewhat by the suppression of this attempt to overturn the male-dominant order through suicide. See Hayward, 1996, pp. 105–6 on cinematic strategies used to control 'threatening' women.

21. 'Lesbian history' is arguably a lesbian (sub-)cultural discourse in itself, in its thematic recurrence in lesbian communities across Britain and the United States. See, for example, Duberman et al., 1989; Hamer, 1996; Lesbian History Group, 1989; Traub, 2002.

22. For further examples of Madonna's cross-dressing, see 'Vogue' (Fincher, 1990) or the 'Bye, Bye, Baby' section in *The Girlie Show* (1993).

23. *Morocco* (1930); *Dishonored* (1931); *Blonde Venus* (1932); *Scarlet Empress* (1934).

24. My main point here is not the extent to which cinematic cross-dressing has survived post-Hollywood Production Code: certainly it has been popular in mainstream cinema in the last twenty years or so (key examples include *Tootsie* (Pollack, 1982), *Victor/Victoria* (Edwards, 1982), *Mrs. Doubtfire* (Columbus, 1993) and *To Wong Foo, Thanks For Everything, Julie Newmar* (Kidron, 1995)). Rather, it is my contention that Dietrich's off-screen cross-dressing was crucial to her style and image as a celebrity, and that – for reasons of fashion – a similar example would not be accepted today in the same way as Dietrich was. See Halberstam, 1998, pp. 175–230, for a more in-depth reading of the cinematic history of female masculinity. Of course, cinematic cross-dressing is located in a long history of literary and dramatic transvestism, a subject about which much has been written (see, for example, Ferris, 1993; Stallybrass, 1992; or Traub, 1992). My point here is a broad one relating to the development of this in twentieth-century popular cultural contexts.

25. Morton reads the monocle first as a 'condensed symbol of mastery, the gaze, and the cinematic apparatus' (1993, p. 229), alongside a discourse of knowledge (*Metropolis* 'constantly equates vision with knowledge. Characters never overhear information' (p. 222)). She goes on to explore some of the gender issues raised by this prop, which she says 'underscores the partial nature of the elite's gaze and an enactment of mastery', the gaze representing phallic power (p. 232). Within this reading, Morton is careful not simply to equate phallus/masculinity/male-ness, writing that even as Madonna 'mimics the phallic swagger of crotch-grabbing rock stars', there may be 'no pretended allusion to a penis', asserting instead 'her own specific adequacy' (p. 233). While I am keen, in turn, not to equate female phallic power/female masculinity/lesbianism, both vestimentary and bodily codes are surely pertinent to the present chapter.

26. As noted, Madonna and her (female) dancers maintained the tuxedos into the 'Bye, Bye Baby' section which followed 'Like a Virgin', and the cabaret style is still perceptible there, although it is most clearly geographically located in 'Like a Wirgin'. See Judy Garland in *Summer Stock* (Walters, 1950) for one example of a woman in men's clothing, but with a clear sense of retaining a feminized and sexualized image. See also (interestingly) Dietrich in *Der Blaue Engel* (von Sternberg, 1930).

27. In particular see *Morocco*, when Dietrich kisses a woman on the lips. Also relevant is the highly camp 'Hot Voodoo' scene in *Blonde Venus* (von Sternberg, 1932). Dietrich's disguise as a pilot in *Dishonored* (von Sternberg, 1931) is also worth noting. See Kobal (1968) for photographic evidence of Dietrich in male-defined clothing off-screen.

28. The dismissal of the walking canes, which by this point in the show have been explicitly constructed as phallic props, can be read variously as female dominance as a replacement for male dominance, or as an assertion of the performativity of all gender formations, or as the exposure of the 'men' here as cross-dressed women. This latter interpretation in particular encourages a lesbian reading of the ensuing scenes of simulated sex between the girls and the 'men', since the audience are forced to confront the fact of the 'men's' female-ness.

29. There may be a point of interest in the fact that Madonna has undertaken several joint projects with her husband, this video being one example (Ritchie has also directed Madonna in *Star* – a 2001 BMW advert – and *Swept Away* (2002)). Arguably, this

professional relationship underlines the personal one, reinforcing their identity as a couple. See also the picture in Taraborrelli (2001, plate section between pp. 286–7) of Madonna and Ritchie wearing T-shirts promoting each other's work (*Music* and *Snatch* respectively).

30.   Although evidence is not available, it is worth noting the rumours surrounding *Up For Grabs*, that the lesbian kiss was one of several changes requested by Madonna to Williamson's original script. See also Madonna's performance of 'Hollywood' with Britney Spears and Christina Aguilera at the 2003 MTV music video awards, during which she French-kissed both Spears and Aguilera. Following this, Spears declared the kisses to have been Madonna's idea. See <http://stacks.msnbc.com/news/962215.asp?0sl=–l0&cp1=1>, last visited 10 September 2003. Hints at the sexual connection were later played out in the video accompanying Spears' single 'Me Against the Music' (Hunter, 2003), in which she and Madonna nearly exchange another kiss, Spears pinning Madonna against a wall, the moment being interrupted by the fading disappearance of Madonna.

31.   See Eisenbach, 1997, p. 69, for a humorous example of this trope's currency in lesbian (sub-)culture.

PART III

Drowned Worlds:
Ethnic Identities

Olivier Tridon

Chapter 6

East is hot!

'Madonna's Indian Summer' and the poetics of appropriation

Michael Angelo Tata

During the long, hot and otherwise aesthetically lukewarm summer of 1998, Madonna, as if picking up a vibe from New York City's collective unconscious, broke with the comparative insipidness of her *Something to Remember* (1995) and *Evita* (1996) personae and burst onto the club scene with a fresh, exciting and incongruous new image: that of the post-Catholic, anti-material/antimatter Indian princess. In the spring of that year she had come forth with the video for 'Frozen' (Cunningham, 1998), which featured her as a virtual vamp exploring the darker side of fashion and love. On Valentine's Day, she had been gracious enough to put in an appearance at New York City's gay mecca the Roxy, at which she also materialized as a Gothed-out version of herself. Despite these images and apparitions, it was the release of July's *Rolling Stone*, in which David LaChapelle photographed her in shot after shot of Hindu finery and posturing, that caught my attention and awakened me from my artistic slumber. Although earlier work had referenced pan-Asian imagery only obliquely, as in her Orientalist performance of 'Like a Virgin' in the eponymous *Blond Ambition* tour (1990), her momentary transformation into a Balinese idol in the video for 'Fever' (Sednaoui, 1993) or the Thai choreography of the 'Vogue' performance in *The Girlie Show* (1993), it was only now that she made the controversial decision to embody 'sincerely' one particular Asian worldview and style, that of Hinduism. As is so often her way, she placed the serious and the frivolous at a chiasm, the result being her signature over-exaggeration and deformation of this new subject position to the point of maximum absurdity: such is her magic.

In the ensuing months, Madonna's incipient Orientalism would fragment, devolving to a skin-deep Beverly Hills spiritualism in the 'Ray of Light' video (Åkerlund, 1998), producing a psychotic Geisha meltdown in the 'Nothing Really Matters' video (Renck, 1999) and, in what for her was surely her pièce de résistance, the film *The Next Best Thing* (Schlesinger, 2000), evaporating such that all that remained was the role of yoga instructor. As far as live performances were concerned, her rendition of 'Ray of Light' at the 1998 MTV Video Music Awards would bring Hinduism to the street, as she and a fleet of dancers worked it to the songs 'Shanti/Ashtangi' and 'Ray of Light' against a backdrop of super-sized images of Hindu deities. After 'Ray of Light', the fun would continue only briefly. In the video for 'Music' (Åkerlund, 2000), the first single to be released from the album of the same title later that year, she would momentarily morph into a cartoon DJ Vishnu, her arms spinning up a commotion at the turntables. During the *Drowned World Tour* (2001), she would eschew the Hindu altogether. Choosing instead to swathe herself in a monstrous kimono out of a Beverly Semmes installation, using Japanimation cartoons as a backdrop for her choreography[1] and even enacting what may have been discarded footage from a parallel-universe variant of the film *Crouching Tiger, Hidden Dragon* (Ang Lee, 2000), she had bid *adieu* to Ganesh, the Hindu pantheon, mendhi body art and the bindhi dot.[2] In the final wash, Madonna's Hindu style would barely make it into the third millennium via the song 'Cyber-raga', a B-side track from various 2000 EPs of 'Music' and 'Don't Tell Me' remixes included on the album *Groundwork 2001*, a musical project the proceeds of which were used to combat world hunger. India, like so many of her other Others, had suddenly become passé.

Perhaps because I'm shallow, perhaps because I am a candidate for Borderline Personality Disorder, perhaps because, perverting Rimbaud, I'm *absolument postmoderne*, when my life seems evacuated of meaning, I look to art to supply me with some extrinsic centre with which I can identify, or at least temporarily occupy until something better comes along. Madonna's *Ray of Light* did the trick, evoking and causing to circulate many surprising, scandalous images: a range inclusive of (but not limited to) Buddhist posing, Hindu self-ornamentation and Gothic chic. I had never thought about wearing a sarong before, but by the time August rolled around, I was about ready to swipe a Gaultier wrap from Bloomingdales and of course I was in search of a mendhi artist to wrap a tribal tattoo around my biceps to match the sarong. I wondered if I, too, should sport a bindhi dot, an external marker pointing to the fact that I had somehow experienced Enlightenment; had, like Madonna, turned myself into a particle of light, a photon. The credits accompanying the *Rolling Stone* photos provided smitten fans with a plan for acquiring items and services such as these, offering what amounted to a Recipe for Hindu Glamour: 'Clear plastic corset by Oliver Theyskens ... Tank Top Jet by John Eschaya ... Python pants by Alexander McQueen by special order ... Head piece by Bhindi Jewellers of Artesia' (LaChapelle, 1998, p. 68). Fortunately for Madonna's emulators, still wannabes after all these years, there was a roadmap of designers, boutiques, stylists and personal shoppers, all to guide one in one's quest to become the new Madonna. Sparking a veritable retail frenzy evocative of the energy of Macy's early 1980s Madonna boutiques, the list drew a map that any Madonna impersonator, from a professional drag performer to someone merely dressing for a social engagement, could follow. Hinduism made easy.

Although Madonna's new aesthetic showings in the videos for 'Frozen' and 'Ray of Light' instantly aroused critical interest and caused many an eyebrow to arch, my attention was not really held captive until the release of July's *Rolling Stone*, since, as I have stated, it was here that I was made to confront David LaChapelle's new photos of Madonna in all her splendour and ludicrousness.[3] I was presented with these photos by Revlene, a Los Angeles-based Madonna impersonator and make-up artist visiting New York.[4] In light of these photos, I was impelled to reflect upon what, if anything, held Madonna's recent manifestations together: to ask the Steinian question, was there any use in a centre? In the video for 'Frozen', she had acted the part of some deviant Marilyn Manson vampire gliding across desert sands, a huge brunette weave extending down past her derrière, dance moves à la Martha Graham freezing her in positions reminiscent of Buddhist sculpture, while in the subsequent video for 'Ray of Light', she had flaunted a newly bronzed body which gyrated in time-delayed motions ridiculously out of sync with a Los Angeles cityscape in which everything moved at triple fast-forward. Adding further confusion to the mix, she had populated LaChapelle's photo spread with images of herself flanked by pink Sarasvati *cygnets* and Chinese dragons. Even more perplexing was her appearance on an episode of *The Rosie O'Donnell Show* (1998, NBC Channel) timed perfectly to coincide with the release of the *Ray of Light* album. 'Mo', as Rosie calls her, commented on the death of the 'Material Girl', a person whom she no longer could claim to be, her ontological flux moving away from a life of cheap Marilyn Monroe dresses and strings of cubic zirconia to one of nirvana-esque peacefulness and post-Vedic placidity. Further disbelief arose when, also on *Rosie*, she raved about the cabbala and mendhi body art, therein putting her in some relation to both Judaism and Hinduism, seemingly irreconcilable ways of apprehending and interpreting the world: in short, one could not help but wonder at what new Gestalt Madonna was trying to create for herself, of how these various units – Gothic chic, modern dance, Buddhist sculpture, trips to the *salon de bronzer*, an interest in Jewish mysticism, the deployment of technologies of Hindu body-ornamentation – could in any way gel together into some coherent bit of arrested experiential flow that could be labelled 'Madonna' (that is, if she had not transcended self-identicality along the way – wasn't that also 'too material?').

The fact that David LaChapelle was responsible for presenting Madonna's Hindu self to her fans was telling, for who else other than LaChapelle, star of the worlds of art and advertising alike, could unify or dis-unify the many disparate elements that comprised Madonna's new image? Who else could perform the feat of reconstructing this bundle of contradictory elements into something that could, if not make sense, at least successfully perform 'not making sense'? The title of the series, 'Madonna's Indian Summer', evoked nostalgia for the slowly evanescing summer, and provoked curiosity as to what Madonna had to do with anything Indian. Consisting of seven images depicting Madonna's new look and a few short paragraphs of text in which she commented on her own corporeal history, the series represented Madonna's gift to her demanding fans, the gift of a new bundle of images to chase away summer melancholia, heat exhaustion, body anxiety. Madonna's image, in its LaChapellian manifestation, presented her as Hindu Goddess; in his photographs, she emerged from a background of emanating light rays and ferocious dragons in bright pink, almost fuchsia or magenta, sarongs and cholis, decked out with gold bangles and spangles, her hair the longest it had ever been, a bindhi dot on her forehead to signify the spiritual enlightenment she had somehow achieved during the sweaty, steamy Manhattan summer months. On her song 'Shanti/Ashtangi' – a song which, alas for the history of camp, would never be released as a single – she grooved to a Bollywood beat while spouting the fundamentals of Eastern Enlightenment: were these images allusive to some sort of Hindu mind-expansion or merely a New Age/California version of that expansion? bell hooks's assessment of Madonna as 'Plantation Mistress' (1992b) once again seemed novel and accurate, causing me to wonder how, as a cultural theorist, I should begin the business of explaining these photographs, to consider which model of appropriation to appropriate, which aesthetic technique to use to sanction the appropriation.

Jamesonian pastiche (1992, pp. 16–19), Hebdigian bricolage (1998, pp. 102–5), Donna Haraway's notion of cyborg implosivity (1991, pp. 151–3): were these the means for justifying her new infractions and obscenities?[5] Perhaps the relevant concept was the idea of media jujitsu (Shohat and Stam, 1994, pp. 328–33), Gloria Anzaldúa's notion of the cultural importance of transliteration (1987, pp. 57–8) or Indian visual artist Chila Kumari Burman's 'Fly Girl' aesthetic.[6] Both sides of the postmodern/postcolonial divide, that invidious split between proponents of global play (for example, Baudrillard) and local responsibility (for example Shohat), beckoned.[7] Furthermore, reading the new constellation of images in light of Slavoj Žižek (1989), the situation seemed to be that, perhaps no longer identifying as American, Madonna had vacated her Material subject position for that of a citizen of the British Commonwealth; and so, choosing to take on the external appearance of the Hindu, she had traversed Lacan's famous Graph of Desire (1977b), one of the more useful methods offered by contemporary psychoanalysis for computing and tracking the identification process in the human psyche, to the effect that a new ego ideal, that of the Eastern-gazing Briton, had crystallized (Žižek, 1989, pp. 100–129).[8] Later on in the summer, at Barrucada, in Chelsea, New York City, I would even see a performance in which Hedda Lettuce, decked out in what could sartorially be referred to as 'Madonna Travesty', spun around in several yards of silk, her face enveloped by a matching purdah, as she pretended to lip-synch the lyrics to 'Shantih' (I say 'pretended' because one could merely detect the movements of her mouth behind the fabric, without being able to discern their accuracy, what words they aspired to pronounce). She claimed she had just married a very rich Indian taxi-cab mogul and that she now had to dress in accordance with these restrictive yet liberating feminine testamentary practices.[9] Tammy Faye, Hedda's sidekick, grimaced at Hedda's improprieties.

What I, in my own improper way, have thus far rather coyly flirted with and skirted are the appropriation debates, those endless volleys of arguments for and against the lifting of what could, if one had the desire, be described as 'cultural property'. The first problem is how, in this complex era of appropriation and counter-appropriation, within the aesthetic confines of what Brian Jarvis has described as the Baudrillardian 'semioticisation of space' (1998, pp. 30–34), one can even begin to assign origins, to return from the simulacrum to 'the real'.[10] Eminent examples of 'lifting', most of which are aesthetically desirable as guilty (or not-so-guilty) pleasures, come to mind: P. Diddy's use of 1980s samples; Warhol's pilfered flowers; Koons' Yorkshires; house remakes of everything from 'The Sound of Music' (Junior Vasquez, 2000) to the *Sesame Street* theme (Smart E's, 1992); Gaultier's controversial use of Hasidim surfaces in his *Les Rabbins Chics* (Chic Rabbis) collection from autumn/winter 1993–4; Cy's 'subway chic' fashion show in the film *Prêt-à-Porter* (Altman, 1994). What also comes to mind is the immense volume of literature for and against the radical detachment of simulacrum from reality, spectres of hooks, Fusco, Mercer, Polhemus, Danto, Derrida, Baudrillard. Like it or not, one must concede that in this cybernetic age, this hyper wired circuitry, this era with its potent mythologies of globalization, its silk-screens of da Vinci and Communist hammers alike, there can be no going back, no Black Panthers mythography of 'the natural',[11] no return to the static supremacy of the copyright, that strange '©' floating after various owned and patented products.[12] Rigoberta Menchú (1998), whose many silences break up the illusory seamlessness of her ethnographer,[13] and fashion theorist Caroline Evans,[14] who predicted that, in the future, cultural innovators would flee the media (1997, pp. 174–5), relegating their productions to a consummate and ever-shifting underground somewhere beneath the huts of the global village, provided a caveat to my glibness. Yes, Menchú's silences, those pockets of cultural information she refuses to provide, and Evans' media-avoidance, the self-imposed exile of the cultural engineer (her example: the Raver), seem like one solution – if you don't want it to be exploited, then don't make it exploitable.[15] However, as the trend in this increasingly globalized world, a de-alienated and de-sublimated entity, is that it will most likely contain fewer of these silences and exiles, the true conundrum hence becomes not how to put the brakes on an appropriative process gone haywire, but how to join in the fun and play; not how to pin down and regulate cultural objects, but how to jettison theory out the window and, following Susan Sontag's example (1986), revel in the object's sensuality. In short, all that remained was immersion in the poetics of appropriation.

For me, the question is thus not how to get beyond appropriation, the reification of ritual in spectacle, or commodity fetishism, all of which are givens, but rather how to describe, appreciate and enjoy the many hybrid, syncretic products that have resulted from cultural border-crossings, copyright infringements, out-and-out raids, tacit complicities, flagrant self-exoticizations, fashion recyclings, orientalisms, Americanisms, whatever have been the processes of cultural production in the late capitalist world(s). In other words, how to listen to Lil' Kim, watch a John Waters film or consume Madonna's new Hindu Goddess persona without guilt. Perhaps what needed to be redefined was the notion of postmodern space, for, examining LaChapelle's Madonnarama, gazing at these radically orientalized and meta/hyper orientalized images,[16] these parodies of orientalism, it appears that, epistemologically, they are based on a certain notion of space – or, to be more precise, that they depend on a certain notion of the obliteration of space, of the repackaging of Enlightenment space, with its discontinuities and rifts (public/private, citizen/foreigner) into the integrated space of the cybernetic, in which distance is at long last overcome, if only within the confines of the aesthetic imaginary. LaChapelle's radical juxtapositions are so bold as to posit a new spatiality, one in which the distances between nations and cultures, those very stretches of space that fuelled classic anthropological and ethnological endeavours, are traversed with the speed of light, the 'c' Madonna manages to turn herself into on her 1998 album and which she, according to the lyrics of 'Ray of Light', transcends, no matter what Einstein's Special Theory of Relativity might have to say about the violation of the laws of physics such a speed would entail (see Hawking, 1996, pp. 27–30).[17] As Caren Kaplan comments, the self-alienating practices of modernism's many flâneurs, dandies, exiles and expatriates are negated by postmodern aesthetic practices which promote the very un-alienated touring of the globe engaged in by the postmodern webcrawler, magazine surfer or mall-shopper (1996, pp. 27–64). Supposedly beyond melancholy and imperialist nostalgia, the pomo cogito enters into a stream of data as a bit of data itself, touring the world with a friction-free easiness unthinkable to the modern, for whom travel functions as the outward sign of alienation and dissent.

One photograph in the LaChapelle portfolio speaks best to the issue of what types of travel Hindu Madonna embodies and enacts: Madonna, costumed in semi-transparent Goth tights and camisole, floats outstretched on a post-apocalyptic red river, against a dragon, a cloud of fire and a Rising Sun symbol.[18] The extremeness of LaChapelle's power pastiche is jarring: how is it that Japan, China, India, London's Brick Lane and New York City's East Village have all come together in this bizarre, distance-annihilating image (that is, this image in which cultural distances are crossed via the logic of pastiche)? Has there been an atomic holocaust, and if so, is it only Madonna who has survived so miraculously unscathed? Is she death goddess Kali? Or is she creator-deity Vishnu, reclining on his serpent as he awaits the production of a new universe?[19] Are the holocaust, the carnage, the destruction, the hecatomb hers? The fire floating detached above her head could have emanated from the dragon's mouth, or it could have been the result of a nuclear explosion. Madonna's hand, reaching out to some imagined viewer of the scenario, disperses several drops of water which appear more like a bunch of diamonds than an aquatic spray. Though many of the photographs in the series present Madonna in and/or dispensing a precious stream of water, it is this particular deployment of the fluid that is most arresting: is she trying to put out the fires that will precede a nuclear winter? Is she dispensing crystallized dodecahedrons of wisdom?[20] Is she climaxing? Taking her too literally is one response to the excessiveness and earnestness of the images: literalizing them and tracing their consequences opens them to the world and to themselves.

Returning to LaChapelle's own words, appended to his book *LaChapelleLand* (a version of La-La Land, Los Angeles, City of Angels), provides some illumination as to the intentionality behind images such as this one. Barthesianly obtuse, emerging from a third space, the image of D-day Madonna (1996, p. 44) begins to reveal its excesses in light of LaChapelle's remarks on his other works (a horizontal or rhizomic reading). The titles alone of his photographs speak volumes: *Frozen Yogurt Cowboys*, *Hot Pants Tragedy*, *Brandi With Boob Cup and Ceramic Leopards*, *Lou Lou in Front of the Sphinx*. Commodification, dieting, sexual paraphernalia, Egyptology – for LaChapelle, the world is one great collection of fragments waiting to be turned into that supreme queer commodity, drama:

> Once we were playing kickball in the apartment complex parking lot when this woman came downstairs with a giant hairdo, halter top, hot pants, cork platform wedgies, and started smashing her husband's new Lincoln with a hammer. We were mesmerized. Seeing her on all fours, screaming, crawling on that car and bashing it, with that outfit, that hair, those fingernails ... well, it was a little bit of heaven. I'll never forget it. I love drama and outrageousness. I love crazy scenes. Always have. (1996, p. 148)

The histrionic image of a bouffant-crowned matron smashing her man's vehicle to pieces seems directly related to the 'Indian Summer' series, for in each tableau, in, for example, the scene of revenge, violence and AquaNet in North Carolina and that of Madonna reclining on the water with her dragon, there is a high-camp juxtaposition of incommensurable images,[21] images which, like those in Burman's *Fly Girl* series, do not compute, indeed, cannot compute without remainder, excrescence, spillover (in essence, they semantically overflow their boundaries, deferring definitive interpretations and readings – a species of visual synergy). A practitioner of postmodern play, LaChapelle, like French photographers Pierre et Gilles or American photographer Aaron Cobbett, fuses sleaze with *haute glamour*, generating sublimity through the reverberations that result from the radical juxtaposition of supercharged traces and clichéd stereotypes.[22] Motivated by his own despair at the prevalence of 'American trash culture', LaChapelle recuperates the abject in order to distil beauty from it: 'And now I'm not bothered by looking at places like McDonald's. I see them and think "Oh, I could do a photo here." They're colourful and bright' (1996, p. 149). *Tori Spelling* (1993). *Kitty G with Hotdogs* (1994). *Sunset Boulevard* (1993). McGlam, McChic, McFly. But also: Mc[McGlam, McChic, McFly].

Trash and meta-trash (trash about trash) – as well as the commodification of commodification itself (the act of creating commodities as the new fetish).

LaChapelleLand contains many images that resonate in interesting and problematic ways with the photos in the 'Indian Summer' series; specifically, his representations of Madonna previous to the 'Indian Summer' series provide insights as to LaChapelle's vision of her. For LaChapelle, Madonna, like other celebrities, represents a piece of exploitable kitsch, a fragment of trash culture: see, for example, two of his photographs which deal directly with Madonna: *Courtney Love and Madonna Look-alikes in Whatever Happened to Baby Jane?* (1996) and *Madonna and Child* (1995). In *Courtney Love and Madonna Look-alikes*, LaChapelle re-stages camp film classic *Whatever Happened to Baby Jane?* (Aldrich, 1962) with Madonna and her musical, cinematic and vestimentary nemesis Courtney Love; in doing so, LaChapelle alludes to the very real rivalry that exists between the two. Sitting in a wheelchair, Madonna, clad in a black and gold bustier with pasties which reference her look in the videos 'Open Your Heart' (Mondino, 1986) and 'Vogue' (Fincher, 1990), still clutching her dumb-bell, reacts in horror as Courtney Love, frozen in the kinderwhore look that made her famous as the lead singer of Hole, acts the part of mentally tortured, washed-up childhood actress Baby Jane, serving her sister Blanche a glorious luncheon *entrée de rat garni*. Courtney's pinafore, festooned with awkwardly gigantic ribbons, her tiara,[23] her ruffle-socks and tap shoes, her thunder thighs, the look of abjection and vengefulness on her powdered, pasty face, platter-top raised triumphantly to expose Madonna's delicious dinner; Madonna's blonde weave, her rosary beads, ridiculously pencilled eyebrows, platform shoes and *Blond Ambition* headset: LaChapelle metaphorizes the real-life battles between Love and Madonna by placing the two into a previous text of sibling hatred and revenge. *Madonna with Child* is tame by comparison, even a little awkward. Gloss-deficient. In this Maryolatric photograph, Madonna lies splayed across the page with a screaming little girl suspended diagonally over her obscured breasts. To the right of Madonna's head floats a beach thong with a huge rainbow ribbon like a sea anemone on the toe. From the top right corner of the photo, a foot protrudes to blot out the first 'N' in the name 'MADONNA'. This photograph represents Madonna parodying a possible new identity as mother; read against images such as Madonna wheeling a gold baby carriage down Gaultier's runway, it is LaChapelle ironizing Madonna, Madonna ironizing herself, motherhood viewed as purely performative.

The meta- or hyper-orientalisms and celebrity-as-*objet* ethos of LaChapelle mark out a territory in which Madonna's Hindu Goddess images can be decoded. Questions of both appropriation and cultural cartography (ways in which work such as LaChapelle's explodes national borders) problematize these images; returning to LaChapelle's previous work on Madonna or to other of his orientally inflected images, such as *Tantric Sex* (1995), *Rachel and Sumo Wrestlers* (1994), or *k. d. lang* (1995), only makes matters worse, for it presents us with an orientalizing system when before we only had detached instances of the oriental.[24] Opposing Madonna's images to the images produced by visual artist Chila Kumari Burman or to the performances of Coco Fusco, reading them against Rigoberta Menchú's disturbing silences, against tropes of the Plantation Mistress or the renegade Raver – all strategies I have thus far suggested – are some approaches to arriving at an understanding of the aesthetic workings of the post-Material Girl. Placing aesthetic approaches from postmodern (LaChapelle, Madonna, Evans) and postcolonial (Shohat, Menchú, hooks) discourses in relation to one another, allowing postmodern techniques of pastiche, *détournement* and *bricolage* to reverberate with and against postcolonial strategies of anthropophagy, the poetics of disembodiment and media jujitsu,[25] we gain the benefit of engaging the contemporary scene of mythmaking at its most dense (an antinomy, given that this is also mythography at its flimsiest). Looking to the awkward interfacing that exists between the global and the local, or, alternately, between that which can be viewed as flat simulacrum and that which demands engagement as 3-D reality, we come to the point at which battles over cultural ownership constitute a rich and enticing field of inquiry. For some, such as Baudrillard (1995), the Gulf War (or even the collapse of the World Trade Center) will be a TV projection of unreal and shimmering images, while for others, such as Shohat and Stam (1994, pp. 130–31), it will represent a real battle in which real blood is spilled and real lives hang in the balance. Similarly, some will receive Madonna's Hindu transformation as fashion-forward and of-the-moment, while others will deem it an act of cultural hijacking and sacrilege. What kind of conversation can these two parties engage in? What dialogue can result? And, most importantly, how can the real and the simulated retain their respective existences qua real and simulated? That each must retain its integrity while opening itself to the other seems evident.

Postscript: transnational street party 2K

In the final image of LaChapelle's series, Madonna kicks it in characteristic street-party fashion – perhaps an anachronistic film still from the street party she would later enact on the stage of the 1998 MTV Video Music Awards and during the performance of 'Ray of Light' in the *Drowned World Tour* (2001). In this photograph, the crowning glory of the spread, the street once again becomes a dancefloor. How interchangeable the two are in all Madonna's work: the breakdancing scenes in the 'Borderline' video (Lambert, 1984), the bongo-drummer and guitarist *en las calles de San Pedro* in 'La Isla Bonita' (Lambert, 1987), the fluidity between freeway and discothèque in 'Ray of Light'. Street Style: I think of Ted Polhemus's observation that it is supereminently mythologies of the street that have influenced haute couture at the end of the twentieth century.[26] How do street and dancefloor or street and runway slide into and out of one another? How do their ontologies mix, overlap, super- and sub-impose? On this particular street, a crowd – different from the head-spinners of 'Borderline', the street musicians of 'La Isla Bonita' and the clubkids of 'Ray of Light' – assembles. Compared to the diversities of Calvin Klein and Benetton ad campaigns, the crowd surrounding Madonna in her Indian Summer Street Party is radically heterogeneous (unlike Calvin Klein's crowds, it is more than a troop of pale heroin devotees or Andy Warhol Factory aspirants; unlike Benetton's, it is not fundamentally an homage to genetic diversity). Action abounds. A gynaecomast arrives pulling a wheelie on a child's Big Wheels toy. An obese white man with several chins clutches a brown paper bag with one hand while using the other to barbecue chicken. A shirtless male dancer swoons in ecstasy while a dog, standing on its hind legs, bestows kisses upon his moaning mouth; behind his head looms a mylar balloon emblazoned with some unreadable wish: Happy Birthday, Get Well, We Hope... And that's not all: a pregnant Latina in a New York Yankees cap, Puerto Rican Pride necklace and chunky gold earrings echoes the fat man grilling chicken. An Indian woman in a cream sari and heavy gold choker raises her arm as if to vogue, while behind her, a shirtless black queen joins in. To the remote left is a highway – the Brooklyn–Queens Expressway? Above the action, a scrawny *papi chulo* in saggy shorts and drooping drawers waves a Puerto Rican flag. Translating the images into words, constructing the verbal photograph, could take a lifetime.

Far off to the right, Madonna dances, straddling a boom box, which is probably playing some new remix of 'Ray of Light'. She stands in front of a fire hydrant which, on this hot July day, someone has mercifully loosened: water spurts out in a gush, transforming to a ray of light as it hits Madonna's pink sequined Alexander McQueen pants. Her hands are posed so as to emulate Hindu symbology, her blonde and hennaed hair draping onto her breasts.[27] Charles Jencks (1996) allies heterogeneity to the peripheralization of centre, its displacement to the margins: is this how to read Madonna's off-centre positioning? Is this how to read Madonna as architecture? Yet though she is off-centre, she still constitutes the focal point of the party scene: occupying the margins, Madonna is still the point of unification, the Lacanian *point de capiton*, the off-centre centre around which all satellite persons and personalities cluster, orbit. The spiritual illumination, the shantih, represented by the water spouting from the fire hydrant, the urban solution to a lack of swimming pool posited as the source of that illumination, sprays Madonna and gynaecomast with its wet wisdom: overcoming Western selfishness and narcissism, Madonna receives streams of enlightenment in an off-centre position isomorphic with the dissolution and displacement of ego produced by that enlightenment. But of course the centre has not dissolved – it has merely moved, slumming in the periphery. Another climax.

The pink of Madonna's sequined, reflecting pants refers back to other applications of that colour throughout the cluster of seven images. The conjunction of 'pinkness' with water in many of these images, their almost perpetual association in this series, gives to the colour the ambience or nimbus of 'Enlightenment'. As the lyrics to 'Ray of Light' seem to indicate, it is Madonna's transformation into a ray of light that gains her 'a universe' and allows her to complete the mourning process. I had never thought of her fashion transitions as involving mourning before – but had she, without my knowing it, subtly, *sub rosa*, mourned the death of the late 1980s *Who's That Girl?* girl, or of the early 1990s *Truth or Dare* fascist bitch? What had died, according to the mentioned late 1990s interviews, was the Material Girl; what had been born was the post-Vedic, spiritually enlightened, bindhi-sporting Hindu Goddess. Is the mourning process complete? Is this scene some sort of after-party, a celebration of the death of self, a post-potlatch carnival? Her hands frozen in Hindu *mudras* indicating peace, her lips chanting '*Om*' like an ad for a Gap fragrance, her hips arrested mid-gyration, she reflects the water-turned-light as the gynaecomast, the only other person to get soaked by the ejaculating hydrant, screams out 'You go, girl.'

Acknowledgements

A version of this essay first appeared under the title 'Post-Vedic Madonnarama' in the journal *Found Object* **9** (Fall, 2000). 'East is Hot!' is a reference to a 1991 advertising campaign for fashion designer Franco Moschino.

Notes

1. See Dorinne Kondo (1997) for her analysis of the equation of 'Asian' with 'Japanese' in the fashion world (and, by extension, the equation of 'Japanese' with the dual poles of cultural modernism, best represented by Issey Miyake's designs, and traditionalism, best represented by the kimono). That Madonna should give the Hindu style the boot and embrace *japonaisserie* is significant, and speaks to the value ascribed to Japanese culture by America.
2. The *bindu* is 'the dot, drop, globule; in philosophy: the metaphysical point out of time and space where the absolute and the phenomenal meet, which is experienced in some types of samadhi; the sacred mark made on the forehead, symbolizing the third eye (the eye of wisdom); in the Tantras: semen; Shiva's semen, the essence of life and the symbol of the nectar of immortality; the symbol of *brahman*, the essence of all reality' (Werner, 1997, p. 44).
3. For Aristotle, 'the ludicrous' occurs within comedy as a species of the ugly: 'Comedy is, as we have said, an imitation of characters of a lower type – not, however, in the full sense of the word bad, the Ludicrous being merely a subdivision of the ugly. It consists in some defect or ugliness which is not painful or destructive' (1961, pp. 59–60). Hence via Aristotle, we apprehend Madonna's relation to that other aesthetic category, the ugly.
4. During spring 2001, in conjunction with my 'Madonna: Emptiness and Emanation' course offered through the English Department of CUNY's Hunter College, both

Revlene and the mother of Voguing, Willi Ninja, performed, Revlene embodying the ethos and styles of the 'Music' and 'Don't Tell Me' videos (both 2000), and Willi providing a Voguing demo. Video available upon request.

5.   Madonna's need for justification, as demonstrated by her hilarious episodes with the Pope or Canadian authorities in *Truth or Dare* (Keshishian, 1991) is crucial, for, like Habermas' prototypical modern aesthetic object, she must forever articulate her own condition of possibility (1998, pp. 7–10).

6.   My reference is to Burman's 1993 series of 'auto-portraits' in which many of the contradictory and incommensurable identities of the split racial self are dramatized. (For a reading of these 'auto-portraits' see Nead, 1995.)

7.   These streams of references are used to demarcate the 'territory' in which both postmodernism and postcolonialism do battle over the appropriation issue. The interspace of that territory is where I plant myself and where this present chapter as lyrical essay proliferates.

8.   One advantage to this schema is that it reveals the imperialist content of Madonna's Hinduism: literally speaking, she positions herself as a Brit and thus is able to view India as imperial commodity. This interpretation also resonates with the material on the *Music* album: Madonna becomes a cowgirl only because, positioned as British, she can appreciate the gaudiness of this foundational American myth. On Madonna's relationship with the USA, see Albiez's piece in this collection (Chapter 8).

9.   See Fusco for a discussion of uses of *tapadas* by the sixteenth-century Peruvian viceroyalty (1995, p. 69).

10.   Yet, since the simulacrum does not ever emerge from the Real, the move is always made in bad faith. Hence there is no return because there never was any departure. See Baudrillard, 2000, p. 41.

11.   See Mercer (1994) for a deconstruction of 'the natural' in the 'Black is Beautiful' movement and a consequent valorization of the conk as non-imitative hair-straightening practice (a 'New World' hairstyle). It seems as if his ideas of 'difference' and 'double take' (p. 119) can also be applied to Madonna: isn't the point that the material she borrows needs to be radically out of place miscontextualized (p. 119)?

12.   Still, the © does matter, though not for the aesthetic imaginary, which, of late, has lulled itself into the charming delusion that all is up for grabs in the game of cultural mopping. Patented gene sequences and trademarked animals, like OncoMouse™, tell a different story: creatures such as these attest to the validity of cultural regulation.

13.   'We Indians have always hidden our identity and kept our secrets to ourselves. This is why we are discriminated against. We often find it hard to talk about ourselves because we know we must hide so much in order to preserve our Indian culture and prevent it from being taken away from us' (Menchú, 1998, p. 20).

14.   Rabine provides a further example of the desire of contemporary fashion theorists to plunge into the postcolonial/postmodern vortex (1997, pp. 147–9).

15.   See the film *Groove* (Greg Harrison III, 2000) vis-à-vis Evans's (1997) interpretation of Rave culture.

16.   'Meta' in the sense of reflexivity: the meta-oriental is the oriental reflected back upon itself. 'Hyper' in the sense of 'hyperrealism'. The meta/hyper oriental is thus the excess of orientalism revelatory of orientalism's artificiality. It is orientalism revealed as high camp.

17.   In Einstein's formula $E = mc^2$, perhaps the most famous prediction of the special theory of relativity, 'c' denotes the speed of light, while 'E' denotes the energy of an object and 'm' denotes its mass. One of the consequences of this formula and of the

theory behind it is that no object may travel at any speed in excess of 'c', or 186 000 miles per second. Hence Madonna's ability to travel 'quicker than a ray of light' places her in violation of Einsteinian physics, and raises questions as to the nature of her existence (what type of materiality does she exhibit if she is able to transgress what Einstein has postulated to be one of the universe's most fundamental and constitutive limits?) as well as to her inertial frame of reference.

18. This image was included in LaChapelle's show at New York City's Tony Shafrazi gallery (4 June–15 September 1999).

19. It seems in some way helpful to scan compilations of Hindu artworks for Madonna analogues. In Dehejia (1997), I found several images which mirror Madonna's poses: Vishnu reclining on his serpent in a sculptured panel of the Vishnu Temple, Deogarh, *c*. AD 500; *Krishna Dallying with the Gopis*, Kangra, *c*.1775; Ravi Varma's *Woman Holding a Fan*, *c*.1895.

20. In Platonic geometry, the dodecahedron has an important place; a 'Platonic solid', or solid of which each face is a regular polygon and which, by virtue of its regularity, constitutes a building block of nature, represented for Plato either 'cosmos' or 'ether' (there are only five Platonic solids: in Plato's estimation, the tetrahedron corresponded to fire, the cube to earth, the octahedron to air and the icosahedron to water).

21. Here I introduce the distinction between intentional and unintentional camp. For Sontag (1986), only that which aspires to seriousness qualifies as camp (a supreme example: the art nouveau object). Whether LaChapelle's images similarly aspire to seriousness or are satisfied with their radical frivolity is a matter to be determined. What rides on this call is the division between camp (*Plan 9 from Outer Space*; Wood, 1959) and camp-about-camp (*Pink Flamingos*; Waters, 1972).

22. For a discussion of the work of French photographers Pierre et Gilles, see Tata, 2000.

23. Compare Baby Jane/Courtney Love's tiara in this photograph to Madonna's tiara in the penultimate image of the 'Indian Summer' series. Madonna, her outstretched hand suspending a Sacred Heart pierced with pins like a voodoo doll, is crowned queen of heaven and earth. Time-lapse photography creates a luminescent nimbus around her head, each tiara point shooting out arcs of light and enlightenment.

24. Like the system outlined by Said (1994), this system provides a means for the Occident to devour, contain and neutralize the East; unlike Said's system, it revels in its superficiality and inorganicism.

25. See Shohat and Stam, where jujitsu is listed as one of six modes of aesthetic resistance (1994, pp. 292–337).

26. See Polhemus (1994) for an examination of the shift from Trickle Down (women buying Dior patterns to make their own New Look dresses) to Bubble Up (Versace raiding punk iconography to produce his notorious gold-safety-pinned Elizabeth Hurley dress). The runway looks to the street for inspiration: La Rue becomes L'Autre.

27. See Hiltebeitel's discussion of the cult of Draupadi for one possible referent to Madonna's new hairstyle (1991). Is she recuperating Draupadi by loosening her own *kuntal*? Reading the sudden looseness of her tresses against Indian folklore contextualizes the style innovation, thus revealing further appropriative activity on Madonna's part.

Chapter 7

Re-worlding the oriental
Critical perspectives on Madonna as geisha

Rahul Gairola

Madonna as postmodern icon

It is hardly a surprise that the opposing impulses to 'wanna-be' and to dislike Madonna derive from the same anxiety over the singer's 'real' identity, giving an ironic twist to the question 'Who's that girl?' Even those deeply influenced by the media spectacles generated by pop culture can become riddled with insecurity when they feel they cannot identify the 'real' person behind the myriad masks of pop stardom. While such an essentializing, self-fulfilling impulse to pigeonhole Madonna into an 'authentic' identity serves as a hermeneutical anchor for *both* those who love her and those who hate her (since those who admire her praise her ability to slip from beneath the rigid umbrellas of signification, while those who condemn her are often threatened by her resistance to a static image), the so-called 'Queen of Pop' eludes both followers and critics by shifting her image before stable identificatory paradigms and criticisms can summarily describe her. In an interview with Madonna, Andrew Harrison observes that the media, even despite the release of *Ray of Light* (1998), maintain an anachronistic desire for the 'pointy-chested global sex dictator' (2000, p. 80) that was the Madonna of *Erotica* (1992). Though she saturated popular media with a reformed 'ambient hippychick' image and sold more copies of *Ray of Light* than any of her other albums in the past decade, Harrison writes that 'nobody quite knows where' the new Madonna is in relation to her past projects (2000, p. 80).

By emulating a wide spectrum of performative looks that can be disorienting, Madonna constantly forces us to re-frame the ways in which we view her. Lynne Layton observes that Madonna straddles a contradictory position by deconstructing the 'humanist notion of a controlled, rational, ego-centred self' by destabilizing her identity while simultaneously asserting and maintaining individual control (1994, p. 143). In becoming, among many other things, a somewhat normative role model for women and a sex object for men, Madonna has also become a sign of the 'darker' aspects of unacceptable femininity. At the same time that anti-pornography feminists have decried her earlier work, politically progressive feminists have hailed her for producing positive role models for women (McNair, 1996, p. 158). Her agency has reached legendary proportions worldwide as she proclaims in interviews that she reveals bits of herself in given moments despite speaking from behind myriad masks (Eccleston, 1998, p. 93; Walters, 1998, p. 76). Like the elusive entity of the myth, Madonna too engages in a 'constant game of hide-and-seek between meaning and the form' (Barthes, 1972, p. 118).

As a result of Madonna's ability to transform her self and experiment with musical styles, a number of theorists (Kaplan, 1987; Bordo, 1993; Schwichtenberg, 1993c) have advanced the notion that Madonna is a postmodern icon who signifies the liberating instability of signification in the twentieth century. Why a 'postmodern icon'? If indeed 'postmodern' as a theoretical adjective describes the evolution of modernity with its fragmentary experiences that bombard the subject and characterize life approaching the twenty-first century, few contemporary performers deserve to be characterized as such more than does Madonna. Her 'identity' cannot be relegated to a single specific look since its most discernable characteristic is the dynamic nature of metamorphosis, change and growth. In this manner, Madonna fragments and dismembers the very stereotypes that the religious Right, censors and other conservative factions tend to evoke in their pathologization of her work.

Through her engagement with this prismatic discourse of popular identity dissemination, Madonna has become the celebrated poster child of pop feminism.[1] This is strongly reflected in Camille Paglia's claim that:

> Madonna has a far profounder vision of sex than do the feminists. She sees both the animality and the artifice. Changing her costume style and hair color virtually every month, Madonna embodies the eternal values of beauty and pleasure. Feminism says, 'No more masks.' Madonna says we are nothing but masks. (1992, p. 5)

This chameleonic virtue leads Paglia to proclaim that Madonna is the 'future of feminism' (1992, p. 5). As revolutionary as Paglia's assertion sounds, being 'the future of feminism' can surely be quite an arduous task considering the criticism by so many scholars of the technological vehicles of capitalism that have given birth to myriad identity possibilities in global media. Some key postmodern theorists have emphasized the negative effects that late capitalism has had on American culture (Jameson, 1998, p. 2; Baudrillard, 1999, p. 386), and attribute the dismemberment of the notion of a hallowed experience to consumerism. A salient aspect of postmodernism is the proliferation of synthetic experiences inextricably bound to the juggernaut of power that is American capitalism (although we might note here that consumers' desires for power, money or, more importantly, the power that money can buy should be further theorized).

Frederic Jameson asserts that postmodernity has spawned the proliferation of the pastiche, or 'blank parody' – a cultural mode of emulation that exists for the sake of itself without the slightest motive of soliciting humour (or any other reaction) from people (1998, p. 5). Expounding on this concept, Jameson claims, 'in a world in which stylistic innovation is no longer possible, all that is left is to imitate dead styles, to speak through the masks and with the voices of the styles in the imaginary museum' (p. 7). Such a process, he argues, inevitably highlights the 'necessary failure of art and the aesthetic, the failure of the new, the imprisonment in the past' (p. 7). Jameson's notions on the postmodern and Madonna as a postmodern icon collate to suggest that the singer herself is a metaphor for pastiche. This qualifies Madonna as a debaser of proper culture who is thus 'destined forever to have little credibility in the eyes of those concerned with "reality" and "identity"; they have no guarantee of an audience' (Lyotard, 1993, p. 41).

My goal hereon is to consider Madonna as a postmodern icon and her relationship as such with ethnicity and the global market in the music video for 'Nothing Really Matters' (Renck, 1999), and to consider briefly the *Drowned World Tour* (2001) – two examples of her wearing the vestments and ethnic mask of a geisha. I hope to demonstrate that, contrary to Lyotard, there is indeed a guarantee of audience, and it is within the space of the 'inauthentic' that we see an emergence of some very real social stakes in terms of ethnicity. It is worth noting here that the notion of ethnicity is itself a historically contested terrain between instrumentalist models that see ethnicity as a synthesized construct of material interests, and primordial models that claim material interest disorients, rather than forms, ethnic collectives (Bentley, 1987, pp. 25–6). Subsequently, the notion of ethnicity is a problematical terrain of identity formulation even before Madonna manipulates it, and is further complicated by the phenomenal ways that global media reconfigure the ways we interact with and internalize ethnicity, culture and identity. Given the fact that Madonna's emulation of geisha occurred at the same time that a number of other cultural texts established relationships with East Asian culture and the world market, I will read visual elements of Madonna-as-geisha in relation to those concurrent cultural texts. Indeed, it behoves us to rethink the ways that Madonna as a postmodern icon operates as a fluctuating cultural discourse in synergy with the advent of global capital and its oscillations. While it is plausible to dismiss Madonna's use of Eastern images as capitalist racism,[2] interrogating the politics of viewers' notions of ethnicity demonstrates that race is not an issue here in the same way that capital and agency are.

Race/sex/market relations and the *Drowned World Tour*

A number of theorists have speculated on the relationships shared between Madonna's persona, her fans and aspects of the market (Fiske, 1987b, pp. 271–2; Frith, 1993, p. 91; Seigworth, 1993, p. 305; Freccero, 1994, p. 181). In an attempt to think over the connection between the postmodern icon's work and the market, David Tetzlaff observes, 'the vicissitudes of glitter and wealth have become a more reliable source of narrative spectacle than anything inherent in the work [of Madonna] itself' (1993, p. 248). Here, Tetzlaff asserts that economics and identity are inextricably bound – we apprehend identities through economic filters. Tetzlaff concludes that 'ultimately, Madonna's power is tied to her ability to have her image reproduced and distributed. Each image dispersed throughout the culture is another validation of worth' (p. 262). This view is one that bell hooks also took with the publication of the book *Sex* (1992), claiming that 'Madonna is really only a link in the marketing chain that exploits representations of sexuality and the body for a profit, a chain which focuses on images that were once deemed "taboo"' (1992a, p. 70). Yet, while the market indeed has a great effect on cultural production, it is not the sole determining factor. Considering Madonna's astronomical income, we should consider elements that complicate an isolated study of economics.[3] Let us thus examine market aspects in relation to questions around sex and race. bell hooks asserts that commodity culture constructs sexual desire for the Other:

> When race and ethnicity become commodified as resources for pleasure, the culture of specific groups, as well as the bodies of individuals, can be seen as constituting an alternative playground where members of dominating races, genders, sexual practices affirm their power-over in intimate relations with the Other. (1992a, p. 23)

While we can see how pop cultural sexualization of the Other can foster a hegemonic discourse, a problem I see with hooks' criticism is that her argument not only presupposes a static conception of ethnicity, and to some degree sexuality, to achieve its argument, but also depends upon a somewhat stable conception of the world market that will unfailingly allow capitalist ventures to wield economic power. Stuart Hall has effectively argued that the traditional Marxist paradigm is not sufficient to explain myriad factors that shape the oppression of peoples since it casts an 'overwhelmingly determining effect' on the social structures around economics and sociology (1996, p. 17). Gayle Rubin has also criticized traditional Marxism for imposing determining effects on economic structures that unjustly downplay the role of gender and domestic labour in capitalist societies (1975, p. 162). All this suggests that we should factor sex, gender and other social elements in surveying the global economy lest we fall victims to an abstraction of economic relations (that ignores human effects) along the same lines that values abstract labour. Once we do this, we see that sex and gender formations also manifest along tropes of capitalism.

Asserting that women are exchangeable commodities circulating in patriarchal capitalism, Luce Irigaray claims that 'the society we know, our own culture, is based upon the exchange of women' through the use, consumption, and circulation of their bodies (1997, p. 174). Irigaray makes a useful distinction between the two 'bodies' that a woman encapsulates: '*A commodity – a woman – is divided into two irreconcilable 'bodies'*: her natural body and her socially valued, exchangeable body, which is a particularly mimetic expression of masculine values' (p. 180, her emphasis). This is to say that there is a distinction between the biological corpus of a woman and the metaphorical body of social indoctrination that 'inscribes' itself on the psychological landscape of the woman through discourses of socialization. Irigaray states that the socially valued body that reflects patriarchal ideals subordinates the natural body, transforming it into 'a value-bearing object', whose 'likeness' is measured in reference to an authoritative model (p. 180).

Madonna complicates this binary of the woman's body when emulating a non-Western woman, and this is most evident in her *Drowned World Tour* show. For the Japanese segment (which covers the performances for the songs 'Paradise (Not For Me)', 'Frozen', 'Nobody's Perfect' and a 'Mer Girl' / 'Sky Fits Heaven' medley), a reversal of traditional male/female gender roles is juxtaposed against projected images of domestic abuse and male-dominated love. A large screen features Madonna-as-geisha singing 'Paradise (Not For Me)' as the backdrop against which four Asian dancers in shorts dangle in the air, then fall onto the stage. The background video of Madonna features her with painted face and lips in a cerise kimono crosscut by silhouettes of samurai with drawn swords and the Japanese flag. 'Paradise' phases right into 'Frozen', where the 'real' Madonna first appears as geisha in a stylized dance complete with synchronized karate moves distributed along all sides of the stage by herself and her dancers. At the middle of the number, the singer spins around as a menacing samurai dancer appears on a raised platform above her.

So far we have encountered Madonna-as-geisha during the *Drowned World Tour* in what seems a non-political performance that reflects the commodification of Other culture that hooks criticizes (1992a). More specifically, the 'Japanese section' of the 2001 tour has been called 'curious' because it 'comes off as too distant' and 'aspires to be a morality tale' (Gallo, 2001). This criticism carries the implication that Madonna-as-geisha (rather than Madonna-as-cowgirl) is visually incoherent. Such an interpretation, however, defaults back to notions of authentic and inauthentic ethnicities, and the sense that Madonna-as-geisha is a mix match. I would like to argue that the Madonna-as-geisha numbers force viewers to reconsider Madonna 'live' by reading this part of the *Drowned World Tour* as a socio-political mode of performance art. Madonna's natural body in the 'Japanese section' becomes a way for critiquing the social bodies that buttress the domination of women by men, and the domination of Western women over Eastern women. Within this critique is also a gesture towards condemning domestic violence towards both women and men. The 'Nobody's Perfect' piece that follows 'Frozen' features the same menacing samurai passionately yet aggressively caressing Madonna-as-geisha, thrusting her towards and away from him as he swings his sword discomfortingly close to the singer's face and neck.

One begins to sense a troubling theme of domestic abuse in this number – clearly a different effect from the exploitation or fetishization of ethnicity for profit. Madonna-as-geisha shadows the samurai with small steps, only to be physically rebuked then pulled back by him in a demonstration of ostensibly ambivalent yet extremely violent love. At the climax of the number, the samurai cuts a braid off her kimono's hood, symbolically stealing her womanhood while killing her. But there is redemption of this symbolically violent act, albeit one that also communicates through violence.[4] Madonna-as-geisha transmogrifies in the number that follows, a medley of 'Mer Girl I / Sky Fits Heaven / Mer Girl II'. She appears in the very same elevated space previously occupied by the samurai during 'Frozen' in what seems to be a reversal of both gender roles and sex power. At the pivotal segue into 'Sky Fits Heaven', Madonna-as-geisha sheds the demure persona of 'Nobody's Perfect' and goes on the offensive. She flies through the sky along with two other female dancers while fighting male samurai dressed in black.

This number ends in a reversal of power positions in the visual field: with all the other samurai killed off, Madonna-as-geisha breaks the neck of the last one and kicks him off the stage – this is the very same samurai who 'kills' her by cutting her braid, and with whom she switches spatial positions onstage. This scene is interesting because it immediately segues into 'Mer Girl II' with just Madonna singing the second part of the song alone on stage. Behind her, however, the big screen flickers back to life with an image of Madonna-as-geisha without the kimono but with a black eye and bruised lips. The 'real' Madonna has vengefully killed the samurai who terrorized her in the previous number, and the physical prowess she displays in metamorphosing from a reticent geisha to one capable of attacking her patriarchal oppressors is juxtaposed by this enormous projected image of her in the black wig receiving blows from an invisible aggressor. Though that physical body of the real Madonna has killed off her tormentor, the flickering screen behind her shows the social body of domestic abuse marking the physical body. In this way, there is no resolution to this performative narrative piece, for it contradicts itself throughout and unto the last instance by beginning with patriarchal violence that ends in the erasure of necessarily patriarchal violence, since a male aggressor is not indexed in the visual field of the screen.

A couple of questions arise: is Madonna's politicization of domestic abuse undermined by her own use of violence against men throughout the Japanese section? Does she substitute violence towards women with violence towards men? We may explore these questions by recalling Irigaray's natural and social bodies while surveying the various movements of violence through which these, the Japanese numbers, are performed. We track the theme of domestic abuse as it begins spatially with the samurai looking down at Madonna-as-geisha, then cutting off her braid in 'Nobody's Perfect', in an act that seems like female castration. The tables turn when Madonna and gal pals fly through the sky and defeat their male oppressors in 'Sky Fits Heaven', especially evident when she breaks the neck of the samurai. Ironically though, while she is finishing the piece solo, the flickering image on the screen depicts a battered Madonna in the geisha wig. We thus end up with the combination of two different contradictory bodies that are themselves not static. In other words, the Japanese sequence offers a dialectical tension between these bodies rather than a resolution between them, highlighting the network of power battles between men and women in the contexts of race, gender and sexual expression. On the one hand, Madonna-as-geisha is reticent and is the victim of patriarchal dominance and domestic violence. On the other hand, Madonna-as-geisha is capable of vengeful violence that symbolizes domestic abuse towards men. The end moment of this violent sequence, which simultaneously portrays the natural body of Madonna-as-geisha and the projected, social body of domestic abuse towards women, deserves some critical attention. The juxtaposition of a victorious Madonna against the large image of a battered Madonna seems to suggest that not only is such violence caught in a cycle that cannot be delineated as just patriarchal or matriarchal violence, but that the two bodies simultaneously contradict and complement one another. The battered face (natural body) of Madonna-as-geisha at the end of the Japanese section signifies a social body – that of domestic abuse. The natural body of Madonna-as-geisha in 'Nobody's Perfect' signifies the social body of female reticence. The number for 'Sky Fits Heaven', in which Madonna-as-geisha is on the offensive, signifies not only the social body of feminist discourse, but also the violent retaliation that often spawns from violence. The resistance of this section to conclude with a resolution while constantly contradicting its own images expresses the hardships that two very different 'bodies' – the natural and social – can endure in the processes that enjoin them. Such visual contradictions highlight a strategic shift away from crystallizing an 'authentic identity'.

All this is to say that this section of the *Drowned World Tour* does not simply emanate a 'guys are bad' or 'girl power' stance, but instead attempts to place both in (violent) dialogue with one another by using the natural body of Madonna as an ideological canvas upon which social bodies are illustrated. Thus natural bodies and social bodies are engaged in an exchange system of their own in which the signifiers that characterize both fluctuate and form one another, and do not privilege patriarchy or whiteness as the sites at which this occurs. Thus, contrary to hooks's views, there can be some political productivity in this process of 'becoming other' on a massive media scale, even when the voices of reason originate from sources that may otherwise seem oppositional. We might here consider the limitations of the parameters of authenticity, especially when one concedes that no person embodies just one single identity or subject position. Gayatri Spivak tells Sneja Gunew:

> For me, the question 'Who should speak?' is less crucial than 'Who will listen?' ...
> There are many subject positions which one must inhabit; one is not just one thing.
> That is when a political consciousness comes in. So that in fact, for the person who
> does the 'speaking as' something, it is a problem of distancing from one's self,
> whatever that self might be. (Gunew, 1990, p. 60)

Spivak's insight in this passage exemplifies that one must strategically become an Other to engage in the intellectual labour that allows distance from one's experiential life. We see this manifested physically in the 'natural body' of Madonna, which potentially transforms from a social body – that of an American cultural landscape – to a Pangea-like cultural landscape upon which ethnic signifiers are placed, erased and replaced. Like Spivak, Madonna seems in her performances to posit less concern with who or what has the right to speak – a mentality that hinges on the metaphysical rites of identity that bestow authorial privilege on a person – than who will listen.

In closing this section, let me mention a brief example that demonstrates how nationalism also becomes an ironic element of the *Drowned World Tour*. After the annihilation of the World Trade Center twin towers in New York City on 11 September 2001, Madonna cancelled her Los Angeles show planned for that day and added an extra date to her schedule on Saturday, 15 September, which consequently became the final world tour date. For those shows Madonna wore, instead of the tartan kilt-like garment with which she had opened previous shows, a pleated American flag. Despite national grief, Madonna was the forerunner of a frenzied reaction of not only Americans to publicly proclaim a neo-nationalism through flag display, but companies to manufacture everything from trinkets to clothing that capitalized on the resurrection of American consumers' patriotism and desire to be perceived as patriotic. Thus an irony underlay these *Drowned World Tour* productions – the geisha number with its Japanese flag was put alongside a dangerous neo-patriotism/American nationalism symbolized by the flag, which became an influential factor on the audience.[5] I mention this in concluding this section to acknowledge that such investment in 'who will listen' can be dangerous even as it is revolutionary when patriotic nationalism is at stake.

Madonna as geisha in 'Nothing Really Matters'

While her early videos including 'Lucky Star' (Pierson, 1983), 'Borderline' (Lambert, 1984) and 'Rain' (Romanek, 1993) contrast the white singer against ethnic Others including blacks, Hispanics and East Asians, Madonna gradually begins to emulate women from non-Western countries in videos like 'Fever' (Thai deity; Sednaoui, 1993), 'Secret' (Black lounge singer; McDaniel, 1994), 'Take a Bow' (Spanish señora; Haussman, 1994) and 'Frozen' (Hindu deity; Cunningham, 1998). As demonstrated in the video for 'Nothing Really Matters' and the images of her in the *Drowned World Tour* programme, Madonna took on the mask of the geisha for a period after her emulation of a Hindu goddess, and recreated it on stage during her 1999 Grammy Awards performance of 'Nothing Really Matters' and, as mentioned, in a segment of her *Drowned World Tour* two years later. 'Nothing Really Matters' is an interesting case study since Madonna is the centred 'Japanese' subject featured in the video while it backgrounds 'real'

Japanese subjects, thus visually marginalized by the pop star's kimono-clad parade as geisha.

Johan Renck directed and shot the video in January 1999, the same month and year that Vintage Books published the second edition of Arthur Golden's bestseller *Memoirs of a Geisha*, which captivated American readers and remained a bestseller for over a year on the *New York Times* list.[6] At the same time, a movement that a number of fashion critics dubbed 'Geisha Glam' became the chic craze in the USA and around the world (Cruz, 1999). According to Ruth La Ferla, the 'American obsession' (though we should here note that this phenomenon was no doubt global as well) with East Asian themes manifested itself in other marketing ventures: *Star Wars: Episode I* (George Lucas, 1999) expressly utilizes costumes that mirror Japanese noblewomen's garments, while the spring collections of Italian fashion designers Dolce & Gabbana and French designer Jean Paul Gaultier proudly featured obis – broad sashes that tie into large bows at the back, usually binding a kimono to the waist (La Ferla, 1999, p. 1). This massive commercialization of East Asian culture, beginning in early 1999 American pop and fashion culture, was followed by smaller companies like Lafco, a soap-maker in New York that cites Madonna, *Memoirs of a Geisha*, *Star Wars: Episode I* and the advent of feng shui as the inspirations for its new soap 'Kimono' (La Ferla, 1999, p. 1).[7]

It is not purely coincidental that all these aspects of East Asian culture manifest themselves in Madonna's work and American commodity culture. Mark Watts observes that Madonna's music videos are postmodern in two distinct ways: the very form of video is a mass-transmitted pastiche and the content of her videos are postmodern since they engage in an intertextual system (1996, p. 101). We clearly see this *intertextual referentiality* in the relationship between 'Nothing Really Matters' and the global market for Americanized East Asian culture. While she did not explicitly profit from Golden's novel, Madonna confesses that her costuming was greatly inspired by the character of Hatsumono, a scheming geisha in the novel, and that her emulation of the character is semi-autobiographical (Chetwynd et al., 1999). There is thus an intertextual referentiality to Golden's novel as well as a reappropriation of it. An article in *USA Today* reported that Madonna intended the video to depict the celebrity's gradual descent into madness from the pressures of being a star, and in doing so resignifies the word 'geisha' from the popular misconception that it means 'prostitute' to its actual Japanese definition – 'artist' (Chetwynd et al., 1999).

Thus Madonna-as-geisha is a market signifier for Golden's *Memoirs of a Geisha*, whose narrative and success in the USA then became a cultural signifier for Madonna-as-geisha. This cultural partnership works in a symbiotic relationship in which the cultural capital, to use Bourdieu's term (1990, pp. 126–7), of both Madonna and Golden's commodified work, like capital itself, amasses from the proliferation and promotion of the other 'text'. This intertexuality of culture even occurred to Golden, who said: 'the thought I kept having was, my goodness, if it wasn't for me, Madonna would be wearing something else' (quoted in Cruz, 1999). Yet 'Geisha Glam' was not restricted to the garment industry – it became a pan-marketing discourse (as with the American flag after 11 September 2001) that established inter-referential relationships between commodities in a number of industries that profited in the USA from the ways in which Madonna marked her body. Robert Miklitsch proposes the formulation of the 'commodity-body-sign' as a way of factoring the physical body into the web of values created by commodity fetishism (1998, pp. 79–80). If we view Madonna's emulation of Hatsumono through the lens of the commodity-body-sign, we must go beyond commodification or fetishization and acknowledge that only certain bodies with a particular tenor of cultural capital can facilitate the dissemination of Americanized East Asian culture. In other words, the global market's susceptibility to geisha glam is an effect of Madonna being 'Madonna the popstar'.

As mentioned, the video for 'Nothing Really Matters' features scenes of Madonna dancing in jerky movements crosscut by images of 'real' Japanese subjects in white garments, mobilized by awkward motions. As such, these 'authentic' Japanese subjects, though visually juxtaposed against Madonna, are auxiliary to the sequences featuring her, and seem to frame Madonna as a paradigm of female Japanese embodiment. The video opens with a Madonna in a shiny, black kimono wearing make-up that masks her eyes in a broad, red band.[8] In her arms, she cradles a transparent bag filled with water. This water bag seems a prosthetic, reflexive extension of her 'natural body' (to re-invoke Irigaray), a symbol of Madonna's first child Lourdes. Whereas Irigaray argues that a woman as a commodity is a 'mirror value of and for man' (1997, p. 178), this claim is countered in the context of this particular video. For, if indeed this water bag symbolizes a child, then it also serves as a referent of the child back to the sexual relations that have created this child, which include the absent patriarchal figure of father.

In this way, absence serves as a vehicle for agency. E. Ann Kaplan's work, crucial in directing film and media studies away from concentration on the 'male gaze', is helpful in leading readers to see that 'the various possibilities for "seeing otherwise" in different figurations of the female body have the potential to reveal "what popular culture *can* do"' (1987, p. 116, her emphasis). If the water bag does serve as referent to the biological product of heterosexual sex, the patriarchal figure of father remains absent from the video (also the case in Madonna's video for 'Drowned World/ Substitute for Love' (Stern, 1998), which contains a cameo of her daughter Lourdes at the end). Like an advertisement for Madonna's new fashion statement and lifestyle, this absence of a male figure and presence of a symbolic child in 'Nothing Really Matters' deviates from many of her past videos, including 'Like a Prayer' (Lambert, 1989) and 'Power of Goodbye' (Rolston, 1998), by signifying not the singer's robust sexuality or body parts, but her dynamic abilities as a shape-shifting maternal figure. This water bag also signifies Madonna as mother rather than wife, drawing emphasis on the product of consummation – her child. In other words, by cradling the water bag in the video, Madonna refers to the child (motherhood) rather than the traditional ways and means that produced it (sex, wifehood).

These elements illuminate Madonna's assertion that she is a biographer whose videos reflect various facets of her self, thus initially throwing into question the signified of the ethnic signifiers. According to Olivia Khoo, 'Madonna's translation of the Asian exotic is ... a fold, whereby the star folds into her own image of herself as different, spectacular' (2000, p. 207). If we allow that Madonna does 'fold' into herself with each new transformation, we see that viewers predicate a system of signs that they then read from the visual text, which may have significations aside from what seems ostensible and/or presumed. Kaplan (1987) cues us in to another aspect of music videos worth exploring – the circulation of videos on the global superpower of music videos, MTV. In reference to sex and gender, Kaplan writes, 'only those female representations considered the most marketable are frequently cycled' and what is most marketable has a direct relationship to dominant ideology, the social imaginary and the phallus as signifier (1987, p. 115). Also exploring reception, Thomas Nakayama and Lisa Peñaloza have studied the hermeneutic responses of Asians and Asian Americans to Madonna's videos.[9] Most Asians and Asian Americans, according to their study, felt alienated by the visual narratives of her early videos, and clearly distanced themselves from politics of the visual texts (1993, p. 46).

Considering Kaplan's assertion, the heavy MTV airplay of 'Nothing Really Matters' suggests that Madonna-as-geisha is sexy, even if the portrayal is, in a sense, codified by both finance and cultural capital. The visual coding of the video itself is riddling, for although Madonna wears the Japanese vestments of the geisha, her jerky dance moves and the jumpy movements of the camera do not reflect the stereotypical virtues of reticence and coquettishness that 'Geisha Glam' fashion experts say the clothing signifies (La Ferla, 1999, p. 1). As demonstrated by the study conducted by Nakayama and Peñaloza (1993), even when Madonna is performing another ethnicity or signifies that ethnicity on her natural body (see Irigaray, 1997, p. 180), those who consider themselves to be part of that ethnic group – in this case Asians and Asian Americans – do not 'relate' to Madonna-as-ethnic-Other (a term I use here to cover her many ethnic emulations). Thus the implication is that they see her as a white performer, despite ethnic signifiers, and even if they do view her as a feasible representative of their ethnic group, that representation is measured against another representation (that of the 'true' ethnic subject).

Thus in the video for 'Nothing Really Matters', Madonna-as-geisha can be read as a hybrid figure that embodies contradictions, whose movements are juxtaposed against the visual landscape of the red kimono and black hair that we measure up against the essentialized notion of *the* Japanese woman. This schism in Madonna's video identity, I believe, argues less for an association with an 'authentic' Japanese woman than it draws attention to consumers' own desires to recognize in the spectacular images of world media culture a reference back to familiar identity formations – a process that is not exclusive to one's ethnicity or gender. In this way, nostalgia concerned with resurrecting familiar ethnic and gender roles (and consequently also notions of nationalism and sexuality) limits rather than expands the field that encompasses them. We develop, from socialization, addictive needs for film and media to offer us such 'copies' of ethnic and gender representations, the latter of which Judith Butler likens to drag performances that do not have an original or primary referent in the 'natural' world (1991, p. 21).

Though Butler, in her criticism of the discourses surrounding identity authenticity focuses on gender, it may be worthwhile to question the ways that ethnicity is implicated in her argument. We undoubtedly apprehend gender within cultural roots informed by nationalities – even in these transnational times that characterize the tenuous boundaries of nation-states – so it is feasible to say that cultural roots themselves are part fantasy constructions from which subject–object positions are informed. This is apparent in 'Nothing Really Matters'. While some viewers may find Madonna's Japanese look offensive for purporting the authentic and performing the inauthentic, we do not apprehend a sense of the 'real' I in this video (and many others) in any way – not even from the 'authentic' Japanese subjects in the video. The camera swings suddenly at sharp angles intended to convey a sense of carnivalesque exaggeration and shock, intensified by jump cuts (sudden sequence changes intended to disorient viewers) that show the 'real' Japanese dancers moving in slow motion. By utilizing camera angles, colours, lighting and other formalistic techniques, Renck posits viewers in a fantasy world that destabilizes rather than confirms any set notion of a stable ethnic identity.

'What it feels like in this world': towards a new hermeneutics of American orientalism

The many manifestations of American pop culture's recent interest in East Asian culture seem to move in a different direction from the pioneering critique of orientalism introduced by Said (1985): whereas the Orient has historically been portrayed in Western art and literature as a timeless and less civilized place in contrast to the Occident (Jhally, 1998), we should rethink what it means when capitalism becomes the very vehicle through which the Orient can culturally colonize the Occident.[10] Indeed, Said has retrospectively emphasized that the division between Orient and Occident is neither unchanging nor simply fictional – it is a fact produced by Orientalists and Orientals alike (Said, 1985, p. 15). What Roland Robertson has described as 'the compression of the world and the intensification of the consciousness of the world as a whole' (1992, p. 8) has occurred along the lines of *a number of discursive terrains*, one of the most salient of which is the movement of peoples across continents. For as Lisa Lowe has strongly argued, 'the immigration of Asians to the United States has been the locus of meanings that are simultaneously legal, political, economic, cultural, and aesthetic' (1996, p. 6).

Likewise, the emigration of multinational corporations into non-Western countries has profoundly affected local culture. Aihwa Ong observes that the influx of consumer goods into the East has, ironically, promoted cultural diversity due to local interpretations and re-appropriations of corporate signs (1999, p. 10). Referring to movements between continents, Ong continues that 'transnational mobility and maneuvers mean that there is a new mode of constructing identity, as well as new modes of subjectification that cut across political borders' (p. 18). No doubt these 'new modes of subjectification' have become influential in the ways people in the USA re-conceptualize American identity. Warren Cohen states that the influx of Asians into the United States has catalysed what he calls the 'Asianization of America', the most immediately pronounced effects of which can be seen in pop culture (2002, p. 83). Citing a wide range of examples, Cohen's point is that corporate appropriations of Asian culture are not simply a testament to American cultural imperialism; rather they are evidence of the profound effect that immigration of East Asians into the USA has had on the evolution of American culture and identity (p. 82). Indeed, American studies has read in the opposite direction for far too long, privileging North American cartography while cutting itself off from the critical study of foreign relations that includes, but is not limited to, European colonialism (Amy Kaplan, 1993, p. 9).

Reading 'Nothing Really Matters' in this context, the natural body of Madonna is a slate upon which the impact of East Asian immigration into the USA and cultural influence is inscribed – East Asians, in this sense, have appropriated her in a dualistic (rather than one-way) shuttling of identities. Saying otherwise risks ignoring the immigration of East Asians into and the birth of diasporic identities within the USA, and thus underestimates the monumental effects of Asian culture in America. In this way, technology and globalization have in a sense facilitated a global awareness of hybrid ethnic identities, many of which are transmitted worldwide through what Arjun Appadurai has dubbed 'mediascapes' (1996, p. 33). For Appadurai, mediascapes 'tend to be image-centred, narrative-based accounts of strips of reality, and what they offer to those who experience and transform them is a series of elements (such as characters, plots, and textual forms) out of which scripts can be formed of imagined lives, their own as well as those of others living in other places' (p. 35). In the context of globalization, Appadurai's 'mediascape' reflects Benedict Anderson's assertion that 'communities are to be distinguished, not by their falsity/genuineness, but by the style in which they are imagined' (1991, p. 6).

We should therefore look into the stylistics of both the mediascape *and* the ways in which we imagine and theorize ourselves within and beyond national boundaries, for they both constitute a synergy of the acquisition of identities. Such a method of re-imagining and re-theorizing could enable cultural theorists to shortstop, for example, the 'rage' that can arise from 'multicultural capitalism – capitalism based on the production and consumption of cultural diversity and the marketing of packaged versions of the "exotic"' (Puwar, 2002, p. 64). Re-imagining, however is not an easy process, and it immediately challenges Anderson's notion of an 'imagined community' when cultural theorists acquiesce that the ways that we imagine are not homogenous or unilateral. This process demands a reflection on the relationship between discourse and the world, as we 'know' it. Citing the diversity of discourse itself, Michel Foucault argues, 'We must not imagine a world of discourse divided between accepted discourse and excluded discourse … but as a multiplicity of discursive elements that can come into play in various strategies' (1990, p. 100). Discourse, for Foucault, is a fluid network of processes shaped by the crosscurrents of their own trajectories, and thus allow for new discourses to subvert, invert and meld with older ones. I mention Foucault here in the context of Appadurai (1996) and Anderson (1991) to advance the point that those very strategies used by profit-making pop culture to sell itself, if one views this as its ultimate goal, are those same cultural hallmarks that pave the way for new groups to re-appropriate representations that too often buttress, form or even oppose our own identificatory imaginings.

This necessitates a multi-faceted, even fragmented way of interpreting pop culture rather than a knee-jerk reaction to it. What I am calling for is a hermeneutical sensibility that, in being postmodern, allows us to interpret culture in the prismatic ways that it is disseminated to us, in the same way that we experience that 'future of feminism' that is Madonna (Paglia, 1992, p. 5). I would like to conclude by emphasizing two concepts – the first is a strategy that those reluctant to foreclose on the notion of authentic ethnic identities may find useful or empowering; the second is helpful in identifying a methodology whose goal is to reconsider the effects of globalization in the context of Orientalist discourse: transculturation, and critical globality. Mary Louise Pratt describes 'transculturation' as the process whereby marginal groups 'select and invent from materials transmitted to them by a dominant or metropolitan culture',[11] using the occasion to locally re-appropriate Western commodities (1992, p. 6). This process not only resignifies the ethnic signifiers in videos like 'Nothing Really Matters', but also creates a space for diasporic identities – first generation Asian Americans among many others – to reclaim agency while casting aside essentialist notions of any ethnic identity. Viewers might then avoid treating Madonna as the simulacrum of the 'real' (Robinson, 1993, p. 343). Though I believe criticism of Madonna-as-geisha should be self-reflexive rather than accusatory, transculturation opens an avenue for appropriating Madonna's appropriations, and is a powerful tactic that manifests cultural irony, sardonic humour, parody and even political dissent.

Spivak has offered the notion of 'worlding' to describe the process through which the 'First' world constructs and subordinates the 'Third' world (1985, p. 128). Prompted to theorize by Spivak's notion of 'worlding', John Muthyala argues that we must revise American Studies by resisting Eurocentric models that predicate America's imaginings of itself, and by rethinking meta-narratives of modernity and border-crossings (2001, p. 114). Yet how might one effectively begin to tackle such a massive task? A pragmatic suggestion lies in the second concept with which I would like to conclude. Alys Weinbaum and Brent Edwards encourage cultural and literary critics to engage in what they call 'critical globality' (2000, pp. 269–70). They write, 'in proposing "critical globality" … we hope to mark the mobilization of a new hermeneutic, a method of reading the idea of the "globe" against the grain, in order to posit a new axis around which a more critical cultural studies might be organized' (p. 270).

In formulating their model of a new hermeneutical paradigm for viewing the world and its relations, Weinbaum and Edwards stress that 'critical globality' describes the process of 'becoming literate in the workings of capitalism and other forms of power' (p. 270) as it marks a historical shift in the ways that globalization catalyses new class formations and reconfigures the boundaries of nation-states (p. 271). The authors also acknowledge that the term needs to be further developed, which is what I have hoped to do throughout this chapter in the context of Madonna-as-geisha. The site of postmodern hermeneutics seems to me a likely place where new tactics of seeing and thinking familiar components of pop culture can benefit from the instability of their signifiers and the fragmentations of their interpretations. It may indeed be that Madonna needs to take more responsibility for the ways that her representations facilitate pan-marketing strategies that exploit other cultures while boosting her record sales. But we can only bemoan the effects of capitalism and orientalism to a certain point – a point at which we risk becoming the very agents of the discourses of marginalization against which we struggle. I do not imply that the singer should avoid responsibility for using ethnic signifiers, but am more invested in the relocation of hermeneutics and critics' own responsibilities in the dissemination of ethnic identities. No amount of criticism of either Madonna or twenty-first-century capitalism can exonerate listeners and viewers from challenging their most beloved notions of the 'authentic', for responsibly coping with globalization demonstrates that re-worlding the oriental also means re-worlding ourselves.

Acknowledgements

Earlier versions of this paper were delivered at the 2002 Design History Conference at the University of Wales, Aberystwyth (UK); the 2002 MELUS-India conference at Osmania University, Hyderabad; the 2001 Cinema Studies Colloquium conference at the University of Washington, Seattle and the 1999 California American Studies Association conference at the University of

California, Santa Cruz. I am grateful to the following mentors for their counsel and support: Bruce Burgett, Johnnella Butler, Michael Cowan, Kate Cummings, Richard Feldstein, Cynthia Fuchs, Robert Miklitsch, Chandan Reddy and Alys Weinbaum. Dialogues with Manthia Diawara and Lisa Patti at the 2002 School for Criticism and Theory at Cornell University helped me to revise my thinking. I also thank Keith Apgar, Jennifer Bendery, David Bradley, Joseph Findeiss and Isaac Phillips. My deepest appreciation, though, is for my sister Sapna, whose love for Madonna's work has critically informed me for many years.

Notes

1. In Chapter 10 in this collection David Gauntlett deals with issues related to Madonna and 'popular feminism'.
2. This is especially the case in light of the outrage publicly expressed by the World Vaishnava Society after Madonna signified her body with the markers of Hindu women, then writhed about in a T-shirt during her 1998 MTV Music Video Awards performance in promotion of *Ray of Light* – the Society demanded an apology from both Madonna and MTV (Luscombe, 1998).
3. Rollingstone.com reports that Madonna's net gross for 2001 was approximately $40.8 million (LaFranco et al., 2002). The British newspaper *The Sunday Times* reported that Madonna was the highest earning pop artist in the UK in 2002, with annual earnings of around £36 million (see the *New Musical Express* online article: 'Material Girl', <http://www.nme.com/news/103386.htm>, last visited 23 January).
4. For an analysis of the use of violence in Madonna's recent work, see Patricia Pisters in this collection (Chapter 2).
5. For a relevant study of Madonna and nationalities, see Chapter 8 in this collection, in which Sean Albiez deals specifically with Americanisms.
6. Random House published the first edition of *Memoirs of a Geisha* in September 1997.
7. Feng shui is the Chinese practice of object placement for optimal energy flows.
8. In February 1999, *Harper's Bazaar* featured a photograph portfolio titled 'Like a Geisha' (Demarchelier, 1999) that showcased Madonna in similar Japanese garments.
9. For an updated retrospective of the consumption of Madonna, see Peñaloza in this collection (Chapter 11).
10. It is worth recalling that when he introduced it Said's notion of orientalism primarily focused on the West's relationship with the Middle East but it has come to signify, in a more general sense, the geographical and cultural binaries between the Occident and the Orient.
11. Pratt (1992) cites the term's first use in the 1940s by Cuban sociologist Fernando Ortiz (1978). Ortiz originally developed the term in describing Afro-Cuban culture in an attempt to move beyond the binary of acculturation/deculturation.

Chapter 8

The day the music died laughing
Madonna and Country

Sean Albiez

> Everyone thinks and writes that I have become a complete Anglophile. They say
> I've got no interest in America ... sometimes you have to go away from
> something to really appreciate and see it ... I certainly have gone through
> periods of thinking, Oh God, you know, I can't deal with America.
> (Madonna quoted in Sischy, 2001a, p. 157)

Madonna's twenty-year career has been founded on the often controversial
appropriation of icons, images and musics derived from the (sub-)cultures of
American and European identity. Through this 'subcultural tourism' (Tetzlaff,
1993, p. 259) she has repeatedly addressed issues of identity and cultural politics.
However, this expedition through alternate ethnic, sexual and gender identities
has left her American national identity and ethnicity relatively unacknowledged.
Madonna is a white, Roman Catholic, northern, urban, half French-Canadian,
half Italian, working-class North American who has transcended her social class
and cultural origins. She has almost consistently refused to address personally or
creatively this litany of specific markers of identity, with the main exception of
her Catholicism. She has embraced her paternal Italian heritage (memorably
asserting 'Italians Do It Better' in the 'Papa Don't Preach' video – Foley, 1986)
but at the expense of her maternal North American roots, reproducing the
patriarchal cycle of the denial of maternal inheritance. After all, we are more able
to recognize Madonna as an Italian-American Ciccone than a French-Canadian
Fortin (her mother's maiden name). Ethnicity and race have been central themes
in much of her work but, arguably, she has been on the whole blind to herself as
a white American. bell hooks specifically has criticized Madonna for this myopia,
encouraging her to look to herself rather than to others in search of an
understanding of cultural politics and power:

> Perhaps when Madonna explores ... memories of her white, working class
> childhood in a troubled family in a way that enables her to understand intimately
> the politics of exploitation, domination and submission, she will have a deeper
> connection with oppositional black culture. If and when this radical critical self-
> interrogation takes place she will have the power to create ... acts of resistance that
> transform rather than simply seduce. (1992b, p. 164)

The academic interrogation of Madonna has focused on her appropriations, subversions and transformations but her motivations in addressing cultural politics are uncertain. She tellingly admits:

> I always approach every project I do with, What am I going to get out of it? What am I going to learn from it? Is it going to challenge me? Is it going to take me to another place? Am I going to grow from it? It always starts there. (Jimenez, 2000)

Recent biographies of Madonna (Taraborrelli, 2001; Morton, 2002) likewise characterize her as selfish and egocentric in motivation, with every decision based on what is good for herself, her career and ambition (and, lately, her children). She is not obviously altruistic and we should be careful of claims that her interventions in cultural politics are more than by-products of a single-minded pursuit of success. The seduction of her demographically diverse audience has been achieved through adroit marketing manoeuvres to broaden her appeal and fan base, and the transformative cultural impact of this work is hard to quantify. Yet, we should not suggest this characterization describes Madonna alone within the music industry, and her consistency of interest in oppressed groups is indicative of a certain political commitment.

By becoming an All-American cowgirl for the promotion of *Music* in 2000, Madonna may have partially begun a new phase of self-analysis, but in what sense is this an interrogation of her ethnicity or nationality? Has she perhaps recognized herself within the All-American cowgirl such that in the early twenty-first century she has felt it necessary to engage with both country (the USA) and Country (music and its associated cultural practices)?

Madonna, the USA and the UK

Madonna's pursuit of self-creation and re-invention works in parallel with the American dream and the foundational myths of American identity. The New World has always represented an opportunity to cut past cultural ties and reconfigure a new national identity that supports freedom, opportunity, meritocracy and democracy – through hard work anybody can become anything or anyone. Madonna reproduces the unfortunate reality of this myth; that it is mainly those with a white European heritage who can fully lay claim to the dream. However, the self-actualization of Madonna closely matches the fundamental philosophy of the United States – to succeed in the face of adversity, to build an identity from the remnants of past conflicts and to embrace the new.

What complicates Madonna's attachment to her nationality and ethnicity is the adoption of England as her home after marriage to Guy Ritchie. This has resulted in her 'dealing with America' while simultaneously adopting a studied English persona. Her self-mocking acceptance speech for the 2001 Brit Awards through an exaggerated Queen's English reflects an awareness of this new 'Britishness' that she has increasingly assumed. Her Scottish wedding at Dornoch Cathedral and Skibo Castle reproduced both the romanticism of the American tourist and the lifestyle of the British monarchy who retreat to Scotland to holiday. Though there was an element of ironic self-parody in the Brit speech, Madonna has fallen for the myths of the British country lifestyle (but apparently not the National Health Service, returning to Los Angeles for the birth of Rocco after criticizing the backward nature of British health care and famously declaring to an American radio station that British hospitals were old and Victorian – see Taraborrelli, 2001, p. 347). Only lately has Madonna begun to locate herself as a white European-American with a matching cultural heritage and reproduced the north-eastern WASP fascination with English and Scottishness. This seems at odds with her French-Canadian and Italian Catholic heritage, but entirely consistent with her tendency to adopt alternate ethnic and national identities. Her adoption of English country life (and the Ritchie aristocratic heritage) inflects her work around America and Country. English country life is a privileged idyll of the well-to-do whereas American Country is a populist form drawing on a specifically working-class heritage. Madonna has formerly distanced herself from Country and what she felt was an unreconstructed, racist and redneck culture (Morton, 2002, p. 212). Yet Madonna is now drawn to both a conservative English country lifestyle that is suspicious of the modernizing tendencies of urban culture, and mainstream conservative elements of American culture against which she has formerly defined herself.

Madonna has rarely wrapped herself (metaphorically or literally) in the American flag, but has often adopted other flags of convenience. For example, changing her kilt during the *Drowned World Tour* (2001) from tartan, to the British Union flag, to the Stars and Stripes; wearing the national football shirt of the country she was playing during *The Girlie Show* tour (1993); criticizing Americans for being unsophisticated when interviewed in Britain, and British workmen for being lazy when speaking to Americans (see, for example, Daly, 2002, p. 168). When she has specifically embraced the American flag, it has been in an undoubtedly ambiguous manner.

In 1990, Madonna's Stars and Stripes-draped contribution to the 'Rock the Vote' campaign (wearing only a flag, underwear and boots) was both an affirmation of liberal representational politics and a youthful send-up of the seriousness of the campaign's message (Mandziuk, 1993, pp. 173–5). Madonna's paradoxical contribution reproduced the notion that American adolescents are both 'violators and precursors of system' (Meyer Spacks, 1981, p. 296) and as such can be trusted to abide by, subvert and contribute to the ongoing renewal of the democratic consensus of American identity. Madonna's characteristic iconoclasm meant she could not easily sustain a serious political address to the American people, finishing the television spot with the line 'If you don't vote, you're gonna get a spanking' (Mandziuk, 1993, p. 174). Madonna then outlandishly failed to vote herself.

During the performance of 'Holiday' in *The Girlie Show* Madonna acted out a military call and response routine with the backdrop of a huge American flag. Both she and her dancers wore long, ceremonial, military trench coats with a red and white-striped lining that alluded to the backdrop. The demand that Australia 'have a good time' was barked out as a command that perhaps suggested only Madonna and America can offer the world this good time. This almost imperialistic display was obviously a parody, but played on America's belief that the world must love the USA as a benevolent provider of global popular culture and protection to the globe; a belief severely shaken in September 2001. After the September 11th attacks on America, Madonna made an intervention at the tail end of her *Drowned World Tour* in the national crisis that engulfed the nation. She opened her postponed Los Angeles show on 13 September wearing a kilt made from the American flag, and called on the audience to pray for President Bush's restraint. She attempted a short, didactic speech on global terrorism followed by a call for a minute's silence that was interrupted by chants of 'USA! USA! USA!': Madonna's response was to distance herself from the overt nationalist sentiment by saying 'if you want the world to change, change yourself'.[1] This refusal to embrace ideologically a US subject position even at this moment of national tragedy (while paradoxically clothing herself in the American flag) is both a testament to Madonna's sincerity in her belief in liberal politics and human rights, and perhaps her inability to accept herself as, in the final analysis, an American. Her donation of $1 million, the proceeds of her Los Angeles shows, to children orphaned by the attacks does indicate something of her non-aligned altruism and compassion.

Madonna and her family temporarily relocated to Los Angeles in late 2002. Her subsequent album and eponymous single *American Life* (2003) promised a critique of contemporary America, but merely pronounced her misgivings with her (celebrity) life. Rather than positioning herself in the American *we*, she sang from the *I* of her unique experience, and this self-conscious strategy was emphasized through her suggestion that the American dream is 'a very powerful illusion and people are caught up in it, including myself. Or I was' (quoted in Rees, 2003, p. 89). The single 'American Life' mapped Madonna's career – her path to success, material gains, entourage of helpers and advisers and her non-aligned religious beliefs. She rails against materialism, and reveals how she has recently woken to the empty illusion of the American dream. But Madonna's perspective is neither 'extreme' (as she suggests) or democratically motivated. Arguably, Shania Twain's 'Ka-Ching!' (2003) was more successful as social commentary in its criticism of the ill-effects of unrestrained consumption and American materialism as experienced by the majority. Madonna's disillusion with *her* experience of the American dream does not result in her withdrawal from public life, but instead heralds the arrival of her latest foray into the global popular music marketplace. Ambivalently and rhetorically she asks whether she is satisfied with her 'American' life suggesting that she believes her ambition is sated, but also that fame and financial success are banal in themselves. Instead of using this moment of heightened awareness to radically reposition herself, she leaves the question of her satisfaction hanging in the ether; apparently happier to pose questions than provide answers no matter how tentative.

However, in the 'American Life' video (Åkerlund, 2003), Madonna ostensibly found a vehicle for her liberal political convictions during the build up to the Iraq War. The video, shot pre-war, represented a military-chic fashion show. Western models, wearing military paraphernalia, are followed onto the catwalk by Middle Eastern child 'victims of war'. Footage of American weaponry in action apparently 'targeting' these children is unequivocally – due to timing and the global political context – an anti-Iraq-War statement. The video also seemed a condemnation of the unethical use of such images by the fashion and news media, while simultaneously and questionably exploiting them in a pop promo. Madonna sings to camera backed by an American flag, and later disrupts the fashion show, leading a group of dancing female paramilitaries to destroy this 'offensive' spectacle. In the final act of the video she throws a grenade/cigar lighter at a seated President Bush look-alike. Despite the obvious allusions to the Iraq War, Madonna initially claimed the video was non-specific and 'anti' the thirty wars taking place across the world at any one time (Rees, 2003, p. 92). This disingenuousness may have marked her discomfort at the prospect of her anti-Bush message hitting international television screens between images of the soon to commence hostilities. By the end of March 2003 after war had begun, Madonna pulled the video, stating that

> I do not believe it is appropriate to air at this time. Due to the volatile state of the world and out of sensitivity and respect to the armed forces, who I support and pray for, I do not want to risk offending anyone who might misinterpret the meaning of this video. (Madonna.com, 31 March 2003)

Unlike her equivocal response to September 11th, when faced with America at war Madonna demonstrated her support for the American and British armed forces, notably without passing comment on the legitimacy of the war. Her motivations for pulling the video may include a reluctant but fundamental patriotism, and fears of a commercial backlash if her *American Life* was denounced as anti-American. Therefore, her deeply uncharacteristic wish not to offend anybody possibly demonstrated her sensitivity to the differences between subverting cultural political norms and meddling in global politics.

Madonna of the trail

So then, what is at stake in Madonna's adoption of the persona of All-American cowgirl? It is first necessary to explore the fundamental importance of the cowgirl/boy myth to American identity in order to appreciate Madonna's appropriation and possible transformation of this myth. But what is equally important is to identify why Country music performers themselves have consciously appropriated the cowgirl/boy image in performance since the 1930s. In the early twentieth century, the National Society of Daughters of the American Revolution placed statues of 'The Madonna of the Trail' at twelve locations on the nineteenth-century Western trails, to celebrate the pioneer women who helped settle the American West. The active role of women in the West, as outlined by Lucey (2002), was underplayed in the 'Cowboy boom' in twentieth-century American popular culture, with women usually represented as homemakers or the victims of Native American or black-hatted brutality. Nineteenth-century Montana-based Evelyn Cameron relished the freedom and challenges the West gave her and other women, writing 'Manual labour … is all I care about, and … is what will really make a strong woman. I like to break colts, brand calves, cut down trees, ride and work in a garden' (Cheney, 2001).

Wright (2001) locates the cowboy, and by implication the cowgirl, as representing American individualism and self-interest based on the maximization of private property, self-preservation and strictly egotistic motivations. The West was democratic, egalitarian, free and provided the opportunity to rise for Americans and immigrant Europeans. Of course, this democracy and equality did not also embrace racial or sexual equality, and white male Europeans were predictably ascendant. It was only through the adoption of the ideologies at the heart of the American dream that women, blacks, Hispanics, Chinese and others were able to promote their own interests. The cowgirl therefore represents the adoption of the American myths of freedom within the Western wide open 'virgin' expanses. However, the cowgirl is a problematic proto-feminist figure, as pioneer women were often denying their sexuality and gender to conform and compete with men, playing them at their own game of market relations and the violent subjugation of difference.

Images of the American wilderness are the backdrop against which American individualism grew (Wright, 2001, p. 187), and these images are continually revisited in American popular culture and lately by Madonna in the 'Don't Tell Me' video (Mondino, 2000) and the Cowboy section of the *Drowned World Tour*. For much of the twentieth century the Western was the most popular film and literary genre of American popular culture. Western iconography remains central to the American experience in the early twenty-first century 'in other areas of culture [such as] clothes, music, dances, rodeos, festivals, vacations, furniture, magazines, advertising [and] art' (Wright, 2001, p. 9).

Since the 1940s Country musicians have transformed and muddied our understanding of the lineage and heritage of Country music through the adoption of Western iconography. The Hollywood singing cowboys (Gene Autry, Tex Ritter, Roy Rogers), Hank Williams and the contemporary Country hat acts (Garth Brooks, Tim McGraw) integrated the Western myth into what is essentially hillbilly mountain music (Tichi, 1994). Peterson (1997) argues that the

Western styling of Country performers, male and female, does not work homologically. Country music generally does not originate in the American West, and Country performers have had little or nothing to do with its geographical, historical or social realities. Country adopted the Western look to counter an inherent American cultural bias against redneck mountain culture, in an attempt to appeal to an urban and national audience. Americans of all regions identified with the cowboy as it 'fitted the American self concept' (see Peterson, 1997, p. 93). Country's adoption of Western style was therefore a marketing strategy which obfuscated its origins, creating an image with dubious authenticity.

Female Country artists also adopted the style. For example, Charline Arthur was an androgynous 1950s rockabilly cowgirl renowned for the irreverence of her provocative performances. Loretta Lynn, an authentic Appalachian mountain girl, pre-empted Madonna's calls for female emancipation in her hymn to the liberatory potential of 'The Pill' (1974). Dolly Parton, a respected Nashville Bluegrass artist and hard-headed business woman, denied the relevance of feminist theory while arguing for personal freedom through self-actualization – a creed not far removed from Madonna's.[2] Madonna is therefore a 'new kid on the block' when it comes to overt image manipulation, a strong head for business and cultural controversy. These Country cowgirls, among many others, proved the ability of women to succeed in their own terms long before Madonna entered the cultural scene (Bufwack and Oermann, 1993). As a cowgirl, Madonna may be parodying and criticizing Country, while missing the irony of her implicit critique of these women. What is crucial to understand is that the cowgirl was not born of vaudeville or Country music as a cross-dressing male/female expression of mythic fantasy and desire, but is a real and vital historical figure and has become an enduring American myth. Like Madonna in the present, when female and male Country artists adopted the Western costume they were undertaking a parodic commentary on this myth while recognizing the potency of the cowboy/girl in the wider culture. Madonna, and Country artists past and present, have recast and utilized the myth as a way to ensure they are a more saleable commodity, perpetuating the currency of this enduring cultural icon. Madonna's specific strategy may have been to tap into the late 1990s success of contemporary female Country artists such as Shania Twain, Faith Hill, LeAnn Rimes, Gillian Welch and the Dixie Chicks.

Madonna does not overtly question or acknowledge the darker side of the individualist cowboy myth (white, male, heterosexual supremacy), and clearly connects with the private, selfish and strictly egotistic motivations of the pioneer European. She has been absolutely reliant on the promise of the American dream as embodied in these American icons. Madonna may have culturally challenged the white, male, north-eastern hegemony of North American social and cultural values, but she has personally benefited from being a metaphorical cowgirl. The statues of 'The Madonna of the Trail' are therefore significant as Madonna has more in common with pioneer Western women than she probably cares to acknowledge through the filter of her liberal politics and global perspectives.

Parody and pastiche

Before moving on, it is important to clarify the parodic terms of engagement of Madonna's work. Jameson claimed it is unfeasible within postmodern culture to talk of parody due to the relativistic nature of cultural value in the flattened cultural hierarchy of postmodernism (1991, p. 17). He argues that there is no normative critical ground from which a specific parodic stance can be taken on a cultural form or practice. Parody can only work if it is measured against a normative set of values, either to ridicule conservatively the new that threatens the established order, or to radically subvert the old through parodic iconoclasm. Jameson prefers the term 'pastiche' to describe the late capitalist prevalence of 'blank parody', but also recognizes that parody, despite the lack of a cultural dominant from which to measure its critical stance, can still be 'more or less playful, critical, ironic, or empty' (see Dentith, 2000, p. 162). From this perspective, Madonna has no stable position from which we can treat her parodic engagement as critical. Her strategy therefore is arguably merely play or pastiche rather than directed critique. Though Madonna's consistent identity transformations and appropriations make her critical position on the USA difficult to ascertain, there is consistency in the specific identification she has made with the subcultural margins of American culture and other ethnic identities (English, Latin-American, Japanese). Madonna therefore uses the margins and her recent adoption of an English upper middle-class identity as critical ground from which to question American hierarchies and values with contradictory and complex outcomes.

Jameson's work on parody is unhelpful as his contention that parody is unachievable – leaving us merely with pastiche – assumes we are crushed by a *flattened world* (see Dentith, 2000, p. 162), where no hierarchy of value remains from which to criticize or engage with culture through parody. It may be more useful to suggest that we are immersed in a *drowned world* where parodic intertextuality does not simply operate in a rhizomic Deleuzian manner, but also in a complex multi-dimensional depth across postmodern popular culture. Within this depth we must strategically assess each parodic act on its own terms, locating it in its specific historical, social and cultural contexts, allowing a mapping of such parodic interventions. It can also be argued that intentionality in parody is not inherent as creative acts always implicitly and explicitly critique former genres, forms and practices. Madonna may have had few clear strategic parodic intentions in her turn to America, but we can interpret and strategically (re)construct the meaning of her work as parodic transformation. Parody as a mode of cultural engagement still has currency, though we need to use it tentatively, and this is well demonstrated in Dentith's suggestion that 'parody includes any cultural practice which provides a relatively polemical allusive imitation of another cultural production or practice' (2000, p. 9). Madonna certainly has polemically alluded to a field of contemporary American experience that she has been previously alienated from in engaging with both country and Country. We may not be able to second-guess Madonna's intentions and motivations, but we can characterize her work as parody. Pastiche is not a particularly useful concept, as all creative acts to a greater or lesser extent are an implicit parodic critique of that which came before due to their inherent inter-textuality, whether or not there is clear authorial intent.

The millennial All-American techno-cowgirl

From 'American Pie' (2000) onwards, Madonna has reflected on the diversity of American identity and the overarching myths of the American dream with ambivalence, ambiguity and discomfort. This exploration may have its origin and critical perspective in an exhaustion of other 'marginal' identities and the perspective that English exile has afforded her. Whatever the origins, there is clear evidence that Madonna has returned to America from 'within' its margins while paradoxically keeping physically distant from it. As a result, Madonna has at the turn of the century engaged with the iconography of America, the West and the Country music formation.[3]

'American Pie' (2000)

In 1971, Don McLean's 'American Pie' represented a key moment in American popular culture where, after late 1960s psychedelic rock, a more spiritual, honest and self-consciously authentic voice was developing in American singer/songwriter folk and Country rock. This was a voice that spoke nostalgically about 1950s Rock & Roll (reflecting on the death of Buddy Holly – 'the day the music died') and black Rhythm & Blues with an evident sense of generational bereavement (the post-war baby boomers then hitting mid-twenties adulthood). 'American Pie' represented a desire for a return to a time of certainties before counter-cultural challenges to mainstream American values, and a fixed consensual sense of national identity and purpose. It is a deeply conservative song which also attempts to acknowledge the importance of the previous decade's struggles and maps the development of Rock & Roll into 'Rock' – music with pretensions to cultural weight that perhaps had lost sight of the fun of Rock & Roll. 'American Pie' is about the death of Rock & Roll, possibly Rock (and probably Brian Jones, Janis Joplin and Jim Morrison, though Lester Bangs felt the word play of the song could mean everything and nothing (1996, p. 130)), and hope of a spiritual and musical rebirth. The film *American Graffiti* (Lucas, 1973) realized the vision of 'American Pie' by concretizing the nostalgic emotional and cultural perspective of the early 1970s, looking backwards but knowing that inevitably we move on relentlessly through time – nowhere more so than in the fields of fashion and popular music.

The recording of 'American Pie' by Madonna was suggested by Rupert Everett due to the song's role in *The Next Best Thing* (Schlesinger, 2000), in which the actors co-starred. The song has been treated as a secular hymn to youth by its American fans and Madonna's version predictably received mixed responses as a kind of sacrilege. Due to the song's themes it appeared an odd choice for Madonna. Acknowledging her consistent identification with the voices of the post-1960s counter-cultural margins, and her challenges to the All-American golden age represented in 'American Pie', the song marked a considerable cultural dis-re-location for Madonna. The song perhaps represents Madonna ceasing to live in the egocentric now of relationships, self-reflexivity and personal exploration (à la *Ray of Light* (1998)), and reaching out to her national culture and its icons and myths for creative sustenance. This appropriation seemed more essentially legitimate than others in her career, as she apparently reclaimed her national heritage through 'American Pie' and her later transformation into the All-American cowgirl.

If in the 'American Pie' video (Stolzol, 2000) Madonna is suggesting America is heterogeneous and diverse without an authentic core, does she place most Americans as excluded from the table of authenticity? Is she reiterating the alienation that gay, black and Hispanic Americans feel while simultaneously alienating 'mainstream America' from the foundations of American identity? The video for 'American Pie' seems to address this with a simple answer that all subject identities are valid aspects of American life and none should be ascendant. The video is mostly in split screen with tiara-wearing 'princess' Madonna performing a playful rendition of the song while dancing exuberantly behind, around and in front of a large American flag on what looks like the stage of a rural village hall (actually shot in England, giving this performance ironic nuances in its representation of homecoming). Madonna seems to reiterate and revisit some of the discomfort she felt in the 1990 'Rock the Vote' television spot by marching, saluting the audience and then irreverently showing us her buttock cleavage to undercut any sense that we view her as seriously taking on the persona of proud American. The rest of the video consists of split screen tracking shots of most possible permutations of regional, class, age, sexual, occupational, subcultural and gender identity at large in the American subcontinent. They are shot in front of American flags, bowling alleys, small town churches, suburban and urban streets. The participants look impassive, troubled or sombre, but are rarely smiling. We are led to believe that the American people are on the whole anxious, distressed or quietly proud. Only Madonna, a former cheerleader, and a college cheerleading team seem at all happy about the prospect of being American at the beginning of the twenty-first century. The video, shot in 2000, does feel at times prescient due to its celebration of the 'the people as heroes' of American society (fire-fighters included) and seems to pre-empt the national embrace of the American flag in the sombre mood post-September 11th. However, the video suggests nothing more profound than the belief that all Americans are equal and valid individuals who should be treated with respect whatever their subjectivity. This liberal message, enshrined in the constitution but meted out variably across American society, seems an abnegation of cultural-political responsibility. If Madonna were a political radical, she would have ensured the video represented more openly the inequities and economic divide at the heart of post-governmental corporate America.

Madonna's 'American Pie' is therefore a simple visual restatement of liberal politics and individualism within the national context. The conservative treatment of the song, with its religiosity, nostalgia and sombre assessment of the national Zeitgeist suggests Madonna has little to add and nowhere to go as a cultural radical. She could genuinely embrace oppositional politics to mark herself as definitively radical in the early twenty-first century, but has instead embraced the trappings of an English aristocratic lifestyle. Maybe it is because American cultural studies, critical pedagogy and Madonna's transformative agenda have succeeded in repositioning the margins at the centre, with the oppositional becoming the norm in American popular culture, that she now needs to look elsewhere to construct a commentary or critique of America. Where were the equivalent of burning crosses, the perversion of bigoted values, the images of abject poverty and social despair? Mainly hidden behind the ubiquitous American flags of the video, it would seem. *The Next Best Thing* dealt more clearly with issues around American family values and gay sexuality, demonstrating Madonna's continued commitment to the exploration of such themes. But such a critical engagement was absent from the 'American Pie' video, with gay and lesbian kisses causing only mild controversy due to their innocuous, honest and underplayed treatment. Instead of oppositional cultural politics, Madonna turned next to mainstream Americana to explore her relationship to the nation portrayed in 'American Pie'.

Music *and the cyberroundupinstallation (2000)*

Released in September 2000, *Music* is vibrantly packaged using images and a typographical style that are immersed in the iconography of the West (as designed by Jean Baptiste Mondino). The design and visual impact owes a good deal to Miss Rodeo America and Lisa Eisner's book *Rodeo Girl* (2000). Miss Rodeo America, part rodeo and part beauty pageant, began in 1955. The cowgirls of these rodeos are alluring remixes of the American past and cowgirl/boy iconography of the twentieth century. The rodeo women embody a nostalgic American cultural and sexual desire. They are dazzlingly glamorous and astoundingly inauthentic in their representation of the past and present of rural American life in the West. These images are for many the source of the recent focus on the reinvention and co-optation of Western style in the fashion world (and by Madonna), and are so rich they almost blind us to the origins, sources and heritage of this style.

For *Music*, Mondino utilizes over-saturated colour images of Madonna as a hyper-real urban/rural cowgirl. Madonna adopts a club version of the Western look while standing in the street outside a single level suburban dwelling, alternately striking a pose, sipping a milkshake and scrutinizing an acoustic guitar. In-between times she is sleeping in a haystack wearing an elaborately embroidered shirt, a pink Stetson with a tiara around the brim, jeans and sequined shoes. The red sequined shoe on the backplate of the CD is an obvious allusion to Dorothy in *The Wizard of Oz* (Fleming, 1939), and her plaintive cries of 'there's no place like home' seem apposite in an album drenched in rural Americana and which embodies Madonna's American homecoming. Fragments of the lyrics of 'Music' are presented over several pages of the CD booklet in a Country and Western nineteenth-century poster font. A repeated image of a cowboy on a bucking bronco specifically ties these images to Miss Rodeo America, though by representing a male rather than a female rider. This, and the overt glamorization of the Western look indicates Madonna is not making any explicit connection with the historical cowgirl to subvert the cowboy myth. But she implicitly parodies the cultural fantasy embodied in this iconic style that is rooted firmly in America's founding myths, and is (still) the popular dress of large sections of the American people, from Presidents to cowhands. Eisner's cowgirls match Madonna rhinestone for rhinestone, and as such Madonna is adopting and popularizing a fashion already in club and mainstream American fashion culture. She further elaborates the style in the video for 'Music' (Åkerlund, 2000) in a specifically ghetto fabulous urban/club setting. What is significant is that Madonna here has turned to Americana, underlining her interest in exploring her relationship to mainstream America through a fashion and cultural style that is rich and multi-layered in its meaning.

The music of *Music* is consistent with this de/reconstruction of Western iconography. Very little in the album announces itself as Country music per se, but the turn to acoustic instrumentation within a digital environment and songwriting that alludes to acoustic singer-songwriting ('I Deserve It', 'Nobody's Perfect', 'Don't Tell Me' and 'Gone') mixes the organic with future machine music, with implicit and explicit allusions to Kraftwerk in 'Music'. This locates Madonna's engagement with Country not as nostalgia but as a contemporary attempt to reconstruct a cyber-folk sensibility, with the introspective environment of these songs cybernetically coupled to digital studio technology and the global audience. Madonna was to further explore this in her promotional mini-tour and webcast at the end of 2000. In November 2000, Dolce and Gabbana created an environment they called a 'Cyberroundupinstallation' which attempted to further elaborate the techno-Western persona of Madonna for her New York launch of *Music* and London Brixton Academy webcast. The Wild West theme park presented a hyper-real vision of a contemporary frontier town with barbecues, beauty pageants, mechanical bulls, a saloon and orbiting horseshoes. This Italian take on the contemporary American West resonates with Sergio Leone's hyper-real spaghetti Western filmic environment in the 1960s, and with the techno-theme park aesthetic of *Westworld* (Crichton, 1973). Dolce stated 'the idea was to create a young person's take on anything Western, add glamorous touches and not take anything literally. Even our haystacks and horses are made of gold' (quoted in Robson, 2000). After performing in this Disney-esque Western playground Madonna went on to further develop the cowgirl in a more complex way for the 'Don't Tell Me' video and the *Drowned World Tour* cowgirl section.

'Don't Tell Me' (2000)

The 'Don't Tell Me' video (again created by Mondino) further questions the cowboy/girl as an American icon, the myths of the American West and Madonna's relationship to them. The video represents three separate levels of experience or reality. West-world 1 is that which Madonna occupies – the performance space of the studio. West-world 2 is the back-projection before which Madonna performs and West-world 3 is the roadside advertising poster site within the Western landscape, which also suggests a drive-in movie screen due to its moving images. Madonna occupies only the ersatz studio space, walking, dancing or riding a mechanical bucking bronco. She walks to camera dressed in an everyday low key, plaid flannel shirt, jeans, boots and dirt, dressed up only with a large buckled belt, representing the West as authentic reality. She dances wearing a hyper-Western-styled black leather shirt and suede chaps costume, representing the West as inauthentic performance. She rides the mechanical bronco wearing a red printed vest top and brown leather tasselled trousers, representing the West as a vicariously experienced cultural playground akin to the Cyberroundupinstallation. Her physical removal or alienation from the open spaces of the West parallels her previous distancing from these aspects of American culture, and represents her at a borderline or frontier that is difficult to traverse.

The cowboy dancers, however, have the licence to roam between these spaces. The video incorporates images of contemporary Country and Western culture with Madonna/Mondino demonstrating the dichotomy of authenticity and inauthenticity in Western iconography through the device of an image within an image (within an image). The posterized/drive-in movie Marlboro Men in denim, clean tucked-in shirts and pristine hats are portrayed dancing alone, and then in competition, placing this key twentieth-century cowboy icon up for interrogation as an inauthentic cultural construct more at home in the world of advertising than on the American plains. When these dancers join Madonna, they too have adopted a club version of Western style and are in black, switching from line dancing in unison with Madonna to offering their pelvic areas to her in deferential subjugation. The dancers have moved from the 'authentic' Marlboro world into an inauthentic contradictory ill-defined space in support of Madonna's performance. The cowboys seem to have thwarted Madonna's attempts to keep a critical distance from Western culture, while she has subverted them by meeting them only on her own terms, and in apparel that would be more at home in a gay club than in a honky-tonk bar.

Yet Madonna's West-world 1 is still located in a studied pseudo-studio space which we are constantly reminded of as the camera tracks backwards to reveal the artifice involved in representing the rich and intoxicating American Western landscape. We are reminded of the measured and constructed nature of this 'reality' which is shown to be highly fraudulent. By implication we are also reminded that the seductive myths of the American West are equally inauthentic. If West-world 1 is so bogus, how much more so are the Baudrillardian simulations of West-world 2 and 3, which represent the filmic and advertising media through which the visual myths of the West are perpetuated? A cowboy rodeo rider in full tasselled costume is continually intercut in slow motion throughout the video and is finally unseated/dethroned as the video ends. This suggests Madonna's debunking of the potency of the cowboy myth as well as questioning its specifically male and camp nature which, as has been demonstrated, exscribes cowgirls from the history of the American West. Madonna/Mondino perpetuates this exscription by failing to have a single cowgirl in her video, but this is maybe an attempt to underline the homoerotic aspects of the myth. The contemporary American moment is therefore demonstrated to be still fascinated by the archetypal cowboy and indicates the importance of Madonna's parody of aspects of this culture in the present. Line dancing, after all, is a systematized parody of frontier and square dancing, and Madonna's choreographed parodic critique of this 'folk' dance allows us to track back and identify the deceit in formalizing spontaneous dance into an invented American tradition.

The Drowned World Tour – *the cowgirl section*

For the *Drowned World Tour* Madonna further explored Country iconography. She wrote a parody of an 'old school' honky-tonk Country and Western track called 'The Funny Song'. She adopted, not always successfully and, as will be argued below, problematically, a southern drawl for the Country section of the show. Madonna wore a version of 'trailer park' chic, with a Stars and Stripes vest top, embroidered jeans, cowboy boots and a racoon's tail. She also donned a cutaway acoustic guitar as a badge of folk/Country authenticity. Choreographed line-dancing and an onstage mechanical bull sustained the visual themes introduced in the 'Don't Tell Me' video. Back projections of lonely American desert landscapes and highways (referencing *Easy Rider* (Hopper, 1969), *Paris, Texas* (Wenders, 1984) and *Thelma and Louise* (Scott, 1991)) were representative of Madonna's further journey into the wilderness and heartland of the myths of America. Dancing in unison around Madonna were multiple 'Marlboro men/women/whatever' of diverse ethnic origin, which scrutinized the under-played reality of ethnic and gender diversity in the historical American West, while alluding to the representation of America's need to embrace its diversity in the 'American Pie' video.

In this section of the show, Madonna opens up questions around authenticity central to Country. Country is diverse and has its own set of internal debates about authenticity, such as Alt. Country being recognized as an anti-Nashville punk-inspired oppositional Country, and the Americana Music Association supporting Bluegrass and heritage Country in Nashville itself. Madonna may not have intended to engage with these issues, but by drawing on folk/Country stylings within overtly synthetic Electronica, the question of musical authenticity opened up in *Music* is further explored. The plastic-wrapped bales of hay Madonna used as a seat during this section of the performance stand as metaphors for the music of *Music* and as indicators of the difficulty in nailing down the authentic. They do this both as a representation of the artificially constructed nature of Madonna's relationship to the organic of folk and Country music in her cowgirl character, and as a representation of the preservation of the organic within this music. Contemporary Country music also walks this line of preservation and re-invention. The parody of Western iconography within the cowboy section of the tour is both a critique and a celebration of aspects of this 'authentic' culture. However, Madonna's critique results in a problematic set of outcomes, not least in her replication of the anti-rural prejudice that has long been at the heart of urban America's attitudes to Country, and Country's attitudes to its origins.

Madonna, through her tone and the vocal inflection of 'The Funny Song' in the *Drowned World Tour,* replicates the northern (urban) disdain for southern (rural) culture that is a key issue in understanding American identity. Madonna becomes regionalist and perpetuates the long American tradition of denigrating the rural redneck, as a result of which Country adopted Western iconography while retaining its accent. It can be argued that in revisiting America, Madonna reproduces the ideological divide at the heart of North American identity, and in choosing a side, alienates not only Southerners, but also the swathe of working-class and lower middle-class white Americans of all regions who look to Country as a vehicle for their dreams, hopes and desires. I would argue that by mocking the culture of these people, Madonna reproduces northern urban intellectual elitism. Madonna's music suddenly dies laughing, like a stand up comedian telling a joke without any inclination of the punch line. The difficulty in understanding Madonna's attempt at parody here is that

The question of the cultural politics of parody is comparable to that of the cultural politics of laughter, which has likewise been claimed both for anti-authoritarian irreverence and as a means of ridiculing and stigmatising the socially marginal and the oppressed. (Dentith, 2000, p. 28)

Madonna irreverently questions the American cowgirl/boy myth while simultaneously ridiculing and stigmatizing the culture of a perpetually denigrated cultural grouping – poor white America. We cannot clearly demarcate a particular punch line that would orientate Madonna's parodic critique, and there are probably many possible conflicting punch lines with the laughter travelling in more than one direction. But if the laughter never materializes due to the ineptitude of the delivery of the joke, the comedian is said to die in the full glare of audience scrutiny.

Why is this apparently innocuous parody of Country so significant? The answer can be found in the role Country has played in the lives of Americans. As Bufwack and Oermann have suggested, Country music is a repository of the lived experience of poor America, which

is a window into the world of the majority of American women. It describes poverty, hardship, economic exploitation, sexual subjugation, and limited opportunities. But it also contains outspoken protest and joyful rebellion. The history of women's country music reveals a rich vein of positive images, self-assertive lyrics, and strong female performers. (1993, p. x)

Madonna's 'The Funny Song' therefore takes on significance due to its lightweight and ill-considered treatment of themes at the heart of Country. The narrative alludes to the symbolic barbecuing of her father's bones after finding him shot through the head, and is sung in an accent that demonstrates perceptible contempt for rural America(ns) and could suggest an ignorance of the depth and history of critical working class women's Country music. Madonna attempts to introduce a narrative of female rebellion into the Country form, when in fact such rebellion has always been a feature of Country music. The song reveals a certain unawareness of the significance of such ignorance when it comes to the amplification and reproduction of anti-rural, poor, white working-class values, and possibly the belittling of the female experience in the West. It is telling that Madonna quickly dropped the song from her *Drowned World Tour* set after September 11th due to its banal violence.

This is dangerous territory for Madonna to become enmeshed within as she perhaps perpetuates some of the prejudices that have a long history in American popular culture. 'As early as the 1840s, popular literature and entertainment had created negative stereotypes of poor white Southerners. Folk humorists characterised male mountaineers as degenerate, inbred, illiterate, dirty, immoral, drunken, foolish, shiftless, and lawless and their female counterparts as pipe smoking, snuff dipping, work-laden, slutty and ugly' (Bufwack and Oermann,

1993, p. 24). This stereotype may no longer be ubiquitous but it is still present within American popular culture even if it is now more variably deployed. The poor swamp- or mountain-dwelling southerner has been inflected differently in films such as the Loretta Lynn biopic *Coal Miner's Daughter* (Apted, 1980) and *Southern Comfort* (Hill, 1981), and the stereotype challenged through the celebration of the dignity of these people, their heritage and culture. This has been most notable in the recent revival of mountain music in the Country world, specifically seen in the success of the Bluegrass and old-school Country of the *O Brother, Where Art Thou?* (Coen Brothers, 2000) soundtrack album at the 2001 Country Music Association awards.

Conclusions

Madonna's engagement with country and Country can be read as a political act that argues for the recognition of American diversity and heterogeneity over the traditional American quest to subsume difference within national uniformity. Paradoxically, Madonna replicates through parody the elitist values that inform the cultural and social hierarchy of class in the United States. These contradictory outcomes are in the nature of parody, and as outlined by Rose:

> most parody worthy of the name is ambivalent towards its targets ... entail[ing] ... a mixture of criticism and sympathy ... the way in which its comedy can laugh both at and with its target, may be traced to the way in which the parodist makes the object of the parody a part of the parody's structure. (1995, pp. 51–2)

Madonna parodies by co-opting, appropriating, recontextualizing and transforming aspects of Americana through the integration of elements of Western style into the structure of her creative works. In 2000–2001 Madonna overtly looked to her American heritage and engaged in a critical assessment of the seductive icons and myths of the American West with both 'sympathy and criticism'. However, Madonna reproduced through tone and perhaps ignorance the denigration of the culture of poor, rural America and the Country culture of many American people. The ambivalence of her attitudes to America are inherent in parody as a strategy, and as Dentith suggests, parody is always 'politically and socially multivalent; its particular uses are never neutral' (2000, p. 28). By parodying the parody of Western style, while adopting elements of Country authenticity, Madonna may be signalling both a desire to ground herself in her white American ethnicity and the problematics of ethnic and national essentialism, a continual theme in the transformations she has undertaken in her own life and career. She also forces us to recognize her personal investment in the American dream as a free-roaming cowgirl expressing herself across the wide open plains of global popular culture.

Notes

1. News stories around Madonna's response to the September 11th tragedy are archived at <www.madonnarama.com/arc8-2001.shtml>, last visited 1 August 2002.
2. Parton's resistance to feminist perspectives were expressed in the programme 'Did I shave my legs for this' (BBC Radio 4, 1 January 2002). Programme produced by Nick Barraclough for Smooth Operations and presented by Liz Kershaw.
3. The 'Country formation' is a concept transposed from Grossberg's 'Rock formation' (1994, p. 41). Neither 'Country' nor 'Rock' as specifically *cultural* formations can be reduced to music alone – both are a complex multi-layered interplay of practices, material culture, technology, fashion, mediation, language and music formed at the intersections and interfaces of industry, text and audience. Therefore Madonna engages with the 'Country formation' but not directly with 'Nashville'.

Chapter 9

Crossing the border(line)
Madonna's encounter with the Hispanic

Santiago Fouz-Hernández

'Hispanic' is one of five ethnic labels adopted by the North American Office of Budget and Management in the late 1970s that, together with other widely generic terms such as 'white', 'black', 'Asian or Pacific' or 'American Indian/Alaskan Native' seem to separate neatly the citizens of the USA on a racial basis (Gracia and De Greiff, 2000, p. 8). Officially, the term 'Latino' (often used interchangeably with 'Hispanic') includes 'persons from Mexico, Central and South America and the Spanish-speaking Caribbean' (Ortiz, 1997, p. xvi) but, as Martín Alcoff has noted, 'Hispanic' has been commonly used in the North American media since the 1960s 'to identify all people of Latin American and even Spanish descent' as a coherent group and, especially, the thirty million or so who live in the USA (2000, p. 29). Needless to say, this 'conveniently' inclusive (and yet highly 'exclusivist') term is hugely problematic, as it ignores the differences and cultural richness of those peoples who fall under such an imposed category. As Mendieta writes, Latinos 'certainly did not begin with these categories' but 'learn to think through them as we become part of the society and culture of the U.S. political structure' (2000, p. 47). He points out that, 'Latin Americans are not just *criollos* or mestizos [but] also mulatos and *negros* … [a mixture] of Spanish, Portuguese, Amerindian, and African' (p. 52), or, as Abalos graphically puts it, '*de colores*' (2001, p. 47).[1]

Oboler has traced the current labelling and degradation of Spanish-speaking people in the USA to the nineteenth century, when newly formed nations struggled to form an identity, which, in the case of the USA, relied heavily on racialized ideological projections of (WASP) superiority and (non-WASP) inferiority – as opposed to birthplace (1997, pp. 32–47). She argues that

> the differentiated experiences and response to the conquest of the South West … reduced both rich and poor to a homogeneous image of all Latin American population as 'Mexicans' who were 'idle', 'shiftless', 'fatalistic' and 'resigned' … described [by nineteenth-century politicians] as '… ignorant, degraded, demoralised and priest-ridden'; an image that was projected nationwide … [and] extended to

include all Spanish-speaking people in the hemisphere and continued to shape both the direction of US police and popular prejudices toward people with ties to Latin America well into the twentieth century. (1997, pp. 47–9)

Oboler's line of arguing is clearly applicable to other racial minorities in the USA, but here she demonstrates the particularly wide dislocation of Hispanics from the broader society there. Perhaps as a defence strategy, and unlike other immigrants in the USA, second and third generations still use Spanish as their main language (Nelson and Tienda, 1997, p. 8).

Much has been written about Madonna's subversion, deconstruction and inversion of gender. With a few exceptions (hooks, 1992a and 1993; Nakayama and Peñaloza, 1993; Patton, 1993; and some of the authors contributing to this collection), critics have paid far less attention to her deconstruction of ethnic identities. Those critics who have done so often relate to these issues as secondary points in essays that focus on camp (Curry, 1990; Robertson, 1996), sex (most of the essays in Frank and Smith, 1993a; Metzstein, 1993) or postmodernity (Tetzlaff, 1993; Freccero, 1999). Furthermore, very little has been written about her take on the Hispanic, which is perhaps the most influential and re-visited 'ethnic' style in her work. Almost every year since 1984 and up to 2003, Madonna has presented either a song, video, photo shoot or live performance displaying a Hispanic influence (Blake, 1993) and she has recorded and performed in Spanish some of her hit singles.

As discussed in the introduction to this book, it has become common place in both academic and journalistic criticism on Madonna to describe her subcultural practices as 'an appropriation of style rather than a substantive politics' (Robertson, 1996, p. 133). Yet most of this criticism, although apparently aware of the obvious implications of commerciality and longevity, seems to bypass the fact that Madonna herself, often hailed as the All-American girl, is in fact half Italian, half French-Canadian and the mother of a half-Hispanic girl. Hence, and despite the recent reinforcement of her Anglo-American identity (especially by means of her marriage to Guy Ritchie in 2000), issues of race, ethnicity and 'national identity' are not exactly unproblematic in her case. Could we interpret her appropriations of, say, Latino or Black culture as a reminder of the multi-racial and multi-cultural make-up of the USA, and indeed of herself as an example of this? If we go a step further, we could argue that Madonna's temporary ethnic transformations form an interesting site in which to explore the thesis that, like gender and sexuality, ethnicity can also be performed (as some of the contributors to Zack, 1997 argue).[2] In this chapter, I will examine each of the stages of Madonna's Hispanic explorations, from mere flirting with Latino men (in the video 'Borderline'), to an arguable involvement in Latino/Spanish culture (in the video 'La Isla Bonita'), and a fetishization of and dissociation from the Spanish Other (in the videos 'Take a Bow' and 'You'll See') to their culmination in her role as perhaps the most famous and powerful Hispanic female icon of all times, Eva Perón.

Borderline: the early years

Madonna's personal interest in Hispanic/Spanish music, art, culture and men is well documented. Not only is the Hispanic influence reflected in her work but it has also had an important influence in her life. Madonna herself has talked about her early links with the Hispanic communities in New York, describing this time of her life with passion: 'I'm very influenced by Spanish music. When I lived in New York for so many years I was constantly listening to salsa and merengue. I mean, that stuff was constantly blaring out of everybody's radio on the street' (quoted in Zollo, 1989).

According to Andersen, shortly after her arrival in New York, Madonna worked and socialized mostly with Hispanic and black people at the American Dance Center (1999, p. 89).[3] She confessed to having rushed the writing of 'Into the Groove' (1985) because 'there was this gorgeous Puerto Rican boy sitting across from me that I wanted to go out on a date with, and I just wanted to get over it' (*FHM*, 1995, p. 93).[4] Two important elements of Madonna's Hispanic connection arise here: the association of Latinos with the streets or public spaces (as evidenced by the early videos that I am about to discuss) and the Latino as an object of desire. The latter aspect is also documented in the film *Truth or Dare* (Keshishian, 1991) – where she declared her interest in Spanish actor Antonio Banderas – and in some of the photographs and stories in her book *Sex* (1992). Real-life Hispanic links include two of her most important relationships: with DJ 'Jellybean' Benitez in the early 1980s (to whom she nearly got married (Connelly, 1997, p. 34)) and with Carlos León in the mid-1990s (the Cuban-born, New York-bred fitness trainer who would become the father of her first child).

In *Madonnarama* (a collection of academic essays published in response to Madonna's book *Sex* and its 'crucial ingredients – sex, race, power and capital' (Frank and Smith, 1993a, p. 13)), Champagne, Lentz and hooks criticize what they regard as Madonna's abuse of power in relation to ethnic minorities in her book. hooks refers specifically to the episode in which Madonna/Dita has a sexual experience with a young, virgin Puerto Rican boy. She reads Dita's comment that he 'gave [her] crabs' as an example of Madonna's 'narrative of pure white womanhood contaminated by contact with the colored "Other"' (hooks, 1993, p. 77). This type of judgement is not unjustified. However, aspects of gender and sex interrelate here and one could easily fall into the trap of over-reading Madonna's treatment of men from ethnic minorities whilst ignoring similar uses and abuses of white men, both in *Sex* and in other examples of her work. Amongst other things, hooks's argument itself perpetuates white supremacy by reaffirming white men as the norm exempt from scrutiny. On the other hand, there are also many positive comments about the Puerto Rican boy, with whom Dita had 'awesome ... excellent' sex, 'probably the most erotic sex [she] ever had'. And yet, despite the undeniable stereotypical potential of those remarks (Latino men as sexual beasts), the characterization of the boy as inexperienced, smooth and 'not very big' defuses and confuses such a stereotype.

These issues provide a useful background for the discussion of one of Madonna's first videos, 'Borderline' (Lambert, 1984), described in *Rolling Stone* as 'pretty straightforward' narratively:

> Boy and girl enjoy simple pleasures of barrio love, girl is tempted by fame (in the person of a British photographer), boy gets huffy, girl gets famous, but her new beau's out-of-line reaction to a behavioral trifle (all she did was to spray-paint his expensive sports car) drives her back to her true love. (*Rolling Stone*, 1997, p. 223)

Yet the clip attracted early critical attention from academics. In a short analysis, Paglia argued that the competition between the Latino boyfriend and the intrusive British photographer in the video presents 'the new dualities of her life: the gritty, multiracial street and the club scene that she had haunted in obscurity and poverty, and her new slick, fast world of popularity and success' (1999, p. 163). This duality is well established in the clip through the men's opposing worlds, in which the Latino men are relegated to the streets and the bar, and the British man is situated in a safer, private space (his studio – with all its associations of productivity and success). The 'British space' is pretentiously decorated with a classical image of masculinity – a Roman-style statue of a nude soldier holding a spear erect – and a series of phallic Palladian columns that, together with the flashy sports car and combat trousers, stand for his position of strength and financial (phallic) power. In sheer contrast, the phallic symbols associated with the Latino man are a shabby street lamp, and a pool cue that he pointedly holds erect while negotiating a possible come-back with the white girl. This, like the virginity and the emphasis on oral – not penetrative – sex in the episode of the Puerto Rican boy in *Sex*, is an ironic statement on Hispanic men, which, as noted by Skeggs, usually 'signify sexually powerful masculinities' (1993, p. 69).

Indeed, as Mirandé has argued, whilst a certain macho attitude applied to Anglo-American entertainers, athletes and other stars can be regarded as positive, signifying 'strength, virility, masculinity and sex appeal' (1997, p. 66), machismo in Latino men is often interpreted as negative, related to 'male dominance, patriarchy, authoritarianism and ... spousal abuse' (p. 66). This attitude was reflected in one study of university students from different ethnic backgrounds who were asked to interpret the 'Borderline' video (Nakayama and Peñaloza, 1993). Both Hispanic and Caucasian respondents emphasized the machismo side of Hispanic cultures. Whilst Hispanics claimed to understand the concept of the video better than non-Latinos (not necessarily agreeing with machismo but understanding it (p. 47)), the Caucasians used the machismo and the portrayal of (non-white) 'gangs' as the basis of their negative assessment of the clip (p. 50).

With the video in mind, the song's lyrics ('Something in the way you love me won't let me be / I don't want to be your prisoner so baby won't you set me free') could be interpreted as a rebellion against the male chauvinistic ways of the

Latino, who (unsuccessfully) tries to stop her from working with the British man. Interestingly, studies on the negative implications of machismo have found that 'the origins of excessive masculine displays and the cult of masculinity in … Latino countries can be traced to the Spanish Conquest, as the powerless colonized man attempted to compensate for deep-seated feelings of inadequacy and inferiority by assuming a hypermasculine, aggressive and domineering stance' (Mirandé, 1997, p. 67). In the clip, the Latino man's attempt to deny his girlfriend's wish to work with the British photographer could be interpreted in this way, where the Briton is the 'colonizer': an outsider who invades the *barrio* (Hispanic quarter) with his photographic avidity, in what appears to be an ethnographic interest in the area as an object of study, and steals the girlfriend of one of the locals. Rodríguez has argued that the 'Latin lover' type, often viewed as someone 'in control', was often the one who 'lost the girl when she met a Yankee' (1997, p. 3).

Schwichtenberg (1993c) cites 'Borderline' amongst a series of early Madonna videos that she sees as 'reflexive commentaries on "male looking" countered by a feminine "look"' (p. 134). Close-up shots of her eyes emphasize her position as a gazing subject. Yet, whilst the Madonna character clearly holds the gaze (if not necessarily the power) when looking at the Latino men (in the company of a 'critical mass' of white girlfriends), the English photographer is the character most clearly in charge of the gaze (literally, given his profession). Hence, issues of gender inversion (white woman looks at Latino man) collide with issues of racial representation (white man looks at white woman). As in so many Madonna videos, we are bombarded with a series of conflicting messages that problematize most interpretations (even when disregarding the issue about Madonna's non-Anglo background). In one sense, Madonna's graffiti on the photographer's car symbolizes her rebellion against the photographer's values, and a reaffirmation of her street life which links her to the *barrio*. The fact that part of her graffiti (on the statue and on the columns) was already 'scripted' into the photo shoot reveals an intention to this 'bridging' effect within the 'pretend' setting of this black-and-white sub-narrative, which associated the Madonna character with the Hispanic through her Spanish-style flounced dress. The same effect is established in the main (colour) narrative through the denim jacket (with graffiti on the back) that the Madonna character wears during her first encounter with the photographer. Hence, one could read Madonna's rebellious spray-painting of the sports car and her final comeback with Latino boyfriend as a triumph of the Hispanic. She seems to feel more at home in the street, apparently well integrated into the *barrio* from the beginning, when she is happily dancing with the Latino kids. Yet, at the end of the video and back in the company of her boyfriend, she wears the hat that the photographer was forcing on her (unsuccessfully) during the photo shoot, hence also suggesting a small triumph of those values represented by the British man. These apparent contradictions emphasize the ambiguity of the Madonna character, who mixes elements of both cultures. Like the song's title, Madonna stays somewhere on the borderline, a concept that would be visually revisited some sixteen years later, in the clip for 'Don't Tell Me' (Mondino, 2000), where a group of ethnically diverse cowboys playfully move in and out of a markedly Western setting as if suggesting their 'in-between' positions with regard to American and 'Other' cultures and identities. If nothing else, both the lyrics and the video for 'Borderline' provide interesting metaphors for Madonna's artistic relationship with the Hispanic: she always comes back to it but is never fully integrated.

Spanish lullaby? Performing Hispanic identities

In 1987, well before the so-called Spanish boom invaded the pop world in the late 1990s, Madonna released what perhaps remains her most Latin-sounding song to date: 'La Isla Bonita'.[5] Described by Madonna as her tribute to 'the beauty and mystery of Latin American people' (Rettenmund, 1995, p. 98), it is characteristic of her work with Pat Leonard in the 1980s. She once declared that 'Latin rhythms' often dominated their 'uptempo' compositions, adding: 'It's like ... we're possessed. We both think that we were Latin in another life' (quoted in Zollo, 1989). The result in this case was a musical pastiche that mixes the sound of Cuban drums with Spanish guitar, maracas and even four lines sung in Spanish (the title's catch phrase, the introductory line '¿Cómo puede ser verdad?' and 'Te dijo te amo / El dijo que te ama'),[6] a successful formula that she would repeat a few months later in the chorus of 'Who's That Girl?' (1987).

If one focuses on the lyrics, the word 'stereotype' comes to mind when we hear words such as 'tropical island breeze', 'samba', 'sun', 'siesta', 'sea', 'warm' or 'wild and free'. Research carried out by the Center for Media and Public Affairs, found that Hispanics on North American television were 'twice as likely as whites to be of "low socioeconomic status", half as likely to be "professional or executive" and 50 percent more likely to be portrayed as "unskilled laborer"' (National Council of La Raza, 1994, p. 28). A 1993 study carried out by the Pitzer College concluded that 'Hispanics and other minorities have replaced blacks in the lower social classes on television', with 75 per cent of Hispanic characters on North American television being of a low socioeconomic status as opposed to 24 per cent of blacks and 17 per cent of whites (p. 28). Ramírez Berg believes that, from a psychological perspective, stereotypes mirror repressed desires and that the representation of Hispanic characters in Hollywood film alternates between degradation and idealization. This follows the Klein scheme of, on the one hand, 'paranoid-schizoid' representations that result from the fear of the bad and, on the other, 'depressive' representations that result from a feeling of guilt and regret about the former type of representation (Ramírez Berg, 1994, p. 108). These contradictions seem to be at play in the song and video 'La Isla Bonita'. The lyrics first position the narrator as a tourist (who prays that 'the days would last, they went so fast'), then isolate the Latin-Others as 'them' ('You can watch them go by'), talking about the 'time for siesta' or people with 'no cares in this world', only to add that they have 'beautiful faces'.[7]

If Madonna and Leonard's musical collaborations often result in Latin-influenced songs, the same could be said of her video collaborations with director Mary Lambert. What was a more or less realistic New York 'street' style setting in 'Borderline' becomes pure pastiche in 'La Isla Bonita'. As in many Madonna videos, she plays two different characters: 'a boyishly-dressed Catholic woman and a colourful flamenco dancer' (Rettenmund, 1995, p. 98). This division is emphasized by two opposing locations. A sparsely decorated room (cold-coloured walls; altar adorned with black-and-white pictures – of Hispanic-looking people, presumably relatives – and a few figures of saints surrounded by just a few candles) matches the first Madonna character: a pale girl also discreetly dressed with a plain white petticoat and short hair brushed back. The austerity and passivity of the first character (who cries in her room upstairs while watching the Latinos dance in the street, and reluctantly ignores their invitation to join them), is contrasted with the passion and activity of the second character, represented by her red and voluminous extravagant Spanish-style dress (with a generous décolletage and middle parting in the skirt) and red carnation decorations in her longer hair (arranged in a Spanish-style netted bun). Complementing this passionate look, the second setting features a bright-red room, with abundant candles and candelabra, as well as a single, large picture of the Sacred Heart, bigger than the black and white images of the previous settings and also, appropriately, bright red. Whilst the spiritual, submissive Madonna watches the Latinos passively from the safety of her room, then kneels down and prays (perhaps to avoid temptation), the passionate Madonna dances, lies on the floor, touches herself and then leaves the room to descend and join the dancers in the street in what is, by all accounts, a memory or a dream sequence ('Last night I dreamt of San Pedro'). Whilst both settings seem to suggest that the Madonna character(s) live in the *barrio* and are integrated in the Hispanic community (the photos on the altar could suggest that she is even a Latina herself), the portrayal of Madonna in the dancing scenes (lush, flashy, brand-new and colourful 'big' dress) contrasts sharply with the Latinos (sparsely dressed with worn-out, shabby clothing). She dances around them and even flirts with the guitarist, but she does not seem to get really involved and, as noted by Tetzlaff, the video ends with Madonna 'dancing off screen' (1993, p. 259).

One of the interesting features of this video is, of course, the link established between Latino culture and Catholicism. The two Madonna characters symbolize the contrast between the restrained and passionate sides of this religion. It would appear that this contrast also recalls what Rettenmund has described as Madonna's take on Catholicism: she rejects it 'for its restrictive attitudes toward women and its even stricter sexual codes, but could never fall out of love with its artifice, high drama, symbolism, and preoccupation with elaborate ritual' (1995,

p. 34). This latter side of religion would become a constant feature in her videos, especially in 'Like a Prayer' (Lambert, 1989), and later in 'Justify My Love' (Mondino, 1990) and 'Secret' (McDaniel, 1994). Speaking in 1991 about 'Like a Virgin' (1984), Madonna declared: 'Passion and sexuality and religion all bleed into each other for me. I think that you can be a very sexual person and also a very religious and spiritual person' (quoted in Deevoy, 1997, p. 162). Although there is little room here to develop the topic of Catholicism and its relation to sex in Madonna's work (a subject already widely discussed in, for example, Scott, 1993; Allen, 1999; Freccero, 1999; and Siegel 1999), it is worth mentioning that in the early 1990s she was persistent in declaring that, whilst she still believed in God, she did not practise Catholicism anymore due to its disapproval of sex and its sexism (see Fisher, 1997, p. 180),[8] openly confessing: 'I've already fallen out of love with Catholicism' (Deevoy, 1997, p. 162), a strong statement possibly motivated by the Vatican's public criticism of the *Blond Ambition* tour in 1990 (as shown in *Truth or Dare*, and documented in Sobran, 1999, p. 126 or Gilbert, 1999, p. 140), which affected ticket sales and resulted in the cancellation of one of her Italian shows (Rettenmund, 1995, p. 22).[9] During the 1980s and early 1990s, prior to her interest in the cabbala, Madonna played publicly with Christian rituals, demonstratively praying with her dancers before and during the *Blond Ambition* and *The Girlie Show* tours.[10]

As well as the obsessive interest in religion, most of the other Hispanic stereotypes described in the above mentioned studies on representation also feature in 'La Isla Bonita'. Latinos are portrayed as indeed having 'no cares in this world': they may well live in an impoverished, crumbling *barrio* (as suggested by the piled up rubbish, vandalized cars and wrecked sofa abandoned in the middle of the street), but they (literally) face the music with maracas, tom-toms, bongo drums and guitars, dancing in the street. The old mix with the young in apparent harmony; the children are not at school, the adults are probably unemployed and dependent on welfare. In her study of the (mis-)representation of Latinas in North American media, Clara Rodríguez (1997) notes that they are often portrayed either as promiscuous or as impoverished mothers with many children. She also observed that Latinas often play roles such as maids or unemployed people dependent on welfare, always with limited presence and speech. She found that, more often than not, music and dance 'replace brains' (p. 2), as in this video.

Richard Dyer has pointed out that stereotypes are, first and foremost, a form of 'ordering'. The social need to 'order' derives from 'a belief in the absoluteness and certainty of any particular order' and is also related to social relations of power (1993, p. 12). For him, 'the role of stereotypes is to make visible the invisible, so that there is no danger of it creeping up on us unaware; and to make fast, firm and separate what is in reality fluid and much closer to the norm than the dominant value system cares to admit' (p. 16). In that sense, the role of the Latinos here could be interpreted as complementary to the Madonna characters, following the pattern that Ramírez Berg identifies in Hollywood film: stereotypes emphasize the positive characteristics of the dominant type (1994, p. 111). On the other hand, Madonna's street dance would be a passing fantasy, a liberating dream of a potential return to unity with the Other, that passionate something 'lacking by the Anglos' (p. 110) that would be left behind once the fantasy is fulfilled and one's own characteristics reaffirmed. Yet, Ramírez Berg also talks about the *barrio* as a useful way of containing the threat of the ethnic Other. The Hispanic Madonna characters seen so far are presented as being part of that *barrio* and, to a certain extent, part of Latino culture. Yet once again, duplicitous meanings problematize the interpretation of ethnic representation here. As in 'Borderline', the Madonna of 'La Isla Bonita' moves in and out of the *barrio*. Even though she lives there, her reality is clearly separated from that of the Latinos, either by staying safely upstairs or, when descending, by marking her difference with her clothing and then leaving the fiesta behind.

Verás: Madonna's gaze, Hispanic bodies

Released in a period of backlash that followed the release of *Sex*, 'Take a Bow' gave Madonna one of her biggest ever hits in the USA, staying at the number one Billboard spot for seven weeks (Madonna's record so far). This unexpected success has been attributed 'to a magnificent video made in Spain replete with a handsome bullfighter' (O'Dair, 1997, p. 20), played by real-life matador Emilio Muñoz (one of Spain's top *toreros* at the time of shooting the video). During the 1990s, Madonna's videos became increasingly sophisticated and whilst 'La Isla Bonita' was pure pastiche, 'Take a Bow' (Haussman, 1994) combined the aesthetics and pace of art cinema with the plethora of stereotypical images and unsubtle phallic and religious symbols that characterized the videos discussed so far. Much of the Catholic imagery seen in 'La Isla Bonita' reappears here, except this time it is associated with the bullfighter even more than with Madonna. Religious images are a strong part of the bull-fighting ritual, as matadors often pray before they face the bull (very much like Madonna-the-performer has done in front of the camera before she faces her audience) and, as seen on the video, the bullfighter attire often has embroidered images of Mary, *the* Madonna. Once again, Madonna's name plays a strong part in the video's semiotics. During the bullfight, she rests her hands on an embroidered print of her namesake, which hangs from her box. Later, after a tiff between her and the bullfighter (apparently ending an affair between them), the Madonna character stands alone by a framed picture of the Virgin Mary, in which she is wearing a dark shawl similar to the one that Madonna wore before the sexual act. The scene is followed by a series of close-ups of Muñoz's bare feet as he walks away from her, stepping on pieces of broken glass that had been scattered on the floor during their fight. These close-ups emphasize a fetishist theme that underlies the whole clip, but could also be interpreted as a reference to the Passion of Christ, linked to the over-present religious imagery. Moreover, some of the glass is part of a framed print of the Immaculate Conception that now lies, torn, presumably blood-stained, on the floor. There are also close-ups of Madonna's bleeding finger (caused by her accidentally pricking it with a hair pin) which could be interpreted as metaphoric stigmata, although more obvious implications would relate to an association between bull-fighting and sexual intercourse, especially with a virgin, and her self-positioning as phallic and penetrative. The apparent links between sex and the *corrida* (*corrida* in Spanish means both 'bullfight' and 'sexual orgasm') are played out to the full in the video. Like in Almodóvar's *Matador* (1986), shots of the couple's sexual encounter are cross-cut with shots of the bullfight, and sexual penetration is suggested through a cut to Muñoz's deadly stab into the bull.[11] The lipstick stain on Madonna's cheek after their final kiss could signify the virgin's broken hymen, a mark for her fetishized body.

Bullfighting, almost by definition, is associated with penetration, ecstasy and male bravado and domination.[12] As summed up by Mexican writer Carlos Fuentes:

> The effrontery of the suit of lights, its tight-hugging breeches, the flaunting of the male sexual organ, the importance given to the buttocks, the obviously seductive and self-appraising stride, the lust for blood and sensation – the bullfighting authorises this incredible arrogance and sexual exhibitionism. (quoted in Stavans, 1998, p. 230)

The drawing of these connections between bullfighting, masculinity, power, death and sex have been widely explored in Hispanic literature and cinema and re-visited in Spanish films of the 1980s and 1990s, most famously perhaps in the above-mentioned *Matador* and in Bigas Luna's *Jamón, jamón* (1992) – both major representatives of post-Franco 'Spanishness' abroad. Due to their connections with both Spanish national identity (bullfighting is 'the' Spanish national fiesta) and masculinity, the figure of the matador and the act of bullfighting are recognized metaphors of specifically Spanish masculinity. The machismo associated with Hispanic men 'implies, above all, the ability to penetrate, and it is associated with being active, closed, unyielding' (Melhuus, 1996, p. 240). The matador's instruments (the *banderilla*, the sword and the knife), the threat posed by the bull's horns and, as Fuentes suggests, the emphasis that the outfit places on the male figure in general (and the genitals in particular) seem to insist on that idea. Earlier, I explained how the episode with the Puerto Rican boy in *Sex* defuses the macho stereotype by focusing on non-penetrative sex and feminizing the boy's body, describing his long hair and smooth skin, and the fact that he is not very well endowed. The masculinity and power usually embodied by the bullfighter had already been downplayed by Madonna in the opening and Spanish sections of the *Who's That Girl?* tour (1987), where a matador was paraded as a circus-clown figure, a decorative Hispanic 'prop', devoid of its connotations of masculine power.

Despite the above-mentioned play with phallic imagery, it could be argued that in 'Take a Bow' the Madonna character once again subverts the gender structure and masculine subjectivity implicit in traditional bullfighting. This effect is achieved primarily through the feminization of the matador and also through the emphasis on Madonna's perspective and her dominant gaze. As mentioned above, the religious iconography often associated with Madonna is linked to the male bullfighter, who wears a cross around his neck, as Madonna did in her early days of fame. This apparent parallel between Madonna and the bullfighter is emphasized at the beginning of the clip, when shots of the matador's dressing-up ritual are cross-cut with similar shots of Madonna adjusting her own tight dress, suggesting a feminization of the bullfighter and of the ritual itself.[13]

As in the two previous videos studied, the use of the gaze in 'Take a Bow' results in a clash of interests and interpretations of race and gender although, unlike in the two previous videos, there is no attempt to integrate the Madonna character in the world of 'the Other'. Here she is most clearly located as an outsider, a division marked by Madonna's strikingly blonde hair and her position as spectator, while watching the *corrida* (in black and white) on television and from the VIP box in the bullring. This time she is, really, a tourist: her room looks like a Spanish guest house and, once again, she is seen to leave the setting towards the end. The issue of blondeness as a strategy of racial separation has been brought up by many of Madonna's critics. hooks has argued that Madonna's success 'is tied to her reputation as a blonde' and that her Marilyn Monroe persona was a public statement of her 'longing to leave behind the experience of her ethnic and bodily history to inhabit the cultural space of the white feminine ideal' (1993, p. 75). Champagne also notes that Madonna is the only blonde woman in the entire *Sex* book, and that her blonde hair and pale skin are part of a strategy to distance herself from some of the dark-skinned types that surround her in various photographs (1993, p. 131). Yet this line of argument ignores Madonna's ever-changing hair colour and ethnic positioning, which, as she has acknowledged, are partly linked to her ancestry: 'I feel more grounded when I have dark hair ... I also feel more Italian' (Zehme, 1997, p. 112).[14] Hence, her darker hair in 'La Isla Bonita' could be read as an attempt to associate her Italian blood with her Hispanic persona, whilst her blonde hair in 'Take a Bow' could reveal an intentional association with the non-Italian in her and a separation from the Spanish bullfighter. Yet, whilst Madonna seemed happy to link her dark hair with her Italian heritage, she described blondeness in the same interview as simply 'a different state of mind', related to sexual attractiveness, not to a particular ethnic identity: 'the artifice of being blond has some incredibly sort of sexual connotation. Men really respond to it' (p. 112). This is indeed suggested in her most famous 'blonde' roles as sex kitten in films such as *Who's That Girl* (Foley, 1987), *Dick Tracy* (Beatty, 1990) or *Body of Evidence* (Edel, 1993), as well as in various videos. Changes of hair colour, then, could be interpreted in terms of both sexuality and ethnic identity.

The strong sexuality that underlies the 'Take a Bow' video becomes explicit when Madonna, semi-naked in bed, watches the bullfighter 'in action' on television. In a scene reminiscent of her simulated masturbation in the *Blond Ambition* tour, she is seen in bed with the television set, covering it with the sheets as if pretending the matador was physically in bed with her. The male body is objectified in the bullring and on the television through the close-ups of various parts of the matador's body, especially the shots of his tight-fitting suit during the dressing-up ritual. Notably, there are various shots of the bullfighter's backside, the most vulnerable part of his body in terms of (visual) penetration. In other scenes, Madonna's own body is fetishized: there are similar instances of her body parts enclosed in tight clothing, close-up shots of her fingers, of her arms as she puts on a pair of long leather gloves, and also at the end when the viewing positions switch and the bullfighter touches a television screen that projects an image of Madonna (perhaps as her real performer self). These instances are arguably efforts to compensate the threat posed by her character (a castrating, voyeuristic, phallic woman) and her domineering narrative perspective, for which her excessive femininity provides a perfect cover for most of the video. Explicit femininity can be empowering in so far as it reveals an awareness of stereotypical femininity (see Riviere, 1929 and Doane, 1992). When used as a masquerade, femininity threatens the disarticulation of 'male systems of viewing' (Doane, 1992, p. 235). Madonna's position as 'spectator' is emphasized through the televised and live bullfights but also through the focus on her eyes, her veil and her overall representation as 'Bardot-esque' (Clerk, 2002, p. 132), as a classic femme fatale. However, I am not suggesting that Madonna's voyeuristic gaze overrides the phallic structure of the visual narrative altogether. As Doane has argued, the veil of the femme fatale 'reveals the limits of an illusory female power, which may pose as a challenge to the phallus, but cannot elude it' (cited in Smith, 2000, p. 69). Thus, Madonna's role-reversals in this video encourage a complex set of interpretations that suggest a less radical challenge to the patriarchal system than may first appear.

The video's concern with the issue of celebrity offers an opportunity for another interesting role-reversal. Madonna's position as spectator in 'Take a Bow' was already established in the song's lyrics, which addressed either a metaphoric 'performer' (a lover who 'acts' in a relationship and 'breaks her heart') or a real one. In an MTV interview recorded on the set of the video, she declared to have thought originally about a film star, but chose a bullfighter instead as it would be difficult to show a film star's profession within the mini-film that is a video clip (*Madonna Videography*, 1998). The focus on a *real* bullfighter as 'a star' facilitates the staging of a chain of simulacra that undoubtedly reflect Madonna's own position as a star in real life: announcing the act with a poster, performing in front of an audience, attracting media attention and so on. In retrospect, this parallel (especially the paparazzi shots) is striking when compared with the later video 'Drowned World/Substitute for Love' (Stern, 1998), in which Madonna's star persona is explored. Proclaimed as 'a queen of undermining masculinity' (Skeggs, 1993, p. 72), in 'Take a Bow' Madonna focuses on an international icon of machismo and male power to reclaim the female gaze. By swapping celebrity/spectator positions with a *macho*, she reflects on her own position as a female celebrity-object.

The visual narrative strategies (female masquerade, fetishistic scopophilia) compensate for a lyrical narrative that talks about male 'masquerade' and male agency in breaking a woman's heart. In the song itself, the female reclaims subjectivity by ending the relationship. These themes are cleverly complemented in the sequel song and video 'You'll See' (Haussman, 1995), in which the Madonna character reinstates her position of superiority in the lyrics ('You think that you are strong / But you are weak' ... 'I'll survive' ... 'I don't need anyone at all'), and also visually by making the bullfighter regret the break-up and follow her train helplessly while *she* leaves *him* behind. Madonna's (real-life) use of the video as a means to show *Evita* director Alan Parker that she could master the 1940s look (a factor of influence in her casting over Michelle Pfeiffer) also complements her fictional position of control in the clip (Clerk, 2002, pp. 132–3).

Evita: Lo que siente la mujer

Playing the role of Eva Perón in the film adaptation of the Tim Rice/Andrew Lloyd Webber musical (1978) was arguably one of Madonna's biggest ambitions of the 1990s. Contemplated and publicly discussed since the early 1990s (Bates, 1991), her efforts to acquire the role are no secret. There was, for example, the well-known handwritten four-page letter sent to director Alan Parker, where she explained why 'no one could play Evita as well as she could' and her willingness to 'sing, dance and act her heart out, and put everything else on hold' (Parker, 1996, p. 13). Once chosen for the role, she trained her voice with coach Joan Layder for three months and learned the score from David Caddick, Lloyd Webber's musical director (p. 16). As documented in her Evita diary entries of January 1996 and in various interviews (Castellano, 1996; Jackson, 1996), Madonna spent three weeks in Buenos Aires prior to the start of filming in order to do her own research, meeting some of the people who had met Eva, including President Menem.[15] Their short but productive encounter resulted in official permission to use the legendary Casa Rosada balcony for one of the climatic scenes of the film.[16]

The reasons why Madonna's star persona was perfectly suited to play the role of 'the most famous woman to ever come out of South America' (Parker, 1996, p. 11) seem almost too obvious to comment. The parallel between the stories of these two self-made women was one of the issues most talked about in the film reviews and also by the director, co-stars and Madonna herself (see, for example, Arroyo, 1997, p. 41 and Jackson, 1996, p. 30).[17] Even their physical resemblance was noticed by President Menem (Madonna, 1996, 8 February). The mixed but passionate reception of Madonna in Buenos Aires (graffiti demanding she 'go home!', as well as people marching through the streets in her support) was perceived by the artist as 'perfect' because 'this is exactly how it was for her when she was alive' (Jackson, 1996, p. 30, see also Gundersen, 1999, p. 76).[18] Co-star Antonio Banderas referred to this incident as 'the story all over again of Eva Duarte' (quoted in Udovitch, 1997, p. 248).

Madonna 'fell madly in love' with her character and during filming she felt 'completely possessed' (Jackson, 1996, p. 29), sometimes even dreaming that she was Evita (Madonna, 1996, 24 February). This process of identification is played out by Madonna in the diaries, reaching remarkable levels of passion. The linguistic style in her account of the filming of 'Don't Cry For Me Argentina' in the Casa Rosada recalls that of magic realism:[19] 'I felt her enter my body like a heat missile, starting with my feet, travelling up my spine, and flying out my fingertips, into the air, out to the people and back up to heaven' … 'she is haunting me' (10 March). The extreme level of identification that the diaries celebrate contrasts sharply with her apparent lack of adaptation to the reality of Argentina, making despotic and suspicious comments about its food (22 January), its lifestyle (23 January) and its men (30 January, 2 February, 8 February). References to Argentina in the diaries are not kind: she refers to the country as 'this place', calling it 'scary' and 'uncivilized' (23 January), a 'godforsaken place', 'chaotic' and 'fickle' (30 January). Her sense of relief when leaving the country is summarized in her gesture of kissing the ground when she gets 'back to America' (19 March). Needless to say, many of the stereotypes referred to above reappear here in both fictional (Savigliano, 1997) and non-fictional contexts. Madonna's diaries describe the Argentinians as loud and lazy. 'Everyone is unemployed', she writes, referring to people screaming outside her hotel room, adding: 'no one has to get up and go to work in the morning' (January 23). She dismisses her (North American) manager's concerns about death threats against her, saying that 'all Latinos exaggerate and are over the top' (January 26). Also revealing is her comment that 'Latin men were put on this earth to charm women. And torture them!' (January 27).

Once again, contradictions arise here in Madonna's approach to Hispanic identities. On the one hand, she identifies wholeheartedly with the Argentinian icon; on the other, she seems to distance herself from the reality of the country and its peoples. Madonna's Evita incarnation recalls the fact that Evita herself looked like one of those 'European' types described by Rodríguez (1997, p. 3).[20] Like Madonna, she was one to change her appearance often, once again suggesting the concept of the female masquerade (as illustrated in *Evita* by Madonna's infinite wardrobe changes (Parker, 1996, p. 23)). Madonna perceived a change as she removed her brown contact lenses: 'It felt funny to be me with green eyes' (5 March), suggesting an almost conscious switch of ethnic identities. One cannot help but wonder the extent to which Hispanic identity is part of Madonna's attraction to Eva Perón. In interview, she insisted that 'Latin culture' was a big part of it: 'its music and art, which I've always been drawn to' (quoted in Jackson, 1996, p. 29). Yet, what comes across in most interviews and also in the diaries is that what Madonna found in Evita was a kindred spirit: an icon of female power and determination over the unfavourable circumstances of women in a highly patriarchal society. Hispanic societies provide a good example: 'misogyny ... runs throughout our society, and [it] says that women who are successful are whores, bitches, immoral ... You do get some solace from thinking ... I'm just one in a long line of women who have been trounced for being individually strong' (quoted in Jackson, 1996, p. 30). In an interview published in one of Spain's national newspapers, Madonna gave some interesting details about the origins of her interest in Eva:

> At school they portrayed her as a cruel, ambitious, corrupt and ruthless woman. It is typical of History to portray powerful women in this way, because they are women that inspire terror. I thought that people also perceived me in that way, so I thought that I owed it to her, as a homage to all women that at different points in history have been misjudged and scorned. (quoted in Castellano, 1996, p. 37, my translation)

Eva Perón's cause was by no means focused on women's issues (although she did campaign strongly, and successfully, for women's right to vote), yet her very position of power in the Argentinian society of the 1940s deserves her a place amongst the most iconic women of the twentieth century. As Melhuus has argued:

> In Latin America, notions of power – el poder – are part of the male discourse. Power ... represents a contested space for the articulation of masculine identity. It belongs to the penetrating realm of machismo and is associated with violence and aggressiveness, a particular form of self-assertion which more than anything implies being in control, being in command, having authority not only – or primarily – over women but also over other men. (1996, p. 240)

Even though some critics have read the staging of Evita's death in the musical as a moralistic and male-chauvinist lesson about the fate of a woman who 'misbehaved' – a classic punishment of the femme fatale (Savigliano, 1997, p. 166; see also Clément, 1988), she is perhaps one of the very few Latina icons with the potential to contradict Rodríguez's findings about the representation of the Latina in North American media as 'passive, feeble, unintelligent and dependent' or 'occasionally ... strong' but 'eventually subdued by a "real" man' (1997, p. 3). Madonna's identification with Evita (or with the late Princess of Wales, in whom Madonna has also found parallels with Evita (Eccleston, 1998, p. 86)) could be interpreted as part of what Canadian feminist Adrienne Rich terms a 'lesbian continuum'. This continuum is 'a range – through each woman's life and throughout history – of woman-identified experience, not simply the fact that a woman has had or consciously desired genital sexual experience with another woman' (1993, p. 239) and can be viewed as a female defence strategy against patriarchy, in so far as patriarchy depends on 'relations between men … which establish interdependence and solidarity among men that enable them to dominate women' (Heidi Hartmann quoted in Sedgwick, 1985, p. 3). This definition of patriarchy seems appropriate in the context of many Latin countries (notice the similarity with the definition of power in Latin America described above by Melhuus). According to Savigliano, in the film the tango (which, like bullfighting in Spain, has strong associations with male power in Argentina) is used to 'mark Evita/Madonna's shameful but obstinate path to the top by manipulating machismo' (1997, p. 162).

An interesting and related issue surrounds Madonna's Evita persona – motherhood – and it is ironic that it would happen on the set of *Evita*: prior to filming, childlessness was yet another shared feature between the two women. As noted by Langer (1966), in *La razón de mi vida* (1951) Eva used her lack of children as a factor that would allow her to become the symbolic mother of all Argentinians. Madonna has referred to her first pregnancy as 'poetic' because 'it happened while I was trying to give birth to another sort of baby' (quoted in Udovitch, 1997, p. 250). She later declared to have conceived of her song 'What it Feels Like for a Girl' while she was trying to hide her second pregnancy from the media (Sischy, 2001b). This song, together with 'You'll See' ('Verás' in Spanish), is one of two that Madonna chose to record in Spanish and performed in that language throughout the *Drowned World Tour* (as 'Lo que siente la mujer'). Both songs can be interpreted as 'female protest' songs addressed at men. In both, the female subject position is claimed, rejecting the (male) assumption that women are weak or submissive.[21] As seen earlier, this discomfort with the traditional female position and its incompatibility with power was one of the reasons why Madonna felt attracted to Evita. Whilst I am by no means suggesting that motherhood was a planned commercial strategy, the truth is that Madonna's 'new' persona as exemplary matriarch in the late 1990s was a decisive step for her recovery after the *Sex* backlash.

As this chapter shows, it is extremely difficult to pin down Madonna's ethnic identities or to give a clear-cut interpretation of her subcultural practices. Her exploration of Hispanic identities offers plenty of examples of simplistic stereotyping, obvious distancing and, at the same time, her continuous engagement with and attention to Latino culture (particularly art and music) expands from the aesthetics of the 'Borderline' video in 1984 to the artwork of her 2003 album *American Life*, inspired by iconic images of Che Guevara.[22] Studies carried out by the National Council of La Raza in the early 1990s showed that in television programmes aired in the USA, representations of blacks nearly tripled from 6 per cent in the period 1995–6 to 17 per cent, whereas portrayals of Hispanics had dropped from 2 per cent to 1 per cent (1994, p. 31). Oboler has noted that 'the way in which US history is presented to school children ... affects the way they are thought to imagine their [invisible] "national community"', adding that 'a significant number of texts continue to present a principally white, Protestant, Anglo-Saxon view of America's past and present, while the nature and problems of minority groups are largely neglected ... even less attention is paid to America's increasingly significant minority groups of Spanish-speaking peoples' (1997, p. 49). Madonna's contribution to the representation of Hispanic identities so far has been, in a sense, one that increases the presence of Hispanic peoples in mainstream global media, often with some sense of respect (Evita, Frida Kahlo).[23] And yet her relationship with Latino men in real life and in the fiction of her videos, films and other performances (which could include the *Vanity Fair*-destined 'private' diaries) seems to reflect a complex and conflictive pattern of attraction and glamorization combined with an active challenge to reaffirm her female position in a macho society. This seems to have had a positive effect on some Latinas. In a personal account, Carmen Lugo-Lugo has described how Madonna became a figure of 'struggle and a source of empowerment' for Puerto Rican women in need of inspiration to resist a fresh injection of (already well-established) patriarchal power in the island with 1980s Reaganism (2001, pp. 122–3).[24] Finally, Madonna's changing ethnic identities can also be read as a reflection of her own problematic relationship with the USA.[25] Mendieta has noted that 'just as Latin Americans dismantled race through five hundred years of *mestizaje* and miscegenation, they are poised to contribute to the remaking and reconfiguration of America by dismantling its racial edifice' (2000, p. 56).[26] Madonna's playful adoption and dismissal of ethnic identities could inspire similarly dismantling thoughts.

Acknowledgements

I would like to thank my co-editor, Freya Jarman-Ivens, and my friend and colleague Ian Biddle (both from the International Centre for Music Studies at the University of Newcastle upon Tyne) for their useful comments and revisions on earlier and longer versions of this chapter.

Notes

1. The problematic natures of the 'Latino' label and 'Hispanic' identity are discussed in recent literature in great detail. See, for example, Romero et al., 1997; Darder and Torres, 1998 (especially parts I and II); Gracia and De Greiff, 2000; and Abalos, 2001. The term *criollo* (creole) has changed its meaning and connotations in different times and areas. Originally, it was used to refer to white men of European

descent born in a tropical colony but it is now used quite widely to refer to various mixing of races. *Mestizo* (now used with increasingly positive connotations) also refers to mixed-raced peoples in South America but it often evokes the early cultural and racial mix between Spanish and Portuguese settlers and the native Indians. *Mulato* is sometimes used interchangeably with *mestizo* but it is also associated with racist slave discourses, to refer to slaves who are 'one half white'. See Ashcroft et al., 1998.

2. Here it would be appropriate to specify my use of the terms 'race' and 'ethnicity'. Following Appiah (1997), I will use 'race' as a biological term and 'ethnicity' as a cultural construct based on the assumption of a shared culture and identity. These terms could be regarded as the equivalent of (biological) sex and (culturally constructed) gender respectively (see Corlett, 1997).

3. The one-hour television special *Madonna Rising* (aired on VH1 in 1998) is also a good testimony to her background and early integration with ethnic minorities in New York's East Village.

4. Another anecdotal but relevant episode of her Hispanic connection was revealed in that same interview, where she declared to have found a 'kind of mother' in a 'very spiritual' older Cuban woman ('the mother of a friend of a friend') with whom she used to talk, eat and go to church (*FHM*, 1995, p. 93).

5. This 'Latin pop boom' peaked with Ricky Martin's hit 'Livin' La Vida Loca', which was quickly followed by Geri Halliwell's debut solo single, 'Mi Chico Latino', and the successful music debut of actress Jennifer López, all in the same year, 1999. The influence of 'La Isla Bonita' on the lyrics and sound of Halliwell's Spanglish single is significant. Madonna also recorded a song in 'Spanglish' with Martin ('Be Careful', featured on his 1999 album *Ricky Martin*). An important aspect of this Latino boom is that, as in Hollywood cinema, most Latinos who have 'made it' into the pop music business are what Rodríguez calls 'European prototypes' (1997, p. 3). Interestingly, Martin was born Enrique José Martín Morales and has clearly felt a need to anglicize his name in order to achieve international celebrity.

6. In its studio version, the song featured the famous Brazilian percussionist Paulinho Da Costa. He was replaced for live performances in 1987 and 1993 by another famous percussionist, Cuban Luis Conte.

7. These stereotypes are reproduced in live performances. 'La Isla Bonita' is one of the songs most often performed live and one of only two pre-1994 hits that Madonna included in her *Drowned World Tour* (2001). It is telling that this song is almost always closely followed by 'Holiday', establishing a casual link between the Hispanic and fiesta or spare time, which could be negatively interpreted as a reinforcement of the stereotype of Hispanic laziness. Alternatively, the fact that all Madonna tours except the first one included a long Spanish section can be perceived as a genuine interest in the Hispanic.

8. Lugo-Lugo celebrates this rejection of Catholic sexual repression as particularly inspiring for Catholic women (2001, p. 127).

9. Humorously, in a typical Madonna move, she went on to call her first greatest hits album *The Immaculate Collection* (1990) and dedicated it to the Pope.

10. During *Blond Ambition* she prayed with her dancers before the shows (while the camera was rolling for *Truth or Dare*) and on the stage during her rendition of 'Like a Prayer' (which directly followed the simulated masturbation and orgasm during 'Like a Virgin'). In *The Girlie Show*, towards the end of the filmed performance in Sydney, she again asked her dancers to thank God for the good weather in a carefully staged prayer.

11. 'Take a Bow' could have been inspired by *Matador*, which starred Antonio Banderas. Madonna declared herself a fan of both Almodóvar and Banderas in *Truth or Dare*. On *Matador*, fetishism and power, see Evans, 1993; Smith, 2000, pp. 65–78; and Allinson, 2001. For a reading of Banderas, see Perriam, 2003.

12. As seen in Almodóvar's *Talk to Her* (2002), female bullfighters in Spain are often the victims of the machismo that characterizes their profession. Cristina Sánchez, perhaps the most renowned Spanish female bullfighter of all time, gave up her career in 1999 partly due to this (see Gooch, 1999, p. 22).

13. One could even argue that Madonna was the metaphoric '*torera*' of the clip. In Spanish, '*torero*' can also be understood as a compliment based on hegemonic notions of masculinity (power, self-confidence, control). It was interesting to witness how, during the world premiere of the *Drowned World Tour* in Barcelona, the Spanish audience received Madonna's cocky attitude in her opening number with screams of '*torera, torera*'.

14. More recently, in an interview with Jonathan Ross broadcast by BBC1 in the UK (2 May 2003), she referred to her brunette hair as 'good strong Italian hair'.

15. For reasons of space, this section of the chapter will focus on the circumstances surrounding the *Evita* film and its interest as part of Madonna's 'Hispanic' persona rather than on an analysis of the film itself, which would require a separate study (such as Savigliano, 1997).

16. Menem's decision could be interpreted cynically: Savigliano's argument is that Parker's *Evita* 'evokes precisely Menem's understanding of a Peronism suited to our times', revealing the utopianism of past Peronism and indirectly helping to 'win elections' (1997, p. 169).

17. See also the examples cited by Savigliano, 1997, pp. 159–60.

18. Parker argued that the anti-Madonna graffiti appeared to be the work of one minority group – The Commandos of the Peronista (1996, p. 18). The rapid release of an Argentinian version of Eva's story, filmed that year with Argentinian director and actors (*Eva Perón* (Desanzo, 1996)), could be interpreted as part of the reaction against the Parker film in Evita's country. Like the musical on which the film was based, Parker's *Evita* has been perceived as devoid of politics and historically blurry, focusing instead on the legendary figure of Evita (Savigliano, 1997, pp. 163–6).

19. The term 'magic realism' describes the narrative technique that combines the real and the fantastic, and is often associated with Latin American authors such as Gabriel García Márquez or Isabel Allende.

20. Rodríguez refers to Parker's *Evita* as an example of a Hollywood film about Latin America with Latino settings and characters 'but no Latinos in major roles' (1997, p. 3). Savigliano notes how Evita's dancing partners become 'whiter and better dressed' as she gets closer to the top (1997, p. 162).

21. My interpretation of the song 'You'll See' as anti-patriarchal is influenced by the promotional video and is not solely based on the song's lyrics, which are non-gender-specific.

22. The withdrawal of the controversial anti-war video clip 'American Life' (Åkerlund, 2003), arguably contradicted and diminished the revolutionary potential suggested by the Che-esque artwork of both album and single.

23. Madonna's genuine interest in Hispanic music is perhaps best illustrated in her creation of a Latin sub-label within her record company (Maverick Música). She is a well-known collector of Hispanic art, including works by Dalí, Picasso, Rivera and especially Frida Kahlo (see, for example, Martin, 1992, p. 16; Fisher, 1997, p. 176; Zehme, 1997, p. 105; or Daly, 2002, p. 224).

24. In the early 1990s, Paglia noted that 'Madonna's most enduring cultural contribution may be that she has introduced ravishing visual beauty and a lush Mediterranean sensuality into parched, pinched, word-drunk Anglo-Saxon feminism' (1999, p. 167).
25. For an up-to-date analysis of Madonna's relationship with American culture, see Albiez's contribution to this collection (Chapter 8).
26. In this context, the term *mestizaje* refers generally to racial mixture through the centuries in South America. As mentioned earlier, the term has been used traditionally to refer to the mixture between the native Indians and the settlers from Spain and Portugal.

PART IV

Blond Ambition:
Consuming Celebrity

Olivier Tridon

Chapter 10

Madonna's daughters
Girl power and the empowered girl-pop breakthrough

David Gauntlett

Madonna has clearly been a uniquely successful and enduring pop phenomenon; the other chapters in this book reflect the ways in which Madonna provides a whole world of ideas and experiences – in music, visuals and expressions of cultural and sexual politics – which can be discussed on their own terms. In this chapter, however, I will be looking at the influence that Madonna has had on other performers who have followed her in the sphere of popular music, and her impact (by implication) upon the pop world in general.[1] Some of the influences Madonna has had upon the world of pop are quite broad: for example, she has provided a recipe for 'longevity' – based on regular self-reinvention, working with talented up-and-coming producers and fostering controversies – which many artists, female and male, may try to emulate. More recently, Madonna introduced European electronic dance music into the mainstream of American pop culture (such as the collaborations with Mirwais on *Music* (2000), and with him and Stuart Price of Les Rhythmes Digitales on *American Life* (2003)), and more generally has always been a ˙mainstream pioneer of dance sounds and electronica, and has worked with interesting producers and remixers (to name but a few: Shep Pettibone, Nellee Hooper, William Orbit, Thunderpuss, BT, Kruder & Dorfmeister, Groove Armada and Deep Dish).

Arguably her biggest influence, however, has been on newer generations of female pop performers. This chapter will discuss the ways in which Madonna opened up avenues, opportunities and themes which were capitalized upon by more recent female artists such as the Spice Girls, Britney Spears, Destiny's Child, Jennifer Lopez ('J-Lo'), Lil' Kim, Anastacia, Missy Elliot, Kylie Minogue, Pink and others. Kelly Osbourne's semi-ironic 'rock' version of 'Papa Don't Preach' (2002) is just one of the more obvious illustrations of the debt that today's female stars owe to Madonna. Many of them are Madonna's daughters in the very direct sense that they grew up listening to and admiring Madonna, and decided they wanted to be like her. Most of them have said so explicitly at some point.

Madonna and Britney

In recent years, the most well-known cross-generational Madonna connection has been that between the fortysomething star and Britney Spears, which came to a head for a few months in late 2000, when the two stars wore each other's T-shirts and were rumoured to be considering a duet, Madonna dedicated the song 'What it Feels Like for a Girl' to her protégé during a New York *Music* promotion gig, and the entertainment newsmedia became almost obsessed with their relationship of mutual admiration. Britney, born in 1981, grew up listening to and idolizing Madonna – even though we might expect that Madonna's controversial image and values would not go down so well in Britney's tiny Bible-loving village of Kenwood, Louisiana. (The *Sex* book was published just before Britney's eleventh birthday, but she is unlikely to have received a copy.) Asked in 2001 about the comparisons with Madonna, Britney told MTV:

> I think that we have the same drive. When we want something, we get it. As far as our music and our talent goes, we're very different. Onstage we have the same drive, too. I just saw her show and she's just amazing. She was flawless ... I think we're very different in a lot of ways. It is flattering that they say we're alike. (MTV.com, 2001)

Possibly wearying of these comparisons by the next year, Britney told *Arena* magazine:

> I look up to Madonna but I don't want my career to follow in her footsteps. I want to have my own identity and do my own thing. If the definition of a woman is someone who has lived her life and has all the wisdom that she needs, I think I'm getting close. (Wilson, 2002, p. 84)

No doubt Madonna would approve of both the assertion of independence, and the bold statement about the meaning of womanhood. Some observers of popular culture, however, feel that the comparisons between the two stars are meaningless and fail to recognize Madonna's unique contribution: Madonna was never 'just another pop star', whereas Britney can more easily be seen as a standard manufactured pop act. In an article on the website *Dark America*, a writer who purports to be a fan of neither artist notes that Madonna struggled up through the tough New York club scene, whilst Britney arrived in the public eye via stage school and the Mickey Mouse Club. Furthermore:

> Madonna, whether you like her or not, started a revolution amongst women in music. She made the female body seem more like a machine with cravings and less like a Barbie doll. Her attitudes and opinions about sex, nudity, style and sexuality forced the public to sit up and take notice ... Britney [on the other hand] makes little girls dress like twenty-something whores. She's made the female body seem more like a spectacle than a shrine. Her attitudes and opinions are one big corporate buy-line and nobody cares what she thinks. ('Cyberpunk', 2001)

Whilst it is true that Madonna was more of a pioneer, and is much more open and challenging about sex, this argument plays down the significance of what Britney means to her fans. Talking to such fans – or viewing a few Britney fan websites – soon shows that it is quite wrong to say that 'nobody cares what she thinks', even though her impact on the wider culture has not (yet) been as great as Madonna's. For instance, articles about and interviews with Britney Spears always emphasize the apparently high level of control she has over her image and career, and her songs contain messages of independence and inner strength, all of which impresses fans (even if cynical critics dismiss it as hype).

Nevertheless, asked in an interview to summarize herself in five words, Britney offered: 'Bubbly, innocent, respectable, fun and responsible' (*Arena*, 2001, p. 105). It seems safe to assume that Madonna – based on her numerous public statements in the 1980s and 1990s – would have taken pride in accepting none of these adjectives for herself. Perhaps the younger Madonna would have accepted 'fun', although recent biographics (Taraborrelli, 2001; Morton, 2002; Thompson, 2002) suggest that Madonna in the 1980s was too *driven* to have much time for 'fun' (see Madonna's statements of independence and ambition in St. Michael, 1999, pp. 15–23). Of course, in reality, Britney must be deeply driven too. Regarding the comparisons between Britney and the early Madonna, Madonna told *Elle* magazine:

> Can I just say that I find it really irritating that everyone beats up on Britney Spears. I want to do nothing but support her and praise her and wish her the best. I mean, she's just 19 years old! It's just shocking. I wish I'd had my shit together like that when I was 19. I was so gawky and geeky and awkward and unsure of myself. I didn't have a tan! I didn't know how to dress! (Carroll, 2001, p. 52)

It could be said that Britney was able to be so successful at such a young age in part *because* Madonna had already cleared the way for that kind of female pop star. In any case, and despite the apparent differences between the two, Madonna was clearly a significant influence upon Britney Spears, and the Britney phenomenon reflects a number of themes in post-Madonna pop that will be considered later in this chapter.

The Spice factor

Now we need to rewind our chronology slightly, to consider one of the most obvious earlier manifestations of post-Madonna pop with a gender agenda. In 1996, the Spice Girls burst onto the scene, shouting (literally) about 'girl power' at every opportunity. Mixing conventional glamour with a feisty, ultra-confident, 'in your face' approach, the Spices, driven by Geri Halliwell, really did push the 'girl power' agenda in the public sphere for a while, celebrating independent womanhood to their young (and older) fans. Their debut single 'Wannabe' (1996) topped the charts in twenty-three countries, and 'girl power' became a catchphrase throughout the media, appearing in newspaper headlines just as often as it did in the pages of teen magazines. In her autobiography, Geri recalls a point in 1994 where she wondered whether the band was going to work or not:

> I asked a DJ friend what I should do. 'Girl bands don't work,' he said bluntly. I disagreed with him. The music scene *needed* young, positive female recording artists. At twelve years old I had Madonna to look up to. The teenagers today needed someone like that. (Halliwell, 1999, p. 221)

Outlining the characteristics of each Spice Girl to a journalist in 1997, Geri explained, 'We've all got balls, but I've got quite big balls, basically' (Heath, 1997, p. 78). Although this remark was no doubt original, it reflects various similar statements made by Madonna during her career, which play on the combination of a bold 'masculine' boast with the tease or promise of female sexuality. Also in 1997 – perhaps thinking of the media success achieved by Camille Paglia in her articles on Madonna (see, for example, Paglia, 1990) – the British newspaper *The Guardian* sent another well-known older feminist, Kathy Acker, to interview the Spice Girls. Whilst rather overwhelmed by their noise and energy, Acker was quite impressed. In the piece, she confesses to being a little concerned about the individualism of their 'do what you want' message, but Geri tells her that the Spice Girls between themselves, and with their fans, are a community more powerful than the sum of its parts. She says:

> Normally, when you get fans of groups, they want to act like you, they copy what you're wearing, for instance. Whereas our fans, they might have pigtails and they might wear sweatclothes, but they are so individual, it's unbelievable. When you speak to them, they've got so much balls! It's like we've collected a whole group of our people together! … I can remember someone coming up to us and going, 'Do you know what? I've just finished with my boyfriend! And you've given me the incentive to go "Fuck this!"' (quoted in Acker, 1997, p. 14)

Acker asks whether the Spice Girls want boyfriends. Mel B replies:

> I think whoever we would choose to be with should respect the way we are – and our job as well. The way we are together. None of us would be interested in a man that wanted to dominate, wanted to pull you down, and wanted you to do what he wanted you to do. (p. 14)

Statements of independence such as this again reflect the Madonna ethos, explained in numerous interviews throughout her career (but particularly in the mid-1980s to mid-1990s), that personal strength and 'doing what you want' are supremely important – not just a nice idea, but absolutely essential to survival – whereas finding a soul mate was not so central, and a boyfriend that told you what to do was out of the question.

The Spice Girls, in the Acker interview as in many others, said many more things about fulfilling your dreams, going against expectations and creating your own opportunities for success. Acker notes that in the 1980s, feminism was represented in Britain and America by intellectual, middle-class women, and was popularly seen as elitist and anti-sex. She notes with pleasure that in the 1990s, the Spice Girls were able to confidently represent 'the voices, not really the voice, of young women and, just as important, of women not from the educated classes' (1997, p. 19). This is true, but of course, again, Madonna was the real pioneer, having created the space for such women to become successful with her popular reinterpretation of feminism seen in the music and videos of hits as diverse as 'Papa Don't Preach' (Foley, 1986), 'Express Yourself' (Fincher, 1989), 'Justify My Love' (Mondino, 1990), 'Erotica' (Baron, 1992) and many others.

The Spice Girls did not simply copy Madonna, though. Their 'girl power' slogan worked like a kind of brand which they stamped everywhere they went – whereas Madonna's indications of a feminist ethos had been, unusually, much more subtle (!). 'Girl power' was a celebration of self-belief, independence and female friendship, and whilst cynics muttered that it was an empty ideology – sneering that its goal seemed merely to be the right to shout 'girl power' a lot – the idea did nevertheless seem to be empowering for young girls. Sheila Whiteley notes that the Spice Girls were 'a challenge to the dominance of lad culture ... they introduced the language of independence to a willing audience of pre- and teenage girls' (2000, p. 215). Putting forward a thesis similar to Acker's, Whiteley notes that although the discourses of feminism were well known in the 1990s, they were assigned a negative image in tabloid newspapers and other popular media, and presented as 'heavy' and opposed to men and sex. She says the Spice Girls changed that:

> The impact of the Spice Girls ... was to provide a new twist to the feminist discourse of power and subjectivity. By telling their fans that feminism is necessary and fun, that it is part of everydayness, and that girls should challenge rather than accept traditional constraints – 'What you looking at boy? Can you handle a Spice Girl?' – they sold the 1990s as 'a girl's world' and presented the 'future as female'. (2000, pp. 216–17)

By the mid-1990s, Madonna's sexual dominatrix image had waned, and even been pointedly replaced with the ballad-crooning softie of the *Something to Remember* compilation album (1995), complaining ironically in the sleeve notes that everyone focuses upon the controversy and images, rather than the music. Furthermore, Madonna's feminist messages were not usually spelt out in the obvious, in-your-face style of the Spice Girls. Whilst it was easy for cynics to criticize the 'girl power' idea as a bunch of banal statements about 'believing in yourself' and 'doing whatever you want to do', the Spice message was still an encouraging confidence boost to young women, and should not be dismissed too readily. At the time, television programmes and magazine articles – as well as letters written to pop magazines, and the anecdote everyone had about the super-confidence of their little sister or daughter – suggested that 'girl power' was more than a phenomenon imagined within the media, and did indeed have an impact in the real world (see also BBC Online, 1997; Vernon, 1999; Bunting, 2001; Williams, 2002). Other female stars and groups subsequently inherited this inspirational mantle, although without the clear hook of the Spices' 'girl power' slogan.[2]

Destiny's Child – independent women

In the first years of the new millennium, as discussed above, Britney Spears had taken Madonna's job of being the super-confident sexy young white girl. Destiny's Child, meanwhile, were putting the 'girl power' ethos into their actual *songs* more clearly than their predecessors had. They were also a massive international success: the album *Survivor* (2001) sold five million copies within five weeks; their previous album, *The Writing's On the Wall* (1999), sold over nine million copies worldwide. Almost all of the songs on *Survivor* were both written and produced by key band member Beyoncé Knowles, rapidly emergent as a Madonna-style control enthusiast. An MTV documentary about the group, *All Eyes on Destiny's Child*, celebrated their '"take no mess" attitude' and gushed that the group communicated a 'message of self-reliance and personal strength in the most *alluring* of packages'. It also noted that this was 'a new kind of act: fierce, foxy and frankly intelligent, proudly shouting out their self-sufficiency' (MTV, 2001). Their big hit 'Bills, Bills, Bills' (1999) was a goodbye note to a boyfriend who didn't pay his way and was always borrowing money from the richer female protagonist. 'Independent Women Part 1' (2000) continued the emphasis on women having their own money and paying their own bills – financial independence – celebrating 'All the honeys makin' money', and asserting 'I depend on me'. 'Independent Women Part 2' (2001) insists that they will never be controlled, and will offer no love or commitment.

These words are notable simply because they are so different to the typical loving or 'I want you' lyrics common in pop music. Whilst Madonna had startled some people with the sexual desire in her performances, Destiny's Child have perhaps produced the greater surprise with the popularity of their 'I *don't* want you' lyrics. One fan comment posted at online store Amazon.co.uk says that Beyoncé is 'truly inspirational' and notes that the group are 'promoting a more sophisticated "Girl Power" message that the Spice Girls failed to carry' (12 May 2001). Another user seems slightly more jaded: 'We've heard the "girl-power" lark time and time before, but Destiny's Child are acutely aware of its selling power and the appeal it has to the "Jerry Springer generation"' (30 May 2001). The first implication of this comment is that the 'girl power' discourse is actually a commercial tool (and therefore, by implication, not actually very challenging).

Of course, it is possible for an ideology, or a set of ideas, to be both thought-provoking and commercially successful; however, the suspicion seems to be that some 'girl power' artists are exploiting the resonance of these popular affirmative ideas in order to achieve the goal to which they are most committed – making money. On the other hand, the 'girl power' ideology would applaud women's commercial success as a triumph in itself anyway. The second notion contained in the comment above is that there is a generation brought up on 'shouty' daytime TV shows, for whom the idea of criticizing and dumping inadequate partners is a source of *pleasure*. The emotional carnival of relationship-clash talk shows like those hosted by Jerry Springer and Rikki Lake in the 1990s seems to have spilled over into a more general enjoyment of the self-worth attained from being a woman who says 'You're not good enough for me' to a man.[3] We can trace a clear line from those audience members shouting advice to Rikki Lake's female guests ('Kick him to the kerb!' they would call, and 'Go Rikki, go Rikki' in scenes of emotional confrontation), to the new audience for empowered, independent female pop music.

In an online interview, Beyoncé said that the group's central message is 'for women to be independent, strong women, and for women to demand respect' (Yahoo! Chat Event, 2000). A fan from Florida, at Amazon.com, agreed that '*Survivor* is a good CD for young women' (11 May 2001). Another American fan comments: '"Independent Women" and "Survivor" are unforgettable … Beyoncé's writing is exceptional, she speaks to our generation – delivering messages in unique ways. The girl is tough. I hope she keeps going going going' (2 May 2001). As with the Spice Girls and Madonna (and, indeed, most pop stars) Destiny's Child use sex appeal to sell their music, and critics would assert that the promotion of a particular image of thin, attractive women is not pro-feminist behaviour. On the other hand, of course, it could be argued that these are positive, attractive images of black women which might counteract the emphasis on beautiful *white* women in the mass media. We can also note that mainstream *male* pop stars are required to be thin and conventionally good-looking too.

The key themes of post-Madonna girl pop

I have traced a brief history, above, of some of the impact that Madonna has had on certain artists who followed in her footsteps. Of course, there will be hundreds of other performers who have been influenced by Madonna in some way – I mentioned a few at the start of this chapter, and there are many others. Similarly, of course, Madonna herself may have been influenced by the work of these artists. Now, however, I will present four key *themes* that Madonna established as central, and that have since been used and emphasized by her pop successors (and imitators):

- a celebration of 'popular feminism'
- women as confident sexual agents
- fluid identities and reinvention of the self
- transformations and contradictions.

These themes represent elements that recur in the music, videos, imagery and interviews of Madonna and other artists that have followed her steps. It is not necessarily the case that the artists in question have consciously or explicitly decided to develop these themes; nevertheless, by doing what they want to do and 'expressing themselves', their work articulates these ideas.

A celebration of 'popular feminism'

Traditionally – in other words, before Madonna – feminist messages were not often a key to success in the mainstream pop charts. Of course, we can think of some exceptions: female singer-songwriters successful in the 1970s, such as Joni Mitchell, were independent, free-thinking women whose lyrics sometimes expressed a feminist ethos. Joan Armatrading was quite successful in the 1980s and was always popular with the feminist magazine *Spare Rib*. In 1985 the Eurythmics and Aretha Franklin had a big hit with 'Sisters Are Doing It For Themselves'.[4] However, it is difficult to point to a *superstar* before Madonna with a feminist agenda, because Madonna was the first person to remix her own populist version of feminism and make it part of a pop music success story.[5] In addition, traditional and patriarchal responses to her work during the course of her career spurred Madonna to be more emphatic in some of her liberatory messages. For example, although the book *Sex* (1992) was in some ways designed to 'shock' conservatives, Madonna was clearly surprised and saddened that a wide range of people and groups (including feminists) found reasons to attack it; this hardened her resolve to express her own reality and identity, as she noted in 'Human Nature' (1995): 'Did I say something true? / Oops, I didn't know I couldn't talk about sex.'[6] In short, Madonna had her own broadly feminist agenda in the first place – albeit a sometimes vague and contradictory cocktail of ideas about independence, assertiveness, sex, fantasy and the need for all people to express themselves – but she was prompted to build on this through her own experiences of being an open, sexual, determined woman within the music industry.

Madonna's expressions of womanhood are close to what Angela McRobbie (1999) calls 'popular feminism' and Natasha Walter's 'new feminism' (1998). These 'versions' of feminism are also similar to the idea of empowered female living celebrated by *Cosmopolitan* magazine for many years: a vision that emphasizes being confident, independent, pleasure-seeking and subservient to no one. This mainstream interpretation of feminism – which may not actually answer to the 'feminist' label – has become a strong element of modern pop culture, and

Madonna was perhaps the single most important figure in putting it there. By always doing her own thing, and insisting upon her right to do so, Madonna made a bold statement. In her film *Truth or Dare* (Keshishian, 1991), fans saw how single-mindedly Madonna stood up to her critics. Today, this level of dedication to independence has become the norm for female stars. For example, when Britney's film *Crossroads* (Rhimes, 2002) was savaged by mostly middle-aged, mostly male critics, the usually polite star declared:

> To be totally honest with you, I think if the critics like it I should be really worried, because everything my critics like, I hate. And everything the critics hate, I like. As long as my fans are touched by it, that's what counts. (quoted in Wilson, 2002, p. 83)

This robust rejection of the views of a critical older generation is typical of the new voice of popular feminism. Such a stance also places a strong emphasis on female pleasure and independent sexuality, which I will discuss in the next section. More broadly, it stands for independence of spirit and not being tied down by other people's expectations – in other words, it is the Spice Girls' idea of straightforward, individualistic 'girl power'. Where traditional feminism worries about the interconnected oppressive networks of patriarchy, capitalism and racism, popular feminism puts a smile on its face and assumes that if women are encouraged to 'go for it' and 'believe in yourself' then liberation will be achieved. These ideas appear frequently in the work of all of the female performers mentioned in this chapter.

Some feminists denounce 'popular feminism' (or 'girl power', or 'feminism lite') as a radical simplification of the original critical feminist thesis. They argue that the new perspective fails to challenge broader social structures such as capitalism, and only tackles patriarchy on a limited, individualistic basis.[7] On the other hand, the upbeat, aspirational message conveyed by female pop stars appears to have a definite impact upon young women, encouraging them to be more assertive and independent – an outcome that feminists could be pleased about. In my email interviews with Britney Spears fans (reported in more depth in Gauntlett, 2002, pp. 224–36), the message of self-confidence seemed to be one of the most important aspects of Britney's meaningfulness. For example:

> I do believe that Britney sends out good messages to girls. She shows self esteem which makes girls believe that they can achieve anything (15-year-old female from Sydney, Australia).

> I think that Britney sends out the message for us girls to have self-confidence. I have a great amount of confidence in myself ... With all these girl power songs coming out, saying how we don't need guys, I have so much confidence – it definitely helped me out. Like 'look at me now, you can't have me, too bad, you lost' (17-year-old female from Belding, Mississippi, USA).

> Britney gives me a message of accepting yourself, and not letting boys push you around ... In ['What You See (Is What You Get)'] she is basically saying that ... if

a boy wants to change her than he better leave. That shows girls not to let their boyfriends boss them around. To be their own woman (15-year-old female from Pennsylvania, USA).[8]

In many more quotes like these, Britney's teenage fans insisted that the star helped them to be strong and independent young women. They hadn't been inspired to initiate the kind of revolution desired by 1970s feminists, of course – nothing of the sort – but the everyday strength of character that they enjoyed and celebrated, fostered in part by their engagement with post-Madonna pop stars, was a triumph of popular feminism.

Women as confident sexual agents

Madonna famously carved out a space for female performers to be unapologetically sexual agents/actors, asserting their own needs and desires, and refusing to be treated as mere sex objects by men. Since then, sexual self-confidence has become a primary component of the representation of positive womanhood projected by successful female performers. Again this is an aspect of 'popular feminism', where the perceived puritanism of established feminism is turned on its head. As McRobbie notes, however, this new-found mainstream sexual assertiveness echoes some of the feminist demands of two decades earlier:

> To [many] young women official feminism is something that belongs to their mothers' generation. They have to develop their own language for dealing with sexual inequality, and if they do this through a raunchy language of 'shagging, snogging and having a good time', then perhaps the role this plays is not unlike the sexually explicit manifestoes found in the early writing of figures like [feminist pioneers] Germaine Greer and Sheila Rowbotham. The key difference is that this language is now found in the mainstream of commercial culture – not out there in the margins of the 'political underground'. (1999, p. 126)

McRobbie is talking here about the sexually assertive language of magazines aimed at young independent women (such as *More* in the UK and *Cosmopolitan* internationally), but her points are just as relevant to the young women inspired by the shameless sexual provocation of Madonna in the early 1990s or more recent stars such as Lil' Kim, Pink, Jennifer Lopez and even the less explicit Britney. Even though some feminists or other critics may not approve of the repetitive association of women and sexuality – even if it only matches the recurring association of *men* and sexuality within the world of popular music – it remains the case that the sexually assertive performances of these pop stars have helped to change attitudes to (and consequently experiences of) women and sex. As McRobbie puts it:

> The idea that sexual pleasure is learnt, not automatically discovered with the right partner, the importance of being able to identify and articulate what you want

sexually and what you do not want, the importance of learning about the body and being able to make the right decisions about abortion and contraception, the different ways of getting pleasure and so on, each one of these figured high in the early feminist agenda. This was the sort of material found in books like *Our Bodies, Our Selves* (Boston Women's Health Collective 1973), the volume which started as a feminist handbook and went on to sell millions of copies across the world. (1999, p. 57)

Madonna's sexual assertiveness has been, of course, one of the most distinctive elements of her life and work. This has been less apparent in recent years, but from the early impact of 'Like a Virgin' (1984), via various videos including the polysexuality of the steamy 'Justify My Love' promo (Mondino, 1990), the *Sex* book and *Erotica* album (1992), and numerous other sexual references in videos and interviews, up to the cheeky 'Music' video (Åkerlund, 2000) and, I suppose, even shagging her gay best friend in *The Next Best Thing* (Schlesinger, 2000), Madonna's image as sexual free spirit has been emphatically defined.

Although Madonna clearly did not invent sexiness in pop, she could be credited with bringing a female desiring gaze to centre stage, and subsequently – as I have already mentioned – stars such as the Spice Girls, Destiny's Child, Lil' Kim, Kylie Minogue and Pink have portrayed themselves as self-assured sex specialists who would decide which of their admirers they would entertain. (This mirrors the behaviour of male 'sex gods' such as Elvis Presley and Mick Jagger in the past, of course, but when women began to take this role it was unexpected and challenging.)

Fluid identities and reinvention of the self

With her numerous changes of visual style and continued musical innovation, Madonna is credited with popularizing the view that identity is not fixed and can be continuously rearranged and revamped. Three different academic books about Madonna published in 1993 all pointed to Madonna's continuous reinventions of herself, and provided theoretical discussion of what this might mean (see Frank and Smith, 1993a; Lloyd, 1993; Schwichtenberg, 1993a). Just three years earlier, in her groundbreaking book *Gender Trouble* (1990), Judith Butler had set out her argument that there were not necessarily any connections between the body that a person is born with (whether male or female or unclear), the gendered personality that they perform in everyday life (whether 'masculine' or 'feminine', or both, neither or something else) and their sexual orientation (whether gay or straight or both or whatever). Since identities are not fixed, Butler suggested, they can change over time or, indeed, we can choose to change our 'identity'. In Butler's model, there is no need to be constrained by certain conventional alignments of these elements: being born male does not mean that one has to acquire a masculine personality, nor does it mean that one has to be attracted to women. Nor, necessarily do the supposedly 'opposite' things apply either – there are no binaries and opposites, just an infinite range of possible personalities. Butler called for 'a radical proliferation of gender, *to displace* the very gender norms' that had previously made traditional sexuality and gender roles appear natural (1990, p. 148).

Butler's book seemed revolutionary and exciting, but it was also very difficult to read, and critics noted that the author failed to provide any examples of how 'gender trouble' could be brought about in everyday life, or what this might look like. For example, Monique Deveaux (1994) complained that Butler did not explain how her idea of everyday resistance would work in practical terms, and in a review of *Gender Trouble*, E. Ann Kaplan (1992) noted that she would have liked 'more concreteness, particularly in relation to Butler's proposed politics of repetitive parodic gender performance' (p. 846). However, the answer was before their eyes, as the contributors to *The Madonna Connection* (Schwichtenberg, 1993a) – who included Kaplan – noticed: Madonna seemed to be the living embodiment of Butler's manifesto. The *Sex* book, the videos for 'Express Yourself', 'Justify My Love' and the whole *Erotica* album, did it all – the blurring and confusion of genders, fluidity of sexuality, transgression of masculine and feminine stereotypes were all what Butler appeared to be calling for. Butler seemed to think that gender boundaries should be challenged on the level of everyday life, whereas Madonna had taken her campaign to the world stage, but nevertheless Madonna's popularity potentially meant that her gender-troubling activities might affect her fans as they found meaning for her work within their everyday lives.

There can be no doubt that Madonna has continued to innovate and to 'reinvent herself' with each album (and to a lesser extent, each single and video) or film. As the DJ/producer Sasha noted in 2000, 'She could have taken the Celine Dion route and gone for horrible ballads, but she really pushes herself' (quoted in Harrison, 2000, p. 83). Other female stars have found that a regular change of theme, image and/or style can help to extend a career – Kylie Minogue, in particular, has stretched her pop career from the 1980s to the present, partly by reinventing herself as 'indie Kylie', 'dance Kylie' and 'disco Kylie' (although the public always seemed to like the 'pure pop Kylie' better than any of her other image excursions). Nevertheless, it has to be admitted that Madonna's presentation of the 'fluid genders'/'fluid identity' idea hasn't really been adopted by many other stars in the years since. However, it seems likely that Britney Spears's popularity is helped by an identity *mystery* similar to that cultivated by Madonna – who is the 'real' Britney? Teenage sex bomb or church-going virgin? Our tantalizing inability to 'pin down' her 'true' identity may add to the Britney appeal.

Transformations and contradictions

As the sociologists Anthony Giddens and Ulrich Beck have argued, citizens in modern Western societies have to make choices of identity and lifestyle (see Giddens 1991 and 1992; Giddens and Pierson, 1998; Beck, 2002). This is the case even if people's preferred options are rather obvious and conventional ones, or are limited due to lack of financial (or cultural) resources; we still have to make *choices* – whether consciously or more passively – about how to present ourselves and how to live our lives. Pop stars like Madonna and her successors are unlikely to have a clear-cut, direct effect on the choices that we make – even if we are fans of these artists – but they may nevertheless influence our ideas and our perception of the range of ways of living available to us. Beck says that in modern Western societies everyone wants to 'live their own life', but this is, at the same time, 'an experimental life' (2002, p. 26). Since the social world is no longer confident in its traditions, every approach to life, whether seemingly radical or conventional, is somewhat risky and needs to be worked upon – nurtured, considered and maintained, or amended. Because 'inherited recipes for living and role stereotypes fail to function' (p. 26), we have to make our own new patterns of being, and again – although this is not one of Beck's emphases – it seems clear that popular media must play a role in this.

Madonna's numerous transformations of style and appearance, as noted above, reflect the lack of fixedness of modern identities, and her ability to seemingly change herself has been an inspiration to her fans (again, see Frank and Smith, 1993a; Lloyd, 1993; Schwichtenberg, 1993a; Faith, 1997; and other chapters in this collection). The transformations enacted by other female stars reinforce this idea: that you don't have to settle for one thing in life, and that you can reach for other more exciting possibilities – again, this was a key part of the Spice Girls' 'girl power' message, as well as being an idea communicated in interviews and songs by Missy Elliot, Pink, Lil' Kim and indeed all of the stars mentioned above. My interviews with Britney Spears fans (Gauntlett, 2002) showed that she communicated to them a message of empowerment, confidence and independence, and the idea that 'anybody' could change their life and become successful. Even if this 'feelgood' notion is not a good representation of reality, it is nevertheless the case that it provided young female fans with confidence, optimism and aspirations which they carried forward into their lives.

Finally, we should note that the 'messages' emanating from pop stars are not always clear and consistent. Madonna's interest in the Catholic church always seemed rather contradictory, for example – she seemed to love it and hate it in equal measure, on the one hand taunting it with her 'shocking' imagery, and on the other hand seeking a connection with the Catholic faith, calling her daughter Lourdes and so on. In another sphere of her life, Madonna's earlier gender-bending imagery and messages of sexual liberation and freedom seem to sit a little uncomfortably with getting married to Guy Ritchie, a film director noted for his obsession with macho gangsters (as we know, he even directed her on a car commercial (*Star* in 2001), a film (*Swept Away* in 2002) and the video for one of her singles ('What it Feels Like for a Girl' in 2001)).[9] Of the 'post-Madonna' stars, Britney, Destiny's Child and others have milked the paradox of their well-behaved Christian values contrasting with the raunchiness of their performances. More generally, the 'do what you want' ideal and the message of freedom articulated by all of these stars contrast with the carefully controlled, workaholic lives that we know they lead from all those magazine articles and MTV specials.

Conclusions

Although Madonna is quite a self-contained phenomenon, being both fiercely independent and uniquely successful, she has had a clear impact upon the careers of the female pop stars who have followed in her wake, partly because she 'opened up' the pop market to certain possibilities and partly in her emphasis upon certain themes. Madonna made it possible to articulate feminist ideas in an accessible (or indeed sexually provocative) style, paving the way for 'girl power' a few years later – both Madonna and the Spice Girls celebrated a feminist attitude to personal freedom, but extended it to cover the right to wear corsets and hot pants as a radical statement. The new female stars were not closely identified with the now established face of feminism, which was often seen by younger women as anti-men and anti-sex, but they created a new language and imagery of female empowerment which began with Madonna's famous pointy bra and soon led to the shockwaves that hit the hip-hop world when Lil' Kim started rapping about oral sex. This new-found sexual self-confidence is also linked to the celebration of personal change and transformation that is found in post-Madonna pop songs, videos, interviews and imagery. Not all of the messages of the new generation of female pop stars add up to a clear manifesto, as we have noted, but more optimistically, we could say that the contradictions are useful and productive, because the multiple messages of pop culture contribute to the idea that in a post-Madonna world there is an open realm of liberating possibilities.

Notes

1. This article includes some material (on Britney Spears, the Spice Girls and Destiny's Child) which previously appeared in a different form in the chapter 'Directions for Living: Role Models, Pop Music, and Self-Help Discourses' in Gauntlett, 2002.
2. Geri went on to be a star, and sub-Madonna-style gay icon, in her own right. Interviewed by *Attitude* magazine in 2001, she was still saying life-affirming and liberal things such as 'I believe that anything is possible for anyone – shutting down possibilities is a waste of living' and 'Last week I was entertaining the idea of becoming a lesbian' (Flynn, 2001, p. 46). In the same month she told *Marie Claire*: 'I'm a tomboy who likes to dress as Barbie' and 'I do get comments about how I look, but I have to try and let that go ... What matters is how I feel about myself' (Forrest, 2001, pp. 43–4).
3. On these talk shows, see Gamson, 1999, and Lunt, 2002.

4. For more on the history of women in rock and pop music, see Sherman, 2000; Whiteley, 2000; Hirshey, 2002; and O'Brien, 2002.
5. Of course, the status of Madonna's attitudes and works as expressions of 'feminism' can be debated. Today it is often recognized that there are 'feminisms' of different kinds. See Whelehan, 1995, and Brooks, 1997, for useful discussions of the development of different strands of feminisms, and post-feminism. Madonna's relationship to feminism is discussed in various chapters in Schwichtenberg, 1993, and also by Patricia Pisters in this collection.
6. For evidence of her disappointment at the critical reaction, see Madonna's remarks quoted, for example, by St. Michael (1999, pp. 97–8). Morton's biography says that Madonna was privately 'distraught' at the negative response to the *Sex* book, and had difficulty sleeping at night, having expected that more people would be supportive of the project (2002, pp. 182–3). The backlash in the wake of *Sex* and *Erotica* (1992) seemed to bring about the end of Madonna's most outrageous period.
7. For example, a few days after I posted a Trading Card about 'girl power' at the website theory.org.uk, I received an email from one (male) viewer, informing me that the 'girl power' concept was 'a virulently reactionary anti-feminist movement'. (Theory.org.uk features a set of 'Trading Cards' that contain concise information about various theorists – such as Judith Butler, Michel Foucault and Anthony Giddens – and concepts such as postmodernism and 'girl power'. See <http://www.theory.org.uk>.
8. Compare these responses with those collected by Lisa Peñaloza in relation to Madonna (see Chapter 11 in this collection).
9. The provocative gender theme suggested by the lyrics in that song seemed largely ignored, with some meaningless violence deployed instead. For further discussion of this video, see Patricia Pisters in this collection (Chapter 2).

Chapter 11

Consuming Madonna then and now

An examination of the dynamics and structuring of celebrity consumption

Lisa Peñaloza

In this chapter I explore the ways in which consumers respond to the work of celebrities as the means for generating insights regarding contemporary consumer culture. Celebrities are a key element in consumer culture. Like products, celebrities are part of the contemporary landscape, and consumers view and employ them in their daily lives in ways similar to those in which people historically have incorporated elements of their environment into stories to make sense of human existence (Macay, 1997). However, our experiences with celebrities carry an intensity and immediacy well beyond many other consumption experiences (O'Guinn, 1991). Part of the reason celebrity commands a transcendent, larger-than-life character is that consumers experience these people predominantly through the media (Dyer, 1986; Stacey, 1994; Moores, 1997). Part fantasy, part reality, celebrity encounters are part of a larger set of social processes through which we work out key social issues of the day (McCracken, 1989; Denzin, 1995). Through contacts with and narratives about celebrities, people develop understandings of themselves, each other and our culture (Walters, 1995).

Madonna was selected as the focal celebrity for this investigation due to her phenomenal success. In making my arguments I draw from literature on celebrity in marketing and consumer behaviour, film studies, Madonna's body of work, critics' accounts of her work and two surveys of consumers' interactions with Madonna. Using a case study format, I develop a model of celebrity consumption by analysing the meanings consumers attribute to Madonna and their uses of these meanings. Celebrity consumption is situated within the multicultural world that this book explores, as I emphasize the ways in which celebrity meanings are deployed and contested by members of subcultural groups. Further, I attend to the larger frame of marketing and media agents and institutions (for example, production and promotion companies, marketers and so on) through which contemporary celebrities are produced and circulated. Finally, implications are drawn in terms of the global economy. Specifically, I extrapolate from subcultural difference in celebrity consumption in the USA to consider global cultural dynamics. At issue are factors influencing heterogeneity in cultural representations and the reception of cultural meanings as they occur within and across various consumer subcultures on a global scale.

Conceptual framework

Early research on celebrity consumption in the field of marketing focused predominantly on product endorsements, and was primarily concerned with celebrities' abilities to provide product information for marketers in their development of product and brand images (Baker and Churchill, 1977; Dholakia and Sternthal, 1977). More recently, researchers emphasize celebrities as carriers of cultural meanings who supply a vast array of these meanings and images to consumers for their use in developing their identities and social relations (Kozinets, 2001; McCracken, 1989). Because celebrity endorsements are a visible, but small, subset of all consumer–celebrity interactions, I broaden the scope of this work to include celebrity appearances in film, concerts, recorded music and videos, television appearances, entertainment magazines, talk shows, tabloids, benefits and other public service activities, awards ceremonies, fan clubs and interpersonal contact. Celebrities operate in and through a number of marketing and media institutions. The links to a product or service distinguish product endorsements within the larger category of celebrity consumption, as they add another set of signifiers (McCracken, 1989). Further, it is likely that celebrity activities and personalities play into the meaning-making process, and their impact on consumers is rendered more complex by the inseparability of on- and off-stage dimensions. That is, so called 'off-stage' and 'on-stage' celebrity appearances are often combined in the media, and as a result are merged in the way they are experienced by consumers.

The second literature useful in this conceptualization is film studies. Observing overlaps between celebrity consumption and film spectatorship, I draw from this body of work to assert that celebrity meanings are attributed by consumers as the result of a complex negotiation between celebrity, market institutions and audience. Film scholars have argued that consumers' perceptions of film stars are based in part on what consumers bring to the celebrity as the result of their particular experiences of age, gender, race/ethnicity, class and sexuality (Fiske, 1987a; Dyer, 1991; Stacey, 1994). Thus, in looking at celebrity consumption, this work highlights the importance of social factors as influences on the meanings attributed to celebrities by consumers and the ways these meanings are intimately tied into their respective dynamics of identity and social difference.

Other sources of key theoretical insights are psychoanalytic studies emphasizing the processes through which celebrities are experienced by members of a film audience. While this work emphasizes Hollywood film stars, it is usefully applied to more general celebrity consumption because media such as film and television are the primary means of consumers' contact with celebrities. In her classic article 'Visual Pleasure and Narrative Cinema' (1975), Mulvey drew from Freud and Lacan to emphasize the psychological dynamics of desire.[1] Mulvey construed the visual pleasures of film viewing as a twofold process of desire experienced through consumers' objectification of celebrities and identification with their images on the film screen. Objectification involves the separation of the celebrity from the image on the screen, important in accomplishing voyeuristic pleasures. Identification involves the unification of the viewing subject with the image on the screen and in a chain reaction, with the celebrity, which allows the narcissistic pleasures of experiencing the subjectivity and action portrayed.

Notably, early work characterized the film spectator position as inherently male-gendered (Mulvey, 1975), due to the so-called 'masculine' pleasures of looking accorded to audiences as the result of film techniques. Of particular importance were strategically selected shots and angles in the creation of the film, the social conventions of male characters looking at female characters recreated within the film genre and the spectator's identification with the main character, who was typically male. Later work emphasized less fixed notions of gender spectatorship (Cowie, 1984). Stacey (1994) was critical of the overemphasis on narrative structures within the film text, directing attention to the activity of audiences in constructing the star. Thus, the literature on celebrity spectatorship mirrors the blurred gender roles in film and incorporates more active, plural subject positions for audiences.

This literature raises a number of issues regarding the nature of celebrity consumption. First, conceptualizations of consumers actively producing cultural meanings from celebrities are in line with the growing body of work on consumer culture highlighting the role of consumer production in adding market value (Arnould and Price, 1993; O'Guinn and Shrum, 1994; Schor and Holt, 2000). Second, psychological processes of desire are brought to the fore.[2] In their review of treatments of desire in consumer culture, Belk et al. (2000) describe consumer desire as always deferred, often accompanied by anxiety and involving complex interactions between celebrity representations and equally problematic notions of consumer identity. I suggest subcultural difference plays an important role in consumer desire as well. In locating celebrity meanings within a multicultural context, I extend identification and individuation processes to consumers who are members of various subcultural groups. That is, consumers draw from celebrities in a matching of their identity and social relations with those depicted by the celebrities. Yet crossovers are just as vital, as consumers draw from symbols of other identities and social groups, and in doing so add to the blurring of gender roles and multiple subject positions (Peñaloza, 2001).

Finally, this chapter situates celebrity consumption within its institutional context. At issue is the means of star construction, in its effects on celebrity meanings and cultural relations. Through techniques of film, video and audio recording, and enhanced graphics, as well as surgery, celebrities perform superhuman feats and aesthetic perfection, and their images maintain an equally superhuman circulation. At the same time, through video news releases, tabloids and talk shows, consumers are inundated with highly personal images and information, often of an intimate nature more characteristic of relations with close friends and family. This humanly superhuman character of celebrities is a fascinating part of the hyper-reality and consumption of the spectacle theorized by Baudrillard (Poster, 1988) and DeBord (1977).[3] Even when simulated, mechanically altered and at their most fantastic and fantasy-filled, celebrities maintain important reality effects for consumers in serving as models and in giving advice on how they should live. In terms of meanings, the potential effect of age and motherhood on the reception of Madonna's recent work is significant. Regarding social relations, contemporary consumers should also take into account perceptions of the impact of Madonna's inclusion of people of colour and various expressions of sexuality in her work.

Celebrity case study: Madonna

Madonna is arguably the most successful female solo pop performer ever. In the two decades of her career, she has had over two dozen consecutive top ten hits, and by 1992 had signed a $60 million contract with Time Warner (Holden, 1992, B1). She is a veritable cultural production industry. She has written songs with an impressive array of co-authors. Her music videos are credited to a score of producers and directors, with copyrights by Warner Brothers, Maverick and Boy Toy Inc.

In early work, dubbed her 'Boy Toy period', Madonna appeared as a bubbly pop performer, her music featured a throbbing dance beat, and her style consisted of the outer-wear of underwear and a plethora of crucifixes. Later, the focus of her work shifted to a quasi-autobiographical format with images of fantasy and reality that incorporated controversial sadomasochistic and homoerotic themes. Examples of this shift include the video 'Justify My Love' (Mondino, 1990), which was banned by MTV; the film *Truth or Dare* (Keshishian, 1991); the *Erotica* album (1992); and her book, *Sex* (1992), which benefited from charges of its scandalous content, its $50 price tag and its propriety for library collections. Regarding her use of ethnic/national cultures, her work has expanded from largely urban African-American and Latino images and rhythms to include international references to Japan, India and the Middle East. Her ambition is legendary. Madonna has been quoted as wanting to become more famous than God (Young, 1992, p. 81). As noted by Turner, 'She made outrageous claims about her ambitions, but invited the world to join her in believing that dreams come true' (1993, p. 8).

As stated above, this case analysis is drawn from Madonna's body of work, scholarly and journalistic accounts of her work, promotional materials, surveys of young adults' responses to eight of her music videos[4] and participant observation and websites of conferences of Madonna fans.[5] These data are appropriate to the study of celebrity consumption given its multi-faceted, multi-media juxtapositions of imagery and meanings. As Dyer notes, 'the star phenomenon consists of everything publicly available about stars. A film star's image is not just his/her films, but the promotion of those films and of the star through pin-ups, public appearances, studio hand-outs, and so on, as well as interviews, biographies and coverage in the press of the star's doings and "private" life' (1986, pp. 2–3).

In making sense of this material I have organized it into three subsections: particular meanings attached to Madonna, uses of Madonna (how she is integrated into consumers' lives) and the institutional means through which the celebrity Madonna is conveyed. These subsections, while distilled from the literature and grounded in data, are not mutually exclusive, nor exhaustive. They are constitutive facets of the Madonna phenomenon that I use to simulate and interpret the celebrity experience in the complex blend of fantasy and reality that consumer desire entails.

The meanings of Madonna

> 'What do I remind you of? Your past? Your dreams?
> Or some part of yourself you just can't love?'
> Madonna, 'Waiting' (1992)

The meanings attached to Madonna are as varied as her dense body of work, laden as it is with multiple and contradictory signs that she invokes and invites us to use. In this section I review four categories of meanings: sex, love, social difference and commercialism.

A central feature of Madonna's work is her expression of sexual desire. In fact, Madonna's success has been credited less to her talent than to her ability to tap into and challenge established social conventions and hierarchies of gender and sexuality (Schwichtenberg, 1993c). Madonna is attributed sexual meanings that range from slut, to manipulating bitch, to sado-masochistic dominatrix, postmodern culture vulture, New Age earth mother, 1970s retro go-go girl and rave techno machine. Examples abound. In 'Crazy For You' (1985) Madonna beckons, 'Touch me once and you'll know it's true / I never wanted anyone like this.' In 'Open Your Heart' (1986) Madonna is more direct: 'If you gave me half a chance you'd see / My desire burning inside of me.'

Through the mid-1980s and early 1990s Madonna's simulations of sex were mainstays; the crotch-grabbing scenes in the 'Express Yourself' video (Fincher,

1989), for example. In live performances of 'Like a Virgin' during her *Blond Ambition* world tour (1990) Madonna simulated masturbating on the stage. Her book *Sex* was critically denounced as 'willfully perverse in its depiction of bisexual, homosexual, and interracial sexuality' (Kakutani, 1992, p. 2). Yet, despite all the hysteria about *Sex*, only Califia (1993) noted that it was simply not obscene, in lacking erect penises, minors and violence.

The sex theme reverberates through her body of music videos in the 1990s. The video for 'Bad Girl' (Fincher, 1993) opens and closes with a murdered Madonna, who, having lived a life of promiscuous sex, presumably joins her dead lover (played by Christopher Walken). The 'Take a Bow' video (Haussman, 1994) features her unrequited love for bullfighter Emilio Muñoz. He leaves Madonna in an unruly state, her tearstained, lipstick streaked face crying at his departure. The 'Human Nature' video (Mondino, 1995) features dancers in latex and bondage. The video for 'Frozen' (Cunningham, 1998) features a darker side of sexuality, with its blue and black hues and mechanical rhythms.

A second theme, as pervasive in Madonna's work as sex, is romantic love. Romanticism pervades many of Madonna's works, especially her early lyrics. For example, in the song 'Cherish' (1989) Madonna sings about devotion and having her lover by her side, her destiny, whom she would never leave. In 'Like a Virgin' (1984) she sings about how she was lost but now, having found love, she feels 'shiny and new'. In the video for 'Express Yourself' Madonna encourages women to hold out for true love, and in 'Rescue Me' (1991) she sings of love as a saviour, 'I believe in the power of love ... / I believe that you can rescue me.'

The adventurous sexuality so often used to characterize Madonna adds complexity to these otherwise simple verses. Taken together, Madonna's romanticism espouses an interesting blend of idealism and worldly pragmatism in her lyrics and visuals. Most of Madonna's lyrics address the audience directly in the second person, although others speak of her lovers in third person and herself. For example, in 'Into the Groove' (1986) she sings, 'Boy, you've got to prove you're up to me', taunting playfully, 'we might be lovers if the rhythm's right'. In 'Live To Tell' (1986) Madonna sings of deceit and mistrust, noting that 'A man can tell a thousand lies', but 'the truth is never far behind'. In 'Papa Don't Preach' (1986), Madonna breaches the complications of family values in the form of pregnancy, reminding her father that she was always his little girl, but is now a young woman, pregnant, who plans to have her child, marry the father and raise a family. In 'Like a Prayer' (1989) Madonna fluctuates between invocations of religious love and its more carnal manifestations, 'I hear you call my name and it feels like home ... / When you call my name it's like a little prayer.'

The theme of love extends to children in Madonna's more recent work. This is not surprising, given the birth of her children in 1996 and 2000, yet this contrasts in interesting ways with her sexual playfulness. In 'Secret' (1994), the secret of Madonna's lover is revealed at the end of the video to be a young son. The 'Drowned World/Substitute for Love' video (Stern, 1998) from the album *Ray of*

Light introduces a young girl. While her face is not shown, this is her daughter, Lourdes, the substitute for love she ponders having waited for. The same album includes a song dedicated to Lourdes ('Little Star').

The third theme relates to Madonna's representations of people and behaviour considered outside of the mainstream in various respects. Inclusions of social difference appear in many forms in her work, in her statements in interviews and in attributions to her made by respondents. Her work has incorporated non-traditional sex roles, inter-racial relationships and homosexuality, and her dancers have consistently included gay men and people of colour. Part of Madonna's appeal rests on the ambivalence that people have towards social difference (Fiedler, 1978). Her work is charged with contradictory messages of progressive inclusion of difference at the same time as she is charged with cultural appropriation with the sole intent of making money (Smith, 1990).

In 'Borderline' (1984) Madonna sings of non-traditional interpersonal relationships. She is demanding yet submissive. In the survey data collected in the early 1990s (summarized in Nakayama and Peñaloza, 1993), students responded generally positively to the video and to her assertions of women's needs in career and relationships. 'I think her message is there is a fine line between a career and love but you *can* do both', wrote Michael, a 20-year-old white male. 'Women need their freedom to make their own choices and can't be smothered' responded Ellen, a 23-year-old white female. Ben, a 30-year-old white male, agreed: 'I believe the video is about women who get in relationships with men who don't respect them yet always seem to come back. Madonna's message is that you should only take so much.'

In contrast, in responses to more recent videos in a similar survey conducted in 2002, although most students exhibited similarly positive responses to more recent videos and live performances, there was also a hint of a backlash, and a few admitted boredom at the repetition in her work. Jenny, a 22-year-old white woman, wrote about 'Human Nature': 'Madonna is saying to be open with your sexuality, and not caring what other people think.' Leanne responded to 'Don't Tell Me' (2000) with: 'her message is that the woman can take control of love and love someone when she wants to and stop when she wants to'. On 'Human Nature', Steve, a 21-year-old white man, wrote: 'When a woman takes the attitude that she's not someone's bitch she becomes a bitch in the eyes of society.' In response to the same video, Mary, a 23-year-old female, wrote: 'I liked that Madonna shows she is strong enough to produce a video with this content, but it seemed there should have been more to it than sex', while James, a 21-year-old male, wrote: 'It's all about sex, like all of her work – how boring.'

Interracial relationships surfaced in her video 'Like a Prayer' (Lambert, 1989), in which Madonna sings with a black choir, kisses a black saint and employs a cultural inversion whereby the 'bad guys' are white. Notably, Madonna has expressed intentions of furthering social tolerance. In an interview she stated: 'I'm a political person ... I'm incensed by the prejudice in the world, and if I can do something with my celebrity to make people see things that ordinarily they may not pay attention to, then I feel responsible to do it. But I want to have fun while I'm doing it' (quoted in Shewey, 1992a, p. 46).

Madonna has done much to promote gay and lesbian visibility, favouring a gay aesthetic in *Sex* and in many videos and live performances. These themes pervaded her last three world tours, as documented in the interviews with the dancers of the *Blond Ambition* tour (in the documentary film *Truth or Dare*), the lesbian-looking dancers and homoerotic dance numbers of *The Girlie Show* (1993) or the sexual ambiguity that characterized the Spanish section of the *Drowned World Tour* (2001). Again, her inclusions create a sense of titillation and spectacle. An example are her comments regarding her relationship with Sandra Bernhard: 'Whether I'm gay or not is irrelevant. Whether I slept with her [Bernhard] is irrelevant. I'm perfectly willing to have people think that I did' (quoted in Shewey, 1992a, p. 51). The lesbian theme has been revisited more recently on the London stage with the famous kiss in *Up for Grabs* (Williamson, 2002) and also in her cameo role as a lesbian fencing instructor in *Die Another Day* (Tamahori, 2002).[6]

The fourth theme concerns commerce and commercialism. Madonna is viewed as a shrewd marketer and a business woman without equal. Several people I encountered in August 1993 at a conference of Madonna fans spoke with admiration of her business sense. Colleagues Tom Nakayama, Laurie Schulze and I had been invited to present our research to the group, and I noted the following reactions at the time. One woman, who appeared to be in her mid-fifties, spoke of her respect for Madonna's business sense. Another man, who seemed about the same age, noted that he had brought his teenage son because he wanted to support him – for which the crowd of about fifty people cheered. He then admitted that he, too, admired her business savvy. Numerous websites (including the official www.madonna.com) feature lengthy compilations of her singles, albums, videos and other merchandise for sale.

Fans' interpretations notwithstanding, depictions of commerce in Madonna's work are ambiguous, suggesting both parody of, and tribute to materialist culture. Many videos juxtapose romantic love, sexual freedom and spirituality with depictions of money, success and glamour. For example, the song 'Borderline' features a rags to riches narrative, while in the video (Lambert, 1984) Madonna chooses the guy and stays in the *barrio*. In 'Material Girl' (1985) she draws our attention to essential economic relations between the sexes, singing smartly: 'The boy with the cold hard cash is always Mr. Right', and foretelling: 'If I don't get proper credit, I'll just walk away.' The videos for 'Material Girl' (Lambert, 1985) and 'Vogue' (Fincher, 1990) feature handsome men in tuxedos, with Madonna in an evening dress. More recently, she has spurned the furs and pearls in the video for 'Music' (Åkerlund, 2000) and performing her *Drowned World Tour*.

There is a dual thrust to her business acumen. Madonna's early responses were to distance herself from her business savvy to claim her status as an artist.

She has been quoted as saying, 'I'm very flattered that everyone thinks I'm such a good businesswoman, but I think that to say that I'm a great manipulator, that I have great marketing savvy is ultimately an insult, because it undermines my power as an artist' (quoted in Kaplan, 1991, p. 20). More recently, perhaps with the growing globalization of popular culture, such divisions of art and commerce may be less an issue; no contemporary students voiced these concerns.

Uses of Madonna

In responding to Madonna's videos, survey respondents moved back and forth between descriptions of her work, characterizations of her personality and life circumstances, directives of what her message means to society, and projections of themselves and their life situations into her work. Using combinations of first, second and third person voices, they write about her in terms of adulation or disgust, with a familiarity more typical of relations with family and close friends.

Uses of Madonna were of two types, personal and collective. Personal uses of Madonna featured her as the subject of imitation and inspiration. At the 1993 conference of Madonna fans, several people competed in dressing like her and mimicking her performances, in a dramatic appropriation of her image, taking pleasure in the movement of their bodies and being watched by others. As examples, two men in wet briefs were led around on all fours by chains to their necks held by one Madonna lookalike. Another contestant, a 15-year-old boy, took the crowd by storm in his rendition of 'Vogue'. In a blend of youthful innocence and bold sensuality, he lowered his jean jacket on his shoulders, 'strutting his stuff'. People in the crowd went wild, grabbing and lunging at him, screaming their approval.

Several inspired confessions were volunteered at the conference. Jaime, a Latino man in his early thirties, stood up and proclaimed, 'She gives me inspiration to get up in the morning.' He credited Madonna for his determination and optimism in being HIV positive for several years, and thanked her for positive portrayals of gays in her work, which he thought helped legitimize gay culture. A white woman in her mid-twenties, a fan since the age of 12, said she identified with Madonna, particularly with her strength, which she used in coping with abuse by her father. Other confessionals were less positive. A white man in his twenties admitted he had lost friends and suffered because of his admiration for Madonna. Another man in his thirties expressed disappointment in *Sex* and in the 'Erotica' video (Baron, 1992), saying that she had gone too far, and that he could no longer be her fan.

For the most part, respondents interacted with Madonna and her work in the form of a storyline. In some responses people projected themselves into her narratives, deriving codes of reality and of behaviour for themselves, including how to relate to work, to others and to their culture. For example, Bill, a

25-year-old white male, wrote about 'Like a Prayer': 'It's about life and how sometimes *we* are mistaken for someone else and the consequences are catastrophic. Almost like a nightmare. This tells you how lost *I* was' (my emphasis). In the most recent study, Gerry, a 21-year-old white male, wrote in response to 'Frozen': 'This video is about being trapped inside yourself and not seeing what's really there. You need to look beyond what you want to see and see what's really there. Don't be afraid of your sexuality.' Others attributed various characteristics to Madonna and events in her life. For example, noted Karin, a 22-year-old woman, in response to the video 'Don't Tell Me' (Mondino, 2000): 'Madonna is obviously in a better spiritual place here. Her message is don't tell her to stop being happy and doing what she loves.'

At a more collective level subcultural members use Madonna to work out and further their interests. Three subcultures were noted: women, blacks and gays. First, Madonna's depictions of women have been discussed at length by feminist theorists for their emancipatory potential in helping women challenge patriarchal, capitalist culture (E. Ann Kaplan, 1993). Referring to her parodies of female sexuality, feminists have revelled in Madonna's chameleon-like appearance and deferral of identity as an antidote to feminist orthodoxy, reifying limited notions of female agency and subjectivity (Schwichtenberg, 1993c; Walters, 1995). While agreeing with these other feminist theorists initially, hooks (1993) suggests that Madonna has redefined her public persona away from feminist issues. Analogously, Madonna's use of black actors and cultural references has been denounced by blacks as white imperialism (hooks, 1993). One of the most strident denunciations is a poem that accused Madonna of being a 'wannabe' who doesn't want it all but 'to pick and choose. Just pull out the appealing, marketable features of contemporary black urban culture … to own, to claim, to white-wash' (Smith, 1990).

Nevertheless, several students from the 1993 survey attributed to Madonna intentions of challenging racism. Mary, an 18-year-old white female responding to 'Like a Prayer', wrote: 'I liked this video because it makes a statement about racism. It says to me that there is still a *lot* of prejudice in this world … The colour of our skin should not determine who we are or limit our goals.' 'She is trying to break apart peoples [*sic*] concepts of religion, racism and sexuality', wrote Jane, a 21-year-old white woman. 'Her message seems to be that people that aren't "white" have all the odds against them. But it is okay to stand up for non-whites' rights when you are white', wrote Chris, a 20-year-old white man, in response to 'Like a Prayer'. Leah, an 18-year-old Hispanic woman, added her interpretation: 'you shouldn't be afraid of having relationships with another person, no matter what race they are'. In contrast, in the 2002 survey, students saw ethnic and racial diversity as something to be expected in Madonna's work, with only a few crediting her work with promoting inter-racial relationships and tolerance. In response to 'Human Nature', Beth, a 21-year-old woman, wrote: 'I don't think ethnicity is an issue for Madonna. Her videos showcase many different races together as equal.' Mary, the 23-year-old woman quoted earlier, added for the same video: 'The fact that she has many races represented in her work makes it seem as though her message is universal.'

Like blacks, Latinos/as and women, gays and lesbians debate Madonna's capacities as their advocate in helping challenge heterosexist culture. The following quote by Musto echoes the paradoxes of celebrity familiarity: 'We don't even know this girl, but we spend more time talking about her than about our real friends ... After an hour with her, we're aroused, but wearing condoms, mad at her for ripping us off, but somehow thanking her for noticing us, legitimizing us, pulling us by our bootstraps up out of hiding and into the public pleasuredome of scrutiny and success' (1991, p. 36). Madonna has openly supported the gay community for over a decade, providing information on AIDS and safe sex, and contributing to a number of benefits, such as for the Keith Haring Foundation. At the 1993 Madonna conference, Jason, a young white man in his early twenties, spoke of her depiction of gays as a crusade, quoting her claim that by the time she finished, Hollywood wouldn't be homophobic anymore (see Shewey, 1992a, p. 50). Gays and lesbians, while relishing her portrayal of them, ponder Madonna's impact. As mentioned earlier, while she is willing to have others *think* she had an affair with Sandra Bernhard, this ambiguity is a luxury not enjoyed by all, and her posturing has been condemned (hooks, 1993). As depictions of gays and lesbians become more common in North American television shows (such as *Ellen*, *Will and Grace* or the popular American adaptation of the British series *Queer as Folk*), hopefully the debate will advance beyond superficial posturing towards more complex distinctions regarding cultural appropriations and demands by gays and lesbians for more sophisticated articulations of queer subjectivity.

What members of each of these three subcultures have in common is that they make demands of Madonna in their own interests. While they acknowledge some benefit, they question her challenges to sexist, racist and homophobic culture, since she benefits economically. These varied perspectives suggest important subcultural nuances in meaning-making, with implications regarding whose voice gets heard, whose interpretations of Madonna circulate and eventually stick, and who benefits.

A final issue regarding the impact of Madonna's work on social relations relates to how the passing of time and key events in the life of a celebrity affect audiences' reception of her work. In the 2002 survey, students were evenly mixed regarding the impact of age and motherhood on their responses to Madonna's work. Many felt her audience was primarily teens and twenty-somethings, while others suggested her work appeals to a general audience. Sally, a 20-year-old white woman, wrote: 'I have more respect for Madonna and what she does now that she has kids, but I respected her a lot before too. I think it's amazing that she can still kick ass after so long.' Uma, a 22-year-old woman from India, wrote: 'I grew up with Madonna. She is the only musician I have constantly and still listen to over my life and think I always will. I think her age and the fact that she has kids have changed her music, I think she sings with more meaning, not just profits.' Dana, a 21-year-old white woman, added: 'It's not as if she has automatically become more respectable just because she's a mom. But it's impressive the kind of shape she's in!' Nan, a 22-year-old white woman, wrote: 'At first Madonna seemed changed, but now she has returned to the same old Madonna. Instead of motherhood changing her work, it has just been a matter of time and what the audience wants; she seems to give it to them.' Jennifer, a 23-year-old Asian female, wrote: 'I like her work and feel like she is never getting old!!' Anne, a 22-year-old white female, noted: 'I don't think she should be doing some of the stuff she does at her age.' Mark, a 22-year-old white male, argued that: 'It'll be odd if she continues to cultivate sexually explicit material at age 65. Will she ever stop rebellion and return to conformity and privacy?'

Means of Madonna

While celebrity success is easily measured in terms of box office receipts, compact disc and concert ticket and merchandise sales, these measures say little regarding the social agents and institutions through which this success is accomplished. In this section the *means* through which the star Madonna is constructed is the focus of discussion. What is most striking about Madonna in this part of the research is the vast network of creative persons and institutions, and the vast scope of resources involved. Production institutions include recording companies, video producers and directors, concert organizers and publishers. Promotional institutions include talk shows, interviews, gossip columns, reviews and fan clubs.

Regarding production, she has shifted from major studio Time Warner to her own operations: Maverick and Boy Toy. The major studios are strongly vertically integrated and increasingly highly concentrated (Schiller, 1992). Institutional features are not limited to Madonna's productions, but rather increasingly characteristic of global popular cultural products companies. Further, links between production and promotion companies are integral to the respective power of each, and their prowess in creating celebrity. For example, *Sex* had a six-figure promotional budget with advance copies distributed to and reviewed by virtually all major consumer publications (Frank and Smith, 1993b, pp. 7–8). Many of the promotional media were subsidiaries of Time Warner. These links likely contribute to her success; *Sex* sold 500000 copies in its first weeks (p. 8). The Madonna fans' conference was attended by an impressive list of press representatives: MTV, Entertainment Tonight, E!, *People* magazine and numerous local media, adding spectacle to the conference. There is a key symbiotic relationship between celebrity and media, as Madonna's presence benefits these media as well. While not as visible as entertainment media, academic studies and college courses dealing with Madonna's work benefited from the aura of her celebrity through the mid-1990s. Cathy Schwichtenberg, editor of *The Madonna Connection* (1993a), now in its third printing, appeared on talk shows, with reviews of the book gracing a score of national and international newspapers and magazines. Courses offered at such universities as Harvard, Princeton, UCLA and the University of Colorado have been put forth on the premise that celebrities have social significance and are therefore important topics of study.

Repeatedly and consistently, a multitude of agents – from journalists and talk show hosts to academics – promise us the 'real' Madonna, recanting elements of her life in relation to her work. Examples include the death of her mother when Madonna was young, her rags-to-riches story, complete with nude photos taken to make ends meet, her Catholic upbringing, her search for paternal approval, her affinity with men and women of colour, gay men and lesbians, and most recently motherhood, Eastern mysticism, cowboy culture and international rhythms and aesthetics. Strikingly, despite this army of promotional agents, Madonna is credited by critics and audience alike with developing and managing her own image. Her control of her projects and image is legendary. After working with her, photographer Herb Ritts was quoted as saying: 'She knew exactly how she wanted to look' (Kaplan, 1991, p. 20). Curious as to the effects of her control, researchers Schulze, White and Brown (1993) found that Madonna was seen more positively by people when they viewed her as in control; she was viewed more negatively when seen as manipulating and embodying stereotypes.

Critic Musto insightfully summed up the qualities of Madonna:

> Madonna has nothing, and everything to do with realness. Aloof, pre-packaged and encased in the heavy artillery of superstar merchandising, she somehow pierces through the machinery to bare her intentions so frankly we feel intimate with her, breaking down barriers between audience and performer as she brings her deepest secrets into our homes with diary-like immediacy. She's both untouchable and alarmingly accessible – the icon next door, the best friend in a glass booth. (1991, p. 36)

Discussion

The results of the previous section are graphically depicted in Figure 11.1. The diagram is divided into three orbs. At the top of the figure is Madonna, the lived celebrity. She is human and more, with larger than life qualities that many scholars have noted (Dyer, 1986; Stacey, 1994). The middle orb signifies celebrity work. For Madonna, this consists of her music, videos, film, interviews and so on; while for other celebrities it might be television, film, sports or even news telecasting, to name a few. The orb at the bottom of the diagram signifies

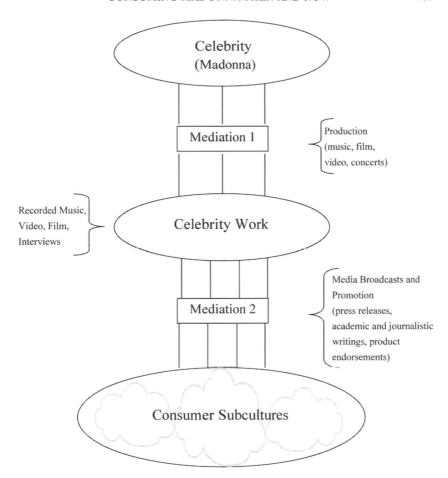

Fig. 11.1 Consuming celebrity

consumers' uses of Madonna and her work, as impinged upon by intercultural relations.

The recursive nature of the relations between Madonna, her work and consumers are conveyed in the lines linking the three orbs. Much agency is noted in the ways in which consumers employ Madonna's work towards their own ends. Two important mediations are noted, depicted as boxes in the diagram. The first mediation is located between Madonna and her work. As discussed earlier, the means of Madonna include her creative ideas and activities, as mediated by production persons and technology. This provides the materials from which meanings of Madonna are derived. A second mediation is posited between consumers and her work. It consists of critics' and journalists' reviews, press releases and the efforts of marketing and advertising companies.

The first point to be gleaned from the diagram is that Madonna is experienced by consumers as a double mediation, a montage of her person, her work and what she says and does, filtered through the two layers of production and promotion technologies. In these ways her persona as artist and business woman, and her work, embody a reflection of our culture. Yet it is a troublesome reflection, as her subjectivity and positionality are blurred by the institutional mediations through which she becomes accessible.[7]

Second, taking into account the means of Madonna is important in understanding the intensity with which some consumers receive her and her work, as well as her larger social significance. Through repeated audio and video broadcasts of her music, videos, interviews, photos and tabloids, we make intimate and frequent contact with Madonna. It is fascinating that so many can profess to know her, even as she is so physically removed from most people's lives as a function of technological advances in an increasingly mediated world. Thus, the means of Madonna create a transcendent zone in which desire and fantasy add important detail and immediacy to the celebrity consumption experience.

In the contemporary global economy it is important to recognize differences and similarities between celebrities and other market-mediated entities. Authenticity is a performance, and it is of the essence. Ironically, celebrities are increasingly simulated people – human yet more, even as products become more personalized through brand images and communities of consumer users (Muñoz and O'Guinn, 2001). The vast network and scope of agents and resources that are involved in producing meanings of Madonna continue to offer us the 'real' her, even as we are presented with an awesome array of polished performances and chameleon-like changes in appearance. But then, reinventions are a fundamental part of many consumer products' marketing strategies as well. Madonna's coup is in pulling it off as celebrity, a person and more.

The third implication of the diagram addresses the socio-cultural dynamics of celebrity consumption. As interpreted by consumers, the meanings in Madonna's work depict complex cultural equations of sex with pornography and the forbidden; love with manipulation and frothy romance; social difference with spectacle, at once exotic, enticing and threatening; and commerce as maker of success and appropriation. In serving cultural elements to her audiences, Madonna encourages us to examine aspects of ourselves and our relations to others in and through her and her work, and the double mediations of each. Key are contestations of consumer cultural identities and presences in the consumption of celebrity, as the result of complex modes of articulation between celebrities and consumers as individuals and as members of subcultural groups. Even as Madonna offers tantalizing images of beauty, wealth and sexual rapture to consumers and academics alike, the view of ourselves and our society depicted by celebrity is necessarily plural and multivocal, even as it is partial and incomplete.

Finally, in a point also related to the appropriation of cultures, it is important to consider the increasing concentration of the culture industry (Jones and Venkatesh, 1992; Schiller, 1992). Cultural products are one of the few areas in which the USA sports a net trade surplus. Strikingly, much of the appeal of Madonna's work lies in the otherness and marginality of other cultures. The early work dealt with cultural differences within the USA, while the later work incorporates international cultural imagery. The reflections of North American and foreign cultures offer tremendous potential for growth in seeing ourselves and how we relate to others, as marketability brings in its wake an ever-expanding array of cultural icons. Yet there is a downside. While promising expansion in the inclusion of international cultures, what may be learned from the experience of blacks, Latinos/as and gays and lesbians in the USA is that the net effect may be more narrow, more limited depictions that are interpreted from an implicit centre position of the white, heterosexual, 'First World' (Lipsitz, 2001). Viewed from outside this mainstream perspective, Madonna and her work are problematic, as members of non-mainstream groups and developing national cultures are much more discerning of cultural appropriations of their cultures than are those positioned outside them. Viewed from the mainstream, her work is no less troubling, as depictions of these 'others' are more targets of projection than understanding. It is a real concern that the complexities of the many cultures she draws from are minimized in their presentation, with value accorded to those aspects that are marketable, while other less attractive, but no less significant features are ignored or discarded. Yet ultimately it is not Madonna, the celebrity, alone who benefits, as many subcultural outsiders and insiders grant some gains in cultural legitimization to her inclusions of those outside the mainstream. Thus, there is a paradoxically inclusive and progressive cultural market dynamic to her cultural transformations, as the market rewards and legitimizes social difference over time.

In sum, any way you approach her, Madonna has amassed an impressive body of work in song, dance, video and film. No less impressive is her talent in keeping us amused, amazed, entertained and challenged over the past twenty years. This work has provided a tentative glimpse into the complex subject of celebrity consumption by investigating the meanings attached to Madonna, as a particular example of celebrity, and the strategic uses of these meanings. Through contacts with and meanings attributed to celebrities, consumers make sense of themselves, their culture and relationships with others. While this work is limited in its scope of intercultural dynamics within the USA, it does offer some insight into the consumption of celebrity and consumer culture. Many questions remain, and further work is called for to investigate the consumption of other celebrities in the USA and in other societies in order to further our understanding of this central aspect of consumer culture.

Notes

1. Lacan's (1977a) work stipulates that a child first comes to self-knowledge by differentiating himself or herself from the mother. This marks a move beyond the initial idealized sense of wholeness labelled the imaginary. At the mirror stage the child experiences the inevitable sense of differentiation and estrangement from the mother as the result of his or her inability to control her, yet gains a sense of himself or herself. In this way the mother embodies the initial 'other' for the child. In the final stage, the symbolic, the child begins to learn social structures and rules. Key among these is the incest taboo, through which primary attachments to the mother are fetishized, repressed and redirected to more socially acceptable avenues. In film studies, researchers generalize the mother–child relation to relationships between an audience and actors/actresses.

2. It is instructive to note how little the term 'desire' is used in consumer research and marketing. Instead, prevalent is the discourse of needs. While this may be explained as a rhetorical strategy that has effectively increased the legitimacy of marketing practices, it has severely limited our understanding of the dynamics of human desire in contemporary consumer culture (Belk et al., 2000).

3. Hyper-reality is characterized as a widespread detachment of signs from their referents and a preference for signs and simulacra over their corresponding objects in the material world (Debord, 1977; Poster, 1988).

4. Some of these data were published elsewhere (Nakayama and Peñaloza, 1993), in a study of grammatical conventions that appeared in interviewees' written responses to the videos 'La Isla Bonita' (Lambert, 1987), 'Borderline' (Lambert, 1984), 'Like a Prayer' (Lambert, 1989), 'Cherish' (Ritts, 1989) and 'Express Yourself' (Fincher, 1989). I carried out the second study in 2002, and report from forty-one students' reactions to the videos 'Human Nature' (Mondino, 1995), 'Frozen' (Cunningham, 1998) and 'Don't Tell Me' (Mondino, 2000), and to questions regarding her audience and whether motherhood and age has affected how they see her work.

5. The 1993 Madonna Expo was held in West Hollywood, California, 13–15 August to coincide with Madonna's birthday. I attended the conference as part of an invited panel of academics with Tom Nakayama and Laurie Schulze. Approximately seventy-five people attended and participated in activities that included Madonna impersonator shows, look-alike contests, displays of memorabilia and parties tied into local clubs.

6. See Jarman-Ivens in this volume for a further discussion of the lesbian theme in Madonna's work (Chapter 5).

7. As a side point, in separating academics from consumers, I acknowledge the detachment of the critical perspective in our profession, yet emphasize the shared nature of our pleasures in using her symbols and imagery towards our personal and professional ends.

Bibliography

Abalos, David T. (2001), *The Latino Male: A Radical Redefinition*, Boulder and London: Lynne Rienner Publishers.

Acker, Kathy (1997), 'All Girls Together', *The Guardian Weekend*, 3 May, 12–19.

Ainley, Rosa (1995), *What's She Like? Lesbian Identities from the 1950s to the 1990s*, London and New York: Cassell.

Allen, Steve (1999), 'Madonna', in Allan Metz and Carol Benson (eds), *The Madonna Companion: Two Decades of Commentary*, New York: Schirmer Books, pp. 144–57. First published 1993.

Allinson, Mark (2001), *A Spanish Labyrinth: The Films of Pedro Almodóvar*, London and New York: I.B. Tauris.

Andermahr, Sonja (1994), 'A Queer Love Affair? Madonna and Lesbian and Gay Culture', in Diane Hamer and Belinda Budge (eds), *The Good, The Bad and The Gorgeous: Popular Culture's Romance with Lesbianism*, London: Pandora, pp. 28–40.

Andersen, Christopher (1999), 'Madonna Rising: The Wilde and Funky Early Years in New York', in Allan Metz and Carol Benson (eds), *The Madonna Companion: Two Decades of Commentary*, New York: Schirmer Books, pp. 87–108. First published 1991.

Anderson, Benedict (1991), *Imagined Communities: Reflections on the Origin and Spread of Nationalism*, London: Verso.

Andreae, Johann Valentin (1973), *Fama Fraternitatis (1614); Confessio Fraternitatis (1615); Chymische Hochzeit: Christiani Rosencreutz Anno 1459 (1616)*, ed. Richard van Dülmen, Stuttgart: Calwer Verlag.

Anzaldúa, Gloria (1987), *Borderlands/La Frontera: The New Mestiza*, San Francisco: Aunt Lute Books.

Appadurai, Arjun (1996), *Modernity at Large: Cultural Dimensions of Globalisation*, Minneapolis: University of Minnesota Press.

Appiah, Anthony (1997), '"But Would that Still Be Me?": Notes on Gender, "Race", Ethnicity as Sources of "Identity"', in Naomi Zack (ed.), *Race/Sex: Their Sameness, Difference and Interplay*, London and New York: Routledge, pp. 75–81.

Arena [unattributed] (2001), 'The Home Girl', *Arena*, August, 105.

Aristotle (1961), *Poetics*, trans. S.H. Butcher, New York: Hill and Wang.

Arnould, Eric and Linda Price (1993), 'River Magic: Extraordinary Experience and the Extended Service Encounter', *Journal of Consumer Research*, **20**, 24–45.

Arroyo, José (1997), '*Evita*', *Sight and Sound*, **7** (2), 40–41.

Ashcroft, Bill, Gareth Griffiths and Helen Tiffin (1998), *Key Concepts in Post-Colonial Studies*, London and New York: Routledge.

Aurnhammer, Achim (1986), *Androgynie: Studien zu einem Motiv in der europäischen Literatur*, Cologne and Vienna: Böhlau Verlag.

Babuscio, Jack (1999), 'The Cinema of Camp (*aka* Camp and the Gay Sensibility)', in

Fabio Cleto (ed.), *Camp: Queer Aesthetics and the Performing Subject: A Reader*, Edinburgh: University of Edinburgh Press, pp. 117–35.

Baker, Michael J. and Gilbert Churchill (1977), 'The Impact of Physically Attractive Models on Advertising Evaluations', *Journal of Marketing Research*, **14**, 538–55.

Bangs, Lester (1996), *Psychotic Reactions and Carburetor Dung*, London: Minerva.

Barber-Kersovan, Alenka (2000), 'Madonna: The Material Girl – Eine amerikanische Karriere', in Alenka Barber-Kersovan, Annette Kreutziger-Herr and Melanie Unseld (eds), *Frauentöne: Beiträge zu einer ungeschriebenen Musikgeschichte*, Karben: Coda, pp. 261–83.

Barber-Kersovan, Alenka, Annette Kreutziger-Herr and Melanie Unseld (eds) (2000), *Frauentöne: Beiträge zu einer ungeschriebenen Musikgeschichte*, Karben: Coda.

Barthes, Roland (1972), *Mythologies*, trans. Annette Lavers, New York: Hill & Wang.

Barthes, Roland (1973), *Mythologies*, trans. Annette Lavers, London: Fontana Press.

Barthes, Roland (1975), *The Pleasure of the Text*, London: Jonathan Cape.

Bates, Simon (1991), 'Interview with Madonna', BBC Radio 1 Broadcast, archived at <http://www.bbc.co.uk/radio1/artist_area/madonna/>, last visited 25 March 2003.

Baudrillard, Jean (1988), 'Die Simulation', in Wolfgang Welsch (ed.), *Wege aus der Moderne: Schlüsseltexte der Postmoderne-Diskussion*, Weinheim: VCH, pp. 153–62.

Baudrillard, Jean (1989), 'The Anorexic Ruins', in Dietmar Kamper and Christoph Wulf (eds), *Looking Back on the End of the World*, New York: Semiotext, pp. 29–45.

Baudrillard, Jean (1995), *The Gulf War Never Took Place*, trans. Paul Patton, Bloomington and Indianapolis: Indiana University Press.

Baudrillard, Jean (1999), 'Simulacra and Simulations', in Julian Wolfreys (ed.), *Literary Theories: A Reader and Guide*, New York: NYU Press, pp. 381–94.

Baudrillard, Jean (2000), *America*, trans. Chris Turner, London: Verso.

BBC Online (1997), 'You've come a long way, baby', 30 December, <http://news.bbc.co.uk/1/hi/entertainment/38786.stm>, last visited 22 October 2002.

Beck, Ulrich (2002), 'A Life of One's Own in a Runaway World: Individualization, Globalization and Politics', in Ulrich Beck and Elisabeth Beck-Gernsheim (eds), *Individualization*, London: Sage, pp. 22–9.

Bego, Mark (1992), *Madonna: Blond Ambition*, London: Plexus.

Belk, Russell W., Guliz Ger and Soren Askegaard (2000), 'The Missing Streetcar Named Desire', in S. Ratneshwar, David Glen Mick and Cynthia Huffman (eds), *The Why of Consumption*, London and New York: Routledge, pp. 98–119.

Bentley, G. Carter (1987), 'Ethnicity and Practice', *Comparative Studies in Society and History*, **29** (1), 24–55.

Biedermann, Hans (1991), *Lexikon der magischen Künste: Die Welt der Magie seit der Spätantike*, Munich: Heyne.

Bingham, Frances (1997), 'Thrilling the Girls in the Gallery', *Diva: Lesbian Life & Style*, **19**, April/May, 26–9.

Blake, Andrew (1993), 'Madonna the Musician', in Fran Lloyd (ed.), *Deconstructing Madonna*, London: Batsford, pp. 17–28.

Bloss, Monika (2001), 'Musik(fern)sehen und Geschlecht hören? Zu möglichen (und unmöglichen) Verhältnissen von Musik und Geschelcht', in Peter Wicke (ed.), *Rock- and Popmusik*, Laaber: Laaber Verlag, pp. 187–226.

Bock, Ulla and Dorothee Alfermann (eds) (1999), *Androgynie: Vielfalt der Möglichkeiten*, Stuttgart: Metzler.

Bordo, Susan (1993), 'Material Girl: The Effacements of Postmodern Culture', in Cathy Schwichtenberg (ed.), *The Madonna Connection: Representational Politics, Subcultural Identities, and Cultural Theory*, Boulder, San Francisco and Oxford: Westview Press, pp. 265–90.

Boshoff, Alison (2003), 'Does Madonna want to get shot of England?', *Daily Mail*, 4 January, 16–17.

Bosma, Hannah and Patricia Pisters (1999), *Madonna: De vele gezichten van een popster*, Amsterdam: Prometheus.

Bourdieu, Pierre (1990), *In Other Words: Essays Towards a Reflexive Sociology*, trans. Matthew Adamson, Stanford, Calif.: Stanford University Press.

Bowers, Jane, 'Current Issues in Feminist Musical Scholarship: Representation and Gender Performance, Identity and Subjectivity, and Telling Stories about Women's Musical Lives', paper presented at the opening conference of the Sophie Drinker Institut, Bremen, 1 June 2002.

Breslow, Norman (1999), 'SM Research Statistical Data, v1.1', <http://www.sexuality. org/l/nb/nbstat.html>, last visited 22 January 2003.

Brill, Stephanie (2001), *The Queer Parent's Primer: A Lesbian and Gay Families' Guide to Navigating the Straight World*, Oakland, Calif.: New Harbinger.

Brooks, Ann (1997), *Postfeminisms: Feminism, Cultural Theory and Cultural Forms*, London and New York: Routledge.

Brumlik, Micha (1993), *C. G. Jung zur Einführung*, Hamburg: Junius.

Bufwack, Mary A. and Robert K. Oermann (1993), *Finding Her Voice: The Illustrated History of Women in Country Music*, New York: Henry Holt and Co.

Buikema, Rosemarie and Anneke Smelik (eds) (1993), *Vrouwenstudies in de cultuurwetenschappen*, Muiderberg: Coutinho.

Bullerjahn, Claudia (2001), 'Populäres und Artifizielles in den Musikvideos von Madonna', in Claudia Bullerjahn and Hans-Joachim Erwe (eds), *Das Populäre in der Musik des 20. Jahrhunderts: Wesenszüge und Erscheinungsformen*, Hildesheim: Olms, pp. 203–68.

Bunting, Madeleine (2001), 'Loadsasex and shopping: A woman's lot', *The Guardian*, 9 February, archived at <http://www.guardian.co.uk/comment/story/0,3604,435623,00. html>, last visited 22 October 2002.

Butler, Judith (1990), *Gender Trouble: Feminism and the Subversion of Identity*, London and New York: Routledge.

Butler, Judith (1991), 'Imitation and Gender Insubordination', in Diana Fuss (ed.), *Inside/Out: Lesbian Theories, Gay Theories*, London and New York: Routledge, pp. 13–31.

Butler, Judith (1993), *Bodies That Matter: On the Discursive Limits of 'Sex'*, London and New York: Routledge.

Butler, Judith (1999), *Gender Trouble: Feminism and the Subversion of Identity*, tenth anniversary edition, London and New York: Routledge.

Califia, Pat (1993), 'Sex and Madonna, or, What Did You Expect from a Girl Who Doesn't Put Out on the First Five Dates?', in Lisa Frank and Paul Smith (eds), *Madonnarama: Essays on Sex and Popular Culture*, Pittsburgh and San Francisco: Cleis Press, pp. 169–84.

Carolin, Louise (1995), 'Effing and Blinding', *Diva: Lesbian Life & Style*, **10**, October/November, 36–7.

Carpenter, Dale (2002), 'Gay Marriage and Women's Equality', <http://www. outsmartmagazine.com/issue/i05-02/outright.php>, last visited 12 February 2003.

Carroll, E. Jean (2001), 'Justify Our Love', *Elle*, February, 52–4.

Castellano, Koro (1996), 'Señora Madonna', *El País Semanal*, **1051**, 17 November, 32–40.

Cersowsky, Peter (1990), *Magie und Dichtung: Zur deutschen und englischen Literatur des 17. Jahrhunderts*, Munich: Fink.

Champagne, John (1993), 'Stabat Madonna', in Lisa Frank and Paul Smith (eds), *Madonnarama: Essays on Sex and Popular Culture*, Pittsburgh and San Francisco: Cleis Press, pp. 111–38.

Cheney, Lynne V. (2001), 'Women and the West', address at an induction event at the National Cowgirl Museum and Hall of Fame, Fort Worth, Tex., 2 November, archived at <http://www.whitehouse.gov/mrscheney/news/20011102.html>, last visited 13 May 2003.

Chesebro, James W. (ed.) (1981), *Gayspeak: Gay Male and Lesbian Communication*, New York: Pilgrim Press.

Chetwynd, Josh, Edna Gundersen and Susan Wloszczyna (1999), 'Madonna's Own Memoirs Mingle with Geisha's', *USA Today*, 12 February (final edition), O1E.

Clément, Catherine (1988), *Opera, or The Undoing of Women*, trans. Betsy Wing, Minneapolis: University of Minnesota Press.

Clerk, Carol (2002), *Madonna Style*, London, New York, Paris, Sydney, Copenhagen, Madrid, Tokyo: Omnibus Press.

Cleto, Fabio (ed.) (1999), *Camp: Queer Aesthetics and the Performing Subject: A Reader*, Edinburgh: University of Edinburgh Press.

Cohen, Warren (2002), *The Asian American Century*, Cambridge, Mass.: Harvard University Press.

Connelly, Christopher (1997), 'Madonna Goes All the Way', in *Rolling Stone* (eds), *Madonna: The Rolling Stone Files*, New York: Hyperion, pp. 25–35. First published 1984.

Cook, Nicholas (1990), *Music, Imagination, and Culture*, Oxford: Clarendon Press.

Corlett, J. Angelo (1997), 'Parallels of Ethnicity and Gender', in Naomi Zack (ed.), *Race/Sex: Their Sameness, Difference and Interplay*, London and New York: Routledge, pp. 83–94.

Corpus Hermeticum (1991), ed. and trans. R. van den Broek and G. Quispel, Amsterdam: In de Pelikaan.

Cosmopolitan [unattributed] (2003), 'Girls Who Love Girls Who Now Love Boys', *Cosmopolitan*, June, 119–20.

Cowie, Elizabeth (1984), 'Fantasia', *m/f*, **9**, 71–104.

Crimp, Douglas and Michael Warner (1993), 'No Sex in *Sex*', in Lisa Frank and Paul Smith (eds), *Madonnarama: Essays on Sex and Culture*, Pittsburgh and San Francisco: Cleis Press, pp. 93–110.

Cruz, Clarissa (1999), 'Geisha Glam', *Entertainment Weekly*, 9 April, 24.

Cubitt, Sean (2000), '"Maybellene": Meaning and the Listening Subject', in Richard Middleton (ed.), *Reading Pop: Approaches to Textual Analysis in Popular Music*, Oxford: Oxford University Press, pp. 141–59.

Currid, Brian (1995), '"We are Family": House Music and Queer Performativity', in Sue-Ellen Case, Philip Brett and Susan Leigh Foster (eds), *Cruising the Performative:*

Interventions into the Representation of Ethnicity, Nationality, and Sexuality, Bloomington and Indianapolis: Indiana University Press, pp. 165–96.

Curry, Ramona (1990), 'Madonna from Marilyn to Marlene: Pastiche and/or Parody?', *Journal of Film and Video*, **42** (2), 15–30.

'Cyberpunk' (2001), 'Britney compared to Madonna?', *Dark America*, <www.dark-america.com/madbrit.html>, last visited 23 August 2002.

Daly, Steven (2002), 'Madonna Marlene', *Vanity Fair*, October, 166–71, 224–6.

Darder, Antonia and Rodolfo D. Torres (1998), *The Latino Studies Reader: Culture, Economy and Society*, Malden and Oxford: Blackwell.

DeBord, Guy (1977), *Society of the Spectacle*, Detroit: Red and Black.

Deevoy, Adrian (1997), '"If You're Going to Reveal Yourself, Reveal Yourself!"': Madonna Talks about Life and *Truth or Dare*', in *Rolling Stone* (eds), *Madonna: The Rolling Stone Files*, New York: Hyperion, pp. 156–65. First published 1991.

Dehejia, Vidya (1997), *Indian Art*, London: Phaidon.

Demarchelier, Patrick (1999), 'Like a Geisha', *Harper's Bazaar*, February, 126–35.

Dentith, Simon (2000), *Parody*, London and New York: Routledge.

Denzin, Norman (1995), *The Cinematic Society*, Thousand Oaks, Calif.: Sage.

Deveaux, Monique (1994), 'Feminism and Empowerment: A Critical Reading of Foucault', *Feminist Studies*, **20** (2), 223–47.

Dholakia, Ruby Roy and Brian Sternthal (1977), 'Highly Credible Sources: Persuasive Facilitators or Persuasive Liabilities?', *Journal of Consumer Research*, **3**, 223–32.

Doan, Laura (1998), 'Passing Fashions: Reading Female Masculinities in the 1920s', *Feminist Studies*, **24** (3), 663–700.

Doane, Mary Ann (1992), 'Film and the Masquerade: Theorising the Female Spectator', in *Screen* (eds), *The Sexual Subject: A Screen Reader in Sexuality*, London and New York: Routledge, pp. 227–43. First published 1982.

Dohm, Burkhard (2000), *Poetische Alchimie: Öffnung zur Sinnlichkeit in der Hohelied- und Bibledichtung von der protestantischen Barockmystik bis zum Pietismus*, Tübingen: Niemeyer.

Douglas, Orville Lloyd (2002), 'What is Equality?' <http://www.americanfeedmagazine.com/douglas10142002.html>, last visited 12 February 2003.

Duberman, Martin B., Martha Vicinus and George Chauncey Jr. (eds) (1989), *Hidden from History: Reclaiming the Gay and Lesbian Past*, London: Penguin.

Dyer, Richard (1986), *Heavenly Bodies: Film Stars and Society*, London: Macmillan.

Dyer, Richard (1990), 'In Defense of Disco', in Simon Frith and Andrew Goodwin (eds), *On Record: Rock, Pop, and the Written Word*, London and New York: Routledge, pp. 410–18. First published 1979.

Dyer, Richard (1991), '*A Star is Born* and the Construction of Authenticity', in C. Gledhill (ed.), *Stardom: Industry of Desire*, London and New York: Routledge, pp. 132–40.

Dyer, Richard (1993), *The Matter of Images*, London and New York: Routledge.

Eccleston, Danny (1998), 'Sexy Mother', *Q Magazine*, March, 84–93.

Eisenbach, Helen (1997), *Lesbianism Made Easy*, New York: Virago.

Eisner, Lisa (2000), *Rodeo Girl*, Los Angeles: Greybull Press.

Evans, Caroline (1997), 'Dreams That Only Money Can Buy … Or, The Shy Tribe in Flight from Discourse', *Fashion Theory*, **1** (2), 169–88.

Evans, Peter (1993), 'Almodóvar's *Matador*: Genre, Subjectivity and Desire', *Bulletin of Hispanic Studies*, **70**, 325–35.

Faith, Karlene (1997), *Madonna: Bawdy and Soul*, Toronto: University of Toronto Press.

Fanon, Frantz (1963), *The Wretched of the Earth*, trans. Constance Farrington, New York: Grove Press.

Ferris, Lesley (ed.) (1993), *Crossing the Stage: Controversies on Cross-Dressing*, London and New York: Routledge.

FHM [unattributed] (1995), 'Has She No Shame', *FHM*, March, 85–93.

Fiedler, Leslie (1978), *Freaks*, New York: Simon and Schuster.

Fischer, Paul (2002), 'Do You Think I'm Funny?', *The Big Issue*, **485**, 22–8 April, 10–12.

Fisher, Carrie (1997), 'True Confessions: The Rolling Stone Interview with Madonna, Part One', in *Rolling Stone* (eds), *Madonna: The Rolling Stone Files*, New York: Hyperion, pp. 170–85. First published 1991.

Fiske, John (1987a), *Television Culture*, London and New York: Routledge.

Fiske, John (1987b), 'British Cultural Studies and Television', in Robert Allen (ed.), *Channels of Discourse: Television and Contemporary Criticism*, London: Methuen, pp. 254–89.

Flynn, Paul (2001), 'Geri: A Glove Story', *Attitude*, April, 36–48.

Forrest, Emma (2001), 'Sugar and Spice', *Marie Claire*, May, 38–44.

Foucault, Michel (1990), *The History of Sexuality: An Introduction (Volume One)*, trans. Robert Hurley, New York: Vintage Books.

Frank, Lisa and Paul Smith (eds) (1993a), *Madonnarama: Essays on Sex and Popular Culture*, Pittsburgh and San Francisco: Cleis Press.

Frank, Lisa and Paul Smith (1993b), 'Introduction: How to Use Your New Madonna', in Lisa Frank and Paul Smith (eds), *Madonnarama: Essays on Sex and Popular Culture*, Pittsburgh and San Francisco: Cleis Press, pp. 7–20.

Freccero, Carla (1994), 'Our Lady of MTV: Madonna's "Like a Prayer"', in Margaret Ferguson and Jennifer Wicke (eds), *Feminism and Postmodernism*, London and Durham, NC: Duke University Press, pp. 179–99. First published 1992.

Freccero, Carla (1999), 'Our Lady of MTV: Madonna's "Like a Prayer"', in Allan Metz and Carol Benson (eds), *The Madonna Companion: Two Decades of Commentary*, New York: Schirmer Books, pp. 184–203. First published 1992.

Frith, Simon (1993), 'The Sound of *Erotica*: Pain, Power, and Pop', in Lisa Frank and Paul Smith (eds), *Madonnarama: Essays on Sex and Popular Culture*, Pittsburgh and San Francisco: Cleis Press, pp. 87–92.

Frith, Simon (1996), *Performing Rites: On the Value of Popular Music*, Oxford: Oxford University Press.

Fusco, Coco (1995), *English Is Broken Here: Notes on Cultural Fusion in America*, New York: The New Press.

Gallo, Phil (2001), '*Drowned World Tour* review', Variety, **384** (5), September, 31.

Gamson, Joshua (1999), *Freaks Talk Back: Tabloid Talk Shows and Sexual Nonconformity*, Chicago: University of Chicago Press.

Gane, Mike (ed.) (1993), *Baudrillard Live: Selected Interviews*, London and New York: Routledge.

Garber, Marjorie (1993), *Vested Interests: Cross-Dressing and Cultural Anxiety*, London: Penguin.

Gardner, Elysa (1997), '*Evita*: The Complete Motion Picture Soundtrack', in *Rolling Stone* (eds), *Madonna: The Rolling Stone Files*, New York: Hyperion, pp. 253–4. First published 1996.

Gauntlett, David (2002), *Media, Gender and Identity: An Introduction*, London and New York: Routledge.

Gelder, Ken, and Sarah Thornton (eds) (1997), *The Subcultures Reader*, London and New York: Routledge.

Giddens, Anthony (1991), *Modernity and Self-Identity: Self and Society in the Late Modern Age*, Cambridge: Polity Press.

Giddens, Anthony (1992), *The Transformation of Intimacy*, Cambridge: Polity Press.

Giddens, Anthony and Christopher Pierson (1998), *Conversations with Anthony Giddens: Making Sense of Modernity*, Cambridge: Polity Press.

Gilbert, Mathew (1999), 'Playing the Shock Market', in Allan Metz and Carol Benson (eds), *The Madonna Companion: Two Decades of Commentary*, New York: Schirmer Books, pp. 137–41.

Ginsberg, Merle (2003), 'Madonna: The Saga Continues', *W*, April, 248–51.

Golden, Arthur (1999), *Memoirs of a Geisha*, New York: Vintage Books.

Gooch, Adela (1999), 'Bullfighter Gored by Male Rivals', *The Guardian*, 22 May, 22.

Gordinier, Jeff (2001), 'Tour de Force', *Entertainment Weekly*, 27 July, 25–33.

Gracia, Jorge J.E. and Pablo De Greiff (eds) (2000), *Hispanics/Latinos in the United States: Ethnicity, Race and Rights*, London and New York: Routledge.

Grigat, Nicoläa (1995), *Madonnabilder: Dekonstruktive Ästhetik in den Videobildern Madonnas*, Frankfurt am Main: Peter Lang Verlag.

Grossberg, Lawrence (1994), 'Is Anybody Listening? Does Anybody Care?', in A. Ross and Tricia Rose (eds), *Microphone Fiends: Youth Music and Youth Culture*, London and New York: Routledge, pp. 41–58.

Guilbert, Georges-Claude (2002), *Madonna as Postmodern Myth: How One Star's Self-Reconstruction Rewrites Sex, Gender, Hollywood and the American Dream*, Jefferson, NC: McFarland & Co.

Gundersen, Edna (1999), 'Face to Face with Madonna', in Allan Metz and Carol Benson (eds), *The Madonna Companion: Two Decades of Commentary*, New York: Schirmer Books, pp. 74–9. First published 1996.

Gunew, Sneja (1990), 'Questions of Multi-culturalism (An Interview with Gayatri Spivak)', in Sarah Harasym (ed.), *The Post-Colonial Critic: Interviews, Strategies, Dialogues*, London and New York: Routledge, pp. 59–66.

Habermas, Jürgen (1998), *The Philosophical Discourse of Modernity*, trans. Frederick G. Lawrence, Cambridge, Mass.: MIT Press.

Halberstam, Judith (1998), *Female Masculinity*, London and Durham, NC: Dale University Press.

Hall, Stuart (1996), 'Race, Articulation, and Societies Structured in Dominance', in Houston A. Baker, Manthia Diawara and Ruth H. Lindeborg (eds), *Black British Cultural Studies: A Reader*, Chicago: University of Chicago Press, pp. 16–60.

Halliwell, Geri (1999), *If Only*, London: Bantam.

Hamer, Emily (1996), *Britannia's Glory: A History of Twentieth-Century Lesbians*, London and New York: Cassell.

Hanegraaff, Wouter J. (1996), *New Age Religion and Western Culture: Esotericism in the Mirror of Secular Thought*, Albany, New York: State University of New York Press.

Haraway, Donna (1989), *Primate Visions*, London and New York: Routledge.

Haraway, Donna (1991), *Simians, Cyborgs, and Women: The Reinvention of Nature*, London and New York: Routledge.

Harrison, Andrew (2000), 'The Further Adventures of Veronica Electronica', *Mix Mag*, March, 78–86.

Hart, Lynda and Joshua Dale (1997), 'Sadomasochism', in Andy Medhurst and Sally Munt (eds), *Lesbian and Gay Studies: A Critical Introduction*, London and New York: Cassell, pp. 341–55.

Hawking, Stephen (1996), *A Brief History of Time*, New York: Bantam Books.

Hawkins, Stan (1997), 'I'll Never Be An Angel: Stories of Deception in Madonna's Music', *Critical Musicology: A Transdisciplinary Online Journal*, <http://www.leeds.ac.uk/music/info/critmus/articles/1997/01/01.html>, last visited 7 January 2003.

Hawkins, Stan (2002), *Settling the Pop Score: Pop Texts and Identity Politics*, Aldershot: Ashgate.

Hayward, Susan (1996), *Key Concepts in Cinema Studies*, London and New York: Routledge.

Healey, Emma (1996), *Lesbian Sex Wars*, London: Virago.

Heath, Chris (1997), 'Top of the World, Ma', *The Face*, March, 74–82.

Hebdige, Dick (1998), *Subculture: The Meaning of Style*, London: Methuen.

Henderson, Lisa (1993), 'Justify Our Love: Madonna and the Politics of Queer Sex', in Cathy Schwichtenberg (ed.), *The Madonna Connection: Representational Politics, Subcultural Identities, and Cultural Theory*, Boulder, San Francisco and Oxford: Westview Press, pp. 107–28.

Hilburn, Robert (1999), 'Madonna is Nobody's Toy', in Allan Metz and Carol Benson (eds), *The Madonna Companion: Two Decades of Commentary*, New York: Schirmer Books, pp. 6–7. First published 1986.

Hiltebeitel, Alf (1991), 'The Folklore of Draupadi: Saris and Hair', in Arjun Appadurai, Frank J. Korom and Margaret A. Mills (eds), *Gender, Genre, Power in South Asian Expressive Traditions*, Philadelphia: University of Pennsylvania Press, pp. 395–427.

Hirshey, Gerri (2002), *We Gotta Get Out of This Place: The True, Tough Story of Women in Rock*, New York: Grove Press.

Holden, Stephen (1992), 'A 60 Million Deal for the Material Girl', *New York Times*, 20 April, B1–4.

Holden, Stephen (1999), 'Madonna Cleans Up Act But Her Music Remains True Blue to Controversy', in Allan Metz and Carol Benson (eds), *The Madonna Companion: Two Decades of Commentary*, New York: Schirmer Books, pp. 48–52. First published 1986.

hooks, bell (1984), *Feminist Theory: From Margin to Center*, Boston: South End Press.

hooks, bell (1992a), *Black Looks: Race and Representation*, Boston: South End Press.

hooks, bell (1992b), 'Madonna: Plantation Mistress or Soul Sister', in *Black Looks, Race and Representation*, Boston: South End Press, pp. 157–64.

hooks, bell (1993), 'Power to the Pussy: We Don't Want to Be Dicks in Drag', in Lisa Frank and Paul Smith (eds), *Madonnarama: Essays on Sex and Culture*, Pittsburgh and San Francisco: Cleis Press, pp. 65–80.

Ikenberg, Tamara (1999), 'Immaterial Girl', in Allan Metz and Carol Benson (eds), *The Madonna Companion: Two Decades of Commentary*, New York: Schirmer Books, pp. 167–70. First published 1998.

Irigaray, Luce (1997), 'Women on the Market', in Alan Schrift (ed.), *The Logic of the Gift: Toward an Ethic of Generosity*, London and New York: Routledge, pp. 174–89.

Jackson, Alan (1996), 'In Her Own Image', *The Times Magazine*, 19 October, 28–32.

Jameson, Frederic (1991), *Postmodernism, or, The Cultural Logic of Late Capitalism*, London: Verso.

Jameson, Frederic (1992), *Postmodernism, or, the Cultural Logic of Late Capitalism*, Durham, NC: Duke University Press.

Jameson, Frederic (1998), *The Cultural Turn: Selected Writings on the Postmodern, 1983–1998*, London: Verso.

Jarvis, Brian (1998), *Postmodern Cartographies: The Geographical Imagination in Contemporary American Culture*, New York: St. Martin's Press.

Jeffreys, Sheila (1994), *The Lesbian Heresy*, London: Women's Press.

Jencks, Charles (1996), 'Hetero-Architecture and the L.A. School', in Allen J. Scott and Edward J. Soja (eds), *The City: Los Angeles and Urban Theory at the End of the Twentieth Century*, Los Angeles: University of California Press, pp. 47–75.

Jhally, Sut (1998), *Edward Said: On Orientalism*, Videocassette, Media Education Foundation.

Jimenez, J. (2000), 'Madonna on *The Next Best Thing*', *Next Magazine*, March, archived at <web.singnet.com.sg/~madonna/madnews86.htm>, last visited 12 March 2002.

Jones, Marc T. and Alladi Venkatesh (1992), 'A Critical Analysis of the Role of the Multinational Corporation in Global Marketing and Consumption', in Russell W. Belk and Nikhilesh Dholakia (eds), *Consumption and Marketing: Macro Dimensions*, Boston: PWS Kent, pp. 282–315.

Jung, Carl Gustav (1963), *Collected Works of C.G. Jung*, Volume 14: *Mysterium coniunctionis*, ed. Herbert Read, Michael Fordham and Gerhard Adler, trans. R.F.C. Hull, London and New York: Routledge and Kegan Paul.

Kakutani, Michiko (1992), 'Madonna Writes; Academics Write About Her', *New York Times*, 21 October, B-2.

Kaplan, Amy (1993), 'Left Alone With America: The Absence of Empire in the Study of American Culture', in Amy Kaplan and Donald Pease (eds), *Cultures of United States Imperialism*, London and Durham, NC: Duke University Press, pp. 1–19.

Kaplan, Caren (1996), *Questions of Travel: Postmodern Discourses of Displacement*, London and Durham, NC: Duke University Press.

Kaplan, E. Ann (1987), *Rocking Around the Clock: Music Television, Postmodernism & Consumer Culture*, New York: Methuen.

Kaplan, E. Ann (1992), 'Review of *Gender Trouble*', *Signs*, **17** (4), 843–8.

Kaplan, E. Ann (1993), 'Madonna Politics: Perversion, Repression, or Subversion? Or Masks and/as Master-y', in Cathy Schwichtenberg (ed.), *The Madonna Connection: Representational Politics, Subcultural Identities, and Cultural Theory*, Boulder, San Francisco and Oxford: Westview Press, pp. 149–65.

Kaplan, James (1991), 'Madonna: The Naked Truth', *Entertainment Weekly*, 17 May, 14–20.

Kaplan, Janet A. (1983), 'Remedios Varo (1913–1963): Spanish-born Mexican Painter, Woman among the Surrealists', unpublished dissertation, Columbia University.

Karentzos, Alexandra (2002), 'Die Goldpanzer der Frauen – Zur Medialität der Geschlechter bei Klimt', in Birgit Käufer, Alexandra Karentzos and Katharina Sykora (eds), *Körperproduktionen: Zur Artifizialität der Geschlechter*, Marburg: Jonas, pp. 145–60.

Khoo, Olivia (2000), 'Folding Chinese Boxes: Asian Exoticism in Australia', *Journal of Australian Studies*, June, 200–208.

Klein, Steven (2003), 'Madonna', *W*, April, 204–47.

Kobal, John (1968), *Marlene Dietrich*, London: Studio Vista.

Koestenbaum, Wayne (1993), *The Queen's Throat: Opera, Homosexuality, and the Mystery of Desire*, New York: Vintage Books.

Kondo, Dorinne (1997), *About Face: Performing Race in Fashion and Theater*, London and New York: Routledge.

Kot, Greg (1999), 'Without the Videos, Her Albums Just Aren't the Same', in Allan Metz and Carol Benson (eds), *The Madonna Companion: Two Decades of Commentary*, New York: Schirmer Books, pp. 15–16. First published 1990.

Kozinets, Robert V. (2001), 'Utopian Enterprise: Articulating the Meanings of Star Trek's Culture of Consumption', *Journal of Consumer Research*, **28**, 67–88.

Lacan, Jacques (1977a), *Écrits: A Selection*, trans. Alan Sheridan, New York: W.W. Norton & Co.

Lacan, Jacques (1977b), 'Subversion of the Subject and Dialectic of Desire', in *Écrits: A Selection*, trans. Alan Sheridan, New York: W.W. Norton & Co., pp. 292–325.

LaChapelle, David (1996), *LaChapelleLand*, New York: Simon and Schuster.

LaChapelle, David (1998), 'Madonna's Indian Summer', *Rolling Stone*, 9–23 July, 62–8.

La Ferla, Ruth (1999), 'Geisha Chic's Allure Derives From Wrapping and Reticence', *New York Times*, 9 May (late edition).

LaFranco, Robert, Mark Binelli and Fred Goodman (2002), 'U2, Dre Highest Earning Artists', 13 June, archived at <http://www.rollingstone.com/news/newsarticle. asp?nid=16113>, last visited 13 May 2003.

Langer, Marie (1966), *Fantasías eternas a la luz del psicoanálisis*, second edition, Buenos Aires: Ediciones Hormé, pp. 79–103.

Layton, Lynne (1994), '"Who's That Girl?" A Case Study of Madonna', in Carol E. Franz and Abigail J. Stewart (eds), *Women Creating Lives: Identities, Resilience, & Resistance*, Boulder, San Francisco and Oxford: Westview Press, pp. 143–56.

Leap, William L. (ed.) (1995), *Beyond the Lavender Lexicon: Authenticity, Imagination, and Appropriation in Lesbian and Gay Languages*, Melbourne: Gordon and Breach Publishers.

Leap, William L. (1996), *Word's Out: Gay Men's English*, Minneapolis: University of Minnesota Press.

Lentz, Kirsten Marthe (1993), 'Chameleon, Vampire, Rich Slut', in Lisa Frank and Paul Smith (eds), *Madonnarama: Essays on Sex and Popular Culture*, Pittsburgh and San Francisco: Cleis Press, pp. 153–68.

Leonardi, Susan J. and Rebecca A. Pope (1996), 'Express Yourselves: Divas Pop and Pomo', in *The Diva's Mouth: Body, Voice, Prima Donna Politics*, New Brunswick, NJ: Rutgers University Press, pp. 205–27.

Lesbian History Group (1989), *Not a Passing Phase: Reclaiming Lesbians in History, 1840–1985*, London: Women's Press.

Lewis, Lisa (1990), *Gender Politics and MTV: Voicing the Difference*, Philadelphia: Temple University Press.

Lipsitz, George (2001), *The Possessive Investment in Whiteness: How White People Profit from Identity Politics*, Philadelphia: Temple University Press.

Lloyd, Fran (ed.) (1993), *Deconstructing Madonna*, London: Batsford.

Loulan, JoAnn (1990), *The Lesbian Erotic Dance: Butch, Femme, Androgyny and Other Rhythms*, San Francisco: Spinsters Book Company.

Lowe, Lisa (1996), *Immigrant Acts: On Asian American Cultural Politics*, London and Durham, NC: Duke University Press.

Lucey, Donna M. (2002), *I Dwell in Possibility: Women Build a Nation, 1600–1920*, Washington: National Geographic.

Lugo-Lugo, C.R. (2001), 'The Madonna Experience: A US Icon Awakens a Puerto Rican Adolescent Feminist Consciousness', *Frontiers: A Journal of Women's Studies*, **22** (2), 118–30.

Lunt, Peter (2000), 'The Jerry Springer Show as an Emotional Public Sphere', paper presented at the 23rd Conference and General Assembly of the International Association for Media and Communication Research, Barcelona, July.

Luscombe, Belinda (1998), 'New Day, New Deity to Offend', *Time*, **152** (13), 68.

Lyotard, Jean-François (1993), 'Answering the Question: What is Postmodernism?', in Thomas Docherty (ed.), *Postmodernism: A Reader*, New York: Columbia University Press, pp. 38–46.

Mackay, Hugh (1997), 'Introduction', in Hugh Mackay (ed.), *Consumption and Everyday Life*, London: Sage, pp. 1–12.

McAuley, Tilly (1995), 'Through the Round Window', *Diva: Lesbian Life & Style*, **11**, December/January, 30–32.

McClary, Susan (1991), *Feminine Endings: Music, Gender, and Sexuality*, Minneapolis: University of Minnesota Press.

McCracken, Grant (1989), 'Who is the Celebrity Endorser? Cultural Foundations of the Endorsement Process', *Journal of Consumer Research*, **16**, 310–21.

MacKinnon, Catherine (1987), *Feminism Unmodified: Discourses on Life and Law*, Cambridge, Mass.: Harvard University Press.

McNair, Brian (1996), *Mediated Sex: Pornography and Postmodern Culture*, London: Arnold.

McRobbie, Angela (1999), *In the Culture Society: Art, Fashion and Popular Music*, London and New York: Routledge.

Madonna (1992), *Sex*, London: Martin Secker & Warburg.

Madonna (1996), 'Madonna's Private Diaries', *Vanity Fair*, November, 175–88, 223–32.

'Madonna on Stage and On the Record' (2003), MTV Music Television Channel Broadcast, 22 April.

'Madonna Rising' (1998), VH1 Music Television Channel Broadcast.

'Madonna Videography' (1998), MTV Music Television Channel Broadcast.

Mandziuk, Roseann M. (1993), 'Feminist Politics and Postmodern Seductions: Madonna and the Struggle for Political Articulation', in Cathy Schwichtenberg (ed.), *The Madonna Connection: Representational Politics, Subcultural Identities and Cultural Theory*, Boulder, San Francisco and Oxford: Westview Press, pp. 167–87.

Manson, Marilyn, with Neil Strauss (1998), *The Long Hard Road Out of Hell*, New York: Regan Books.

Martin, Gavin (1992), 'Madonna's Cabaret', *New Musical Express*, 26 September, 16–19.

Martín Alcoff, Linda (2000), 'Is Latina/o Identity a Racial Identity?', in Jorge J.E. Gracia and Pablo De Greiff (eds), *Hispanics/Latinos in the United States: Ethnicity, Race and Rights*, London and New York: Routledge, pp. 23–44.

Melhuus, Marit (1996), 'Power, Value and the Ambiguous Meanings of Gender', in Marit Melhuus and Kristi Anne Stølen (eds), *Machos, Mistresses, Madonnas: Contesting the Power of Latin American Gender Imagery*, London and New York: Verso, pp. 230–59.

Menchú, Rigoberta (1998), *I, Rigoberta Menchú: An Indian Woman in Guatemala*, ed. Elisabeth Burgos-Debray, trans. Ann Wright, London: Verso.

Mendieta, Eduardo (2000), 'The Making of New Peoples: Hispanizing Race', in Jorge J.E. Gracia and Pablo De Greiff (eds), *Hispanics/Latinos in the United States: Ethnicity, Race and Rights*, London and New York: Routledge, pp. 45–60.

Mercer, Kobena (1994), *Welcome to the Jungle: New Positions in Black Cultural Studies*, London and New York: Routledge.

Mertin, Andreas (1999), *Videoclips im Religionsunterricht: Eine praktische Analyse zur Arbeit mit Musikvideos*, Göttingen: Vandenhoek & Ruprecht.

Metz, Allan and Carol Benson (eds) (1999), *The Madonna Companion: Two Decades of Commentary*, New York: Schirmer Books.

Metzstein, Margery (1993), 'SEX: Signed, Sealed, Delivered', in Fran Lloyd (ed.), *Deconstructing Madonna*, London: Batsford, pp. 91–8.

Meyer Spacks, Patricia (1981), *The Adolescent Idea*, New York: Galaxy.

Miklitsch, Robert (1998), *From Hegel to Madonna: Towards a General Economy of Commodity Fetishism*, Albany, NY: SUNY Press.

Milano, Brett (1999), 'Like a Veteran: Madonna's Tour Reveals Her Savvy, Show-Biz Side', in Allan Metz and Carol Benson (eds), *The Madonna Companion: Two Decades of Commentary*, New York: Schirmer Books, pp. 8–11. First published 1987.

Mirandé, Alfredo (1997), *Hombres y Machos: Masculinity and Latino Culture*, Boulder, San Francisco and Oxford: Westview Press.

Moores, Shaun (1997), 'Broadcasting and its Audiences', in Hugh Mackay (ed.), *Consumption and Everyday Life*, London: Sage, pp. 213–57.

Morris, Mitchell (1993), 'Reading as an Opera Queen', in Ruth A. Solie (ed.), *Musicology and Difference: Gender and Sexuality in Musical Scholarship*, Berkeley: University of California Press, pp. 184–200.

Morris, Mitchell (1999), 'It's Raining Men: The Weather Girls, Gay Subjectivity, and the Erotics of Insatiability', in Elaine Barkin and Lydia Hamessley (eds), *Audible Traces: Identity and Music*, Zurich: Carciofoli Verlagshaus, pp. 213–29.

Morris, Mitchell (ed.) (forthcoming), *Disco's Distinctions: Essays on Music, Race, Sexuality, and the Market*, Berkeley: University of California Press.

Morton, Andrew (2002), *Madonna*, London: Michael O'Mara Books.

Morton, Melanie (1993), 'Don't Go For Second Sex, Baby!', in Cathy Schwichtenberg (ed.), *The Madonna Connection: Representational Politics, Subcultural Identities, and Cultural Theory*, Boulder, San Francisco and Oxford: Westview Press, pp. 213–35.

MTV (2001), *All Eyes on Destiny's Child*, television documentary, MTV Europe, 22 September.

MTV.com (2001), 'Britney Spears: Pop Rocks!', 10 September, <http://www.mtv.com/bands/s/spears_britney/news_feature_091001/index3.jhtml>, last visited 22 October 2002.

Mulvey, Laura (1975), 'Visual Pleasure and Narrative Cinema', *Screen*, **16** (3), 6–18.

Muñoz, Albert M. Jr. and Thomas C. O'Guinn (2001), 'Brand Community', *Journal of Consumer Research*, **27**, 412–32.

Musto, Michael (1991), 'Immaculate Connection', *Outweek*, 20 March, 35–41.

Muthyala, John (2001), 'Reworlding America: The Globalisation of American Studies', *Cultural Critique*, **47**, Winter, 91–119.

Nakayama, Thomas K. and Lisa Peñaloza (1993), 'Madonna T/Races: Music Videos Through the Prism of Color', in Cathy Schwichtenberg (ed.), *The Madonna Connection: Representational Politics, Subcultural Identities, and Cultural Theory*, Boulder, San Francisco and Oxford: Westview Press, pp. 39–56.

National Council of La Raza (1994), 'Out of the Picture: Hispanics in the Media', in Gary D. Keller (ed.), *Hispanics and United States Film: An Overview and Handbook*, Tempe, Ariz.: Bilingual Review Press, pp. 21–35.

Nead, Lynda (1995), *Chila Kumari Burman: Beyond Two Cultures*, London: Kala Press.

Nelson, Candace and Marta Tienda (1997), 'The Structuring of Hispanic Ethnicity: Historical and Contemporary Perspectives', in Mary Romero, Pierrette Hondagneu-Sotelo and Vilma Ortiz (eds), *Challenging Fronteras: Structuring Latina and Latino Lives in the US*, London and New York: Routledge, pp. 7–29.

Newton, Esther (1999), 'Role Models', in Fabio Cleto (ed.), *Camp: Queer Aesthetics and the Performing Subject: A Reader*, Edinburgh: Edinburgh University Press, pp. 96–109.

Oboler, Suzanne (1997), 'So Far From God, So Close to the United States: The Roots of Hispanic Homogenization', in Mary Romero, Pierrette Hondagneu-Sotelo and Vilma Ortiz (eds), *Challenging Fronteras: Structuring Latina and Latino Lives in the US*, London and New York: Routledge, pp. 32–54.

O'Brien, Lucy (2002), *She Bop II: The Definitive History of Women in Rock, Pop and Soul*, London: Continuum.

O'Dair, Barbara (1997), 'Introduction', in *Rolling Stone* (eds), *Madonna: The Rolling Stone Files*, New York: Hyperion, pp. 1–22.

O'Guinn, Thomas C. (1991), 'Touching Greatness: The Central Midwest Barry Manilow Fan Club', in Russell W. Belk (ed.), *Highways and Buyways: Naturalistic Research from the Consumer Behavior Odyssey*, Provo, Ut.: Association for Consumer Research, pp. 102–11.

O'Guinn, Thomas C. and L.J. Shrum (1994), 'The Role of Television in the Construction of Consumption Reality', *Journal of Consumer Research*, **23**, 278–94.

O'Hagan, Andrew (1993), 'Blonde Ambition the American Way', in Fran Lloyd (ed.), *Deconstructing Madonna*, London: Batsford, pp. 29–34.

Ong, Aihwa (1999), *Flexible Citizenship: The Cultural Logics of Transnationality*, London and Durham, NC: Duke University Press.

Orth, Maureen (1992), 'Madonna in Wonderland', *Vanity Fair*, October, 92–100, 160–64.

Ortiz, Fernando (1978), *Contrapunto Cubano*, Caracas: Biblioteca Ayacucho.

Ortiz, Vilma (1997), 'Demographic Overview of Latinos', in Mary Romero, Pierrette Hondagneu-Sotelo and Vilma Ortiz (eds), *Challenging Fronteras: Structuring Latina and Latino Lives in the US*, London and New York: Routledge, pp. xvi–xix.

O'Sullivan, Sue (1994), 'Girls Who Kiss Girls and Who Cares?', in Diane Hamer and Belinda Budge (eds), *The Good, The Bad and The Gorgeous: Popular Culture's Romance with Lesbianism*, London: Pandora, pp. 78–95.

Paglia, Camille (1990), 'Madonna – Finally, a Real Feminist', *New York Times*, 14 December, A39.

Paglia, Camille (1992), *Sex, Art, and American Culture: Essays*, New York: Vintage Books.

Paglia, Camille (1999), 'Venus of the Radio Waves', in Allan Metz and Carol Benson (eds), *The Madonna Companion: Two Decades of Commentary*, New York: Schirmer Books, pp. 161–7. First published 1990.

Parker, Alan (1996), *The Making of Evita*, London and Basingstoke: Boxtree.

Patton, Cindy (1993), 'Embodying Subaltern Memory: Kinesthesia and the Problematics of Gender and Race', in Cathy Schwichtenberg (ed.), *The Madonna Connection: Representational Politics, Subcultural Identities, and Cultural Theory*, Boulder, San Francisco and Oxford: Westview Press, pp. 81–105.

Peñaloza, Lisa (2001), 'Consuming the American West: Animating Cultural Meaning and Memory at a Stock Show and Rodeo', *Journal of Consumer Research*, **28**, 369–98.

Perón, Eva (1951), *La razón de mi vida*, seventh edition, Buenos Aires: Ediciones Peuser.

Perriam, Christopher (2003), 'Antonio Banderas', in *Stars and Masculinities in Spanish Cinema – From Banderas to Bardem*, Oxford: Oxford University Press, pp. 44–69.

Peterson, Richard A. (1997), *Creating Country Music: Fabricating Authenticity*, Chicago: University of Chicago Press.

Pokorny, S. (1989), 'Obsess Yourself! The Root of My Obsession with Sandra and Madonna is Unbridled Lust', *Gay Community News*, 30 July–5 August, 9–10.

Polhemus, Ted (1994), *Street Style*, London: Thames and Hudson.

pop-music.com (2003), <http://mp3.pop-music.com/article350.html>, last visited 26 April 2003.

Poster, Mark (ed.) (1988), *Jean Baudrillard: Selected Writings*, Stanford, Calif.: Stanford University Press.

Powers, Ann (1999), 'New Tune for the Material Girl: I'm Neither', in Allan Metz and Carol Benson (eds), *The Madonna Companion: Two Decades of Commentary*, New York: Schirmer Books, pp. 79–83. First published 1998.

Pratt, Mary Louise (1992), *Imperial Eyes: Travel Writing and Transculturation*, London and New York: Routledge.

Pribram, Deirdre E. (1993), 'Seduction, Control, and the Search for Authenticity: Madonna's *Truth or Dare*', in Cathy Schwichtenberg (ed.), *The Madonna Connection: Representational Politics, Subcultural Identities, and Cultural Theory*, Boulder, San Francisco and Oxford: Westview Press, pp. 189–212.

Puwar, Nirmal (2002), 'Multicultural Fashion ... Stirrings of Another Sense of Aesthetics and Memory', *Feminist Review*, **71**, 63–87.

Queen, Carol A. (1993), 'Talking About *Sex*', in Lisa Frank and Paul Smith (eds), *Madonnarama: Essays on Sex and Popular Culture*, Pittsburgh and San Francisco: Cleis Press, pp. 139–51.

Rabine, Leslie L. (1997), 'Not a Mere Ornament: Tradition, Modernity and Colonialism in Kenyan and Western Clothing', *Fashion Theory*, **1** (2), 145–68.

Ramírez Berg, Charles (1994), 'Stereotyping in Films in General and of the Hispanic in Particular in Media', in Gary D. Keller (ed.), *Hispanics and United States Film: An Overview and Handbook*, Tempe, Ariz.: Bilingual Review Press, pp. 104–20.

Ratliff, Ben (2003), '*American Life* review', *Rolling Stone*, 15 May, archived at <http://www.rollingstone.com/reviews/cd/review.asp?aid=2046406>, last visited 19 May 2003.

Rees, Paul (2003), 'Listen Very Carefully, I Will Say This Only Once', *Q*, **202**, May, 84–92.

Rettenmund, Matthew (1995), *Encyclopedia Madonnica*, New York: St. Martin's Press.

Rich, Adrienne (1993), 'Compulsory Heterosexuality and Lesbian Existence', in Henry Abelove, Michèle Aina Barale and David M. Halperin (eds), *The Gay and Lesbian Studies Reader*, New York and London: Routledge, pp. 227–54. First published 1986.

Rideout, Ernie (2001), 'Mirwais on Music', *Keyboard*, **57**, United Entertainment Media, Inc., archived at <http://archive.keyboardonline.com/features/mirwais/index.shtml>, last visited 23 January 2003.

Riesman, David (1993), 'Listening to Popular Music', in Simon Frith and Andrew Goodwin (eds), *On Record: Rock, Pop, and the Written Word*, London and New York: Routledge. First published 1950.

Riviere, Joan (1929), 'Womanliness as a Masquerade', *International Journal for Psychoanalysis*, **10**, January, 303–13.

Roach, Joyce Gibson (1990), *The Cowgirls*, Denton: University of North Texas Press.

Roberts, Robin (1990), 'Humor and Gender in Feminist Music Videos', in Diane Raymond (ed.), *Sexual Politics and Popular Culture*, Bowling Green, OH: Bowling Green State University Press, pp. 173–82.

Robertson, Pamela (1996), *Guilty Pleasures: Feminist Camp from Mae West to Madonna*, London and New York: I.B. Tauris.

Robertson, Pamela (1999), 'Guilty Pleasures', in Allan Metz and Carol Benson (eds), *The Madonna Companion: Two Decades of Commentary*, New York: Schirmer Books, pp. 268–90. First published 1996.

Robertson, Roland (1992), *Globalisation: Social Theory and Global Culture*, London: Sage.

Robinson, Amy (1993), 'Is She or Isn't She?: Madonna and the Erotics of Appropriation', in Lynda Hart and Peggy Phelan (eds), *Acting Out: Feminist Performances*, Ann Arbor: University of Michigan Press, pp. 337–61.

Robinson, Paul (1994), 'The Opera Queen: A Voice From the Closet', *Cambridge Opera Journal*, **6**, 283–91.

Robson, J. (2000), 'Madonna Makes the Cowgirl Look Cool', *The Age*, 30 November, <www.theage.com.au/entertainment/2000/11/30/FFXX83UU3GC.html>, last visited 5 July 2002.

Rodríguez, Clara (1997), *Latin Looks: Images of Latinas and Latinos in the US Media*, Boulder, San Francisco and Oxford: Westview Press.

Rolling Stone (eds) (1997), *Madonna: The Rolling Stone Files*, New York: Hyperion.

Romero, Mary, Pierrette Hondagneu-Sotelo and Vilma Ortiz (eds) (1997), *Challenging Fronteras: Structuring Latina and Latino Lives in the US*, London and New York: Routledge.

Rose, Margaret A. (1995), *Parody: Ancient, Modern and Post-modern*, Cambridge: Cambridge University Press.

Ross, Andrew (1993), 'This Bridge Called My Pussy', in Lisa Frank and Paul Smith (eds), *Madonnarama: Essays on Sex and Popular Culture*, Pittsburgh and San Francisco: Cleis Press, pp. 47–64.

Ross, Andrew (1999), 'Uses of Camp', in Fabio Cleto (ed.), *Camp: Queer Aesthetics and the Performing Subject: A Reader*, Edinburgh: Edinburgh University Press, pp. 308–29.

Rubin, Gayle (1975), 'The Traffic of Women: Notes on the "Political Economy" of Sex', in Rayna R. Reiter (ed.), *Toward an Anthropology of Women*, New York: Monthly Review Press, pp. 157–210.

Said, Edward (1985), 'Orientalism Reconsidered', in Francis Barker, Peter Hulme, Margaret Iversen and Diana Loxley (eds), *Europe and Its Others: Volume 1*, Colchester: University of Essex, pp. 14–27. First published 1979.

Said, Edward (1994), *Orientalism*, New York: Vintage Press.

St. Michael, Mick (1990), *Madonna in Her Own Words*, London: Omnibus.

St. Michael, Mick (1999), *Madonna in Her Own Words*, London: Omnibus.

Savigliano, M.E. (1997), 'Evita: The Globalization of a National Myth', *Latin American Perspectives*, **24** (6), 156–72.

Scharff, Sue (2001), 'Madonna Denied the Right to Rage', <http://www.saidit.org/archives/may01/mediaglance.html>, last visited 8 January 2003.

Schiller, Herbert (1992), *Mass Communication and American Empire*, Boulder, San Francisco and Oxford: Westview Press.

Scholes, Percy (1993), *The Oxford Companion to Music*, tenth edition, Oxford: Oxford University Press.

Schor, Juliet and Douglas Holt (eds) (2000), *The Consumer Society Reader*, New York: New Press.

Schulze, Laurie, Anne Barton White and Jane D. Brown (1993), 'A Sacred Monster in her Prime: Audience Construction of Madonna as Low-Other', in Cathy Schwichtenberg (ed.), *The Madonna Connection: Representational Politics, Subcultural Identities, and Cultural Theory*, Boulder, San Francisco and Oxford: Westview Press, pp. 15–37.

Schwichtenberg, Cathy (ed.) (1993a), *The Madonna Connection: Representational Politics, Subcultural Identities, and Cultural Theory*, Boulder, San Francisco and Oxford: Westview Press.

Schwichtenberg, Cathy (1993b), 'Connections/Intersections', in Cathy Schwichtenberg (ed.), *The Madonna Connection: Representational Politics, Subcultural Identities, and Cultural Theory*, Boulder, San Francisco and Oxford: Westview Press, pp. 1–11.

Schwichtenberg, Cathy (1993c), 'Madonna's Postmodern Feminism: Bringing the Margins to the Center', in Cathy Schwichtenberg (ed.), *The Madonna Connection: Representational Politics, Subcultural Identities, and Cultural Theory*, Boulder, San Francisco and Oxford: Westview Press, pp. 129–45.

Scott, Ronald B. (1993), 'Images of Race and Religion in Madonna's Video *Like a Prayer*: Prayer and Praise', in Cathy Schwichtenberg (ed.), *The Madonna Connection: Representational Politics, Subcultural Identities, and Cultural Theory*, Boulder, San Francisco and Oxford: Westview Press, pp. 57–77.

Sedgwick, Eve K. (1985), *Between Men: English Literature and Male Homosocial Desire*, New York: Columbia University Press.

Seigworth, Greg (1993), 'The Distance Between Me and You: Madonna and Celestial Navigation (or You Can Be My *Lucky Star*)', in Cathy Schwichtenberg (ed.), *The Madonna Connection: Representational Politics, Subcultural Identities, and Cultural Theory*, Boulder, San Francisco and Oxford: Westview Press, pp. 291–318.

Seligmann, Kurt (1988), *Das Weltreich der Magie: 5000 Jahre Geheime Kunst*, Eltville: BechterMünz.

Sexton, Adam (ed.) (1993), *Desperately Seeking Madonna: In Search of the Meaning of the World's Most Famous Woman*, New York: Delta Books.

Sherman, Dale (2000), *Women in Rock*, Burlington, Ontario: Collector's Guide Publishing.

Shewey, Don (1992a), 'Madonna: The Saint, The Slut, The Sensation', *The Advocate*, March, 42–51.

Shewey, Don (1992b), 'The Gospel According to St. Madonna', *The Advocate*, October, 40–45.

Shohat, Ella and Robert Stam (1994), *Unthinking Eurocentrism: Multiculturalism and the Media*, New York and London: Routledge.

Siegel, Ed (1999), 'Madonna Sells Her Soul for a Song', in Allan Metz and Carol Benson (eds), *The Madonna Companion: Two Decades of Commentary*, New York: Schirmer Books, pp. 131–4. First published 1989.

Silberman, Seth Clarke (1997), 'Cross-Dressing', in Claude J. Summers (ed.), *The Gay and Lesbian Literary Heritage: A Reader's Companion to the Writers and Their Works, From Antiquity to the Present*, London: Bloomsbury, pp. 179–84.

Sischy, Ingrid (2001a), 'Madonna Exclusive!', *Interview*, March, 155–9.

Sischy, Ingrid (2001b), 'Interview with Madonna', <http://www.eecs.harvard.edu/~zhwang/Madonna/arIntv0103.html>, last visited 10 March 2003.

Skeggs, Beverly (1993), 'A Good Time for Women Only', in Fran Lloyd (ed.), *Deconstructing Madonna*, London: Batsford, pp. 61–73.

Smelik, Anneke (1992), 'Meneer Madonna en mevrouw Prince: Carrousel der Seksen', *De Groene Amsterdammer*, 12 August, 16–17.

Smith, Paul Julian (2000), *Desire Unlimited: The Films of Pedro Almodóvar*, London: Verso.

Smith, Stephanie (1990), 'Why Madonna and All White People with Dread Locks Should Burn in Hell', *Akhé*, **2**, 33.

Sobran, Joseph (1999), 'Single Sex and The Girl', in Allan Metz and Carol Benson (eds), *The Madonna Companion: Two Decades of Commentary*, New York: Schirmer Books, pp. 124–30. First published 1991.

Solie, Ruth (2001), 'Feminism', in *The New Grove Dictionary of Music and Musicians*, London: Macmillan, pp. 664–7.

Sontag, Susan (1986), *Against Interpretation*, New York: Anchor Books.

Sontag, Susan (1999), 'Notes on Camp', in Fabio Cleto (ed.), *Camp: Queer Aesthetics and the Performing Subject: A Reader*, Edinburgh: Edinburgh University Press, pp. 53–65. First published in 1964: *Partisan Review*, **31** (4), 515–30.

Spivak, Gayatri (1985), 'The Rani of Simur', in Francis Barker, Peter Hulme, Margaret Iversen and Diana Loxley (eds), *Europe and Its Others: Volume I*, Colchester: University of Essex, pp. 128–51.

Stacey, Jackie (1994), *Star Gazing: Hollywood Cinema and Female Spectatorship*, London and New York: Routledge.

Stallybrass, Peter (1992), 'Transvestism and the "Body Beneath": Speculating on the Boy Actor', in Susan Zimmerman (ed.), *Erotic Politics: Desire on the Renaissance Stage*, London and New York: Routledge, pp. 64–83.

Stavans, Illán (1998), 'The Latin Phallus', in Antonia Darder and Rodolfo D. Torres (eds), *The Latino Studies Reader: Culture, Economy and Society*, Oxford and Malden: Blackwell, pp. 228–39.

Stein, Arlene (1994), 'Crossover Dreams: Lesbianism and Popular Music Since the 1970s', in Diane Hamer and Belinda Budge (eds), *The Good, The Bad and The Gorgeous: Popular Culture's Romance with Lesbianism*, London: Pandora, pp. 15–27.

Sykora, Katharina (1999), 'Androgynie als "Genus tertium", in Magnus Hirschfelds Theorie der "Geschlechtsübergänge"', in Ulla Bock and Dorothee Alfermann (eds), *Androgynie: Vielfalt der Möglichkeiten*, Stuttgart: Metzler.

Taraborrelli, J. Randy (2001), *Madonna: An Intimate Biography*, New York: Simon and Schuster.

Tata, Michael Angelo (2000), 'Post-Vedic Madonnarama', *Found Object*, **9**, 67–88.

Teeman, Tim (2000), 'Teenage Kicks', *Attitude*, January, 60–64.

Tetzlaff, David (1993), 'Metatextual Girl: → patriarchy → postmodernism → power → money → Madonna', in Cathy Schwichtenberg (ed.), *The Madonna Connection: Representational Politics, Subcultural Identities, and Cultural Theory*, Boulder, San Francisco and Oxford: Westview Press, pp. 239–63.

Thompson, Douglas (2002), *Madonna: Queen of the World*, London: Blake.

Tichi, Cecilia (1994), *High Lonesome: The American Culture of Country Music*, Chapel Hill: University of North Carolina Press.

Traub, Valerie (1992), 'The (In)Significance of "Lesbian" Desire in Early Modern England', in Susan Zimmerman (ed.), *Erotic Politics: Desire on the Renaissance Stage*, London and New York: Routledge, pp. 150–69.

Traub, Valerie (2002), *The Renaissance of Lesbianism in Early Modern England*, Cambridge: Cambridge University Press.

Turner, Kay (ed). (1993), *I Dream of Madonna: Women's Dreams of the Goddess of Pop*, London: Thames and Hudson.

Tyler, Carole-Anne (1991), 'Boys Will Be Girls: The Politics of Gay Drag', in Diana Fuss (ed.), *Inside/Out: Lesbian Theories, Gay Theories*, London and New York: Routledge, pp. 32–70.

Udovitch, Mim (1997), 'Madonna', in *Rolling Stone* (eds), *Madonna: The Rolling Stone Files*, New York: Hyperion, pp. 247–52. First published 1997.

Vernon, Polly (1999), 'Girls at Our Best', *The Guardian*, 27 October, archived at <http://www.guardian.co.uk/tv_and_radio/story/0,3604,258349,00.html>, last visited 22 October 2002.

Walter, Natasha (1998), *The New Feminism*, London: Little, Brown.

Walters, Barry (1998), 'Madonna Chooses Dare', *Spin*, April, 70–76.

Walters, Suzanna Danuta (1995), *Material Girls: Making Sense of Feminist Cultural Theory*, Berkeley: University of California Press.

Watts, Mark (1996), 'Electrifying Fragments: Madonna and Postmodern Performance', *New Theatre Quarterly*, **12** (46), 99–107.

Weinbaum, Alys Eve and Brent Hayes Edwards (2000), 'On Critical Globality', *Ariel: A Review of International English Literature*, **31**, 255–74.

Weissberg, Liliane (1994), 'Einleitung', in Liliane Weissberg (ed.), *Weiblichkeit als Maskerade*, Frankfurt am Main: S. Fischer, pp. 7–33.

Werner, Karel (1997), *A Popular Dictionary of Hinduism*, Chicago: NTC Publishing Group.

Whelehan, Imelda (1995), *Modern Feminist Thought: From the Second Wave to 'Post-Feminism'*, Edinburgh: Edinburgh University Press.

Whiteley, Sheila (1997), 'Seduced by the Sign: An Analysis of the Textual Links Between Sound and Image in Pop Videos', in Sheila Whiteley (ed.), *Sexing the Groove: Popular Music and Gender*, London and New York: Routledge, pp. 259–76.

Whiteley, Sheila (2000), *Women in Popular Music: Sexuality, Identity and Subjectivity*, London and New York: Routledge.

Wicke, Peter (2001), 'Sound-Technologien und Körper-Metamorphosen: Das Populäre in der Musik des 20. Jahrhunderts', in Peter Wicke (ed.), *Rock- und Popmusik*, Laaber: Laaber Verlag, pp. 11–60.

Williams, Zoe (2002), 'Just Fancy …', *The Guardian Weekend*, 5 January, 14–19.

Wilson, Ben G. (2002), 'Platinum Blonde', *Arena*, April, 78–84.

Worrell, Denise (1999), 'Madonna!', in Allan Metz and Carol Benson (eds), *The Madonna*

Companion: Two Decades of Commentary, New York: Schirmer Books, pp. 35–47. First published 1985.

Wright, Mary Ann (1998), 'The Great British Ecstasy Revolution', in George McKay (ed.), *DIY Culture: Party and Protest in Nineties Britain*, London and New York: Verso, pp. 228–42.

Wright, Will (2001), *The Wild West: The Mythical Cowboy and Social Theory*, London: Sage.

Yahoo! Chat Event (2000), 'Destiny's Child', 6 July, archived at <http://uk.docs.yahoo.com/chat/destiny.html>, last visited 23 August 2002.

Young, Tracy (1992), 'Madonna Without Pictures', *Allure*, December, 78–81.

Zack, Naomi (ed.) (1997), *Race/Sex: Their Sameness, Difference and Interplay*, London and New York: Routledge.

Zehme, Bill (1997), 'Madonna: The Rolling Stone Interview', in *Rolling Stone* (eds), *Madonna: The Rolling Stone Files*, New York: Hyperion, pp. 99–113. First published 1989.

Žižek, Slavoj (1989), *The Sublime Object of Ideology*, New York: Verso.

Zollo, Paul (1989), *SongTalk*, **2** (11), Summer, archived at <http://www.eecs.harvard.edu/~zhwang/Madonna/arLAPwri.html>, last visited 24 March 2003.

Index

Abdul, Paula 59
abuse, domestic 108, 109, 110
'access sign' 24, 72
Acker, Kathy 164, 165
'Addicted to Love' video 60
advertising 17, 132, 133, 190
'Age of Aquarius' 48
Ahmadzï, Mirwais xvi, xxii, 6, 161, 195
Aida 65
Åkerlund, Jonas xvi, 44, 81, 84 n.6, 85
    n.19, 91, 92, 124, 131, 156 n.22, 171,
    183
alchemy 44, 47, 48
alienation 132
Almodóvar's *Matador* 147
ambiguity, sexual 29
American dream 121, 126
American Graffiti 129
Americana Music Association 134
amplified voice, the 14
Anastacia 161
Anderson, Benedict 116, 117
Andreae, Johann Valentin 46–7
androgyny xix, 16, 36, 38, 41, 43, 44, 45,
    46, 50
    Platonic conception of 43, 48
Andy Warhol Factory 100
anger 31
Anzaldúa, Gloria 94
Appadurai, Arjun 116
appropriations 16, 33, 75, 82, 83, 91, 94,
    95, 98, 116, 117, 120, 121, 127, 129,
    139
    camp 18
    cultural 182, 186, 191
    gender 17
    of Madonna's image by fans 184
    stylistic 10
Arena magazine 162

Argentina 151
Armatrading, Joan 168
art deco 40
artifice 4, 10
artificiality 5
Arthur, Charline 126
assertiveness, sexual 170, 171
Australia 123
authenticity xx, 6, 22, 23, 27, 28, 34, 110,
    115, 126, 129, 132, 134, 136, 190
Autry, Gene 125

BT 161
backlash xv, 176, 182
Baker, Susan 56
Banderas, Antonio 140, 151
Bangs, Lester 128
Barber, Samuel *Adagio for Strings* 65
Baron, Fabien 11, 38, 165, 184
Barthes, Roland 12, 20 n.10
Baudrillard, Jean 22, 28, 33, 34, 35, 49,
    94, 95, 99, 133, 179
Beatty, Warren 35 n.4, 74, 75
Beck, Ulrich 172, 173
Bee Gees 38
Beethoven's *Appassionata* sonata 61
Benetton 100
Benitez, DJ 'Jellybean' 140
Berg, Ramírez 143, 146
Bernhard, Sandra 70, 73, 74, 75, 81, 85
    n.17, 183, 186
Bigas Luna's *Jamón, jamón* 147
Birmingham Post, The 82
bisexuality 73, 75
Bizet's *Carmen* 57
blasphemy 31
blondeness 148
Bloss, Monika 38
Bluegrass 134, 136

body, the
  as an object of desire 39
  presentation of 36, 40
  representation of 38
  woman's
    natural 107–8, 109, 110, 111, 113,
      114, 116
    socially valued 107–8, 109, 110, 111
'body of light' 45
Bollywood 94
Bond films 82
Bourdieu, Pierre 112
Boy Toy Inc. 179, 187
Brit Awards 2001 121
Brooks, Garth 125
bullfighting 147–8
Burman, Chila Kumari 94, 97, 99
  'Fly Girl' 94, 97
Butler, Judith 11, 17–18, 25, 37, 115,
    171–2, 175 n.7
  Gender Trouble 171–2

cabbala xx, 93, 145
Callas, Maria 58
Cameron, Evelyn 125
camp xviii, 3–19, 94, 133, 139
  aesthetic 58
  expression 9
  heterosexual 16
  language 65
  pop 4, 6, 10, 18
  post-1960s 16
  sensibility 16, 69
capitalism 105, 107, 115, 118, 169
Carolin, Louise 71–2
Catholic church 173
Catholicism 120, 144, 145
celebrity xx, 149, 176, 178, 187
Cement Garden, The 30, 34
Cher 58
children 181
Chopin 61
chymical marriage, the 44, 46
Ciccone 120
classical music 57, 61, 64
Close, Glenn 62
Cobbett, Aaron 97

Cohen, Warren 116
commercialism 183
commerciality 139
commodification 98, 113
consumerism 105
consumers 176, 189, 190
consumption xx, 11, 12, 73, 107, 123
  celebrity 176–91
control 25, 29, 60, 71, 76, 77, 104, 150,
    163, 188
Cosmopolitan magazine 75, 168, 170
Country music xx, 120–36
Country Music Association 136
cowboy 13, 126, 132
cowboys, singing 125
cowgirl(s) xx, 6, 13, 108, 121, 124, 125,
    126, 133
critics xvi, 17, 56, 139, 148, 163, 167,
    169, 170, 176, 188, 189
cross-dressing 78–81, 126
Crouching Tiger, Hidden Dragon 92
Crowley, Alistair 42
Cubitt, Sean 14
culture
  American 105, 112, 125
  Black 139
  bourgeois 12, 13
  commodity 107, 112
  consumer 176, 178
  contemporary pop 13
  cowboy 188
  dance 4, 8, 19 n.5
  drag king 78
  East Asian 106, 112, 115
  gay 59, 65, 184
  Hispanic 58, 62–3
  Latin 152
  Latino 139, 144
  Latino/Spanish 139
  materialist 183
  pop 13, 18, 118, 168
  popular 123, 125, 136, 184
  rodeo 59
  world media 115
cultural cartography 98
Cunningham, Chris 44, 65, 91, 111, 181
Currid, Brian 66

'Cyber-raga' 92
'Cyberroundupinstallation' 131, 132

Dan-O-Rama xvi
dance
    music 9, 58, 61, 65, 161
    scene 18
    song 64
    trends 10
Danto, Arthur 95
Dark America website 162
Davis, Bette 13, 16
Dayne, Taylor 59
de Beauvoir, Simone 24
de Lempicka, Tamara 39, 46
    Andromeda 39
death 147
Deconstructing Madonna 55
Deep Dish 161
DeMann, Freddy xvi
dependency 30
Derrida, Jacques 95
desire 178, 192 n.2
    consumer 178
    sexual 180
Desperately Seeking Madonna xviii, 22,
    31
Destiny's Child xx, 161, 166–7, 171, 174
    albums:
        Survivor 166, 167
        The Writing's On the Wall 166
    songs:
        'Bills, Bills, Bills' 166
        'Independent Women Part 1' 166
        'Independent Women Part 2' 166
Deveaux, Monique 172
Dietrich, Marlene xvii, 16, 78, 79, 80, 86
    n.24
    Der Blaue Engel 80
    Morocco 80
difference 16, 25, 125, 136
    social 177, 182, 190, 191
    subcultural 178
digital editing 10
Dirty Dancing 75
disco xix, 6, 10, 64, 65, 66
'discovery sign' 24, 25, 72

disguise 38
Dixie Chicks, the 126
Dolce & Gabbana 112, 131
dominance 76
    patriarchal 110
domination 108
dominatrix
    imagery 73
    sado-masochistic 180
    sexual 165
    trickery 15
Dornoch Cathedral 122
drag 4, 11, 12, 13, 15, 16, 17–18, 21 n.20,
    59, 78, 92, 115
drag queens 78, 115
'drowned world' 48, 127
drugs 45, 59
Dyer, Richard 64, 66, 145, 180

E! 187
East Asian immigration into USA 116
Easy Rider 134
economics 107
Edwards, Brent 118
Eisner, Lisa 130
    Rodeo Girl 130
electronica 6
Elle magazine 163
Ellen 186
emancipation, consequences of 31, 34
Entertainment Tonight 187
epigraph 42, 43
eroticism 18, 24
ethnicity xvii, xix, 106, 107, 108, 114,
    115, 120, 139, 177
    commoditization of xx
Eurythmics 168
Evans, Caroline 95
Everett, Rupert 69, 129
exploitation 75, 108

fatherhood 60
female Country music artists 126
female surrealist painters 48
feminism 24, 25, 34, 71, 76, 81, 84 n.9,
    165, 174
    'lite' 169

popular xvii, 168–70
second-wave 23, 71
traditional 169
feminists 73, 104
femininity 12, 15, 22, 23, 24, 26, 31, 104,
    149
femme fatale 149, 152
film stars 177, 178
film studies 176, 177
film theory 25
Fincher, David 11, 25, 38, 69, 78, 86 n.22,
    98, 165, 180, 181, 183
Fitzgerald, Ella 59
flag
    American 111, 113, 122, 124, 129, 130
    British Union 122
    display 111
    Japanese 108, 111
fluidity 57, 58, 99, 172
Foley, James 24, 120, 148, 165
Fortin 120
Foucault, Michel 117, 175 n.7
Franklin, Aretha 168
Freud, Sigmund 52 n.35, 178
Frith, Simon 10–11, 62
Fuentes, Carlos 147
funk 10
Fusco, Coco 95, 99

Gainsbourg, Charlotte 30, 31
Garbo, Greta 16
Gardner, Elysa 63
Gaultier, Jean-Paul 65, 112
gay
    audience 59, 69
    chic 69
    community xix, 56, 58, 69, 74, 186
    male imagery 69
    men 57, 58, 59, 61, 65, 69, 75, 182
    subtext 65
gaze, the 142
    dominant 148
    female 150, 171
    male 13, 17, 40, 113, 142
    use of 148
    voyeuristic 149
geisha xxi, 106, 108, 111, 114

'Geisha Glam' 112, 113, 114
Geisha, Memoirs of a 112
gender xix, 11, 57, 66, 107, 110, 115, 139,
    177, 180
    agenda 163
    ambiguity 11
    and voice 38
    as performance 25
    boundaries 172
    construction of 41
    conventions 29
    fluidity 26
    inversion 142
    parody 16
    roles 109, 172
    socially constructed nature 11, 25, 37
    subversion 11
Gibson, Debbie 59
Giddens, Anthony 172, 175 n.7
'girl power' 163, 164, 165, 166, 167, 169,
    173, 174
'girlhood' 22, 24, 28, 30
'Girls Just Want to Have Fun' 72
global economy 177, 190
global market 106, 113
globality, critical 117, 118
globalization xx, 95, 116, 117, 118,
    184
Golden, Arthur 112
Golden Globe award 63
Grammy Awards 1999 111
Grey, Jennifer 75
Groove Armada 161
Guardian, The 164
Gundersen, Edna 62
Gunew, Sneja 110

Hall, Radclyffe 79, 82
Hall, Stuart 107
Halliwell, Geri 163, 164
Haraway, Donna 11, 94
Harrison, Andrew 104
Hatsumono 112, 113
Haussman, Michael 111, 146, 150, 181
hermeticism 36, 38, 43, 45, 47, 48
Hinduism 91, 93
Hill, Faith 126

Hispanic 138
  characters in Hollywood film 143, 146
  identities xx, 143, 151, 152, 153, 154
  literature and cinema 147
  music 61
  portrayals on US television 154
  research 143
Holly, Buddy 128
homosexuality 182
hooks, bell 11, 32, 70, 94, 107, 108, 110,
  120, 140, 148, 185
Hooper, Nellee 161
humour 18, 77, 105, 117
hyper-reality 179, 192 n.3

I Dream of Madonna 23
icon
  camp 18
  contemporary xxi
  cultural xviii, 70, 126
  feminist xvii, 72, 76
  for gay men 58, 70
  postmodern 105, 106
  sex xvi
  with a conscience 59
iconoclasm 12
iconography
  Country 133
  cowgirl/boy 130
  gay male 69
  Hindu xix
  of America 128
  pornographic 73, 81
  religious 148
  Western 125, 130, 131, 132, 134
identification 178
identity 8, 24, 106, 107, 120, 138, 177,
  185
  American xx, 116, 120, 121, 122, 124,
    128, 129
  as a social construction 38
  camp 14
  choices 173
  consumer 178
  ethnic 116, 117, 118, 120, 127, 149, 152
  female 25, 37
  formulation 106

gender 49, 120
  lesbian 70, 71
  North American 134
  racial xx
  sexual xix, 37, 120
  Spanish 147
Ikenberg, Tamara 63
impersonation 4, 12, 17, 79
inauthenticity 5, 70, 132
independence xv, 30, 164, 166, 168, 169,
  173
India xvii, 92, 179, 186
individualism 125, 130, 164
intimacy 7, 8, 15, 29
Irigaray, Luce 107–8, 109, 113
irony 77, 111, 117, 126

Jackson, Michael 38
Jagger, Mick 171
Jameson, Frederic 105, 127
Japan xvii, 179
Jarvis, Brian 95
Jencks, Charles 100
Jones, Brian 128
Joplin, Janis 128
Judaism 93
Jung, Carl Gustav 46, 47

Kahlo, Frida 46, 52 n.34, 154
Kaplan, Caren 96
Kaplan, E. Ann 37, 113, 172
Kaplan, Janet A. 46, 47
Keith Haring Foundation 186
Keshishian, Alek 27, 60, 84 n.14, 102 n.5,
  140, 169, 179
Khan, Chaka 59
Khoo, Olivia 114
Klein, Calvin 100
Klimt, Gustav 49
Knowles, Beyoncé 166, 167
Koestenbaum, Wayne 58
Kruder & Dorfmeister 161

La Ferla, Ruth 112
labour, domestic 107
Lacan 178, 192 n.1
  Graph of Desire 94

mirror phase metaphor 14
point de capiton 100
LaChapelle, David xx, 91, 93, 96, 97
LaChapelleLand 97, 98
Lake, Rikki 167
Lambert, Mary xx, 24, 31, 99, 111, 113,
    141, 144, 145, 146, 182, 183
Lang, Fritz 27
lang, k.d. 58
Late Show with David Letterman, The xxii
    n.8, 74
Latinas 145, 154, 180
Latino 138
Latinos 145, 186
Lauper, Cyndi 72
Layder, Joan 56, 62, 150
Layton, Lynne 104
León, Carlos xx, 75, 140
Leonard, Pat 143, 144
Leone, Sergio 132
Les Rhythmes Digitales 161
'lesbian chic' 70
'lesbian continuum' 152–3
lesbianism xv, xix, 69–83
lesbians 61, 65, 69
Lewis, Lisa 24, 25, 72
Lil' Kim 161, 170, 171, 173, 174
line dancing 133
'lipstick lesbian' 75
Little Richard 38
Lopez, Jennifer 161, 170
Los Angeles Times 63
Lourdes, Madonna's daughter xx, 25, 58,
    113, 173, 182
Love, Courtney 98
love, romantic 181, 183
Lowe, Lisa 116
Lugo-Lugo, Carmen 154
LuPone, Patti 62, 63
Lynn, Loretta 126, 136

McClary, Susan 40, 56–7
McDaniel, Melodie 111, 145
McGraw, Tim 125
MacKinnon, Catharine 11
MacLaine, Shirley 44
McLean, Don 128

McQueen, Alexander 100
McRobbie, Angela 168, 170
machismo 141–2, 147, 150
Madama Butterfly 65
Madonna
    abuse of her power 140
    AIDS charities, support for 69
    aggression 32, 34
    aggressive image 25
    albums:
        American Life xvii, xxi, 59, 66, 123,
            153, 161
        Bedtime Stories 14, 63
        Erotica xv, xix, 45, 62, 73, 81, 104,
            171, 172, 179
        Evita, see films
        GHV2 xxii n.5
        I'm Breathless 76
        Immaculate Collection 155 n.9
        Like a Prayer 22, 63, 65
        Like a Virgin 60
        Madonna 59
        Music xvii, xx, 6, 13, 22, 30, 55, 58,
            59, 65, 130–32, 134, 161, 162
        Ray of Light xix, 30, 32, 55, 59, 63,
            65, 92, 104, 129, 181
        Something To Remember xvi, 91, 165
        True Blue 22, 60
    ambition 179
    American heritage 136
    arrogance 13
    artistic credo 66
    as cowgirl 124, 129, 134, 136
    as geisha 104–19
    as role model xv, xvii, 72, 104
    as the future of feminism 56, 105, 117
    biographies of 121, 163
    birth of daughter 25, 58
    bisexual following 10
    book: *Sex* xv, xix, 62, 70, 73, 81, 107,
        140, 146, 147, 148, 153, 162, 168,
        171, 172, 179, 181, 183, 187
    boyfriends 74
    'Britishness' 121–3
    college courses relating to 188
    children 181
    comparisons with Britney Spears 162–3

concerts xviii, 6, 11
daughter xx, 25, 58, 113
depictions of women 185
editing of her music 5
empowerment 12, 15
ethos 164, 165
Evita diaries xvi, 150, 151
feminist agenda 168
films:
    Body of Evidence xv, 85 n.20, 148
    Dick Tracy 76, 148
    Die Another Day xvii, 81–2, 83, 183
    Evita xvi, xix, xx, 55, 59, 62, 63, 65,
        91, 150–154
    Next Best Thing, The 91, 129, 130,
        171
    Swept Away 86 n.29, 173
    Truth or Dare 27, 60, 101, 140, 145,
        169, 179, 183
    Who's That Girl 148
first child xvi, 113, 140
gay following 10
identity 12, 13, 14, 18, 104, 105, 139,
    171
image 72, 91, 104, 188
impersonator 93
influence on female pop performers
    161–74
Italian heritage 120, 148
lesbian following 58
links with Hispanic communities 110
'little-girl' voice 60, 67 n.13
marriage xvii, 75, 81, 82, 121, 139
mother, death of 60, 188
motherhood xvi, 25, 75, 82, 98, 114,
    153, 179, 18, 188
music videos 49, 112, 145, 146, 179,
    181, 184
musical expression 2
musical styles 105
narcissistic traits 17
performance of songs in Spanish 31,
    139, 153
play: Up for Grabs xv, xvii, xix, 81, 83,
    183
positive portrayals of gays 184
pregnancy xvi, 153

record company xvi
relationship with her father 58, 60, 68
    n.17
relationship with gay men xix, 56
role in the studio 5
scholarly studies on xviii, 16
sexuality 181
simulations of sex 180
singing style 45
songs:
    'American Life' xxi, 55
    'American Pie' xx, 128–30
    'Angel' 60
    'Bad Girl' 22
    'Be Careful' (with Ricky Martin) 155
        n.5
    'Borderline', see videos
    'Burning Up' 59
    'Bye Bye Baby' 80
    'Candy Perfume Girl' 22
    'Cherish' 181
    'Crazy for You' 180
    'Dear Jessie' 22
    'Deeper and Deeper' xxii n.6, 84 n.5
    'Die Another Day' xxii n.6, 85 n.19
    'Don't Cry for Me Argentina' 63, 151
    'Don't Tell Me' 92, 131
    'Dress You Up' 55, 60
    'Drowned World/Substitute for
        Love', see videos
    'Erotica', see videos
    'Everybody' 66
    'Express Yourself' xvii, 25, 26, 27,
        32, 38, 42, 56, 62, 64, 72
    'Falling in Love Again' 80
    'Fever' 45
    'Frozen' xix, 64, 65, 108, 109
    'Gone' 131
    'Hanky Panky' 76, 77
    'Holiday' 72, 123
    'Hollywood' 87 n.30
    'Human Nature' 14, 168
    'I Deserve It' 131
    'I'd Be Surprisingly Good for You'
        56, 63
    'Impressive Instant' 81, 83
    'In This Life' 69

'Into the Groove' 140, 181
'Justify My Love' 63
'La Isla Bonita' 32, 99, 100, 143, 145
'Like a Prayer' 57, 181
'Like a Virgin' 22, 24, 41, 80, 91, 145, 171, 181
'Little Star' 22, 58, 182
'Live to Tell' 56–7, 181
'Lo que siente la mujer' 31, 153
'Lucky Star' 24, 59
'Material Girl' 22, 55, 56, 60, 61
'Me Against the Music' (with Britney Spears), *see* videos
'Mer Girl' 32, 33, 108, 109
'Mother and Father' 60
'Music' xvi, xviii, 6–8, 10, 12, 55, 56, 66, 121
'Nobody's Perfect' 108, 109, 110, 131
'Nothing Really Matters', *see* videos
'Oh Father' 58, 60
'Open Your Heart', *see* videos
'Papa Don't Preach' 22, 56, 60, 61, 64, 161, 181
'Paradise (Not for Me)' 65, 108
'Power of Goodbye', *see* videos
'Rain', *see* videos
'Ray of Light' 91, 92, 96, 99, 100, 101
'Secret', *see* videos
'Shanti/Ashtangi' 63, 92, 94
'Shoo-Bee-Doo' 60
'Sky Fits Heaven' 32, 108, 109, 110
'Swim' 63
'Take a Bow' 55, 64, 146, 148, 149, 150
'The Funny Song' 133, 134, 135
'Till Death Do Us Part' 62, 72
'True Blue' 67 n.13
'Verás' 153
'Vogue', *see* videos
'What it Feels Like for a Girl' xvii, xix, 22, 23, 24, 30, 31, 33, 81, 153, 162
'Who's That Girl?' xxii n.6, 22, 143
'You Must Love Me' 63

'You'll See' 150, 153
Star commercial 173
tours:
    Blond Ambition tour 27, 73, 77, 91, 98, 145, 149, 181, 183
    Drowned World Tour xv, xvi, xix, xx, 13, 31, 32, 33, 48, 65, 81, 92, 99, 106, 108, 110, 111, 122, 123, 125, 132, 133, 134, 153, 183
    Re-invention Tour xv, xvi, xviii
    The Girlie Show xix, 22, 69, 70, 80, 91, 122, 123, 145, 183
    Virgin tour 24
    Who's That Girl? 22, 101, 147
videos:
    'American Life' 81, 124
    'American Pie' 129, 134
    'Bad Girl' 11, 181
    'Bedtime Story' xix, 44–9
    'Borderline' xx, 24, 99, 100, 111, 139, 141–3, 144, 146, 153, 182, 183
    'Don't Tell Me' 125, 132, 134, 143, 185
    'Drowned World/Substitute for Love' 113, 150, 181
    'Erotica' 11, 38, 165, 184
    'Express Yourself' 78, 79, 80, 165, 172, 180, 181
    'Fever' 49, 91, 111
    'Frozen' 44, 65, 91, 92, 93, 111, 185
    'Human Nature' 11, 15, 16, 73, 77, 181, 182, 185
    'Justify My Love' xv, xix, 11, 28–9, 31, 41–4, 45, 46, 47, 70, 145, 165, 171, 172, 179
    'La Isla Bonita' 139, 143, 144, 146, 148
    'Like a Prayer' 31, 113, 145, 182, 185
    'Lucky Star' 111
    'Material Girl' 183
    'Me Against the Music' 87 n.30
    'Music' xvi, 92, 131, 171, 183
    'Nothing Really Matters' xx, 63, 91, 106, 111, 112, 113, 114, 115, 116, 117

'Open Your Heart' xix, 38–41, 42, 43, 44, 45, 46, 47, 80, 98, 180
'Papa Don't Preach' 24, 120, 165
'Power of Goodbye' 113
'Rain' 49, 111
'Ray of Light' 44, 91, 92, 93
'Rescue Me' 181
'Secret' 111, 145, 181
'Take a Bow' 111, 139, 181
'Vogue' 11, 69, 91, 98, 183
'What it Feels Like for a Girl' 23, 24, 30, 32, 34, 72, 81, 173
'You'll See' 139, 150
vocal style 59, 60, 61, 63, 134
voice 14, 15, 40, 41, 55, 56, 61, 62, 65–6
voice lessons 56, 62, 150
wannabes and look-alikes 24, 92
websites 183
Madonna Companion, The xviii
Madonna Connection, The xvii, xx, 55, 172, 188
'Madonna of the Trail', The 125, 126
Madonna Queens 56, 58, 66
Madonna: The Rolling Stone Files xviii
'Madonna's Indian Summer' 91–100
Madonnarama 140
Magritte, René 46, 52 n.34
manga animation 32, 33, 34
Mannin, Ethel 82
Manson, Marilyn 38, 93
marketing 176, 190
Marxism 107
masculinity 42, 147
mask(s) 37, 40, 104, 105, 106
masquerade xix, 27, 36, 37, 38, 41, 42, 43, 49, 50, 149, 150, 151
'Material Girl', the 93, 101
materialism 123
materiality 30
Maverick 179, 187
meanings 176, 177, 180
  attached to Madonna 180–87
Mel B 164
Menchú, Rigoberta 95, 99
Metropolis 27, 79
Miklitsch, Robert 113

Minogue, Kylie 161, 171, 172
minorities
  ethnic 140
  racial 139
Miss Rodeo America 130, 131
Missy Elliot 161, 173
Mitchell, Joni 168
Mondino, Jean Baptiste xv, 11, 15, 28, 38, 41, 70, 73, 98, 125, 130, 131, 132, 143, 145, 165, 171, 19, 181, 185
monocle 79, 80, 86 n.25
Monroe, Marilyn 60, 93, 148
More 170
Morris, Mitchell 57, 58
Morrison, Jim 128
Motown 60
mountain music 125, 136
Mozart 61
MTV 17, 24, 28, 42, 59, 114, 149, 162, 166, 174, 179, 187
  1984 music awards 60
  1998 Video Music Awards 91, 99
  2003 music video awards xix
Mulvey, Laura 25, 178
Muñoz, Emilio 146, 147, 181
music business 59, 66
music industry 12, 17, 18, 24, 72, 121, 168
Musto, Michael 58, 69, 186, 188
Muthyala, John 118
myth
  American 125, 126, 134
  cowboy 133
  cowgirl/boy 124–9, 135
  individualist 126
  of the American West 125, 132
Nakayama, Thomas 114, 183
nationalism 111, 115
Nashville 126, 134
National Society of Daughters of the American Revolution 125
Neo-Romantics 65
New Age 36, 42, 44, 45, 48, 49, 94
Nightline 42

'O Brother, Where Art Thou?' 136
objectification of celebrities 178

occult, the 48
occultism 43
Ong, Aihwa 116
opera 57, 65
opera queen 56, 57, 58, 66
opera singers 57, 58
Orbit, William xvi, xxii, 19 n.5, 63, 161
orientalism 96, 115, 118
Osbourne, Kelly 23, 161
Ovid 43

Paglia, Camille xvi, 56, 105, 141, 164
Palmer, Robert 60
Paris, Texas 134
Parker, Alan xx, 55, 150
Parlo, Dita xvii, xxii n.7, 73, 76, 77,
    140
parody 77, 80, 105, 117, 123, 127–8, 133,
    134, 135, 136
Parton, Dolly 126
pastiche 96, 105, 106, 112, 127–8, 143,
    144, 146
patriarchy 153, 169
patriotism 111, 124
Peñaloza, Lisa 114
Penn, Sean 74, 75
People magazine 187
performance 5, 27, 28, 32, 34
performativity 11, 22, 80
Péron, Eva xvi, 62, 63, 139, 150–53
Péron, Juan 63
Pettibone, Shep 161
Pfeiffer, Michelle 62
Pierre et Gilles 97
Pierson, Arthur 111
Pink 161, 170, 171, 173
Plato 43, 44
Polhemus, Ted 95, 99
politics
    cultural 120, 121, 161
    feminist 71
    gay 16
    gender xix, 25, 35
    global 124
    identity 14, 16, 18
    lesbian 71
    liberal 122, 130

queer 16
    sexual 161
pop 3, 4, 5, 10
pop music 17, 161, 166
pornography 71, 73, 190
post-feminism 17
postmodernism 26, 105, 127
postmodernity 105, 139
power 105, 142, 147, 153
    female 152
    patriarchal 154
    sex 109
    white Western 70
Pratt, Mary Louise 117
Presley, Elvis 171
Price, Stuart 161
Prince 38, 57, 59
Princess of Wales 152
product endorsements 177
projection 191
Pryce, Jonathan 63

Queer as Folk 186
queer listener 65
queer subtext 61
queer texts 83
queer theory 11
queering, process of 18

race xix, 66, 106, 110, 120, 139, 148,
    177
racism 106, 169 185
rape 33
recording
    process 5
    techniques 29
religion 145
Renck, Johan xx, 91, 106, 112, 115
revenge fantasies 34
Revlene 93
Rhythm & Blues 128
Rich, Adrienne 152
Rimes, LeAnn 126
Ritchie, Guy 30, 31, 60, 72, 75, 81, 82, 86
    n.29, 121, 139, 173
Ritter, Tex 125
Ritts, Herb 188

Riviere, Joan 36–7, 41
Robertson, Pamela 16, 18, 19, 58, 76
Robertson, Roland 115–16
Robinson, Paul 58
Rocco, birth of 122
rock 4, 10, 17, 29, 57, 128
Rock & Roll 128
'Rock the Vote' 122, 129
Rodríguez, Clara 145, 151
Rogers, Roy 125
role reversal 30, 149
Rolling Stone 63, 74, 91–9, 141
Rolston, Matthew 113
Romanek, Mark 44, 49, 111
Rosie O'Donnell Show 93
Ross, Andrew 4, 81
Rubin, Gayle 107

sadomasochism 71, 73, 75–8, 81, 85 n.20
    consensual 77
    gay 75
    heterosexual 76
    lesbian 73, 75, 76, 77, 85 n.18
samurai 108, 109
Sasha 172
Satanists 42
Scharff, Sue 34
Schulze, Laurie 183
Schwichtenberg, Cathy 51 n.19, 52 n.38,
    142, 175 n.5, 188
Scottish wedding xx, 122
Sednaoui, Stephane 49, 91, 111
seduction 28, 29, 33, 121
self-actualization 126
self-confidence 169
    sexual 170, 174
self-mockery 4, 18
self-parody 122
self-reinvention 161, 171
self-respect 30
September 11 111, 123, 130, 135, 137 n.1
sex
    lesbian 71
    objects 104, 170
    Sex, see Madonna, book
    wars 70–71
sexualities, queer xvii

sexuality xvii, xix, 11, 16, 25, 30, 31, 57,
    66, 81, 107, 115, 139, 149, 172, 177,
    179, 180
    female 24, 25, 26, 28, 164, 185
    gay 130
    independent 169
    traditional 172
signification 104, 105, 114
signifier(s) 112, 118, 177
simulacra xx, 28, 33, 34, 49, 149
simulacrum 22, 95, 99, 117
simulations 23, 28, 33
'Sisters Are Doing It For Themselves' 168
Skibo Castle 122
songs, pop 11
Sontag, Susan 13, 17, 95
Spanish dress 32
Spanish-speaking people 138
Spare Rib 168
Spears, Britney xx, 23, 161, 162–3, 166,
    170, 172, 173, 174
    Crossroads 169
spectatorship, gender 178
Spice Girls, the 23, 161, 163–6, 167, 169,
    171, 173, 174
spirituality 183
Spivak, Gayatri 110–11, 117, 118
Springer, Jerry 167
Star Wars: Episode I 112
stereotypes 25, 143, 145, 146, 151, 172,
    188
Stern, Walter 113, 150, 181
Stolzol, Philip 129
street(s), the 99–100, 140
studio production 5
'subcultural tourism' xvii, 58, 120
subjectivity 16, 33, 150, 178, 186, 190
supremacy, white 140
surrealism 36, 38, 44, 46
surrealist paintings 44
survey data 182, 185, 186
Sutherland, Joan 58

Tchaikovsky's *Symphony No.4 in F Minor*
    57
Tetzlaff, David xv, 106, 107
Time Warner 187

Thai choreography 91
Thelma and Louise 134
Thunderpuss 161
Traktor 85 n.19
transculturation 117
transformation(s) xix, xxi, 55, 56, 69, 114,
    136, 172, 173, 174
  cultural 191
  ethnic 139
  gender 14
  identity 127
  subcultural 69
Troubridge, Lady Una 79
Turner, Tina 58
Twain, Shania 123, 126
tweed 82

values 127, 130, 136
Vanity Fair 80, 82, 154
Varo, Remedios 46, 47, 48, 52 n.35
  Los amantes 46
Vatican, the 145
'Veronica Electronica' 63
victimization 32, 33, 34
video, music 24, 38, 114
violence 32, 34, 109, 110
  against men 109
  domestic 108, 110
  patriarchal 109

von Sternberg, Josef 78
voyeur(s) 39, 40, 42

Walken, Christopher 181
Walter, Natasha 168
Ward, Tony 69, 74
Warner Brothers 179
Watts, Mark 112
Weinbaum, Alys 118
Welch, Gillian 126
West, Mae 16, 21 n.21
Westworld 132
Whiteley, Sheila 165
Will and Grace xvii, 186
Williams, Hank 125
Wizard of Oz, The 131
womanhood 162, 168, 170
'womanliness' 37, 40, 41, 42, 43, 48
  as a masquerade 36, 38, 49
  stereotype of 36
women
  as exchangeable commodities 107
  position in contemporary media 23
  role in the West 125
world market 106, 107
'worlding' 117–8
Wright, Mary Ann 66

Žižek, Slavoj 94